Contents

Youth, Citizenship and Empowerment

LEARNING RESOURCES
CENTRE
Havering College
of Further and Higher Education

Edited by

HELENA HELVE and CLAIRE WALLACE

Ashgate

Aldershot • Burlington USA • Singapore • Sydney

Published by
Ashgate Publishing Limited
Gower House
Croft Road
Aldershot
Hampshire GU11 3HR
England

Ashgate Publishing Company
131 Main Street
Burlington, VT 05401-5600 USA

Ashgate website: http://www.ashgate.com

British Library Cataloguing in Publication Data
Youth, citizenship and empowerment
    1. Citizenship 2. Youth - Social conditions
    I. Helve, Helena II. Wallace, Claire, 1956-
    323.6'0835

Library of Congress Control Number: 00-111838

ISBN 0 7546 1646 0

Printed in Great Britain by
Antony Rowe Ltd, Chippenham, Wiltshire.

vii

List of Figures

List of Tables

List of Contributors

Pat Allatt is Professor of Sociology at the School of Social Sciences, University of Teesside. She has researched and published on crime prevention, community development, family ideology, social policy and women's magazines in wartime, childhood and youth – focusing particularly on family relations and labour markets, and the delivery of education, training and other services. She is co-author with S. M. Yeandle "Youth Unemployment and the Family: Voices of Disordered Times" (1992).

John Bynner is Professor and Director of the Centre for Longitudinal Studies, Institute of Education, University of London. He directs two major UK longitudinal research programmes, the "National Child Development Study" and the "1970 British Cohort Study". He also directs the UK Government Department of Education Research Centre on the "Wider Benefits of Learning". His main research interests are in economic and political socialisation and social research methodology. He has researched and published widely in the field of youth transitions including: "Twenty Something in the 1990s" with Elsa Ferri and Peter Shepherd (1997) and "Comparative Youth Transition Research" with Lynne Chisholm (1998).

Lynne Chisholm, PhD, is a Sociologist of Education and Youth, and currently works at the European Commission's Directorate-General for Education and Culture in Brussels, having previously spent twenty years as University Lecturer and Professor at universities in Northern Ireland, England, Canada and Germany. She is a widely published specialist in education, training and youth transitions in comparative and intercultural research and policy context. She is also 1998-2002 President of Resarch Committee 34 (Sociology of Youth) of the International Sociological Association.

David Everatt is Senior Partner in Strategy & Tactics, at a Johannesburg-based research consultancy. He has held research Fellowships and/or taught at the Universities of Rhodes and Cape Town. Everatt is Vice-President of

Africa in RC34 (Sociology of Youth), International Sociological Association. He has served on policy drafting teams in the areas of safety and security, public works programmes and youth development.

Christian Haerpfer is Visiting Professor in Comparative Political Sociology at the University of Strathclyde (Glasgow) and Head of the New Europe Centre at the Institute for Advanced Studies (Vienna). He is Principal Investigator of the "New Democracies Barometer 1991, 1992, 1994, 1996, 1998" and one of the Principal Investigators of the "World Value Study 1997/98". He is consultant for the European Commission (Brussels), European Bank for Reconstruction and Development (EBRD, London) and OECD (Paris). He was Visiting Professor at the Central European University (Prague) and held Fellowships at the European University Institute (Florence) and the University of Essex (Colchester). His most recent books are "Democracy and its Alternatives" with Richard Rose and William Mishler (1998) and "Post-Communism and Democracy" (2000).

Sue Heath is Lecturer in Sociology at the University of Southampton, UK. Her current research is focused on leaving home and processes of household formation in the wider context of youth transitions, and the growing appeal of non-familial living amongst young adults. She is a member of the Youth and Generation study group of the European Sociological Association, the Youth Study Group of the British Sociological Association, and is on the editorial board of "Sociology", the BSA journal. Recent publications include "Preparation for Life? Vocationalism and the Equal Opportunities Challenge" (1997) and "Sociological Research Methods in Context" with Fiona Devine (1999).

Helena Helve, PhD, Docent (Associate Professor) at the University of Helsinki is also a Visiting Research Fellow at the Centre for Longitudinal Studies, Institute of Education, University of London. She is Co-ordinator of the Nordic Youth Research of Nordic Council of Ministers and President of the Finnish Youth Research Society. She has directed several research projects e.g. The Finnish Youth Research 2000 Programme. She is editor in International Bulletin of Youth Research IBYR of Research Committee 34 (Sociology of Youth), International Sociological Association. She has written, co-authored and edited a number of books including "The World View of Young People" (1993), "Youth and Life Management: Research

Perspectives" with John Bynner (1996), "Unification and Marginalisation of Young People" (1998) and "Rural Young People in Changing Europe" (2000).

Tarja Hilden works as Researcher at the Carelian Institute (University of Joensuu, Finland). Her study is a part of a research project called "The Skinheads of Joensuu – A Product of Community?". Her contribution in this project is to examine crimes committed by 15 to 20 year olds.

Liisa Horelli, PhD, is an Environmental Psychologist who is currently Senior Research Fellow at the Helsinki University of Technology in which she leads her research team focusing on young people's participation in urban improvement and in the construction of the information society. She has also written several books and articles about these subjects.

Gill Jones is Professor of Sociology in the School of Social Relations at Keele University. She has undertaken extensive research on young people's transitions to adulthood, their social and economic relations with their parents, and the policy frameworks affecting young people. Publications include "Leaving Home" (1995), "Youth, Family and Citizenship" with Claire Wallace (1992) and "Balancing Acts: Youth, Parenting and Public Policy" with Robert Bell (2000).

Sakari Karvonen is Docent (Associate Professor) in Medical Sociology at the University of Helsinki and works presently in the Finnish Research and Development Centre for Welfare and Health. He has conducted and published a number of studies on young people's health-related behaviour and well-being, focusing particularly on local and regional variation. His current research interests include cross-cultural comparisons (Finland, Scotland, Switzerland) on lifestyle and health. He also collaborates with the Helsinki Health Study that aims at a comparison with the British Whitehall Study.

Liz Kenyon is Lecturer in Sociology at the University of Portsmouth (UK) and Visiting Fellow at the University of Southampton (UK), where she is currently working with Sue Heath on the ESRC project "Young Adults and Shared Household Living" on which the article in this book draws.

Ladislav Macháček, PhD, Prof. Ass., is Senior Researcher at the Institute of Sociology at the Slovak Academy of Sciences, Bratislava. Currently he is working in the field of youth research paying special attention to the question of professional orientation, preparing youth for marriage and parenthood, and relations between the state and youth movements. Macháček is Head of the research group Preparedness of Citizens of the Slovak Republic for European Citizenship (1997-2002). At the same time, he is President of the Sociology of Youth, Slovak Sociological Association, Editor in Chief of the Slovak Sociological Review – SOCIOLÓGIA, and a board member of RC34 (Sociology of Youth), International Sociological Association. His latest books are "Youth in Slovakia" (1998) and "Longterm Unemployed Youth in Europe and Slovakia", (ed.) with K. Roberts (1998).

Sari Näre is Doctor of Social Sciences from the University of Helsinki and Researcher in the Finnish Youth Research Network. Her current research themes are "economy of emotions", sexual violence against adolescent girls and gender culture. Her previous themes are girls' and boys' hero idols, sex trade and Islamic gender culture, and she has also published books on these topics. Näre is main editor of "Nuorisotutkimus" (The Finnish Journal of Youth Research) and Vice-Chairman of the Youth Committee of the City of Helsinki.

Marianne Nylund, MA in Social Sciences, is Researcher at a Local Community project funded by the Finnish Academy and located at Department of Social Policy, University of Helsinki, Finland. She is Contact Person for the Nordic Network on Third Sector Research, European Network on Self-Help Groups, and Researcher at a Nordic Research Project on Volunteers' Motives. Her research interests are third sector, voluntary action, and self-help groups. She has finished her doctoral thesis on Mutual Support and Voluntary Action.

Kari Paakkunainen is Researcher in the Finnish Youth Research Network and works at the University of Helsinki, Department of Political Science. He is a board member of the Finnish Youth Research Society. His main themes of research have been European intellectual history, hermeneutics and the political culture of youth in Europe. He has also published numerous books and articles on these topics.

Ossi Rahkonen, PhD, is Senior Lecturer in the Department of Social Policy at the University of Helsinki, Finland. He has written numerous articles on the history of public health and medical sociology in Finland and on health inequalities in Nordic countries and in the UK. He is Editor both in the Finnish Journal of Social Medicine and Finnish Journal of Social Policy and Social Work.

Mojibur Rahman is Doctoral Candidate at the University of Helsinki, Department of Political Science and Institute of Development Studies. His research interests include for example the rights of the child in developing countries, the role of Non-Governmental Organisations working in the field, the status of girls and women, and intercultural communication. He has also written articles about these subjects.

Reingard Spannring, MA, has been working as Student Assistant at the Institute for Sociology, University of Vienna. She was involved in the creation of "European Youth Surveys Information Data Base" and is currently Researcher in a project "Ways of Integration of Young People in the European Societies"; Claire Wallace has been the leader of both projects.

Leena Suurpää, M.S.Sc, works as Co-ordinator in the Finnish Youth Research Network. She is preparing a doctoral thesis to the University of Helsinki, Department of Sociology on the themes related to young people, politics of difference, immigration and racism. She has worked also at Centre National de la Recherche Scientifique/IRESCO in Paris in 1998-99. Suurpää has co-ordinated a Nordic research project on young people and racism, financed and published by the Nordic Council of Ministers (1998). She is the Finnish Editor of the "Nordic Journal of Youth Research – YOUNG", and belongs to the editorial board of "Nuorisotutkimus" (The Finnish Journal of Youth Research).

Arseniy Svynarenko graduated in 1998 from Odessa Mechnikov University (Ukraine), and in 2000 from the University of Tampere (Finland). His studies focus on the issues of collective identities, social citizenship, and cross-generational comparisons. He has published articles on cultural and national identities and problems between generations in Ukraine.

Timo Virtanen is Researcher at the Åbo Academy University, Turku, Finland and has belonged to the Finnish Youth Research Network. He has researched skinheads and their violent action and worked on a project dealing with racist violence and youth, financed by the European Commission and the Finnish Youth Research Society. He has also published books and articles on this subject.

Claire Wallace is Professor at the University of Derby and Researcher at the Institute for Advanced Studies in Vienna. She has been researching in the field of youth for some twenty years. Since 1992 she has been studying the transformation process in Eastern Europe and was head of sociology at the Central European University in Prague. She is author of numerous books on youth including "Youth, Family and Citizenship" with Gill Jones (1992) and "Youth in Society: The Construction and Reconstruction of Youth in East and West Europe" with Sijka Kovatcheva (1998). She has had a particular interest in cross-national research and has undertaken studies about young people for example in Germany, Austria, Poland and Ukraine.

Acknowledgements

First we wish to thank those who attended the international youth research conference "Youth, Citizenship and Empowerment" held in Helsinki in December 1998 for the ideas developed in this book. The theme of the conference was taken from the Finnish Youth Research 2000 programme, with its emphasis on how young people adapt to and cope with the problems produced by social change. The conference would not have been possible without the financial support of the Finnish Ministry of Education. This book is also supported by RC34 (Sociology of Youth) of the International Sociological Association. Finally we wish to thank Juhana Heikkilä for his untiring dedication and thoughtfulness in putting the book into its final form.

PART 1

INTRODUCTION

1 The State and Prospects of Youth and Citizenship

HELENA HELVE and CLAIRE WALLACE

The ideas of citizenship and empowerment have become powerful policy concepts in the last years, but their meaning is ambiguous. The articles in this volume represent a range of approaches to both issues. The definitions of citizenship, for example have been broadened from the narrow meaning of political, legal and welfare rights analysed by T. H. Marshall fifty years ago (Marshall 1950). The welfare rights which he predicted would represent the final evolutionary stage of modernisation have in fact been everywhere under attack. Instead, new meanings of citizenship have emerged which stress more the active elements, and this is the connection also to empowerment. Even this active meaning of empowered citizenship can have many elements. For some it means the membership and activity in "civil society", that is, voluntary and non-profit associational activities which has been on the rise amongst young people. For Robert Putnam, this kind of activity contributes to "social capital" which is an important element of modernisation and economic development (Putnam 1986). For some Eastern Europeans and those in developing countries it also means more than just joining sports clubs and choral societies. It means the active mobilisation of citizens to defend their interests and even to topple unwanted regimes, something in which youth have been very active (Wallace and Kovatcheva 1998). In the words of Ladislav Macháček (this volume) it means the mobilisation of young people as a *citizenry* as well as a democracy. However, such a citizenry can be demobilised again under changing circumstances. David Everatt, for example, describes the many years of mobilisation of young South Africans as opposition to the dominant apartheid regime, who now prefer different roles as consumers, so that much of the revolutionary energy which had the potential to shape a new youth politics at a national level, was lost.

Another meaning of citizenship is in the sense of rights, usually human rights, which have a transnational dimension, introduced and guaranteed by international organisations which are represented in "civil society" at an international level (Soysal 1996). This sense of citizenship is discussed by Mojibur Rahman in this volume. These rights can be important in introducing formal recognition of the situation of children and young people into states where they are not necessarily respected or even by bypassing the nation states altogether through the networking of international organisations and NGOs (Non-Governmental Organisations) which build partnerships with local organisations to meet the needs of children and young people.

A further meaning of citizenship is the membership of a nation state. This has become ever more meaningful as with increasing international mobility, rich states (including the European Union) try to keep out people from poorer states or to grant them some kind of partial citizenship status as refugees, guest workers and so on. Even this does not prevent the rise in irregular and illegal migration. Many of the articles in this volume describe the interaction between native citizens and these newer arrivals in the culture and mind set of young people. This is the case for example with the article of Leena Suurpää and also those of Tarja Hilden and Timo Virtanen.

The debates about citizenship and empowerment take place in the context of more general social value-shifts in late modern (or postmodern) societies which include the increasing importance of individualisation and reflexivity. This shapes not just the values and aspirations of young people, but also the policy environment in which issues are dealt with. Kari Paakkunainen deals with the relationship between value changes and policy climate at a more abstract level, whilst Helena Helve and Marianne Nylund look at the evidence for them in more detailed empirical studies.

Young people are not only the passive recipients of rights or holders of values. Many of the articles in this volume describe how programmes in which young people participate in shaping their environment (Liisa Horelli) or in helping in programmes for street children and socially marginalised young people (Mojibur Rahman). The current emphasis of both the Council of Europe and the Directorate for Youth, Culture and Education in the European Commission is upon educating young people for citizenship. In other words ways of incorporating them into decision making structures and encouraging them to become active citizens not just at a local, but also at a European level.

Young people are also empowering themselves, without any help from international organisations, in developing new lifestyles and living arrangements, as we see in the article from Sue Heath and Liz Kenyon.

4

However, there can also be negative, a-social aspects of empowerment. In Finland, as in other European countries, young men who are marginalised in the modernisation process and threatened by international or global changes respond by constructing skinhead gangs which gain their strength from developing a brutal culture of masculinity and attacking people they regard as outsiders (Roma, refugees and asylum seekers and others). This is described by Tarja Hilden and Timo Virtanen.

Citizenship can imply a variety of rights and these rights are subject to different kinds of mobilisation at different times. The women's movement, for example, has been very active in putting on the agenda women's rights and pointing out the deficiencies in the idea of citizenship as it applies to women (Summers 1991; Lister 1990). However, one aspect of this is the recognition of sexual abuse and the corresponding right for women to define their own sexuality. This issue is addressed in the article by Sari Näre.

Despite the debates about transnational citizenship, citizenship rights usually inhere to national communities (Bauböck 1995; Joppke and Lukes 1999). However, the definition of this community can itself be problematic. In the many newly forming states around the world, young people have to find a national identity as citizens and this issue is described by Arseniy Svynarenko in the case of Ukrainian young people and Ladislav Macháček for Slovakia. The orientation of young people to European citizenship, on the other hand is tackled by Claire Wallace.

The book is one of the few volumes that brings together a European focus on youth with articles from other parts of the world. Admittedly, there are not many papers from other parts of the world: this is something that will remain a challenge for later volumes on youth research. The main bulk of articles reflect youth research in the Nordic countries, where youth citizenship is most developed and where there has been a well established tradition of research, encouraged by the Nordic Youth Research Network of which Helena Helve is currently the leader. However, the volume also covers the broader new Europe stretching to Russia in the East and Bulgaria and Romania in the south. The volume is organised together with RC34, the Research Committee on Youth of the International Sociological Association, from which the discussants for the different parts of the volume are drawn.

This volume is organised in a number of different parts, with critical discussions and summaries by leading youth scholars. Part 2 provides an overview of the issues with a more conceptually oriented chapter from

Claire Wallace and then an empirically oriented chapter showing the forms of citizenship participation in East and West Europe by Reingard Spannring, Claire Wallace and Christian Haerpfer.

Part 3, about citizenship and power, is introduced by John Bynner. It contains chapters about the participation of young people in environmental planning (Liisa Horelli), a theoretical critique of dominant concepts (Kari Paakkunainen), an account of Nordic volunteers and new living arrangements of young people (Marianne Nylund and Sue Heath and Liz Kenyon).

Part 4 is about citizenship and marginality, with an introduction by Lynne Chisholm. It includes two accounts of new skinhead gangs in Nordic countries (Tarja Hilden and Timo Virtanen), a chapter about sexual citizenship (Sari Näre) and about the views of foreigners (Leena Suurpää).

Part 5 concentrates mainly upon detailed analysis of value shifts with a critical discussion by Gill Jones. The chapters are written by Helena Helve and Sakari Karvonen and Ossi Rahkonen who provide a complementary debate about these changes and how to analyse them. This is followed by an analysis of the construction of national identity among young people in Ukraine by Arseniy Svynarenko.

Part 6 is called "New Actors, Networks and Empowerment" and brings in a more global perspective. This is introduced by Pat Allatt. The chapters include a perspective from Slovakia by Ladislav Macháček as well as an account from developing countries (mainly Asia and the Indian sub-continent) by Mojibur Rahman, whilst South Africa is covered by David Everatt.

The issue of young people's empowerment is deeply political. The chapters of the book focus on the phenomena in societies which differ in their political and economic cultures. The age range covered by the articles extends from street children and child workers in the developing countries to the official definition of youth up to age 35 in South Africa. In a globalising world, the political involvement of young people is ambiguous. Its absence, or apparent absence, is critically linked to people's circumstances and the changes through which they are living. For instance the fall of Communism has served to push the Slovakian youth off the stage (Macháček in this volume). They have lost their institutionalised role in the former regime as political actors. They are victims of rising unemployment and job insecurity. However the new movements – NGOs, such as environmental groups, show that many of the young are politically aware if not politically active. Yet the political activity of young people may also lead to marginalisation, as we can see in the example of skinhead groups and fringe activities. In a globalising world, the new communications technologies and the opening of formerly closed societies offer new opportunities which have strengthened the political role of NGOs. Perhaps they will be able to draw upon new forms of power as well as reach new groups of young people in future.

References

Bauböck, R. (1995), *Transnational Citizenship: Membership and Rights in International Migration*, Edward Elgar, UK.

Joppke, C. and Lukes, S. (eds.) (1999), *Multicultural Questions*, Oxford University Press, Oxford.

Lister, R. (1990), 'Women, Economic Dependency and Citizenship', *Journal of Social Policy, 19(4)*, pp. 445-67.

Marshall, T. H. (1950), *Citizenship and Social Class and Other Essays*, Cambridge University Press, Cambridge.

Putnam, R. D. (1986), 'The Prosperous Community: Social Capital and Public Life', *The American Prospect, 13*, pp. 35-42.

Soysal, Y. N. (1996), 'Changing Citizenship in Europe: Remarks on Postnational Membership and the National State', in D. Cesarani and M. Fulbrook (eds.), *Citizenship, Nationality and Migration in Europe*, Routledge, London.

Summers, Y. (1991), 'Women and Citizenship: The Insane, the Insolvent and the Inanimate?', in P. Abbott and C. Wallace (eds.), *Gender, Power and Sexuality*, Macmillan, London.

Wallace, C. and Kovatcheva, S. (1998), *Youth in Society: The Construction and Deconstruction of Youth in East and West Europe*, Macmillan, London.

PART 2

YOUTH, CITIZENSHIP AND EMPOWERMENT IN COMPARATIVE PERSPECTIVE

2 Youth, Citizenship and Empowerment

CLAIRE WALLACE

Introduction

Empowerment and citizenship have become attractive concepts for developing changes in youth policies and the welfare state. This because they can accommodate the fragmentation of social groups, the movement from collectivistic towards individualistic beliefs, the retreat of the welfare state and the scepticism of "grand narrative" solutions to social problems which are all part of a general "postmodernisation" of societies (Inglehart 1997; Wallace and Kovatcheva 1998). They promise a participatory and democratic response to problems of social exclusion and marginalisation of young people. However, these terms reflect a range of meanings embedded in different debates. In this chapter I shall develop a critical review of some of these meanings first of citizenship and then of empowerment and consider the ways in which they might be relevant for young people.

Young People and Citizenship

Citizenship is of fundamental importance to everyone because it defines an individual's legal, political and social relationship to the society of which they form a part. However, it is also an essentially contested concept.

There has been a recent revival of interest in the concept of citizenship for a number of reasons. Firstly, the pressure towards system integration in Europe due to the convergence of economic institutions and the expansion of supra-national political institutions, such as the European Union and the Council of Europe poses the question: what political entity is the European person a citizen of? Secondly, the struggle for political recognition by marginalised groups such as women, ethnic minorities, gays and lesbians and others means that "citizenship" appears to offer the possibility for social integration in diversified societies. Finally, the struggle over the welfare state and criticisms of the scope of welfare (for example in Britain and the USA) has lead to a reconsideration of what "rights" citizens can expect from their state. The developments in East and Central Europe however, add a new dimension to this debate. Since the opening of Europe to the East and the new waves of migration experienced in the 1990s another aspect of citizenship which has become important is that of national identity – to which state one belongs. Although all these debates developed along separate lines, they are also in many ways essentially related, as I shall show. Hence, the next part of the chapter is divided into four categories: European citizenship; citizenship and marginality; citizenship and the welfare state; citizens and non-citizens.

Young people, as new citizens, have a particular relationship to each of these meanings of citizenship. However, many young people are also excluded from becoming full citizens in various ways. Below I shall examine each meaning of citizenship and its relevance for young people.

1. Young People and European Citizenship

Young people in both Eastern and Western Europe are more likely to identify themselves as European citizens. However, they may hold other – local and national – identities simultaneously.

Figure 2.1 (see p. 31, Appendix) shows that for the European Union countries covered by the Eurobarometer of 1996, older people were more likely than younger people to see their nationality only as a source of identity, whilst young people were more likely to espouse a European identity, but alongside of their national identity.[1] In post-communist Eastern and Central Europe, as measured by the New Democracies Barometer, in 1998, there was likewise a clear tendency for young people to be more pro-European – the further East and South, the more this is the case (see p. 31, Appendix, Figure 2.2).[2] Furthermore, our analysis of the World Values Survey indicates that young people are identifying more and more with Europe over time and this tendency is especially strong in the former Communist countries (Wallace, Spannring and Haerpfer 2000).

Nevertheless the idea of citizens of Europe is still rather vague and abstract. Europe remains a supra-national state without a well established identity. Even the boundaries of Europe are continually under discussion:

does Europe extend from the Ural mountains to the Atlantic Ocean, as General de Gaulle claimed? How far south does it extend? The cold war division of Europe which divided Europe into two halves has disappeared and now a range of new nations also claim to be "European". This is not just an emotional but also a material issue as the European Union is also a "rich mans club" which is trying to exclude its poorer neighbours and is defined vis-à-vis its poorer neighbours.

It is now impossible for nation states alone to control every aspect of citizenship. Environmental and economic connections across the world make regulation by nation states alone unrealistic and anachronistic. However, the globalisation of citizenship is accompanied paradoxically by increased national chauvinism. Thus, the creation of supranational organisations such as the European Court of Human Rights, the European Community, the Council of Europe and so on has helped to create an arena for universal human rights above and beyond the nation state. However, attempts to introduce social citizenship as an element of these supra-national organisations (such as through the Maastricht Treaty or acceptance of the Community Charter of the Fundamental Rights of Workers) have been strongly resisted by nation states themselves. The deepening of ties in the European Community itself serves to create protectionist divisions between citizens who are members of a privileged group of countries and those who are not – and to keep the latter out. The citizens of the European Community are able to enjoy those citizenship rights which can be guaranteed by secure political systems and economic prosperity by virtue of their membership of one of those member states. In practice, most forms of citizenship are tied to the nation state.

However, it is also clear that young people have very different rights and responsibilities in different parts of Europe as well as different kinds of transition – in and out of the family for example. The more individualistic notion of youth characteristic of Northern Europe is not found in the more family-centred concepts of young people in Southern Europe (Pais 1995; Wallace and Kovatcheva 1998). Thus according to the Young Europeans survey of 1990 (Chisholm and Bergeret 1992), young people in Northern Europe wanted to leave home and set up independent households – living separately from their parents was their ideal. However, in Southern Europe, young people did not tend to leave home until they got married. Few young people aimed to live away from home. In Southern Europe and in Eastern Europe there is strong interdependency between children and their parents, whilst in Northern Europe this is not so much the case. These expectations affect gender roles too. In different parts of Europe both the welfare provision and the cultural expectations of what it is to be young, vary. This leads us to ask if there is one model of youth or several?

2. Young People, Citizenship and Marginality

For a range of marginalised groups, citizenship represents a way of gaining universal recognition for their rights in the liberal individualist tradition. Thus, gay couples argue they should have the right to marry or adopt children in the same way as heterosexual couples. Equal rights legislation in most countries can be appealed to in order to uphold these kind of individual citizenship rights. In the political struggles of these marginalised groups, citizenship is appealing because it represents a universal ideal.

However, the liberal individualistic notion of citizenship disguises the fact that different citizens have differential access to citizenship which depend upon not them as individuals but upon their position in the family. Hence this model of citizenship has been challenged by feminist writers who argue that it is undermined by the principle of dependency which is implicit within it (Lister 1990; Summers 1991). This critique focuses on the fact that because women are dependants they are not citizens in the same way as men – they are citizens only through their husbands who claim benefits and pay taxes on behalf of the family. Lister (1990) argues that full social citizenship must recognise women's position as carers within the family in order to be universal. Their access to social welfare depends in some instances upon their relationship to a man. The liberal individualist concept of citizenship assumes a free, individualistic competitor, a model which women with dependants cannot meet.

This critique of liberal notions of citizenship also apply to the situation of young people. Many aspects of social citizenship and other rights also, are defined through the family. They have what we have termed a "proxy" citizenship (Jones and Wallace 1992). Their situation applies also to other groups who have potentially differentiated rights within employment, legal, political and social security systems, or are excluded from the labour market such as the disabled, mentally handicapped and the retired. The association of access to citizenship with full employment tends to relegate those who are not fully employed to lesser forms of citizenship and here the difference between having a right to something and having access to it can be important. For some of these groups state protection, either through guaranteeing negative freedoms or through social support, can be particularly important if their rights or positive freedoms are to be ensured (Fraser and Gordon 1994). Feminists have therefore argued for a version of citizenship that also recognises these differences (Jones 1990).

Differences also occur through poverty. Thus it is that although people may have equal rights, they do not necessarily have equal access to those rights (Jones and Wallace 1992). Hence, people have the right to travel, to buy houses, to change jobs – but cannot necessarily afford to do so. Citizenship is therefore limited by the market as T. H. Marshall recognised (Marshall 1950).

Ethnic minorities have struggled for equal treatment under the law. Although these rights are mostly recognised in Europe it is often the case that the different lifestyles of particular ethnic groups exclude them from such rights. Thus Roma, by not being registered as members of the state they are living in, can be discriminated against, as is the case in the Czech Republic with Roma that came originally from Slovakia and then found themselves stateless. Roma have been universally in conflict with governments who have found their itinerant existence to be problematic as it does not conform to their model of a "good citizen" and have tried to suppress or incorporate them (Crowe 1996). Other ethnic minorities in Europe have been subject to assimilation, discrimination, expulsion and extermination so that recognition of equal citizenship rights with the majority population can be an important human rights achievement. Nevertheless it does not necessarily prevent a range of non-formal forms of discrimination. Furthermore it does not prevent people forming subjective assessments about who should belong to the society independent of legal status (see chapters by Suurpää, Hilden and Virtanen, this volume).

People from marginalised ethnic groups suffer discrimination also as a result of institutionalised racism which may prevent them having access to citizenship rights which they in fact possess. Here we need to look at the models for defining citizenship in different societies. Examples are first France where there is a predominantly civic model in which everyone born in the state is a member of the state but where there are strong assimilationist tendencies. Secondly, Germany where there is a predominately ethnic model whereby citizenship is conferred by descent rather than place of residence. Despite the exclusionary nature of this model, it does help to recognise rights to separate schooling and other provisions for ethnic minorities, because the assumption is that they are not citizens and will eventually return home. Ironically, this system is therefore better at recognising "difference". Third, there is a predominantly imperial model exemplified by countries such as Britain, Netherlands and the former Soviet Union, whereby a multi-national empire claims a range of people as its citizens, both those who live in the state and those who live elsewhere. Although a range of different nationalities and cultures may be seen as citizens, there is nevertheless a hegemonic domination by the "mother" country. In Central and South-Eastern Europe, according to some authors, a "patchwork" model is the predominant one whereby ethnic groups live in patches of territory and make claims for rights to language, schooling and other collective goods according to their own culture (Brubaker 1994; Brubaker 1996).

Members of ethnic groups have struggled over the last years to win rights for themselves as groups rather than as individuals. They have argued for example for education in their own language, for official documents to be written in their language and so on. Examples of this are the Welsh in Britain, the Austrian minority in Italy, the Basques in Spain and the Hungarians in Romania. However, the institutionalisation of collective rather than individual rights also poses problems for a liberal model of citizenship where all people should in principle have the same rights. If an Austrian in Italy is allowed an education in her own language, then why not a North African or an Albanian?

In this sense the recognition of citizenship by marginalised groups can be ambiguous. It can serve to recognise that group, but it can also serve to submerge them in a collective citizenship, which does not recognise individual rights.

3. Citizenship and the Welfare State: Social Citizenship

In T. H. Marshall's (Marshall 1950) conception of social citizenship, he envisaged an evolutionary expansion of citizenship rights as part of a process of modernisation, whereby all members of the polity would acquire rights to various kinds of social benefits. This was based upon a post-war model of the welfare state stabilised by Keynesian policies of full (male) employment. It was also predicated upon the idea of "normal" standardised family transitions from childhood to adulthood, from singlehood to marriage and parenthood, from pupil/trainee to worker etc. However, since the 1970s many of the benefits of social citizenship have been reversed rather than increased as welfare states have attempted to cut back the amount of entitlements but also to reduce the numbers of people who are entitled to benefits. This has important implications for young people who in some states have been thus excluded from entitlements which they had won in former decades. The example would be the UK where young people have lost the right to claim benefits after leaving school and lost also many housing benefits and France where there have been successive attempts to exclude young people from the benefit system.

Social citizenship would be provided or guaranteed by the state. Thus, each form of rights was guaranteed by a set of institutions. On the one side there were "negative freedoms" – freedom from arbitrary interference by the state, freedom to follow one's own wishes and desires – on the other side there were "positive freedoms", or the right to receive sufficient support to participate as an citizen in the same way as others.

Citizenship rights seemed to provide a source of social integration in post-Second World War society because these were in principle both universal and equal for everyone. Despite the institutionalisation of these rights however, access to citizenship is not universal since it is determined not only by legal rights but also by the ability of individuals to mobilise their resources (Barbalet 1988). There is an important difference between rights which people have in principle and the ones they have in practice.

The social welfare system in many welfare states is also based upon what Crompton (1998) calls a "breadwinner model" (e.g. the UK) whereby the benefit entitlements of the family are organised through the (male) breadwinner who pays social insurance. This model has even been reinforced in recent years despite the fact that it is undermined by the many new types of family forms and rising unemployment. In societies with a "family model" of welfare (e.g. France) this is not such an important issue. However, even in the latter societies, access to welfare entitlements is restricted through access to the labour market (Pateman 1989). Many benefits are paid through insurances and the insurances are paid by deductions from employment. Even in societies like the Scandinavian ones with more "universal" models of welfare (Esping-Andersen 1990), benefits are a reward for work. This is particularly problematic for young people because they are less and less likely to be working, and if they are working are likely to be found in casualised or informal jobs which do not

17

necessarily give them access to full benefits. They may spend long periods outside of the labour market.

This exclusion from employment-based forms of citizenship is a product of several factors. First, the increasing tendency of young people to continue in full time education and training for longer and longer periods of time. Second, the increasing numbers of young people who are unable to enter the labour market due to high unemployment, something which has particularly affected the young. Third, many of the jobs they do enter may be casual ones or those in the informal economy. This is particularly the case in some inner city areas where a section of young people simply disappear from the formal system (Coles 1995) and in Southern Europe where youth unemployment is very high.

These factors have lead to an increasingly extended transition for young people so that family and life course transitions are also likely to be postponed or to be embarked upon before entering the labour market as full time workers. This has helped to redefine what is meant by "young" and leads to a move away from the standardised transitions upon which the post-war welfare state was built. This has lead some to hypothesise a 30:30:30 model. For the first 30 years of one's life there is studying and training and courting – outside the labour market. For the second 30 years one is inside the labour market and for the last 30 years outside of it again. The 30 years in the middle have to support a lot of people on either side of the age divide.

This has provoked something of a crisis in the welfare and support of young people – who is going to support them during this long transition? To a great extent it is the family of origin who is responsible for this support. They have a paradoxical situation whereby their children are increasingly autonomous and independent from an earlier age (Büchner 1990; Postman 1983) but are economically dependent for longer and longer periods of time. This can create many tensions in families which might have had other expectations of their children. They are subject to a process of "individualisation" in the words of Ulrich Beck (Beck 1986).

Furthermore, citizenship varies across the life-cycle. The situation of young people has always been ambiguous with regard to citizenship since it is not clear at what age people should acquire this package of rights and they tend to acquire different rights at different ages (Jones and Wallace 1992). The increasing recognition of the rights of children as decision-making persons is accompanied by the removal of welfare rights from groups of young people, who, like married women, are deemed to have rights via their families.

Thus, citizenship as defined by the welfare state – social citizenship – is something which is being eroded and undermined in many countries and young people are at the sharp end of this.

4. Citizens and Non-Citizens

All the discussions described above refer mainly to the nation-state. The rights one acquires are rights which are granted by the nation-state and the duties or obligations which one has as a citizen (serving in the army, paying taxes) are those to the nation state. Here we can indeed distinguish two meanings of citizenship: *formal* citizenship or the membership of a particular nation-state and *substantive* citizenship, or the rights and obligations which one assumes as a citizen.

The post-war patterns of migration of labour and people in Europe have created new problems of citizenship and here the idea is used mainly as a device for excluding some people. Waves of migration from the South to the North, from former colonies and Commonwealth countries to the European colonisers and now from the East to the West mean that lack of citizenship excludes members who might want to join and enjoy the full citizenship rights of the country where they are living. Citizenship rights, developed over a period of time through social insurance and taxation, make citizens unwilling to divide their national cake into smaller pieces by sharing it with what they might consider to be "outsiders". This is fuelled by speculation about "welfare migration" of which there is in fact very little. In Britain "citizenship" became a subject of legislation in the post-war period in order to limit the rights of former Commonwealth members by progressively narrowing the eligibility of citizenship. In Germany and Austria new legislation is being enacted to limit the rights of candidates for citizenship, migrants and asylum seekers who are arriving into these countries. Even within nation states, citizenship has been used to marginalise or exclude ethnic and migrant minorities as the case of the Slovak Roma in the Czech Republic illustrates. The position of migrant workers in many European states was subject to this kind of definition. Under some circumstances citizenship, rather than being universal, becomes a policy instrument for institutionalised racism.

The influx of foreigners in the post-war period means that there are many residents of each state who do not count as full citizens. Yet there are many versions of non-citizenship and of semi-citizenship. To begin with there are the migrants from inside the European Union, then there are guest workers from outside the European Union. For many of these young people who may have grown up in Western European countries, they identify more with their host society than they do with the country of which they are nominally "citizens". This is the case with many guest workers in Germany, Austria and Switzerland for example. It is also the case that asylum seekers and refugees have a form of ambiguous partial citizenship – in the former case as applicants and in the latter case as special exceptions which have to be proved.

It is furthermore the case that even if they are accepted as "citizens", they may find themselves socially excluded on grounds of race, religion or nationality as is the case with young people of North African origin in France, for example. For these young people, a renewed national militancy, expressed for example by wearing headscarves in school, is espoused in opposition to the dominant integrationist tendencies. Often the idea of the migrant excites fear and loathing in the minds of many Europeans (even if they were themselves migrants in the not-too-distant past) in the same way as "welfare scroungers" – people abusing their rights or without any right to benefits. Draconian measures against them are justified along with ever more desperate attempts by migrants to get in. This imagery is further inflamed by politicians of the far right who help to make fear of migrants and the reinforcement of citizenship against them a part of mainstream politics.

The increased mobility of recent years has lead some such as Rainer Bauböck (1994) to formulate a concept of "transnational citizenship" which would better fit the realities of the situation. Instead, exactly the opposite concepts of citizenship are being emphasised, ones which are more restrictive and based more than ever upon the nation state. Migration also throws into a new light the problems of nationality and citizenship as people can be formally members of a given nation state (for example one to which they have migrated) but not want to relinquish their former nationality. This is the case with British-Asians for example. This reinvigoration of national claims within formal citizenship is also reflected in the claims of various indigenous nationalities. The example of someone having Flemish nationality but Belgian citizenship for example, or Scottish nationality and British citizenship.

A further group of non-citizens in Europe are the illegal immigrants. Irregular migration is increasing at a global level (Gosh 1998). As citizenship regulations have become more strict over the last century and entitlement to welfare a more and more contested issue, this has tended to create a group of people who are excluded altogether from political, civic and social citizenship. The tightening of asylum regulations has had the same effect, since those fleeing various kinds of oppression know that they have little chance of being officially recognised and may prefer to go underground, or officially "disappear" at some point during the asylum seeking process. Others are economic migrants seeking better lives but excluded from legal migration due to restrictive immigration laws. The majority of these "non-citizens" are young people and they are thought to number several millions in Europe. They are not officially entitled to education, health care or any kind of social benefit. They are mainly "invisible". They represent a casual, highly exploitable work force.

Increasing European integration is likely to increase these exclusionary tendencies as the model of European citizenship which is being developed tends to be a predominantly white, Christian one which renders non-white, non-Christian Europeans as invisible. These exclusionary tendencies may be further exacerbated by the deflationary consequences of the Maastricht Treaty and the introduction of the European currency because welfare states would cut their budgets by further decreasing welfare and restricting citizenship, something from which already disadvantaged (often non-white and ethnic minority) groups are likely to suffer more (Baimbridge, Burkitt and Macey 1994). This was illustrated in a recent visit by a group of visitors from Central and Eastern Europe to the Council of Europe in Strasbourg. One member of the group pointed to some black representatives in the Council of Europe and exclaimed: "But what are they doing here!" For him, as for many people, the vision of Europe did not include black people. The hard-won recognition of racism and of the situation of people of colour would have to be fought all over again at a European level.

More Active Models of Citizenship

Many of the ideas of citizenship outlined so far imply a rather passive notion of citizenship. Citizenship is granted by the nation state, rights are conferred and so on. Whereas many discussions of citizenship assume that these rights would somehow be automatically bestowed by the course of history and a benevolent welfare state, in fact these rights were the outcome of struggle by different social groups and were won rather than bestowed over a long period of time. Such a struggle was brought about by organised bodies representing different interest groups and the trade unions had an important role to play in this. More recently women's groups, agitational groups representing the poor or the politically marginalised and ethnic organisations have been important in bringing rights to public attention through what has been termed "civil society" (Keane 1988). New rights are coming onto the political agenda as protest groups are organised, so that we could arguably now claim that the right to a clean environment should be added to the list of universal rights of citizens as a consequence of the popular mobilisation of environmental pressure groups.

Furthermore, citizenship is interpreted in different ways by different political lobbies. The neo-liberal and New Right political constellation of parties have tended to emphasise the negative freedoms of citizenship – freedom to own property, to legally form contacts, freedom from the arbitrary authority of the state – whereas the more communitarian and socialist constellations of parties have tended to emphasise the more positive freedoms, guaranteed by social rights such as the right to work, the right to education, housing and social assistance.

One factor that has emerged in these debates has been the criticism of citizenship as something bestowed by a benign state on a passive population. The issue was not just what the society gives to the individual, but what the individual gives to the society. There have therefore been efforts to encourage "active citizenship". A further model for "active citizenship" is the idea of the individual taking responsibility for the welfare of herself and her family rather than relying on the state (Green 1987; Murray 1988). This then emphasises the responsibilities of citizens rather than their rights and stands in stark contrast to the original notion of social citizenship. From the left of the political spectrum, communitarians and socialists have emphasised too the more active integration of citizens in the provision of services, but they have also stressed the importance of state involvement and support in this (Keane 1988). More recently, discussions of social capital have tended to praise a model of active citizenship as one which can assist social and economic development (see Spannring, Wallace and Haerpfer, this volume).

22

The idea of citizenship has therefore been shaded in different political colours as it is espoused by parties across the political spectrum but there is no necessary agreement on what it should be. The concept of citizenship is politically contested because it is essentially a normative concept: that is, it describes what should be, rather than what is, in much of this rhetoric. However, the normative goal of citizenship has served to raise expectations of what citizens expect from the state and these lead governments to increase public expenditure and taxation, which can in turn weaken the economy. In this way the normative aspirations of citizenship can lead to an inherent crisis of unfulfilled expectations (Turner 1990). The universal promise of citizenship is in fact always undermined by various inequalities.

This more active model of citizenship brings us to the issue of empowerment.

Young People and Empowerment

Let us now look more closely at the idea of empowerment. The idea of empowerment has been developed in the context of the culturally engineered work place where the employee is supposed to serve out of intrinsic motivation rather than as a result of external hierarchical control. The idea of empowerment has also been developed in radical social work and community work to encourage the self-help of client groups (disabled etc.) to help them out of a dependency role. It was also applied to the mobilisation of community groups and neighbourhoods as well as individuals.

Here we can distinguish between an idea of empowerment as it is usually used in the US context and that which is usually used in the European context. In the US context, empowerment is a more individualistic notion, one based upon more psychological assumptions. People should be empowered to be individually socially mobile and improve their situation – to climb out of the disadvantaged group that they are in (see for example Yowell and Gordon 1997). In the European context, empowerment usually refers to social groups and to structural problems such as poverty, ethnicity, race and so on. In the European discussions, people should be empowered to improve the conditions of their social group generally (rather than leaving it behind them) (see for example Wise 1995). In this latter view, empowering someone is to help them to address their problems and according to some feminists this is best done through showing them that they are part of some more collective oppression in order to "enable them thereby to take back some control in their lives" (Wise 1995, 108).

Empowerment is usually used in the context of more marginalised groups to enable them to address their problems and to find a voice. It is argued in the case of young people that it should help them to become more mature. However, it is also the case that if marginal young people are empowered, this is also likely to challenge adult or dominant values (Nessel 1988).

In reviewing the literature on empowerment, I found the following examples (mostly from North America) illustrating different kinds of empowerment in different contexts. In the study of Yowell and Gordon (1997) the issue was how to address the dissonance between the informal cultural values of urban young people and the official institutional cultures with which they are confronted. The authors were concerned with how young people could acquire the skills to adapt to these institutional environments whilst utilising the resources of their families and neighbourhoods. They come to the conclusion that a certain kind of "adaptive defiance" is possible. In another study, young people were used to evaluate the programmes in which they participated, being used rather like a research assistant (Penwell and Freeman 1996). In another study, gay and lesbian young people were invited to "tell their own stories" in therapeutic workshops (Mallon 1997). In European Union programmes such as that of DG XX11 "Youth for Europe" the participation of young people is also seen as a requirement. In the British Economic and Social Research Council programme on "Youth, Citizenship and Social Change" this is also the case. When I inquired as to what this meant exactly, I was informed that in some research projects, young people were involved in collecting and evaluating the data (rather like the study of Penwell and Freeman cited above) and in other projects, they were recruited as a monitoring group to comment upon the research as it evolved. The empowerment and participation of young people is also seen as essential in a recent initiative by the Carnegie Foundation in the UK.

However, amidst all this euphoria about empowering youth, we should be aware of some of the limitations. First, the idea of empowerment can be used as a way of individualising social problems and cutting services. This reflects the meaning of empowerment used by the New Right (Abbott and

Wallace 1992). Thus, persons should be empowered to solve their own problems and to manage their own social mobility, or even to solve the problems of the entire social group. This shifts responsibility from statutory agencies to the client. Second, not all young people want to be empowered. Empowerment can only be effective in the right circumstances and with the right kind of training and support. Some young people may be looking for more leadership and control rather than empowerment. It would not suit every kind of young person and every kind of ethnic culture (Nessel 1988). Third, we need to ask ourselves where empowerment will lead. Will empowered young people find better jobs? Will they become community leaders? The question is whether the empowerment of individuals or social groups can really lead to any long term change. In addition, there can be anti-social forms of empowerment. The skinheads described by Hilden and Virtanen in this volume have taken it into their own hands to "clean" the streets of foreigners and restore what they saw as the rightful values and morals. Finally, empowerment is also a form of social control. It shifts the locus of control from the external agencies to the internal moral agency of the individual. It could therefore be seen as a form of discipline in a Foucauldian sense (Foucault 1975). In the critique of the engineered work cultures, it is evident that this kind of empowerment can lead to a "colonisation of the self" and self-exploitation (Hochschild 1997).

Citizenship and Empowerment

Let us now reconsider our four notions of citizenship and the implications they have for empowerment.

1. European Citizenship and Empowerment

At the level of European citizenship, youth has been an important issue. Whilst some governments, such as the UK refused to recognise "youth" as a social group (thereby avoiding any discussion of welfare for this group), at the European level there are a number of initiatives and even a Directorate General which is responsible for youth affairs. Education and exchange programmes are targeted at youth. At a European level, youth have received recognition, but most provisions for young people are nevertheless at a national level and therefore very variable. Thus whilst some countries have a "youth ministry" for example, others do not. However, it remains problematic the extent to which young people participating in European programmes can influence a community of 350 million people. At an institutional level there is little representation for young people and in Eastern Europe the "token" representation which young people held formerly has disappeared. Although young people played an important part in toppling the former Communist regimes in 1989 and can still mobilise to bring down governments, in fact these youth movements tend to evaporate after they have achieved their goals. Youth are more likely to mobilise against some authority and are much less likely to mobilise around things which affect them directly, such as cuts in student grants, the introduction of fees in education and so on (Wallace and Kovatcheva 1998). Thus the formal empowerment of young people in Eastern Europe through youth has declined and as we see in the chapter by Spannring, Wallace and Haerpfer, their participation and integration into society has declined as well.

2. Citizenship, Marginality and Empowerment

Here youth empowerment has more meaning. The struggles by various groups for recognition is indeed a form of empowerment, but it affects young people only indirectly, if they are members of such groups. However, young people are often members of these marginalised groups.

3. Social Citizenship and Empowerment

Although there are campaigns by pressure groups to restore or to improve welfare benefits, including groups representing young people, these are of limited success in a climate where welfare benefits are being generally reduced. What is more significant, perhaps is the empowerment of young people *within* different branches of welfare – in children's homes and hostels, in youth clubs and so on. Here there is a considerable literature (see the Journal of Youth and Policy, the Deutsche Jugendberichten etc.).

4. Non-Citizens, Semi-Citizens and Empowerment

Young people who are not citizens are automatically excluded from having a political voice. They cannot of course vote, but even by drawing attention to themselves, they are in danger of being deported. They are subject to many kinds of material and sexual exploitation and have little opportunity to protest against this. The organisations who would normally help young people in these situations, such as trade unions, are closed to them. It was various NGOs (Non-Governmental Organisations) who managed for example to assist young women who were working as forced prostitutes in Western Europe, but this was only possible in certain contexts. The plight of young non-citizens should be something that perhaps different ethnic and religious organisations should accommodate. The ethnic and religious organisations from the migrants' own community are those most likely to know of their situation and be in the best position to empower them. In the case of the semi-citizens, their self-empowerment can lead to resentment among the local population as is described in the cases of the Somali refugees in Finland (see Suurpää, Hilden and Virtanen, this volume).

Until now we have looked at young people as though they are static entities in the European polity. In fact youth is a passing phase (although it takes longer and longer to pass) and this transient status means that youth are more difficult to mobilise as youth in search of citizenship rights. Nevertheless, their increasing involvement in civil society, especially in civic participation, is evidence of the increasingly mobilised and empowered citizenship of young people in many parts of Western Europe (see Spannring, Wallace and Haerpfer, this volume).

Furthermore, we have to be aware that the idea of the "good citizen" can also be a form of oppression, as those who lived through Communism in Eastern Europe are aware. Not all young people want to conform to the model of the good citizen, neither do ethnic communities. The history of youth sub-cultures has been one of successive waves of young people challenging notions of cultural conformity in each generation, including models of the good citizen to which they are expected to conform. For some young people for example, homelessness was a form of freedom and they would reject the provision which tried to turn them into "good citizens" in return for welfare (Carlen 1996). We should bear this in mind as a warning not to assume that if people are not conforming, then they should conform. Citizenship should be flexible enough to allow a range of definitions to exist.

Conclusions

In this chapter I have discussed four kinds of citizenship and their implications for young people and empowerment: European citizenship; the recognition of diverse identities; social citizenship and the welfare state; formal citizenship status. Citizenship and empowerment start to converge in the more recent reconceptualisations of citizenship which have tended to emphasise the idea of citizenship not as a static set of rights and obligations which a person merely steps into but as something active, which has to be seized and transformed (see also the contributions by Ladislav Macháček and David Everatt, this volume). Rather, what is emphasised is the way in which citizenship is an emergent process which is defined by different social groups in different ways in the course of growing up. However, there is also some divergence in these notions when we consider that empowering youth may lead them to challenge notions of the "good citizen".

Finally we should look at citizenship, as at empowerment, at a number of different levels. At the macro-level of the European Community there are attempts to recognise the rights of young people and to empower them, albeit rather weakly. Whilst empowerment can only be weak at this level, citizenship can be formulated cross-nationally with the help of the EU. At the meso-level of the nation there are wide variations as to what is meant by citizenship and empowerment for young people and the extent to which either would be desirable. At the micro-level of the local community, training scheme, youth club etc., it seems that the ideas of empowerment might be most effective although citizenship, depending as it does on national policies, rather less so.

Notes

1. Question wording: "In the near future do you see yourself as....?", p. B24, Eurobarometer No. 44, Spring 1996.

2. Question wording: "With which of the following do you most closely identify yourself? Europe, Country, Region, Local community, Other." Question measures people who put Europe as their first or second choice. Central Europe = Poland, Hungary, Czech Republic, Slovakia, Slovenia. South-Eastern Europe = Romania, Bulgaria, Federal Republic of Yugoslavia, Croatia, Belarus and Ukraine. N = 12643.

References

Abbott, P. A. and Wallace, C. (1992), *The New Right and the Family in Britain and America*, Pluto Press, London.

Baimbridge, M., Burkitt, B. and Macey, M. (1994), 'The Maastricht Treaty: Exacerbating Racism in Europe?', *Ethnic and Racial Studies, 17 (2)*, pp. 420-441.

Barbalet, J. M. (1988), *Citizenship*, Open University Press, Milton Keynes.

Bauböck, R. (1994), *From Aliens to Citizens: Redefining the Status of Immigrants in Europe*, Avebury, Aldershot, Brookfield USA, Hong Kong, Sydney.

Beck, U. (1986), *Risikogesellschaft: Auf dem Weg in eine andere Moderne*, Suhrkamp, Frankfurt.

Brubaker, R. (1994), *Citizenship and Nationhood in France and Germany*, Harvard University Press, USA.

Brubaker, R. (1996), *Nationalism Reframed: Nationhood and the National Question in the New Europe*, Cambridge University Press, Cambridge.

Büchner, P. (1990), 'Growing up in the Eighties: Changes in the Social Biography of Childhood in the FRG', in L. Chisholm, P. Büchner, H-H. Krüger and P. Brown (eds.), *Childhood, Youth and Social Change: A Comparative Perspective*, Falmer Press, Taylor and Francis, Hants.

Carlen, P. (1996), *A Political Criminology of Youth Homelessness*, Open University Press, Buckingham.

Chisholm, L. and Bergeret, J. M. (1992), *Young People in the European Community: Towards an Agenda for Research and Policy*, European Community, Youth Task Force, Brussels.

Coles, B. (1995), *Youth and Social Policy: Youth, Citizenship and Young Careers*, UCL Press, London.

Crompton, R. (1998), *Address to the Conference 'Work, Employment and Society'*, University of Cambridge, September 1998.

Crowe, D. (1996), *The History of the Gypsies of Eastern Europe and Russia*, St. Martin's Griffin, New York.

Esping-Andersen, G. (1990), *The Three Worlds of Welfare Capitalism*, Polity Press, Cambridge.

Foucault, M. (1975), *Discipline and Punish: The Birth of the Prison*, Penguin, Harmondsworth.

Fraser, N. and Gordon, L. (1994), 'Civil Citizenship against Social Citizenship: On the Idea of Contract vs. Charity', in B. Steenbergen (ed.), *The Condition of Citizenship*, Sage Publications, London.

Gosh, B. (1998), *Huddled Masses and Uncertain Shores: Insights into Irregular Migration*, Nijhoff, The Hague, Netherlands.

Green, D. (1987), *The New Right: The Counter-Revolution in Political, Economic and Social Thought*, Wheatsheaf, Sussex.

Hochschild, A. R. (1997), *The Time Bind: When Work Becomes Home and Home Becomes Work*, Henry Holt and Company, New York.

Inglehart, R. (1997), *Modernization and Postmodernization: Cultural, Political and Economic Change in 43 Societies*, Princeton University Press, Princeton.

Jones, G. and Wallace, C. (1992), *Youth, Family and Citizenship*, Open University Press, Milton Keynes, UK.

Jones, K. B. (1990), 'Citizenship in a Woman-Friendly Polity', *Signs, 15 (4)*, pp. 781-812.

Keane, J. (1988), *Democracy and Civil Society: On the Predicaments of European Socialism, the Prospects for Democracy and the Problem of Controlling Social and Political Power*, Verso, London, New York.

Lister, R. (1990), 'Women, Economic Dependency and Citizenship', *Journal of Social Policy, 19 (4)*, pp. 445-67.

Mallon, G. P. (1997), 'Entering into a Collaborative Search for Meaning with Gay and Lesbian Youth in out-of-home Care: An Empowerment-Based Model for Training Child Welfare Professionals', *Child and Adolescent Social Work, 14 (6)*, pp. 427-444.

Marshall, T. H. (1950), *Citizenship and Social Class and other Essays*, Cambridge University Press, Cambridge.

Murray, C. (1988), *In Pursuit of Happiness and Good Government*, Simon and Schuster, New York.

Nessel, L. (1988), 'A Coalition Approach to Enhancing Youth Empowerment', *Social Policy, 19 (1)*, pp. 25-27.

Pais, J. M. (1995), 'Growing up on the EU Periphery: Portugal', in L. Chisholm, P. Büchner and M. du Bois-Reymond (eds.), *Growing up in Europe: Contemporary Horizons in Childhood and Youth Studies*, Walter de Gruyter, Berlin and New York.

Pateman, C. (1989), *The Disorder of Women*, Polity Press, Cambridge.

Penwell, W. R. and Freeman, T. (1996), 'Participatory Action Research in Youth Programming: A Theory in Use', *Child and Youth Care Forum, 26 (3)*, pp. 175-185.

Porter, E. (1999), *Feminist Perspectives on Ethics*, Longman Addison Wesley, London.

Postman, N. (1983), *The Disappearance of Childhood*, Allen and Unwin, London.

Summers, Y. (1991), 'Women and Citizenship: The Insane, the Insolvent and the Inanimate?', in P. Abbott and C. Wallace (eds.), *Gender, Power and Sexuality*, Macmillan, London.

Turner, B. S. (1990), 'Outline of a Theory of Citizenship', *Sociology, 24 (2)*, pp. 189-217.

Wallace, C. and Kovatcheva, S. (1998), *Youth in Society: The Construction and Deconstruction of Youth in East and West Europe*, Macmillan, London.

Wallace, C., Spannring, R. and Haerpfer, C. (2000), *Youth and Civic Integration in East and West Europe*, Institute for Advanced Studies, Vienna.

Wise, S. (1995), 'Feminist Ethics in Practice', in R. Hugman and D. Smith (eds.), *Ethical Issues in Social Work*, Routledge, London.

Yowell, C. M. and Gordon, E. W. (1997), 'Youth Empowerment and Human Service Institutions', *Journal of Negro Education, 65 (1)*, pp. 19-29.

Appendix

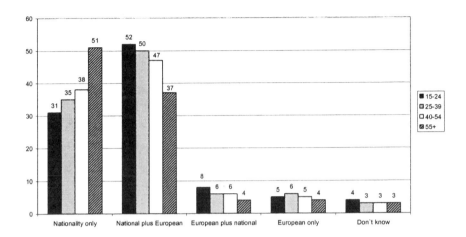

Figure 2.1 European and national identity. Eurobarometer 1996

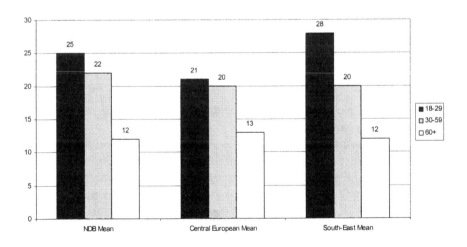

Figure 2.2 Those espousing European identity as first choice

31

3 Civic Participation among Young People in Europe

REINGARD SPANNRING, CLAIRE WALLACE and
CHRISTIAN HAERPFER[1]

Introduction

Discussions about citizenship and empowerment often hinge upon the contribution of young people to different aspects of civic life, either as active volunteers or as members of organisations. Whilst this does not exhaust the ways in which young people can be active "citizens", it is an important element and one which can be analysed quantitatively or qualitatively as other chapters in this volume show (see Nylund, this volume). However, whilst the other chapters in this volume concentrate more upon what kinds of people are active and for what reasons, we would like to stand back and consider how the activity of young people differs across the different countries and regions of Europe. Furthermore, given the anxiety about the decline of "social capital" (in the sense of civic participation) in the USA and the consequences that are alleged to follow in terms of poor educational results, anomie and economic disadvantage (Coleman 1988; Coleman 1988-1989; Putnam 1995a; Putnam 1995b; Putnam 1996), we would like to consider if this is also the case in Europe, especially for young people.

Civic participation is nearly always regarded as a "good thing" whether it is in the context of the development of the Third Sector between state and market (Offe and Heinze 1992; Beck 1997) or in the context of the revival of "civil society" as a layer of associational life between the government and the people (Keane 1988). Most recently, this discussion has tended to hinge around "social capital" and this is usually taken to mean the extent of public participation, which is thought to create a moral climate, enabling the self-regulation of citizens, assisting in turn economic development and modernisation. The classic text in this respect is that of Robert Putnam, who has argued that it was the participation in civil society through such activities as joining football clubs and choral societies which helps to account for the different levels of development in Northern and Southern Italy (Putnam 1994).

In Europe, we could develop a range of speculations regarding social capital and civic participation more generally. For example, there are countries where there has always been a strong tradition of associational life, such as Germany and Switzerland, and others where this has not traditionally been the case – as in Southern Europe. Is civic participation, therefore, simply part of a very long-term tradition, implying a certain historical determinism in this kind of activity? The European Union and the Council of Europe have both been developing programmes to encourage the active involvement of young people in their societies through "Education for Citizenship" programmes, but does membership of such supra-national organisations really make any difference? On the other hand, the participation in civil society could simply reflect levels of affluence: those with more money have more time to think about doing something for the community.

Such issues are of particular importance in Eastern and Central Europe. The collapse of Communism has meant a decline in the formal organisations representing "youth" as a category and young people are no longer compelled to give up their free time for "voluntary" activities which formed part of the communist socialisation programme (Wallace and Kovatcheva 1998). In the process they also lost privileged access to sports, recreation and travel programmes. The conditions of life have become much harsher as many young people are unemployed or forced to look for extra income in the informal economy (Wallace and Haerpfer 2000). However, in our empirical research we have found that there are also great differences between Central and Eastern European countries in terms of their paths of transition (Wallace and Haerpfer 1998; Agh 1998). Whilst the Central European countries, the countries in the first round of accession to the European Union, have generally come through the transition well, other countries to the South and especially to the East in the former Soviet Union have been more characterised by economic and social deterioration in conditions. The Baltic countries, claiming a closer affinity with Scandinavia, may also be in a different transition trajectory. What implications do these changes have for young people? How might it affect their civic participation and the development of social capital?

Methods of Research

To answer these questions, we have turned to the World Values Survey (WVS). The WVS was carried out in most Western European countries in three waves: 1980, 1990-3, 1997-8. Here we have concentrated mainly on waves 2 and 3 because most Central-Eastern European countries were not included in wave 1. The questions in the WVS distinguish between active membership (which we take as an indicator of "civic participation") and passive membership (which we take as an indicator of "civic integration") (Wallace, Spannring and Haerpfer 2000). Thus, we can look at changes over the period of the 1990s, which has seen the opening of Eastern and Central Europe and the widening and deepening of the institutions of the European Union. The WVS for 1990 covers the following European countries: France, Britain, West Germany, Italy, Netherlands, Denmark, Belgium, Spain, Ireland, Hungary, Norway, Sweden, Iceland, Finland, Poland, Switzerland, Belarus, Czech Republic, East Germany, Slovenia, Bulgaria, Romania, Portugal, Austria, Lithuania, Latvia, Estonia, Russia and Slovakia. The WVS for 1997-8 covers the following European countries: Britain, West Germany, Spain, Hungary, Norway, Sweden, Finland, Poland, Switzerland, Belarus, Czech Republic, East Germany, Slovenia, Bulgaria, Romania, Lithuania, Latvia, Estonia, Ukraine, Russia, Moldova, Albania, Serbia, Montenegro, Macedonia, Croatia, Slovakia and Bosnia Herzegovina. This means that not all countries took part in both waves. Moreover, not all countries, which participated in both waves, asked the same questions again in wave 3. As a result we were only able to include the following countries with respect to participation in organisations: West Germany, Switzerland, Spain, Norway, Sweden, Finland, East Germany, Slovenia, Hungary, Bulgaria, Romania, Lithuania, Latvia, Estonia and Russia.

The questions which we are considering here are those about membership of different organisations and we have analysed: church or religious organisations, sport or recreation organisations, art, music or educational organisations, environmental organisations, professional organisations, charitable organisations, voluntary organisations, political parties and labour unions.

One problem, which we encountered when comparing waves 2 and 3, was that the question wording for these questions was changed. In the 1990 survey it was asked if one "belonged to" any of these organisations and then, if one did unpaid work for any of them. In the third wave it was asked whether one was an "active member", an "inactive member" or "not a member" of the organisations in question. This would have had the effect of encouraging more people to count themselves as members in 1995-98 than in 1990 and before. Thus, we must treat the general rise in civic participation, which we describe here as being rather exaggerated. Nevertheless, the fact that there is in fact a decline on some variables in some countries and large differences in the degree of increase between regions, inclines us to accept that at least some of the changes are "real" ones and not just an artefact of question wording.

Since there were so many countries in the third wave, we grouped them according to geo-political regions. In fact we first examined the tables of results to see if this regionalisation made sense, and found that in general it did. Furthermore since the numbers of young people were quite low (the surveys were based upon face-to-face interviews with a representative cross-section of the population – usually about 1000 people in each country),[2] in this way, we could raise this number of respondents to make the statistical analysis more reliable (see Wallace, Spannring and Haerpfer 2000).

Thus, for these purposes, West Germany and Switzerland represented Central-Western Europe; Spain represented South-Western Europe; Finland, Norway and Sweden represented North-Western Europe; East Germany, Slovenia and Hungary represented Central-Eastern Europe; Romania and Bulgaria represented South-Eastern Europe; the Baltic States of Lithuania, Latvia and Estonia represented North-Eastern Europe; Russia represented Eastern Europe. Some regions and countries are missing because we included only those countries, which were in both the second and third waves of the survey.

Results: The Growth of Citizenship?

The results are set out in the form of Figures 3.1-3.9 (see pp. 42-46, Appendix). Here we can see that for nearly every question, the membership and participation in organisations of civil society had grown between 1990 and 1997 in most countries (although some of this growth may be accounted for by the changed question wording). If we begin with Figure 3.1 (see p. 42, Appendix), we can see that membership of religious organisations has grown very dramatically between 1990 and 1997. Furthermore, active membership has grown even more than passive

35

membership (this difference is not shown here). In Central-Western Europe and in North-Western Europe, church membership has increased five-fold. In South-Western Europe, it has increased ten-fold. In the post-communist countries, the rise was not so dramatic: church membership increased three-fold in Central-Eastern Europe, and about the same in North-Eastern and South-Eastern Europe. In Eastern Europe, it declined slightly. This was a very dramatic result, especially for Western Europe, but some of it may be a consequence of the change in question wording (that means that the decline is even more dramatic in Eastern Europe than is pictured here). Has there really been a dramatic religious revival in Western Europe? The increase was the same for all religious denominations, so this cannot be accounted for by a sudden interest in cults and sects on the part of young people. However, increased religious participation reflects the increased participation in other sectors of civil society, as we shall see.

If we turn now to sport and recreational organisations (see p. 42, Appendix, Figure 3.2), we notice that this has also increased, although active membership seems to have decreased. Although the rates of increase are not as dramatic as for religious organisations. It has still increased by about one third in Central-Western Europe whilst in North-Western Europe, it has remained stable – but at high membership. The North-East has also remained stable with about one fifth of young people being members of sports clubs. In Central-Eastern Europe it has increased from 24 % to 35 %, whilst in the other post-communist countries there has also been a rise. The most astonishing growth in civic participation, however, is in the South-West – here represented by Spain, where it has increased from 9 % to 35 %.

Membership in art, music or educational organisations has also increased in Western Europe (see p. 43, Appendix, Figure 3.3). In Central-Western Europe it increased three-fold, from 8 % to 23 %, in South-Western Europe more than four-fold from 6 % to 27 % and in North-Western Europe it increased from 14 % to 27 %. In the post-communist countries this had also increased, although not so dramatically as in Western Europe.

Membership of professional organisations has also increased, although not by the same amount. In Central-Western Europe, this had increased from 7 % to 10 %, in South-Western Europe from 1 % to 12 %, in North-Western Europe it has remained stable at 7 %. On this variable, there was also a rise in the post-communist countries by a few per cent, although in Russia it has declined from very low to almost nothing at all (see p. 43,

36

Appendix, Figure 3.4).

Membership in charitable organisations (see p. 44, Appendix, Figure 3.5) has increased very dramatically, especially in the South-West, where it jumped from about 1 % to 13 % – the biggest rate of increase of all. However, in all other Western European countries, as well as in Central-Eastern Europe, there has been a rise in membership of charitable organisations (although only a small number of the population belongs to such organisations). Furthermore, the active participation has increased even more than the passive participation in these organisations (this is not shown here). Even in the post-communist countries of the Baltic Republics, along with Bulgaria and Romania, there has been an increase. Only in Russia has it declined from already low levels. We could say therefore, that this type of Third Sector activity has been of increasing importance in most parts of Europe.

In voluntary organisations, we find that the Central-Western European countries are more or less stable at about 12 % over the 1990s (see p. 44, Appendix, Figure 3.6), whilst the South-West has shot up from 3 % to 13 % and the North-West has stayed in the lead by rising from 12 % to 17 %. In Central-Eastern Europe, such membership has also increased from 4 % to 9 %. However, in the other post-communist regions, we find a decline over the 1990s so that membership of voluntary organisations is now almost negligible among young people.

Membership of environmental organisations has increased in Western Europe, especially in South-Western Europe where it rose eight-fold. In Central-Eastern Europe it also rose, although in the other post-communist regions, it has declined (see p. 45, Appendix, Figure 3.7). This reflects the fact, perhaps, that environmental activism was important as part of the politics of opposition during the perestroika period of the 1980s; now, along with other kind of political activism, this has declined among young people in these regions (Wallace and Kovatcheva 1998).

Membership of labour unions is one variable where there has been a general decline or not much increase, in most countries. Whilst in Central-Western and North-Western Europe, membership has been rather stable (See p. 45, Appendix, Figure 3.8), in South-Western Europe it has risen considerably. However, in all the post-communist regions there has been a dramatic decline in membership of labour unions, reflecting perhaps the fact that these organisations formed part of the communist state administration in the past and this is no longer the case. Therefore membership of labour unions in the past was a duty; now it is not.

37

The membership of political parties has declined or remained the same (very low) level in the post-communist countries, probably for the same reasons and this is especially the case in the North-Eastern countries. In Western Europe, however, membership of political organisations has generally gone up. In Central-Western Europe from 4 % to 6 % and in Spain from less than 1 % to 12 %. In the North-West it has remained more or less stable (see p. 46, Appendix, Figure 3.9).

Thus whilst civic participation and integration has increased in general among young people over the 1990s, it has not increased everywhere in the same way and in some places it has decreased (despite the more inclusive question wording). In general, the highest membership tends to be of religious and sports organisations, but charitable, voluntary, art/music/educational and professional organisations have all seen a rise, at least in Western Europe. The political parties and trade unions show slightly different pattern with membership having declined steeply in the post-communist world as part of the collapse of the former regime. However, membership of labour unions did not increase much in Western Europe either, indicating the collapse of traditional class alignments in favour of individualised biographical paths (Beck 1986; Heinz 1991; Furlong and Cartmel 1997).

Regional Differences

The regional differences are very interesting. We find in the Nordic countries a consistently high membership of all forms of organisation and this has been stable or rising. The Nordic youth, it appears, were always civic participants and well integrated compared with youth elsewhere, but now the other Western European countries are catching up with them. Participation and integration was also traditionally high in Central-Western Europe and there it has tended to increase. However, the most dramatic changes have been in South-Western Europe where participation in everything has increased very strongly, sometimes even overtaking the traditionally highly integrated societies such as Germany, Switzerland and the Nordic countries. Here we can see the trend towards a convergence in Western European countries, with the South-West catching up as a result of integration into the European Union which has taken place over the last years and catching up with the Nordic countries who were previously a long way ahead of everyone else.

In Eastern Europe there has been the most decline recorded on 7 out of our 9 indicators of civic participation. In the post-communist North-East and South-East, membership is also very low but has not declined on most indicators, and shows a modest increase. This is especially the case with art and educational associations, professional associations and religious associations, so in these areas we can see some promise of civic integration, although levels in general are low. In Central-Eastern Europe there is a general rise in civic integration and we could say that young people in these regions are increasingly integrated except in the case of labour unions and political parties.

The Central-Eastern region is also following the pattern towards convergence with Western Europe through increasing levels of participation and integration (except in labour unions). However, what we see in the rest of the post-communist region there is more a process of decline in participation and integration from very low levels. This is reflected in the decline in the more or less obligatory membership of various organisations by young people and the lack of establishment of a free and voluntary civil society in those countries. Civil society seems to be strongest in the case of religious organisations in these regions. This has very important implications for the situation of young people in those countries who are unprotected by organisations and associations and increasingly less integrated into public life.

Citizenship and Youth

Further analysis of this data set has revealed that young people are more active in civil society than elderly people, but not as active as the middle aged group. Civic participation and integration declines after 50 years of age (Wallace et al. 2000). Thus, if young people are increasingly engaged in civil society, then we would expect this participation if anything to increase during the next stage of their life-course. Indeed, it was often the case (not shown in the data here) that active participation increased even more than passive participation. This is very positive in terms of civic participation and integration in Western Europe, and especially in the South-West. We could say that there is evidence that with the deepening of ties between the Western European EU-member countries, there is a convergence between them in terms of civil society. Central-Eastern Europe seems to be on the same path of integration and could leap ahead very suddenly, if they follow the example of Spain. However, there is an increasing divergence between young people in these countries and those in the former Soviet Union and in the South-East Balkan peninsula.

In interpreting these data, we are inclined to reject the idea of historical determinism. Although traditionally high levels of participation do not decline (as we see in the case of the Nordic North-West), it is evident that countries where this tradition was not established or even destroyed, such as Spain, can catch up and even overtake the more traditionally integrated countries. These trends could reflect increasing affluence, as the Western European countries are the richest ones. However, the per capita income in the South-West, which has shown the most dramatic rise in civil society, is still lower than in the other Western European countries described here and indeed below the EU average when the survey was carried out.[3] We can instead perhaps point to the consequences of strategies of EU integration and the targeting of young people as active citizens, which may well have played a part in the stimulation of this kind of active citizenship. If this is the case, then we would expect to find in future increasing divergences between those countries integrated into the "lucky circle" of EU countries and those which are not and where modernisation is taking quite a different direction.

It would appear therefore, that rather than social capital disappearing in Western Europe, as is claimed to be happening in the USA, it seems to be on the rise, at least amongst young people. This is maybe a reflection of the "European" path of modernisation involving relatively high and redistributive social protection, along with the targeting of youth in integration policies and initiatives.

Notes

1. This project was funded by the Jubilee Fund of the Austrian National Bank and we are grateful for their sponsorship.
2. 1990: West Germany (n = 308), Switzerland (n = 187), Spain (n = 761), Norway (n = 173), Sweden (n = 153), Finland (n = 52), East Germany (n = 156), Slovenia (n = 151), Hungary (n = 107), Bulgaria (n = 122), Romania (n = 158), Lithuania (n = 171), Latvia (n = 146), Estonia (n = 144) and Russia (n = 256).
    1997: West Germany (n = 108), Switzerland (n = 133), Spain (n = 196), Norway (n = 142), Sweden (n = 145), Finland (n = 167), East Germany (n = 85), Slovenia (n = 153), Hungary (n = 103), Bulgaria (n = 133), Romania (n = 189), Lithuania (n = 146), Latvia (n = 195), Estonia (n = 125) and Russia (n = 185).

3.   Per capita GDP purchasing power parity levels in 1997 were 606,578 in Spain and 17,881,183 USD equivalent (WIIW 1998). The EU average at this time was 7,396,810.

References

Agh, A. (1998), *The Politics of Central Europe*, Sage Publications, London, Thousand Oaks, New Delhi.

Beck, U. (1986), *Risikogesellschaft: Auf dem Weg in eine andere Moderne*, Suhrkamp, Frankfurt.

Beck, U. (1997), *The Reinvention of Politics: Rethinking Modernity and the Global Social Order*, Polity Press, Oxford.

Coleman, J. (1988), 'Social Capital, Human Capital and Schools', *Independent School, Fall 88, 48, No. 1*, p. 9.

Coleman, J. (1988-1989), 'Social Capital and the Creation of Human Capital', *American Journal of Sociology, 94* (Supplement), pp. 94-120.

Furlong, A. and Cartmel, F. (1997), *Young People and Social Change: Individualization and Risk in Late Modernity*, Open University Press, Buckingham.

Heinz, W. (1991), *The Life-Course and Social Change: Comparative Perspectives*, Deutsche Studien Verlag, Weinheim.

Keane, J. (1988), *Democracy and Civil Society: On the Predicaments of European Socialism, the Prospects for Democracy and the Problem of Controlling Social and Political Power*, Verso, London, New York.

Offe, C. and Heinze, R. G. (1992), *Beyond Employment: Time, Work and the Informal Economy (Labour and Social Change)*, Temple University Press, USA.

Putnam, R. D. (1994), *Making Democracy Work: Civic Traditions in Modern Italy*, University of Princeton Press, Princeton, USA.

Putnam, R. D. (1995a), 'Bowling Alone: America's Declining Social Capital', *Journal of Democracy, 6*, pp. 65-78.

Putnam, R. D. (1995b), 'Tuning, Tuning out: The Strange Disappearance of Social Capital in America', *PS: Political Science and Politics, 28*, pp. 638-664.

Putnam, R. D. (1996), 'The Strange Disappearance of Civic America', *American Prospect, Winter*, pp. 34-48.

Wallace, C. and Haerpfer, C. (1998), *Three Paths of Transition in Post-Communist Societies*, Institute for Advanced Studies, Vienna.

Wallace, C. and Haerpfer, C. (2000), *The Informal Economy in East-Central Europe, 1991-1998*, Institute for Advanced Studies, Vienna.

Wallace, C. and Kovatcheva, S. (1998), *Youth in Society: The Construction and Deconstruction of Youth in East and West Europe*, Macmillan, London.

Wallace, C., Spannring, R. and Haerpfer, C. (2000), *Youth and Civic Integration in East and West Europe*, Working Paper, forthcoming, Institute for Advanced Studies, Vienna.

Appendix

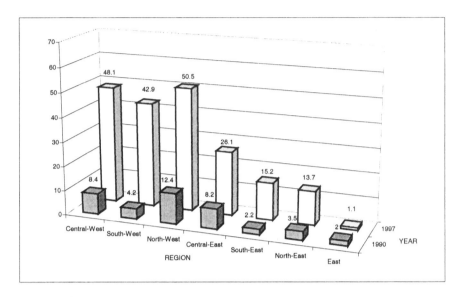

Figure 3.1 Membership in church or other religious organisation

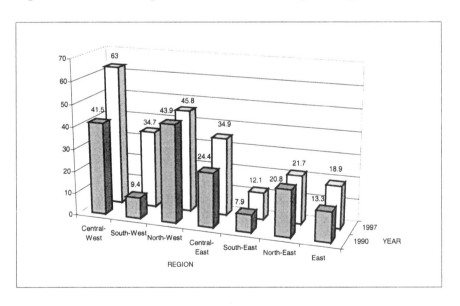

Figure 3.2 Membership in sports or recreation organisation

42

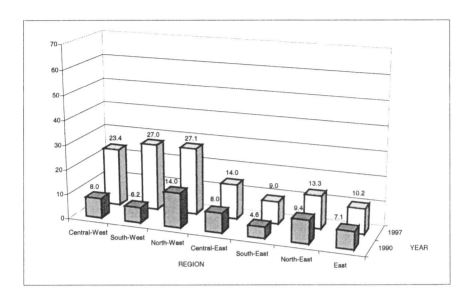

Figure 3.3 Membership in art, music or educational organisation

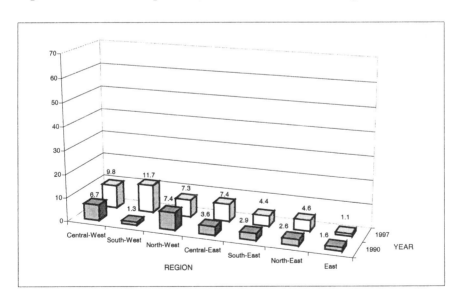

Figure 3.4 Membership in professional organisation

43

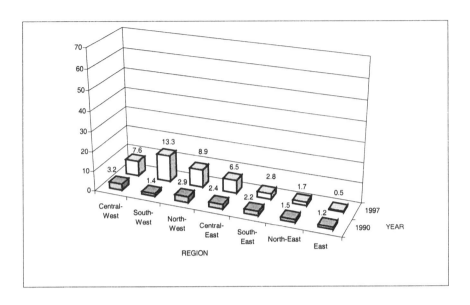

Figure 3.5 Membership in charitable organisation

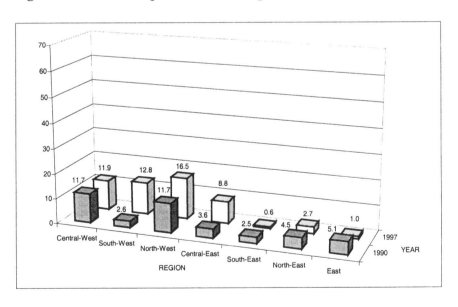

Figure 3.6 Membership in other voluntary organisation

44

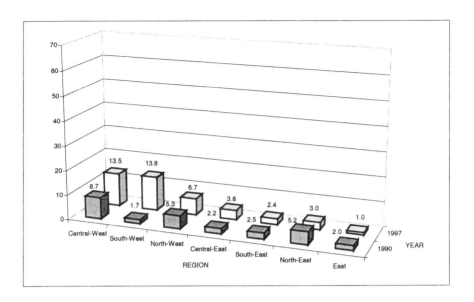

Figure 3.7 Membership in environmental organisation

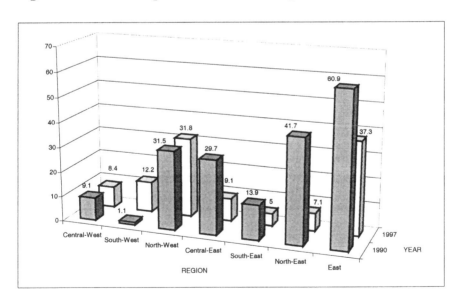

Figure 3.8 Membership in labour union

45

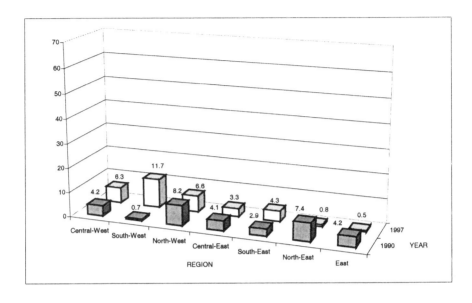

Figure 3.9 Membership in political party

PART 3

CITIZENSHIP AND POWER

4 Critical Discussion: Empowerment or Exclusion?

JOHN BYNNER

The prominence in recent years of the idea of citizenship, as applied to young people, reflects a stage in political, social and economic movements in which citizenship has had a central role to play. The collapse of Communism in the countries of Eastern and Central Europe and its replacement by free market capitalism, has redefined the relationship of the individual to the State (Bynner and Silbereisen 1999; Crocket and Silbereisen 2000). With the establishment of the European Union's parliament based in Strasbourg and the more recent extension of the common market, post-Maastricht, into social policy, increasingly raises questions about what defines a European citizen. The influx of migrants from the ex-communist countries brings issues of membership and boundaries onto the forefront of the European stage. The common feature of all these developments, as Fraser and Emler (1997) argue, is the rights that a citizen can expect and the limitations on access to these rights for those who do not qualify for citizenship.

Marshall's classic account of the evolution of citizenship rights (see Bulmer and Rees 1996) identified the historical sequence of first civic rights (right to own property, right to freedom of speech), then political rights (right to choose who governs) and finally, social and economic rights (right to a minimum standard of living and to equal opportunities). More recently the focus has shifted away somewhat from citizenship towards exclusion from, in the broadest sense, access to the kinds of rights that citizenship represents. In relation to young people, because of the extended dependency, which now typifies the "youth phase" of life (Jones and Wallace 1992), the meaning of citizenship becomes increasingly unclear. Though they may be able to vote at some age between 18 and 21 (depending on the country they live in), the exercise of other rights often occurs mainly through their parents – "citizenship by proxy" as Jones and Wallace (1992) described it. Whether these rights are pursued on their behalf is part of the "private sphere" of family life and is open to scrutiny and regulation by government bodies, only to a very limited extent. Coles (1995) in perhaps the most challenging response to this state of "quasi citizenship" extends the limited number of young people's rights as set out in the Maastricht Treaty to a whole range of *social and economic rights, rights to protection and representational rights*. In his terms, it is the ever-present challenge of the exclusion of a large proportion of young people from these rights, as manifested in the lack of material, education and emotional resources that demands their having the force of law.

Though none of the chapters in this part of the book address the exclusion issue directly, it does represent in one way or another, the sub-plot of all of them. The subject addressed is forms of empowerment among young people, via examples of engagement in the processes through which citizenship is acquired. In a number of ways the research reported illustrates mechanisms which are both liberating and controlling in the sense that typically the adult generation's approach to young people's empowerment comes across as a means of ensuring that they exercise it in (adult) society's way. In this respect much Western European citizenship education is not totally dissimilar from the somewhat extreme forms of it that prevailed in Eastern Europe under Communism (Wallace and Kovatcheva 1998). The voice of youth was heard at the highest levels of the soviet system, yet only accepted when in conformity with communist state ideology and policies as dictated by the adult party chiefs. Instead youth exercised its empowerment through the growing forms of protest arising through the manifestation of youth culture explicitly linking young people across boundaries throughout the whole of Europe. It has been strongly argued that the communist state system's ultimate inability to control the changing values of youth led to their downfall. In many countries the catalyst for the process of collapse of the old regimes were demonstrations spearheaded by young people (Wallace and Kovatcheva 1998).

The first chapter by Liisa Horelli, demonstrates some of these same controlling tendencies on the part of adults in a comparative study of environmental education projects in Finland, France and Switzerland. The aim of these was to involve young people in the planning decisions about environmental renewal initiatives that would affect them. The target populations were generally quite young, children barely in secondary school in Switzerland and France, for example. Even when they extended upwards to 15 and 16 year olds, in a couple of the Finnish examples, much the same story emerged. Decision makers welcomed the input of young people to a certain extent, but there was no evidence of any lasting commitment to their interests or a wish to see their involvement established on a permanent basis. In this sense the attractive idea of a "ladder of participation", in which young people could be enabled to participate increasingly in decisions about planning of the local environment, failed fully to materialise. Basically the adult generation conceived the experiments as not so much as empowering, but educating – improving young people's sense of "environmental competence" but going no further towards full integration in the planning process itself.

Horelli draws an interesting analogy between the feminist struggles for women's emancipation in the political and economic world (Arnot, David and Weiner 1999) with that of young people's struggle for recognition, but this forces us to confront another set of boundaries this time those that lie between childhood, youth and adulthood. In feminism, to paraphrase Jean Jacques Rousseau's dictum, women could be seen as "born free but everywhere they are in chains", in the sense that their economic dependence on husbands during periods of childcare effectively disenfranchised them from many of the social rights of independence identified with citizenship (see Lister 1990). In the case of children, particularly, and young people partly, while still at school, the role is still one of learner rather than teacher and helper rather than full partner. We might see the planning process as being "impoverished" by failing to hear young people's voices, but the economic dependence of young people whilst still at school is only a part of their dependency. They are still acquiring cognitive resources through which their competence to make decisions will be exercised. How far therefore, does it make sense to demand the feminist ideal of equal rights in decision making for them?

Kari Paakkunainen's chapter looks at an older age group, where in principle engagement in the adult political process might be expected. These are young people who have at least left the education system and have already, in British terms, passed the threshold of adult life. The question he addresses is the changing nature of their forms of engagement in the "risk society" (Bynner, Chisholm and Furlong 1997; Furlong and Cartmel 1997) and in the situation prevailing more widely in the "postmodern" (or "late modern") world as elucidated by Bauman (1992), Giddens (1991) and Beck (1992). Paakkunainen notes the main shifts in the life course that this world is said to imply: most notably a breaking down of old structural divisions concerned with class and gender and a withering away of the institutional forms of political expression through trade unions and political parties. Identities need to be adapted to the variety of roles demanded at work and at play. Central to these are the networks to which young people belong. These comprise both the extended sets of social relationships of the conventional kind and more recently, those engendered in virtual reality through the Internet. Politics transforms from ideology into issues. The (young) citizenry fight to resist societal power structures, not to replace the current occupants with new ones to represent their interests, but to defeat the system over issues of concern. Gay rights, animal rights, protests directed at targets from nuclear power stations to new airports and motorways, exemplify the new forms of political expression (Helve 1997).

Periodically the two worlds come face to face through explosions of the kind that occurred in the anarchist vandalisation of the City of London in 1998 and the ecological protests that all but wrecked the meeting of the World Trade Organisation in Seattle in 1999. Such upheavals challenge the very idea of the State or certainly the Super State being erected in Europe. Rather, according to Paakkunainen, government becomes more localised through dialogues and partnerships between local institutions and young citizens. But local does not necessarily imply any geographical restriction on where these dialogues and actions take place. In the (postmodern) risk society, boundaries get weaker and mobility increases, so the action points move, as do the issues. The job of youth workers is to facilitate and develop the competencies in young people that are needed to exercise the new forms of political engagement and to fight ceaselessly, against the marginalisation of protests, which is the official response.

Another main feature of citizenship education in all European countries (e.g. Fogelman 1997) is the encouragement of "volunteering". This is seen as a "safe way" of promoting citizenship to young people: getting across the obligations that go with rights (Williamson 1997). Access to employment and affluence carries with it a civic obligation: donation of services free to worthwhile causes in return. Marianne Nylund analyses data from comparative survey research across all the Nordic countries that examined the motives of young volunteers.

As Nylund acknowledges, there are difficulties in drawing comparative conclusions from the data, because the survey was not based on representative samples of young people in the different countries, but just those engaged in volunteering as identified through voluntary organisations. Moreover, in some cases, the sample sizes were very small, only 36 for example, in the case of Finland. Any generalisations about one country as compared with another cannot therefore really be sustained.

However from analysing the dataset as a whole, some useful insights are gained into the motives of young volunteers: what sort of people they are and how volunteering really does fit into the exercising of citizenship.

Two kinds of values underpinning the volunteering motive are identified: altruistic and egoistic. Altruistic values are to do with volunteering basically to help other people. Egotistical values are those to do with gaining experience and skills that are primarily of value to oneself. Inevitably the two overlap for many young people: there is ambiguity and outright contradictions in the volunteering situation itself. Notably, the great majority of volunteers were volunteering through the same medical charity, the Red Cross. Most were either students or in employment, hardly any were unemployed. This points to the exclusion from volunteering of many, who in theory, would be in the best position to undertake it. What volunteering seems to provide for the young people doing it, often encouraged by adults who persuade them to take it on, is gaining a useful career-enhancing experience. It involves doing something worthwhile, during full time higher education or the interregnum between full-time education and career commitment. Increasing numbers of young people, in fact, have little option but volunteer following completion of education as this provides an accepted route to employment. Employers increasingly expect young people to gain this kind of experience as a prelude to employment, especially if they are not in education or in employment. Volunteering is seen by them as worthwhile work-related experience and also gives young people something useful to do while adding extra items to their CVs.

In this sense there is some personal empowerment because the "ladder of participation" is improving human and social capital as part of the entry to a job. The question remains however, of what happens to those who do not have the opportunity to volunteer. High correlations between volunteering and educational level suggests that those without qualifications are the least likely to get the experience which is increasingly being expected. Also, activity which could in theory, draw in the whole cohort at some stage of their lives is effectively closed off to many young people.

The final contribution from Sue Heath and Liz Kenyon moves into a quite different area of empowerment, that of independent living. Their fascinating research on young people sharing accommodation after leaving the family home, breaks new ground in showing the value of this kind of experience in its own terms to the young people doing it. Rather than being a transitional status, marking time between the parents' family home and forming a partnership and starting a family of ones own, Heath and Kenyon reveal clearly that participating, in the "quasi-family" that a flatshare represents is seen by participants as of considerable benefit. Such an arrangement offers a much truer form of independence than moving into a new partnership and family arrangement in which one form of dependency gives way to another. They note, interestingly, that much of the move towards this form of living which is occurring throughout the whole of Europe is prompted by the glamorised view of flatshare, presented through soap operas on television like the American "Friends" and the UK's "Men Behaving Badly".

This is an example of where a media promoted image of a form of living gives it not only an attraction to young people, who in the past would not have considered it, but makes them actively seek it as the ideal form of living for themselves. The prominence of sharing is of course, in part a response to the high cost of accommodation and the extension of the transition to employment. It takes much longer than in the past to move through such transitional statuses as trainee, boyfriend, girlfriend, quasi-dependence. And the (adult) outcome statuses of established employee, spouse and parent are continually postponed. Shared living gives a breathing space, time for experimenting with communal living free of the judgmental gaze of parents, yet not involving the commitment that cohabitation or marriage entail.

But again, elements of the flat share, at least in this study, reveals that sharers are typically young people who were students together, well educated, and most with good qualifications. So a key question raised by the research is again: "what about the others?" Those who leave school at the minimum age, fail to gain training and a proper job, have limited money and no qualifications, are likely to live at home, if they are men and leave to cohabit or marry and have children at the earliest opportunity, if they are women. What is becoming a normative lifestyle for that increasing section of the population that gains qualifications, becomes an "excluded lifestyle" for those who fail to get them.

It is no accident, that the negative side of empowerment, emerging in these examples, is the biggest threat to true citizenship in Western societies. It is not so much an extension of dependency status, but the exclusion of those without the resources to engage with it fully that challenges the idea of citizenship most. Writers such as Jones and Wallace (1992) and Coles (1995) are at pains to stress the consequence for citizenship of the ever-increasing polarisation that is taking place in all Western societies. Those on the margins move in and out of casual work and unemployment; a quasi-criminal lifestyle, often associated with drugs, may well follow. Mobilisation of such young people, if it occurs at all, is usually in the direction of extreme right wing political movements, not the pursuit of democratic liberal ideals of the kind that environmental protests represent.

Concerns in Britain, about the growing divide, have led to major policy initiatives to give young people access to continuing opportunities and the support and guidance they need to take advantage of them (Social Exclusion Unit 1999a; 1999b; 2000). Financial support is also part of the package. Such policies are premised on the belief that *all young people* need to have access to the full range of resources that they need – described in the Scandinavian context as the pre-requisite for *life management* (Helve and Bynner 1996). Only then can they be expected to engage fully in the political process and local decision-making. In this sense, concerns about citizenship give way to concerns about social cohesion and its counterpart social exclusion (Atkinson and Hills 1998). The route to cohesion is opportunity, not only to participate in the labour market, but to exercise the full range of familial responsibilities and democratic rights that citizenship entails.

References

Arnot, M., David, M. and Weiner, G. (1999), *Closing the Gender Gap: Post War Education and Social Change*, Polity Press, Cambridge.

Atkinson, A. B. and Hills, J. (1998), *Exclusion, Employment and Opportunity*, London School of Economics, CASE paper 4.

Bauman, Z. (1992), *Intimations of Postmodernity*, Routledge, London.

Beck, U. (1992), *Risk Society*, Sage Publications, London.

Bulmer, M. and Rees, A. M. (eds.) (1996), *Citizenship Today: The Contemporary Relevance of T. H. Marshall*, UCL Press, London.

Bynner, J., Chisholm, L. and Furlong, A. (eds.) (1997), *Youth, Citizenship and Social Change in a European Context*, Ashgate Publishing Ltd., Aldershot.

Bynner, J. and Silbereisen, R. K. (eds.) (1999), *Adversity and Challenge in Life in the New Germany and England*, Macmillan, Basingstoke.

Coles, R. (1995), *Youth and Social Policy*, UCL Press, London.

Crocket, L. J. and Silbereisen, R. K. (eds.) (2000), *Negotiating Adolescence in Times of Social Change*, Cambridge University Press, Cambridge.

Fogelman, K. (1997), 'Citizenship Education', in J. Bynner, L. Chisholm and A. Furlong (eds.), *Youth, Citizenship and Social Change in a European Context*, Ashgate Publishing Ltd., Aldershot, pp. 214-227.

Fraser, L. and Emler, N. (1997), 'Participation and Citizenship: A New Agenda for Youth Research', in J. Bynner, L. Chisholm and A. Furlong (eds.), *Youth, Citizenship and Social Change in a European Context*, Ashgate Publishing Ltd, Aldershot, pp. 171-195.

Furlong, A. and Cartmel, F. (1997), *Young People and Social Change: Individualisation and Risk in Late Modernity*, Open University Press, Buckingham.

Giddens, A. (1991), *Modernity and Self-Identity: Self and Society in the Late Modern Age*, Polity Press, Cambridge.

Helve, H. (1997), 'Perspectives on Social Exclusion, Citizenship and Youth', in J. Bynner, L. Chisholm and A. Furlong (eds.), *Youth, Citizenship and Social Change in a European Context*, Ashgate Publishing Ltd, Aldershot, pp. 228-233.

Helve, H. and Bynner, J. (1996), *Youth and Life Management: Research Perspectives*, Helsinki University Press, Helsinki.

Jones, G. and Wallace, C. (1992), *Family, Youth and Citizenship*, Open University Press, Buckingham.

Lister, R. (1990), 'Women, Economic Dependency and Citizenship', *Journal of Social Policy, 19*, pp. 445-467.

UK Government Social Exclusion Unit (1999a), *Teenage Pregnancy (Cm 4342)*, The Stationery Office, London.

UK Government Social Exclusion Unit (1999b), *Bridging the Gap: New Opportunities for 16-18 Year-Olds not in Education, Employment or Training (Cm 4405)*, The Stationery Office, London.

UK Government Social Exclusion Unit (2000), 'National Strategy for Neighbourhood Renewal', *Report of Policy Action Team 12: Young People*, The Stationery Office, London.

Wallace, C. and Kovatcheva, S. (1998), *Youth in Society: The Construction and Reconstruction of Youth in East and West Europe*, Macmillan, London.

Williamson, H. (1997), 'Youth Work and Citizenship', in J. Bynner, L. Chisholm and A. Furlong (eds.), *Youth, Citizenship and Social Change in a European Context*, Ashgate Publishing Ltd, Aldershot, pp. 196-213.

5 Young People's Participation in Local Development: Lip Service or Serious Business?

LIISA HORELLI

Introduction

A decade of experiments involving the participation of nearly 700 children and young people in neighbourhood improvement in Finland, Switzerland and France indicate that young people are sharp analysts of their settings and creative producers of ideas for planning. However, the gatekeepers of local development – the municipalities – are reluctant to expand their top-down, expert-based mode of urban planning to include new groups, such as young people. This chapter discusses the mechanisms for inclusion and strategies to mainstream intergenerational equality in local and regional development.

The fierce societal changes brought about by the globalisation of markets and the challenge implied by the diffusion of information and communication technology should encourage researchers to reanalyse the situation of young people and their roles in the information society. These global events have contributed to paradigm shifts which are currently taking place in many social and scientific fields. For example, institutional structures are being moulded by networking organisations. Traditional education has been invaded by life long learning and new models of individual and collective learning systems. The concept of knowledge is no longer considered merely as "a well argued belief" but something that solves social and practical problems (Stehr 1994; Gibbons et al. 1994). Hierarchical, coercive planning is being replaced by a polyphonic communicative dialogue. The shared paradigm shift behind these phenomena is the transition from a one-way form of communication into two-way, and then from many-to-many. This conscious and systematic transition might imply a shift from the information society into a network-based knowledge society (Castels 1996). The latter requires not only the provision for and access of citizens to information technology and communication networks but also new social, institutional and methodological arrangements for people to participate in the creation and maintenance of this knowledge society.

Participation is the least recognised of the three "Ps" – provision, protection and participation – in the UN Convention on the Rights of the Child. The first two rights, which are rather passive by nature, have received general acceptance. The third, participation, which is one of the most important dimensions of citizenship, has been largely ignored in most countries (Sgritta 1997). In fact, there is evidence that barriers to participation and even the marginalisation of children and young people are increasing all over the world (Chawla 1997).

A survey of the literature on young people's participation in local planning and development indicates that the phenomenon of participation is rare in the Western industrialised countries (Hart 1992; Horelli 1998). The mechanisms of exclusion of young people have been much more frequently analysed and documented (cf. the European Union programmes for fighting social exclusion). Thus for instance, the mechanisms for marginalising local actors – young and old – are complex, having many dimensions. This is evident from a range of different but interrelated elements, such as young people's discourse about alienation and lack of influence, the physical and cultural separation of children's and adults' worlds as well as the barriers to collaboration between different welfare sectors (childcare, social work etc.). The technocratic language and style of negotiation in the planning process along with the resistance towards the application of pragmatic and hermeneutic knowledge, for example in the programming of mobility systems, make it difficult for young people, and lay persons in general, to define issues in a way that would be accepted. Thus, the process of marginalisation and exclusion contains emotional, cognitive, conative and structural elements (Horelli and Vepsä 1995).

But how would we create mechanisms and strategies for the inclusion of young people? What would such a model of participation look like? The aim of this chapter is to conduct a brief meta-analysis of a series of case studies in the participation of children and young people in local development in Finland, Switzerland and France over a decade. We will then present for discussion a strategy for mainstreaming intergenerational equality into local and regional development.

Action Research Design of the Case Studies

Since the participation of young people in planning and development is aimed at achieving change, it calls for an action-oriented design of the change process integrated with research, one which is open and emergent. The design and implementation of this kind of environmental development and research consists of a combination of critical constructivist inquiry, planning, implementation endeavours, and theory-driven evaluation (Guba and Lincoln 1989; Chen 1990; Chisholm and Elden 1993; Horelli 1997).

An integrative approach comprising theories and concepts from environmental psychology, environmental education and collaborative planning and governance has been applied as a loose framework to guide the implementation and analysis of the case studies.

Environmental psychology, dealing with the socially mediated experiences and interactions of people with their physical environment, offers some core concepts that are useful in studying young people in real contexts. They are the following:

- *the construction of the self* as a dynamic, multidimensional and multilevel self-regulation system, which is managed by the means of psychic work, physical (somatic) and social action as well as transactions with the natural and the built environment (Vuorinen 1997; Horelli 1993; Aura et al. 1997). Emotionally significant elements of the environment, such as parks, one's own room, the computer, peers and beautiful buildings, serve as support structures (affordances) for the construction and maintenance of the self. Although this construction is highly dependent on the exterior context, it is recognised here as a purely psychological process of becoming a subject. The construction of the self is evolutionary in the sense that there are age-specific phases and characteristics. For example, children are frequent users of their near environment and their physical affordances until their teens, whereas young people tend to turn to the social affordances of the environment in the construction of the self;

59

- *environmental competence*, which means the knowledge and skills, as well as the courage to use them, in taking responsibility for the environment in accordance with one's own aims and those of the community (Hart 1979; Horelli et al. 1998b). The conditions for inculcating environmental competence in children and young people presuppose a physical and social space of action for children and young people, including such things as opportunities to move around, to manipulate the milieu and to take on meaningful roles in the community (Kyttä 1997; cf. Uzzel's action competence 1998). Opportunities to acquire environmental competence can be measured by the "ladder of participation" which demonstrates how different levels of participation offer space for varying kinds of psychological and learning experiences (Shier 1997). A modified version of Arnstein's (1969) ladder ranges from adapting children to the planning process (which is not real participation) by listening to them, children taking part in adults' planning, co-operation between children and adults, through to children's real participation with adults as assistants (Horelli 1998; Hart 1992). Different steps of the ladder require varying amounts of accommodation to young people by adults. The notion of children's agency (children as agents of their lives, cf. Alanen 1997), for instance, which depends on the external context described above, is closer to sociological thinking than the psychological concept of "the construction of the self".

Environmental education, in an expanded form, has been taken as the framework here. The expanded form means that as well as covering the natural sciences and the protection of the ecological environment, environmental education should extend to take in the built environment and also the understanding of socio-cultural, economic, and even political processes affecting the environment (cf. Uzzel 1998). Since environmental education also includes the fight against "action paralysis" and "learned helplessness", one of its horizontal themes is the empowerment of children and young people to become competent and responsible citizens. This model of learning has been modified by Kolb (1984) to create a circular model of experiential and reflexive learning in which action, experience and critical meta-cognition alternate, leading to a qualitative change in the subjects' understanding. This circle, in the case of environmental improvement, has to be aided by a variety of enabling methods or tools

60

which assist girls and boys to journey from different stages of environmental awareness to that of empowered citizenship. The role of the school is of utmost importance here. Ideally, the school must become an active social development agent, which works in partnership with parents and families, business, industry and labour, community-based organisations and other schools. Thus, the school should make learning in real life settings up-to-date and meaningful (Copa and Paese 1992).

Collaborative planning and governance (Healey 1997) aims to produce a relevant socio-cultural and material infrastructure in local communities through the participation of different partners – politicians, authorities, entrepreneurs, researchers, and local groups among whom young people are important players. This collective endeavour brings about an institutional capacity (collective know-how), which would help to master the challenges of "glocalisation", i.e. the tensions between the effects of globalisation and the local responses. The scope of collaborative planning is larger than that of traditional planning since it integrates the arrangement of physical space with ecological management, preventive social work, economic initiatives, and local governance. The core of collaborative planning is an inclusionary interactive approach in which problems are negotiated with the stakeholders – young and old – to achieve consensus and common strategies. The use of enabling techniques allows the inclusion of children and young people in the process of creating more supportive and relevant environments.

Results of the Meta-Analysis of Case Studies

The research which was conducted on experiments with the participation of children and young people in neighbourhood improvement in Finland, Switzerland and France, between 1989 and 1999, took place in lower-middle class neighbourhoods or suburbs, dominated by social housing. The sites of experiments were the following:

- Malminkartano (Helsinki, Finland), a suburb of 10 000 residents, built in 1980s;
- Kilta (Kerava, Finland), a suburb of 2500 residents, built in 1970s;
- Kekkola (Jyväskylä, Finland), a suburb of 1000 residents, master-planned in 1997-1998;

- Kitee (Finland) or its central neighbourhood Rantala with 3000 residents, built in 1970s;
- Locarno (Switzerland) or its neighbourhood Saleggi with 7000 residents;
- Darnétal (France) or its southern part with 2000 residents;
- Ristinummi (Vaasa, Finland), a suburb of 9000 residents, built in 1970s.

The Finnish experiments lasted between two and three years, whereas the Swiss and the French experiments lasted only half a year. Two "snapshots" of the experiments are briefly described below.

- The first snapshot is taken from Finnish *"Ecoagents of Vaasa"*. Vaasa is a medium-sized Finnish town whose suburb, Ristinummi with 9000 residents, was the object of a national architectural competition for the ecological rehabilitation of suburbs. The Finnish Academy funded two experimental projects: Children as ecoagents in their environment and "The School Yard" as an ecological text-book in which 7-14 year old children participated in the planning of the school yard and the neighbourhood between 1995 and 1997. At the beginning of the project, a methodological package was prepared by the researchers and school teachers which facilitated both the planning process and environmental education. The package comprised different types of diagnostic, expressive, conceptual, organisational, and political methods, which structured the teaching material according to different planning phases. The phases of analysis and planning went well. The children analysed their settings and produced ideas which dealt with nature, the aesthetic quality of the built environment, peers, services and the urban community. The children's approach was eco-social by nature. Nevertheless, children's impact on the implementation process was minor, mainly because young people do not seem to have appropriate channels by which to influence the decision makers.

  The impact of the project and the environmental education on children could be observed in an increase in cognitive and reflective skills, such as improvement of cognitive distinctions concerning the neighbourhood and in a more positive and active view of their environmental role. The use of the school yard did not, however, change. Nor did the project change municipal practices. But it did influence the orientations of the school towards promoting environmental entrepreneurship by young people and to include children's ideas in the local plan "Agenda 21". The methodological package helped to empower children during the different phases of planning and implementation, and to enhance some of the objectives of environmental education. The results challenge the traditional planning theory to be more open. They also challenge environmental education to expand its focus from natural sciences to the teaching of the psychosocial appropriation of the natural and built environment. Last but not least, the experiment confirmed that research on children should consider their participation as part of the phenomenon of children as citizens.

- The second snapshot is taken from French *"Child-Architects of Darnétal"*. Darnétal (10 000 residents) is the neighbouring town of Rouen, the capital of Normandy. L'Ecole d'Architecture, which is situated in Darnétal, organises a yearly seminar and an exhibition of art and architecture connecting French and Nordic culture. In the spring of 1995, the professor in charge of the exhibition invited the elementary school of the neighbourhood, with 2000 residents, to participate in the exhibition. Ecole Marcel Pagnol lies in the southern part of Darnétal in a lower-class neighbourhood with huge blocks of social housing. The school consists of 130 students, aged 7-11. A class of 10-year-olds were assisted by their teacher and two students of architecture, who applied to the French situation the methodological package prepared by the Finnish researchers. The children examined their neighbourhood from the historical point of view, studied animal architecture and wrote an essay "If I were an architect". They also made drawings of both good and bad spots. Finally, they built a model together with the students of architecture. Their products were then displayed along with the "plans" of the Finnish children, at an exhibition called "The Child and Architecture". The design and layout of the exhibition were made by the professor who had been responsible for the exhibitions of the case study. The children, however, participated eagerly in the construction of the exhibition.

The local authorities, present at the opening of the exhibition, promised to create a local council of young people in Darnétal in order to enhance children's perspective in the renovation of the neighbourhood. The students of Marcel Pagnol assessed their experience later on by writing about what they liked and did not like in the project and what they had learnt from it. Most children liked the planning exercise and especially the fact that some of their wishes – new sport areas and play equipment as well as safer traffic solutions – were implemented. A youth council was created and functioned for a year, but after local elections it was dismantled, which ended the consultations with children.

In the analysis of the case-studies the products (drawings, photos, models and plans) of children and young people as well as the researchers' observations of the process have been content analysed according to a modified version of the constant comparative method (Strauss and Corbin 1990; Patton 1990; Miles and Huberman 1994). The main research results of the case studies (Horelli 1994; 1997; 1998; Horelli and Vepsä 1995; Horelli et al. 1998b), indicate that young people are sharp analysts of their settings and creative producers of ideas for planning in general. Irrespective of individual, gender and cultural differences, young people tend to define local supportive structures multi-dimensionally. This includes a strong ecological dimension (greenery, clean air, wildlife), at least in Finland. The physical aspect of the supportive structures comprises beautiful buildings, spaciousness, safe roads, playgrounds as well as rough, unkept ground and abandoned areas. The functional dimension stresses the importance of different kinds of activities, hobbies, work and opportunities for participation. The psychosocial and organisational aspects include peers, friendly adults and collaboration between different age groups and institutions. Children and young people also focus on abstract characteristics, such as safety and communality. Most participants loved beauty, but children's sense of aesthetics differs greatly from that of adults. The creation of environments of this kind would mean a shift towards more ecological and socially supportive settings with opportunities for the involvement of different groups.

Let us now turn to the meta-analysis of all the seven experiments, mobilising nearly 700 children and young people in three different countries, by focusing upon the structural features of the experiments. These are summarised in Table 5.1 (see p. 65) and include the initiators, partnerships, age, number and level of participation of the young people, the objectives of the experiment, its organisation, use of methodological tools, and the tangible results.

Table 5.1 Summary of the findings of the meta-analysis of the experiments

Place of experiment	Initiator	No. and age of young partici-pants	Level of partici-pation 1-3	Objectives	Methods	Results
Malmin-kartano (Helsinki, Finland)	Residents	125 (4-15)	1	Exploring the setting	Diagnostic and expressive techniques	Exhibition and panel
Kilta (Kerava, Finland)	Local authorities	38 (7-12)	1	Exploring the setting	Colour analysis, drawings	Social process
Kekkola (Jyväskylä, Finland)	Ministry of Environ-ment	14 (4-12)	1	Childfriendly master plan	Model building	A master plan
Rantala (Kitee, Finland)	Local council	146 (7-12)	3	Children's participation in planning	Many creative methods	Traffic safety plan, exhibition
Ristinummi (Vaasa, Finland)	Teachers and researchers	348 (7-17)	2	Children's participation in planning	A methodo-logical package, project-organisation	Alternative plan for the renovation of neigh-bourhood
Locarno (Switzerland)	Teachers and researchers	40 (10)	1	Children's participation in planning	3-dimensional model	Exhibition, some improve-ment
Darnétal (France)	Teachers and researchers	21 (10)	1	Children's participation in planning	3-dimensional model	Exhibition, some improve-ment

All the case studies focus with varying depth on the holistic improvement of the residential area or living environment. The age of the participant children and young people range from 4 to 17 years. The initiators of the experiments vary from the local residents to the local and national authorities. None of the cases were initiated by young people themselves. The actors include, however, residents of different ages, community-based organisations, teachers, local authorities, researchers, and politicians. The organisation is usually informal except for two formal project organisations, which lacked representation from young people.

None of the case studies had extra financial resources, beyond the voluntary work of the participants. The objectives of the experiments extend from exploring the environment with children to the aim of producing alternative or new plans for the neighbourhood. The level of participation of young people ranges from 1 (listening to children), to 2 (children taking part in adults' planning) and 3 (co-operation between children and adults).

The methods applied in the case studies extend from a few creative techniques to a whole methodological package of diverse planning tools including model building and computer-aided design. The monitoring and evaluation system has, however, been unsatisfactory in all of the cases.

The tangible results include exhibitions with 3-dimensional models for the improvement of the neighbourhood, alternative plans for the residential area (in the case of Ristinummi, some of which are being implemented), a traffic safety plan (of Kitee which has been implemented), and the contribution (by consultation) to a childfriendly master plan (in Kekkola). In addition, the intangible results include children's increased cognitive skills and environmental competence as well as their conspicuous capacity to adopt an eco-social approach to development. The conditions for the successful production of tangible results seem to depend, besides sufficient length of the endeavour, on the external, structural arrangements of the experiment, such as the involvement of decision makers and high level authorities (Kitee and Kekkola), and the organisation of the development process into a formal project organisation (Ristinummi).

Summa summarum, the results of the experiments are not trivial, although the main finding is that none of the cases have succeeded in changing the practice of not including young people in local development as part of normal procedures. The gatekeepers of urban and rural planning are the municipalities (local authorities and decision makers) who are so far reluctant to expand their top-down, expert-based mode of functioning into collaborative planning and governance, which could also include young people.

It is evident that the cognitive capacity and environmental competence of young people is not enough to legitimise them as relevant partners in development. However, there are signs, at least in Finnish society, that the challenges of glocalisation and the approaching information society would require the contribution of this group of citizens. Consequently, the research design of future experiments would need to take these contextual demands into consideration.

The research questions have so far been exploratory, addressing what urban improvement processes and outcomes are like from the children's perspective or under what conditions and with what methods can young people take part in "urban planning". Now it is time to explore the gap between the competence of the young and the reluctance of the municipalities to recognise their willingness to participate. The next question will be: how to bridge this gap? How can we change the conditions in order to include young people?

Mainstreaming Intergenerational Equality into Local and Regional Development

Next, we shall address the issue of how to include young people in the emerging information society in the context of urban planning. Until now, the most powerful force fighting for inclusion is that of the women's movement. The long history of women's liberation has produced many concepts, approaches and strategies for attaining equality between women and men, which might be useful also for the inclusion of young people. Mainstreaming gender equality is a special strategy aiming at the integration of women into all spheres of policy and levels of decision making. It focuses on the gender system which consists of many interconnected elements produced by the varying activities of women and men in their daily lives (Horelli et al. 1998a). These take place within the individual, as interaction between individuals, as well as on the symbolic and structural levels (Acker 1990).

Changing our non-linear, complex world by rationalistic planning seems rather illusionary. Nevertheless, observing and nurturing multilevel processes and relationships are a necessity, if favourable change in the situation of young people is to be achieved. Therefore, the next five year long experiment, which involves girls and boys between 8 and 18 years old in local and regional development in Pihlajisto (Helsinki) and North Karelia (a region in Eastern Finland), will apply the mainstreaming strategy. Since the mechanism of successful mainstreaming presupposes methodological interventions on different levels, the research efforts of the four person team will focus on the following elements (see p. 68, Figure 5.1): the intrapersonal (space for the construction of identity and

67

environmental competence), the interpersonal (opportunities for weaving local and regional partnerships and networks which include young people), the symbolic (nurturing the image of young people as computer literate experts), and the structural level (negotiating with local authorities, influencing youth parliaments, mainstreaming the national youth policy; cf. Horelli 1999).

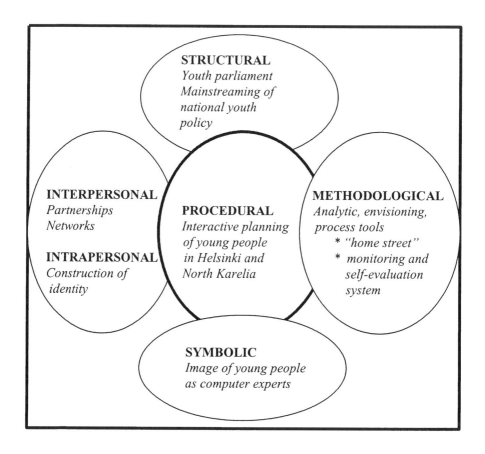

Figure 5.1 The mechanism for mainstreaming young people into local and regional development in the experiments of Pihlajisto and North Karelia, Finland

In practice, the collaborative planning and development of the project will take place both concretely and indirectly via the web. A special computer- and internet-based device, "The Home Street", has been developed at the Department of Architecture of the Helsinki University of Technology (Staffans et al. 1998). This tool will allow the young and other community members to communicate not only with their environment but also with local authorities and decision makers. Therefore the methodological package will comprise, in addition to analytic and envisioning tools, digitalised process techniques for constructing "The Home Street" as an experimental planning site.

This kind of multilevel and multidimensional interdisciplinary research design requires another methodological innovation, namely an empowering monitoring and self-evaluation system. This will not only provide the researchers valuable information about the progress of the projects but above all it increases the young participants' awareness and understanding of the complex structures in which they are living.

Conclusions

We can now return to our title question: is young people's participation in urban planning only lip service or is it serious business? It is serious business in the sense that the status of children in culture and society is the result of continuous negotiation or even struggle. The manipulation of space is not only an indicator of how young people "organise culture" but it also reveals how adults place the young in society (Lönnqvist 1992). As children expand their own territory through participation, it threatens to alter their cultural status, one which adults have tended to relegate to "play and leisure".

If young people's participation is taken truly seriously, it affects the underlying layers of society ranging from the intrapersonal to symbolic meanings and structures. One piece of research will not of course change the situation of young people, but it will be interesting to see whether the multidimensional strategy of mainstreaming intergenerational equality and the application of information technology will assist in making the young more visible in the local context. It is evident, however, that if communities are not built on the basis of young people's expectations and their opportunities to participate, then the solving of urban and rural problems will be even more difficult in the future.

References

Acker, J. (1990), 'Hierarchies, Jobs, Bodies: A Theory of Gendered Organizations', *Gender and Society, 2(4)*, pp. 139-158.

Alanen, L. (1997), 'Children's Childhoods and Kinder und Kindheit', *Childhood 4(2)*, pp. 251- 256.

Arnstein, S. (1969), 'The Ladder of Participation', *Journal of the Institute of American Planners, 35(4)*, pp. 216-24.

Aura, S., Horelli, L. and Korpela, P. (1997), *Ympäristöpsykologian perusteet* (Basics of Environmental Psychology), WSOY, Helsinki.

Castels, M. (1996), *The Information Age: Economy, Society and Culture, Vol. 1: The Rise of Network Society*, Blackwell Publishers, Oxford.

Chawla, L. (1997), *Growing up in Cities*, Project report presented at the 'Urban Childhood Conference', Trondheim, Norway, 9-12 June.

Chen, H-T. (1990), *Theory Driven Evaluation*, Sage Publications, London.

Chisholm, R. F. and Elden, M. (1993), 'Features of Emerging Action Research', *Human Relations 46(2)*, pp. 275-97.

Copa, G. H. and Paese, V. H. (1992), *New Designs for the Comprehensive High School*, Executive Summary Report, NCRVE, University of Minnesota Site, College Education, St. Paul.

Gibbons, M., Limoges, C., Nowotny, H., Schwartzman, S., Scott, P. and Throw, M. (1994), *The New Production of Knowledge*, Sage Publications, London.

Guba, E. G. and Lincoln, Y. S. (1989), *Fourth Generation Evaluation*, Sage Publications, London.

Hart, R. (1979), *Children's Experience of Place*, Irvington, New York.

Hart, R. (1992), *Children's Participation: From Tokenism to Citizenship: Innocenti Essays*, Unicef, Florence.

Healey, P. (1997), *Collaborative Planning: Shaping Places in Fragmented Societies*, Macmillan, London.

Horelli, L. (1993), *Asunto psykologisena ympäristönä* (The Dwelling as a Psychological Environment), Helsinki University of Technology, Department of Architecture, Espoo.

Horelli, L. (1994), *Lasten näköinen ympäristö* (Childfriendly Environment), Ministry of the Environment, Helsinki.

Horelli, L. (1997), 'A Methodological Approach to Children's Participation in Urban Planning', *Scandinavian Housing and Planning Research 14*, pp. 105-15.

Horelli, L. (1998), 'Creating Childfriendly Environments: Case Studies on Children's Participation in three European Countries', *Childhood 5(2)*, pp. 225-239.

Horelli, L. (1999), *Success Criteria for Mainstreaming Equality*, Unpublished manuscript.

Horelli, L., Booth, C. and Gilroy, R. (1998a), *The EuroFEM Toolkit for Mobilizing Women into Local and Regional Development*, EuroFEM, Helsinki.

70

Horelli, L., Kyttä, M. and Kaaja, M. (1998b), *Lapset ympäristön ekoagentteina* (Children as Ecoagents of the Environment), Helsinki University of Technology, Department of Architecture, Espoo.

Horelli, L. and Vepsä, K. (1995), *Ympäristön lapsipuolet* (Environmental Stepchildren), ITLA, Helsinki.

Kolb, D. A. (1984), *Experiential Learning: Experience as a Source of Learning and Development*, Prentice Hall, Englewood Cliffs, NJ.

Kyttä, M. (1997), 'Children's Independent Mobility in Urban, Small Town and Rural Environments', in R. Camstra (ed.), *Growing up in a Changing Urban Landscape*, Van Gorcum, Assen, pp. 41-52.

Lönnqvist, B. (1992), *Ting, rum och barn* (Things, Space and Children), Kansatieteellinen arkisto 38 (Finnish Literature Society, Archives of Folk Tradition), Helsinki.

Miles, M. B. and Huberman, A. M. (1994), *Qualitative Data Analysis, an Expanded Source Book*, 2nd Edition, Sage Publications, London.

Patton, M. Q. (1990), *Qualitative Evaluation and Research Methods*, 2nd Edition, Sage Publications, London.

Sgritta, G. B. (1997), 'Provision: Limits and Possibilities', in P. L. Helistö, E. Lauronen and M. Bardy (eds.), *Politics of Childhood and Children at Risk: Provision, Protection and Participation*, International expert meeting, Finland, European Centre for Social Welfare Policy and Research, Vienna, pp. 35-47.

Shier, H. (1997), *A New Model for Enabling Children to Participate in Decision-Making*, Unpublished manuscript, Scotland.

Staffans, A., Rantanen, H. and Zielinski, J. (1998), *Asukkaat verkossa – vaan ei satimessa: Raportti Kotikatu-projektista* (Residents in the Net but not in the Trap – A Report from the Homestreet-Project), Helsinki University of Technology, Department of Architecture, Espoo.

Stehr, N. (1994), *Knowledge Societies*, Sage Publications, London.

Strauss, A. and Corbin, J. (1990), *Basics of Qualitative Research: Grounded Theory Procedures and Techniques*, Sage Publications, London.

Uzzell, D. (1998), *Education for Environmental Action in the Community: New Roles and Relationships for Youth*, A paper presented at the International Seminar 'Youth, Citizenship and Empowerment', Helsinki, December 7-8, 1998.

Vuorinen, R. (1997), *Minän synty ja kehitys* (Birth of Self and Its Evolution), WSOY, Porvoo.

6 The Operative Contingency of Institutions and the Young Fortuna in the Risk Society

KARI PAAKKUNAINEN

To Youthful Companionship and Ulrich Beck

The steam engine trains of Ruhr and Riihimäki live on in films,
and still they choke on their economic miracle,
pass on and teach us about the challenges of life,
the ABCs of accomplishment from Heimaat and Pentinkulma

And we hate and love our risks together
in the new deal this side of Viipuri and Checkpoint Charlie
still a bit dusty
and hard to find in one's own head
new breznevian teachings, simultaneous-calculators
and leftovers of the world's distribution
already start to terrify us

And it is necessary to find the Other, Learn
to protect and pacify
the young margins of this Europe
among strutting youth and all the stuff

Humility, screaming, whimpering
lessons and powers
by life's bits are prepared
and the ABC book's enlightening pages are presented again

The lines are jumping already
mixing up
beginnings and endings
risks and challenges

(Kari Paakkunainen, March 23, 1998).

"Internal Enterprising" – the Slogan of the Late Twentieth Century

Many gods and traditions of participation are dying. Clear principles and strict authority structures have disappeared from young people's lives. People as individuals fall into, or are lead to choose, many patterns by which to live. Talk about life politics, from possibilities to principle patterns for one's own life, is not just fashionable conversation among sociologists. Many market-based possibilities for consumption and selection, as well as convenience producing cultures, are part of our lifestyle and even our governmental structures, along with their principles of public sector competitiveness and responsibility for productivity. Utilitarian principles are shoving their way into the world of politics, government and wavering societies in other ways as well (Paakkunainen 1998d). Expert and media-based self-help consultants are available to discuss, council and provide tailor made life-guidance and life-services.

At the same time convenience based services and expert practices replace old participatory organisations; collective life choices, common traditional activities and electoral procedures are ploughed under. Consultants, (Euro)evaluations and barometers have, in many ways, replaced democracy and self-government. In a sense our society functions merely as a collection of individuals. At the level of European Union it is a common way to speak about deficiency of democracy and the lack of collective and representative mobilisation. Even adolescents and teenagers must handle decision-making and all the consideration which it requires for themselves, including finding firm grounds for their life decisions and for dealing with many ethical and practical issues and threats – ranging from loss of gainful employment and lack of standard career options to ecological risks.

Schools also produce radical divisions and competitive pressures between young people: multi-valued pacifistic up-bringing and universal utopias in school and social politics have long since been replaced with the idea of "internal enterprising". In addition to these new negative threats though, the world is a more open place, with both the necessity and possibility to choose. Differences between groups of young people are growing, and at the same time lifestyles are becoming more individualised. Though differences may grow (Karisto 1998) we still must live together. Tolerance for alternatives is expanding. Consensus, common culture and unanimity no longer bind us; they have lost their significance and have become ambivalent.

What Does the Contingency of an Activity Mean?

We have been thrown into a situation of uncertainty, or in other words, contingency. The challenges of commodification and enterprising are only one part of the contingency and the feelings of risks and situation of choices. Individuals are, also, responsible as political and ethical citizens. Paradoxically, when life is out of control (in terms of the old structures of "God", imperial principles, political patriarchs, teachers, social inspectors or expert evaluators) it has room for choice – for politics: politics have always required space for openness, for diving into the play of responsibility – in situations with a tense, uncontrolled, unclear and uncertain future. Now especially, life is a game in which openness means that it is under no one's control. The final results are open. Fatalisms and prognoses have, in their collapsing, opened doors for political freedom.

The "crisis" of the risk society has two chances, as shown in the Chinese characters for this word: you can either contemplate and learn and win, or you can drop out of the game, put your survival at risk and even be lost. Confronting lady luck, classically known as Fortuna, is never a certain thing in this game. The politics of individuality may be, in the most genuine form, such a game of uncertainty, contingency: finding Fortuna in risk. This, however, is a question of modern competencies: virtuoso skills in this game – in the politicking of life and in politicising of issues of life and fortune, career span, significance and schedule (Paakkunainen 1998a, 172-197; inspired by Palonen 1993).

The positive growth and enlightenment ideals of the old industrial society, the idea of techno-rational world control and paradigms of linear progression are dead. From young people's perspective, the project of building up a common, shared social welfare state has become incomprehensible and ambivalent – neutralising young people's critiques and cynicism on the basis of various experiences and contexts which are not shared by all. Only the hopeless defenders of the growth of industrial society – the historical compromise between the political left and right and the sovereignty of the colossal party and corporate power structures – are blind enough to deny this (Beck 1993 and 1995).

In the midst of despair and the loss of standards to live by, there is talk of abnormal a-typical or uncontrolled life circumstances and resources. The object here is to point to all that is not part of the mobilisation and governmental goals of the industrial and modern structure; of the "Väinö Linna revival movement" (just like the generation of the economic miracle in Germany or the generations of socialdemocratic "folkrörelse" in Sweden via Hansson-Erlander-Palme). We are routinely faced with the classical questions of confronting clear risks and reflecting on freedom, individuality and the changing group dynamics. Reconsidering one's premises and showing the desire and ability to negotiate and build one's own life projects are part of everyday life.

New Space for Individual Choices: Empiria

The lack of national, collective and traditionally shared cultural codes is reflected in "empirical" studies as well. In addition to life decisions based on consumption, education and employment, ethical and political choices are matters decided within and between individuals. The political writings of young people point to a rise in non-institutional and individualistic activities and rhetoric, taking an ironic distance from the traditional political machinery. Less than half of Finland's "thirty-somethings" voted in the last national elections, and of those over half based their choices on the individual candidates rather than on party ideologies; 1 - 2 % of them are members of political parties, yet most of them belong to at least one – usually athletic – organisation. Nine out of ten unemployed Finnish young people still believe that the individual makes his or her own fortunes (whereas during the economic boom years of the eighties only eight out of ten held this view).

Life horizons and identity work built by the individual emphasise many interpretations: seven out of ten young people consider trade union membership unnecessary, and four out of ten consider trade unions to be "more of a brake than a motor for development". Contingent consideration and risks have not, however, lead to hopelessness: three out of four young people agree with the statement, "even though the (recent economic) recession caused a great deal of human suffering, it has also made the Finnish society and mentality healthier in many respects" (Pesonen, Sänkiaho and Borg 1993; Nuorisobarometrit [*Youth Barometer* reports] 1995, 1996, 1997 and 1998; NUORA 1998; EVA 1995a and b).

The Government and Bureaucrats as well Must Negotiate: The Operative Uncertainty of Institutions in the Risk Society

Ten years ago many researchers were still pessimists, speaking of the governmentalising and bureaucratising of all politics in a spirit of economic functionalism (concerning the modernist paradigm see Hirsch 1980). Nowadays it is more obvious that strict Weberian principles of government no longer hold up; this too is becoming an uncertain, wind-tossed, paper tiger (Beck 1993). Official training to maintain the lordship of officialdom, legalities, strict divisions of labour and hierarchies of power and responsibility, naive concepts of officials' objectivity and unconditional ethico-political convictions, as well as the confidentiality of records, all appear to be rather shaky at the moment (primary inspiration here from Palonen 1994).

The division of labour within administration (in the context of this chapter, youth policy administration in particular), fixed terms and productivity requirements for administrators, the informality and practices of reflexive justice of many new functionaries and partners, confusions of sector divisions, flexibility and dynamism, the expansion of welfare operations into "reconciliation projects", unofficial "networks" and consultation resources, at least preliminary new functionary positions, tertiary sector partnership models as well as project and net budget considerations, all point to the dubious positions and informational dissemination of the machinery of officialdom. The seats of officials are shaky as well, questionable – their informational base is also situational and subjective, condition and problem-centred. It must be renewed and re-legitimised in relation to different problems and points of departure. The uncertainty of administration opens up areas of political conflict and consideration: when seats are wavering and knees shaking it's time for politics and change (Paakkunainen 1998a and 1998d).

Governments must also justify their actions in different incomparable contexts (from "multi-cultural", regional partnership models and workshops to dealing with regional rebels, ecological alternatives, extreme movements and skinheads, animal protection groups and homosexual political movements). In order to make their actions acceptable governments have to submit to new forms of negotiations and fashionable campaigns, which leave their mark. There is little left of the centralised welfare and non-aligned international co-operation projects from the time of Urho Kekkonen's presidency (1956-1981), or of the meta-ideologies of expanding democracy and well-being, or of the government's strict "rural" legalism, after the shifts towards accountability and productivity and the campaigns for networking, partnerships and alliances with the tertiary sector which followed (Review of National Youth Policy: Finland 1997).

On the level of national government these campaigns have been referred to as "the national (business) concern" and "action of state-community (valtioyhteisö)". Youth work, which was marginalised, suffering from an identity crisis and even questioning the purpose of its own existence, had to take these things seriously, to legitimise through reform. In different ways the late-modern bureaucrat must handle and shape the uncertainty which surrounds him after a politician's fashion (Weber's classical political attributes) to play at diving into responsibility, make choices and be committed – as the means of having a rough idea about a future which remains open. The action and its results are in the forefront.

Pluralistic Truths, Contexts and Actors

The extent to which governmental information is problematic, subject to interpretation, a question of perspective and politically motivated also leads to a new form of governmental image and competition in operational methodology: reflexivity and innovation, complex operative relationships, always raise uncertainties and risks in governments as well. Liberal politics, given and received benefits, questioning and politicising settings forcefully bring globalism and the welfare state to their limits. The snowballing effect of public sector growth and its cheese slicer cutting after the fact have not been politically rational innovations, but seemingly going in opposite directions. (Compare this with the media breakthrough, even in Finland, of sociologist Anthony Giddens' and Prime Minister Blair's study club discussion of the "Third way", which seems to be at least temporarily at a dead end.) The paradigm of liberal politics points here to a clear responsibility for change in governmental politics through elections and parliamentarianism. In this way the monumental responsibilities to which the welfare state is committed in terms of services and re-distribution are limited, after the Nordic fashion, to maintaining "established" benefits, in such a way that 90 % of the state budget is automatically allocated in advance.

Nor are crises always learned from. The game format changes: the hardest example of this was the state share reform in Finland, in which the traditional structures for participation in youth politics were sold off in a round of political horse trading in order to balance reduced state shares (regarding municipal structural reforms). Already suffering an identity crisis, the (youth) administration had to appeal to international models and forms of support, to show its significance in them and to take seriously the newly marginalised and tailor more or less autonomous programs to their needs, which have been out of the reach of other branches of government. In the nature of these actions old democracy, parliamentary oversight and justice are no longer generally accepted principles: new "participants" with their stated points of view have stepped into the picture.

The nation state no longer absorbs protests. Neutralised "doctrines of general equality" no longer recognise new risks and participants, possibilities and conflicts – the nature of which is always connected to a given problem or regional context. New conflicts cry out for the logic of individual life politics and solutions in which new compromises are possible. New participants and conflicts are born, for example (Thompson-Hoggett 1996), by creating oppositions between particularism and universalism, diversity and value equality, and by the conquering of "other" groups rising up in place of a principle of standardised treatment (Bauman 1992).

New Professions Finding New Political Alternatives

In addition to this, there appear legions of evaluators and economic efficiency technologies, consultants, barometers and survey technicians; new pedagogues, philosophers and interactive participation producers; psycho-technicians and provocative pedagogy publishers, researchers, media; (post)modern project and organisational sharks, as passionate initiators step onto the stage. It is not at all a question of just petty bourgeois life control and self-help technologies, but of pedagogy and activities relating to the margins of society, and the independence and autonomy of learning practices. These may appeal directly to publicity and specialised audiences; use their information and discussion technologies to move the apparatus of government, its value and thematic organisations; operate within and between as an ally and opponent, even more than political operatives and parliamentary interests. For example, producers of partnership models or "learning by doing" workshop pedagogues are able to design projects for the spirit of the age and select content innovatively. The tailoring principles of the social welfare state thus realise genuine organic intellectuals in spirit and in initiatives (Gramsci 1967).

Government, parliamentary operatives and youth policy interventionists are rather pressured to go down the level of unofficial operatives from diverse regional contexts and the tertiary sector – to set up a certain type of networking – into dialogue and contract dependent organisational culture (Paakkunainen 1995). New, often charismatic, professions like the organisers of the youth training schemes, tailoring projects and methods and the researchers of evaluative strategies could deliver the conventional political culture from the scrutinisation and establishing tendencies. They have strong and mobilisative positions for new alternatives among youth cultures and thematisations introduced via media.

It is a question of knowledge concerning the government's base of information, projects and procedures just this side of "general overview". The significance of old principles changes. "Postmodern specialisation" is, according to Maffesoli, "*specifically that it bonds together opposites, brings them synergy, forcefully makes the age distinctive*" (Maffesoli 1995, 166). A direct linear concept of history fails. "*Self-confident history is replaced by pluralistic and diverse ideologies.*" For example, the key officials in the Finnish Ministry of Education's culture and youth departments represent a diverse range of ideological histories and networks inspired by the avant-garde, researchers and "new professions". Despite that they are able to operate together in a rather nostalgic fashion, to say the least, and their open government mentality is filtered by various principles from different periods and inspiring sources of our country's recent history of governmental combinations, as a game with many players: flexible developmental work of the social welfare ideology in the spirit of common justice, rapidly opening "welfare-mix", and the unclear connections between movement towards the tertiary sector, sporty and creative marketing and computer activities, individual competition and equal rights...

New Light Communities and Dancing Round Table: The Young Setting of the Game and Fortuna

Young people must also through their individual considerations and convictions enter into the world of ethical decisions, commitments, experiments and projections. Here they can find and define themselves as the new operatives, partners and fiery souls of government in the risk society as well. Though politico-ethical communities are no longer camps, collective structures and "party homes" in any way (Gramsci 1967), when people do not have anything else and strong operators have the necessary economic possibilities and cultural hegemony, they live on. The new communities and inspiring networks are more light, projectionary and elastic. At the very latest, in meeting "the other" a young person must make a unique decision as to whether he or she can harm others or limit their freedoms in realising his or her own life politics.

"New politics" can emerge from below, spontaneously, unofficially and without institutional ties. It has its connections with ethico-political aspects of youth identity work, training program selections and professions, citizen initiatives, expressions of feelings and new forms of participation in "spectacular media-democracy" and in its risk-societal sense of drama between moral choices (Paakkunainen 1998a, 122-126). We can speak of social figures which arise from personal familiarity being part of people's initiatives. According to Beck, we should look for forms of sub-politics on the basis of which a new round table of responsible and dynamic participants in confrontation with all different sorts of concrete problems can be created: a group of those which want to confront the challenges of the risk society by "not lying in the dust", but rather, "...*I must step into the politics concerning my own life, since otherwise it will step into me and I will become the game ball of public disputes and confrontations*" (Beck, based on the Finnish translation of 1995, 68-69). These individual projects aren't happening in a political void. Young people have to meet others and social contradictions reflected in a new and open way by the conventional political operations. As we have seen the position of the public operations in the youth policy is nowadays unstable, experimental and depending on equal action relations of companionship.

Reflexive, dialogical and communicative youth politics and its models of round table participation can only be possible when the participatory process of youth politics is outlined as a (reciprocal) relationship between conflicts, games (Spiel) and power (Macht), and when each actor involved has his or her own agreed/agreement-based autonomy. The problem then is to define the "concerned parties" in relation to decision making, solution finding and agreement building: conflicts between the "obstinacy" of young participants, the expert interpreters, regional youth structures, organisers and "self-help" groups is continuously cited by formal decision making and policy operatives in opposition to "confounded-head-banging-participation".

Youth politics as well is an open power game and dance, where individuals and groups must take their own (reflective) places. "Together with partners anything at all can be accomplished; diving into open play could lead to a common Destiny." Youth government must protect its autonomy (and peace) from the utilitarianism of the world of economics. Down with instrumental centralised power and functional divisions of labour! Habermas has in the same spirit emphasised that "*the public sphere of politics... must be conquered by distance (autonomy) from political organisation, equivalent to that which political organisation formerly attempted to keep from economics*" (Habermas 1985, 52-53; Paakkunainen 1998a, 172-197).

On thematic, regional or expert opinion bases, new partnership models can only build visions (e.g. Beck's "round table model") in which the power monopoly of those specially skilled in the field begins to waver, and practices of informal and social and ecological relevance become part of contemplative justice. May the principles of reflexive justice in existing "reconciliation" projects be spread throughout all of society! Decisions cannot be delivered "already made", "only to be sold" or "to be implemented"; decision making structures must be opened further. One condition for uncontrolled and dialogical space is the breaking of the shadowy silence of closed spaces: the goal of transparency. The norms of the process must be bound to self-government, participation in legislative work and personal commitment (Beck 1993). Abilities and cultural capital in professional life, bureaucracy and even commercial operation have major significance here; no one (individual or light community or group of ethical importance to him or her) can avoid responsibility for the risk society (e.g. loss of employment, ecological challenges or destruction of traditional standards in the world).

Examples of the New Networks

Maffesoli, on the other hand, seeks imaginary communities, the beginnings of new tribalism: *"From theoretical, conceptual and distant ideals of democracy towards a communal ideal of a picture and form commonly lived on a day to day basis."* Maffesoli also (1995, 176) goes beyond ego-centrism in searching for a common stylistic and aesthetic basis for new communalism and its common contextualisation and significance. Critical researchers thus search for different sorts of fields of temporary, imaginary and negotiable communal "round table" experiences, which could function as a source not only for new communalism, but also for new political participation, restoring the life of conventional political institutions.

Young people also confront government in a new political fashion, usually precisely when they live in the borderland between passivity and smothering the autonomy of others: we find the Janus-faced tensions and functionality of solidarity. Government and business, in their massive power, are not differentiated ethically – their dissolution, uncertainty and responsibility for the decisions of the risk society spread among all professionals break this facelessness. At the same time the spectacular publications of the risk society give everyone the role of Robin Hood and his merry band. When everything is in motion, closeness forms a functionally important possibility for some to even find functional doors to the meaning of life. Locality becomes more important as some young people at the margins of society form temporary homes together with their comrades in fate.

This thesis searching for a reflective and unofficial new communalism is also supported by fresh research, on which the following generalisations concerning groups of young people and operational initiatives are based: for example our own comparative studies of youth politics in Austria, Sweden, Germany, Italy and Finland (Paakkunainen 1998a and b); young people's courses of action, workshop study (Paakkunainen 1995) and the evaluation of the Youth Academy's "Mahis" campaign (Paakkunainen 1998c). In Finland the welfare state and its historical compromise between young people's changing organisations and working groups live on in a vital way through many new activities. Many unofficial and "welfare mix" sector actions have come into the picture. And here the way is open for the "round table" meetings: *the operative contingency of institutions and the youth's fortuna will meet in the risk society.* The competent individuals in the competition society are co-operating and linking in these projects with the more marginalised youth, losers in hard games of competitions in social and cultural arenas.

Janus-Faced Politics without Black-and-White Values

Traditional collectivism and institutionalism are fading into history. Youth initiatives are learned from crises. They are more risk taking and elastic, providing a network culture with more room than before for individuals to manoeuvre. They also evaluate the successfulness of their actions according to postmodern and reflective principles. They have two-faced, multi-valued and radically contextual political concepts (changing according to backgrounds, themes and situations). On the one hand politics is considered to be "the self-regulated game of dirty old men" and on the other hand there is the individualistic, even radical action of day to day life politics, displaying a rather broad spectrum of views.

This constructivism has a style, form and operational strategy which is rebuilt for every occasion. In the spheres of youth initiatives there are even significant group projects in which learning from uncertainty and conflict – "playing with contingency" – serves as a paradigm for life politics. We can even speak of radical contextualism, plunging into each group's own idiosyncratic horizon of experience to boldly investigate and build a world from there. Besides this, some openings for play and possibilities for influence are still to be seen in the mobilisation structures of industrial society. For this many adolescent and youth organisations have developed their own rhetoric and repertoire of provocation techniques.

This Janus-facedness in political concepts should be a door opening for young people to the political playing fields and sovereignty. The world is no longer black and white, but rather it opens ambiguously and often with irony. The political world and playing fields open before young people finally as imperfect and ambiguous. According to the Bogart theorem, a good person and a good world have stunted growth – are only halves – and they are dispensed with accordingly. On independent playing fields "ego" can show itself without shame as well. According to Seel, an "entirely-good-person" is still not so good and interesting as a "not-so-good-person" (Seel 1996, 779-80; see also Eräsaari 1998, 103-104). In the group initiatives of the nineties not all political playing fields remained lost to pure distinctions of absolute moral rejection, by which politics would be left to "those dirty players". In these sprouting new partners we can see more and more institutional reflections of the risk society. Thus government, unofficial youth cultures and initiatives learn from each other, bringing them closer and creating conditions more conducive to reconciliation and even co-operation (in the germ of the national salary initiative). *Here the uncertain operationalism of the public sector and real-politics and flexible modern (social) politics confront the spirit of the political game and the fortuna of young people in the risk society.*

Two Cultures of Action

Youth networks and initiatives have as their own unique resource and means in (early) youth support in the margins of society. The recent economic recession in Finland gave these cultures a further push. These groups have provided an environment for marginal young people, they have built new communities which even have radical and traditional operational arsenals, and they have developed principles for evaluating "feel-good" type activities both qualitatively and emotionally, and for generally experienced therapeutic repertoires. In the uncertainty of the risk society there are no longer any standard measures for the "success" or "maturity" of a functional culture. Often for these initiatives' members need strong temporary communities, the safety and image of a traditional community, or perhaps a return to the spirit of the French Revolution. *Most often the possibility for these marginal projects to confront the fortuna of the risk society depends on support from the strong arms of the public sector* (see Paakkunainen 1998a and b).

In individual games the operational culture of successful young people is more unofficial and flexible. The drama of the members arises from gifted and unofficial skills and areas of virtuosity. A desire to stand out within social or ecological movement does not require a safe community environment. These sorts of operational motivations do not need general or communal evaluations for their operations, and their political concepts are basically just more individualistic and idealistic versions of what they learned in school. *They have confronted the fortuna of the risk society with their own reflexivity.* Besides school, many sorts of (un)official advisory units, discursive technologies, consultants and more sensitive organisational cultures have given them their room to function. Among others in this category we have Finland's Scouting troops, which fulfil in particular the age-specific needs of early youth, especially in terms of identity and socialisation at this sensitive stage, basing their work on a compromise between church, family and school: safe isolation, individuality and unique, suitably controlled risk taking. The principle of pedagogical responsibility in many organisational cultures brings them to the point where they fulfil public tasks and assistance eligibility requirements in terms of producing balanced young people capable of competition and decision making.

Some National Features

A specific national tendency in Finland, in comparison with mainland Europe even, has to do with the rapid deterioration of formal officialdom; network forming, incitement to action and initiatives coming from young people or young people's and older folk's co-operation on the grass roots level have become more common. This is a blow to the head for our old imperial discipline and national fear of taking initiatives. The beneficiaries and functionaries in these initiatives are often one and the same group: the here-and-now nature of action and the pleasure principle in particular are emphasised. As in international trends, local initiatives are predominant, but still in Finland every tenth initiative is global in scale (as in the EU member state of Italy). Group operations here still depend on public assistance more than in other countries though. But on the other hand, scarcity sends the message of the new action culture's committed nature, "hanging on", or of being a new partner in the dialogue of power.

In terms of political goals and horizons, however, there are still state centred features evident: discussions of decision-making structures, negotiations and publicity are more centralised than direct. The old *etatism* is still evident in contemporary Finland's central organisational dependence. There are many types of decision makers involved in flexible initiatives, involving more professionals than in most countries. More than in comparative countries though, there is a dependence on leaders and central organisational leadership. Trends of change are not necessarily in the direction of member-democracy either, but confronting problems of internal co-operation and overcoming schedule and financial shortages are the most immediate "practical" problems. A stressed atmosphere and a somewhat hopeless demand for professionalism is directed towards the leadership of many projects.

Our public administrative and newly enabled professions have not become problems and sources of alienation for national initiatives as they have in Central Europe: in Finland we don't see organisational professionalism as a problem for voluntary action and spontaneity in national society; on the contrary, at times the tertiary sector legitimises its role through its "professionalism". The means of operation are, in the same spirit, very electric and at times at least rhetorically radical, even though Internet does not mobilise Finns to act as much as myth would suggest. Internet has remained a regrettably technical and commercial gadget for us (Paakkunainen 1997); its uses in building democratic awareness, preparedness and participation are, with the exception of a few individual radicals, still in infant stages of development here. Finnish "Nokia style ingenuity and courage" also remind us of co-operative networks: educational co-operation, professionalism and tradesmen's benefits are (relatively) high; old collectivist and religious world pictures are crumbling and being replaced by individualism and ambiguity, forming a sort of common (convergent) paradigm for most cultures of participation.

Illustration of Operative Contingency of Conventional Operations and a New Action Logic of Risk Society

Following Figure 6.1 (see p. 86) illustrates the playing fields and relationships of youth work and more informal politics. The direction of change illustrated by the horizontal axis shows phases of movement (hopelessly growing, regardless of attempts to restore compromise between the political right and left) from old collective mobilisation and ideology of economic growth towards the risk society and facing challenges on an individual basis: in one way the failure of personal responsibility in margin, in another way the Fortuna of life politics in positive contingency. The vertical axis makes an attempt to visualise the positions of actors in youth politics and their methodological and operational repertoires in reference to old government and planning structures on the one hand, and in reference to modern sub-politics on the other, with reflexive action between the extremes.

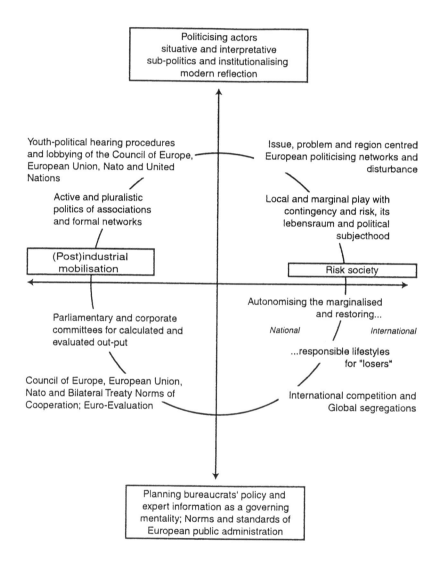

Figure 6.1 Fields of action in youth politics in the crisis of the risk society

The national and European institutions (down in the left quarter) and their universal tools of policy are in the legitimation crises and in front of the requirements articulated in the other fields (three other quarters). And the activity of associations, networks and the international lobbying (up in the left quarter) have to rebuilt their action by the informal, open and "live" responsibilities and dialogue with different life-political (sub-political) experiences.

The status quo articulated with formal associations is nowadays dynamic and many-faced. The learning processes of institutions and associations (the levels on the left hand) mean here the modern reflection (in the spirit of Bauman, Giddens and Beck) that has, also, institutional transformations. It is clear that it is not abstractly possible in the modern welfare society to take down or throw away the decision making structures of integral state; they must rather be renewed in their vital parts and radically joined together with other operations and companions acting in the other three fields.

The field of international and marginal play with contingency and risk (up in the right quarter) is a sub-political arena full of situated, problem-centred and often local or para-national projects and round tables. We could speak here about radical contextualism. This sphere of action could be understood as positive marginalisation and unique base for institutional reflexivity rising up in the other fields. The projects looking for the new choices in front of the risks of everyday life and playing with the contingency have, often, new touches and ideas in reconstructing the life motivations and repressed lifestyles of "losers" (in the lower right quarter). The Finnish examples described above, informal networks working with marginalised youth in the spirit of "pleasure" and "new communities", are projects of this life-political combination, unique play with the contingency.

This "positive marginality" and its life-political projects are living near by the concrete life situations and contexts of marginality, where the stressed competition of individuals is producing individual losers who are autonomising their marginality and their self-responsibility in unsuccessful play of the life. The universal campaigns of EU and nation states are, easily, objectifying marginality. Here the "marginality" is not the term of repressed people, themselves. It is a universal term of functionalised policy for the problems situating "somewhere there" and waiting the social or civilising integration (as in the cases of unemployed ethnic groups, simple-minded supporters of Haider or ghettos in developing East Europe). And the initiatives of corporatives and powerful associations are trying to get the marginal in the dialogue but they often fail because of their own established, historically institutionalised or overtaken interests and privileges.

This illustration and interpretation produce four quadrants, each with both "national" and "international" aspects, within the overall field of youth work, in which individual, networked and institutional reflection and learning processes are taking place. All types of actors within this field are subject to change and are in need of each other, but they are not independent (sub)political actors or experts in each other's methods and means of interpreting their problems. The different subjects have to interfere in other people's business and by the free ways learn and reflect with the others. According to this scheme the most radical change needed in contemporary youth politics, in both Central European and Scandinavian systems, is in recognising actors on the international (the "new-regionality" breaking the boarders of nation states) level as well as the sovereignty of sub-political participants. Concrete steps towards a politically active and autonomous "round table" forum form the nucleus of this strategy for change.

Modern individualised risk society can no longer be governed from one national or European centre. Citizens' initiatives are increasingly defined by the participants, locations, issues and situations on which societal agreement is reached. These situational modern reflexive learning practices can enter into institutionalisation, in which official actors (professions and municipalities, for example) find new dialogical relationships and horizontal dynamics (partnership models, workshops and the germ of a civic salary). New politically active round table forums on the national level are in a position of contingency and playing with risk; and internationally on the field of Euro-networks and disturbance.

Means of operating and participating which identify the fields are given as examples in the Figure 6.1.

References

Allardt, E. (1998), 'Hyvinvointitutkimus ja elämänpolitiikka' (Research of Welfare and the Life Politics), in J. P. Roos and T. Hoikkala (eds.), *Elämänpolitiikka* (Life Politics), Gaudeamus, Tampere.

Bauman, Z. (1992), *Intimations of Postmodernity*, Routledge, London and New York.

Bauman, Z. (1993), *Postmodern Ethics*, Blackwell, Bodmin.

Bauman, Z. (1995), *Life in Fragments*, Blackwell, London.

Bauman, Z. (1997), *Postmodernity and its Discontents*, Polity Press, Cambridge.

Beck, U. (1993), *Die Erfindung des Politischen: Zu einer Theorie reflexiver Modernisierung*, Suhrkamp, Frankfurt.

Beck, U. (1995), *Eigenes Leben, Ausfluge in die unbekannte Gesellschaft, in der wir leben*, C. H. Beck, München.

Borg, S. (1996), *Nuoret, politiikka ja yhteiskunnallinen syrjäytyminen* (Young People, Politics and Social Marginalisation), NUORA, Ministry of Education, Helsinki.

Bourdieu, P. (1984), *Distinction: A Social Critique of the Judgement of Taste*, Harvard University Press, Cambridge, Massachusetts.

Eräsaari, R. (1998), 'Mikä ihmeen elämänpolitiikka?' (A Wonderful Life Politics – What's the Reality), in J. P. Roos and T. Hoikkala (eds.), *Elämänpolitiikka* (Life Politics), Gaudeamus, Tampere.

EVA (1995a and b), The Centre for Finnish Business and Policy Studies, Reports.

Gramsci, A. (1967), *En Kollektiv Intellektuell* (Original title: Avviamento allo studio della filosofia e del materialismo storico), Cavefors, Uddevalla.

Habermas, J. (1985), *Die Neue Unübersichtlichkeit: Kleine Politische Schriften V*, Suhrkamp, Frankfurt am Main.

Hirsch, J. (1980), *Der Sicherheitstaat: Das "Modell Deutschland", Seine Krise und die neuen sozialen Bewegungen*, Europäische Verlag, Frankfurt am Main.

Hoffmann-Lange, U. (1995), *Jugend und Demokratie in Deutschland*, Leske + Budrich, Opladen.

Karisto, A. (1998), 'Pirstoutuvan elämän politiikka' (The Politics in the Fragmentation of the Life), in J. P. Roos and T. Hoikkala (eds.), *Elämänpolitiikka* (Life Politics), Gaudeamus, Tampere.

Maffesoli, M. (1995), *Maailman mieli: Yhteisöllisen tyylin muodoista*, Gaudeamus, Helsinki. (The next reference is the same book in English.)

Maffesoli, M. (1996), *The Contemplation of the World: Figures of Community Style*, University of Minnesota Press, Minneapolis - London.

NUORA 1998, Nuorten järjestökiinnitteisyys: Yhteenvetoraportti 1998 (The Associative Mobilisation of Youth: Summary Report 1998), Nykypaino, Helsinki.

Nuorisobarometri 1995, 1996, 1997 and 1998 (Youth Barometer Reports in Finland), Ministry of Education, Helsinki.

Paakkunainen, K. (1995), *Nuorisopaja: Tehdashallin hämärästä autonomiseen oppiin* (Youth Training Scheme: From the Dark Labour in to the Autonomous Learning Practices), Nuorisotutkimus 2000, 2/95 (Finnish Youth Research 2000 Programme), Hakapaino, Helsinki.

Paakkunainen, K. (1997), *Commodification and Professionalization of Finnish Youth Policy: Contradictions in the Development of Multimedia as a Democratic Publicity and Dialogue*, 'European Symposium on Democracy and Multimedia Networks': Workshop IV, entitled 'The World and Citizens' Networks' organised in Parthenay, France, September 25-27, 1997.

Paakkunainen, K. (1998a), *Kama-Saksan ihailusta kumppanuuteen: Onko saksalaisesta nuorisopolitiikasta meille malliksi?* (Construction of German Youth Policy – A Modell for Us ?), Hakapaino, Helsinki.

Paakkunainen, K. (1998b), *Käsikirjoitus Itävallan, Ruotsin ja Suomen nuorisojärjestöjen vertailusta* (Manuscript for the Comparison of Austrian, Swedish and Finnish Youth Policy), Autumn 1998.

Paakkunainen, K. (1998c), *Political Participation of Youth – A Remedy Against Marginalisation?*, Paper presented in 'NYRIS VI'-seminar, Reykjavik, June 11-13, 1998.

Paakkunainen, K. (1998d), 'Commodification and Professionalisation of Youth Policy', in H. Helve (ed.), *Unification and Marginalisation of Young People*, Finnish Youth Research 2000 Programme, The Finnish Youth Research Society, Helsinki, pp. 136-150.

Palonen, K. (1993), 'Introduction: From Policy and Polity to Politicking and Politicization', in K. Palonen and T. Parvikko (eds.), *Reading the Political: Exploring the Margins of Politics*, The Finnish Political Science Association, Tammer-Paino Oy., Tampere.

Palonen, K. (1994), 'Onko Max Weberin byrokratisoitumisen läpitunkevuuden teesi vanhentunutta?' (Is Max Weber's Idea of Bureaucracy Actual and Correct?), in *Tutkimaton uudistus? Julkisen sektorin uudistukset tutkimushaasteena* (Public Sector's Reforms as a Research Challenge), Ministry of Finance, Public Management Department, Helsinki.

Pesonen, P. , Sänkiaho, R. and Borg, S. (1993), *Vaalikansan äänivalta* (The Power of People in Elections), WSOY, Juva.

Review of National Youth Policy: Finland (1997), Council of Europe and Ministry of Education in Finland, University Press, Helsinki.

Rose, N. (1996), 'Governing "Advanced" Liberal Democracies', in A. Barry, T. Osborne and N. Rose (eds.), *Foucault and Political Reason*, UCL Press, England.

Seel, M. (1996), 'Über das Böse in der Moral', *Merkur 570/571*.

Sgritta, G. (1987), 'Normalization and Project', *International Journal of Sociology, Vol. 17, No. 3*.

Thompson, S. and Hoggett, P. (1996), 'Universalism, Selectivism and Particularism: Towards a Postmodern Social Policy', *Critical Social Policy 46, Vol. 16*.

7 Mixed Motives of Young Nordic Volunteers

MARIANNE NYLUND

Introduction: Voluntary Action and Motives

Earlier studies have dichotomised volunteers' motives into altruistic and egoistic. At the same time, some of them also recognise that motives to volunteer are often a mixture of both altruism and egoism (Clary, Snyder and Stukas 1996; Davis Smith 1996, 22; Van Til 1988, 19-33). In moral philosophy, an altruist is defined as an unselfish person helping others, and an egoist is a person who cares only of her/his own rights (Airaksinen 1993, 118-119). Some youths think that voluntary work is charity work performed by elderly people, often middle and upper class housewives with altruistic motives (Gaskin 1998, 12). Thus, altruism still has the "burden" of philanthropy: rich people helping the poor. According to recent studies, this type of voluntary work is rare in West European countries (Gaskin and Davis Smith 1995). Today, voluntary work or voluntary action can be seen as an activity embodying postmaterial needs and values (Davis Smith 1993, 14; referring to Inglehart 1990). Such values for example, include working for social needs, self-fulfilment, self-development, belonging somewhere, and developing oneself educationally (Helve 1993, 101-102). Everyone has his or her own goals in voluntary work (Helve 1997, 7). Since it is short-term, people volunteer as long as it suits them (Gillespie and King 1985, 802-803; Lähteenmaa 1997). This does not apply only to young people but also to adults (Gaskin and Davis Smith 1995; Omoto and Snyder 1993, 173).

There is an assumption that young people are selfish, and think only about themselves (Lähteenmaa 1997, 47). For example, earlier studies have shown that young people have more egoistic motives than adult volunteers (Andersen 1996; Frisch and Gerrard 1981; Gillespie and King 1985). These egoistic motives include, for example, learning new things, feeling important and needed, exploring career options, and meeting new people. Although young volunteers seek personal satisfaction to fulfil their needs, they also want to do something useful in the community (Gaskin 1998; Lähteenmaa 1996). Thus, voluntary work can also be called a "value based" activity (Davis Smith 1993, 10).

In a British study, adolescents (both volunteers and non-volunteers) were asked why they think young people volunteer (Gaskin 1998, 80). They considered that a personal connection with the cause, helping people, getting work experience, finding out about career options, and to broaden their experience in life were the most crucial reasons to volunteer. On the other hand, the reason why young people are not volunteering is that they do not have enough time, do not want to work without being paid, and their friends do not think that it is "cool". The opinions of friends are particularly important for those under 20 years. Nevertheless, there are also young people who are willing to volunteer but do not have access to, or cannot approach, voluntary organisations (Gaskin and Davis Smith 1995, 109).

During the recession in the early 1990s, Finnish politicians and other decision-makers started to be interested in knowing how to get young people to participate in the community. The issue was: how can young people acquire skills needed in working life when many of them could not find a paid job. In 1994, the unemployment rate among Finnish young people aged 15 to 24 years went up to 34 %, but it decreased to 27 % in 1996 (Labour Force Statistics 1997). How important a motive is career development for young people themselves? The motives of volunteers in Nordic countries have been studied only in the 1990s (Andersen 1996; Júliúsdóttir and Sigurðardóttir 1998), and the motives of young people have received even less attention from researchers (Lähteenmaa 1996). In 1994, the proportion of young people (under 25 years) volunteering, at least once a year, was 26 % in Denmark, 32 % in Sweden (Gaskin and Davis Smith 1995, 29), but only 12 % in Finland (Living Conditions 1994). Figures for Iceland and Norway were not available.

In this chapter, I define volunteering as unpaid work, in other words, organised voluntary action (often personal help) that is performed in voluntary social welfare organisations or in public social and health institutions.[1] I do not relate volunteering to help given to friends, relatives, or neighbours. My aim is to find out what kinds of motives encourage young people to volunteer in Finland, Denmark, Iceland, Norway, and

Sweden with the emphasis on Finnish volunteers. Do young people lack altruistic motives or do they engage in volunteering also because of unselfish reasons? Are they more interested in self-seeking motives, for example, to gain skills and new friends than in offering their time to help others? Based on a questionnaire, I investigated whether there are "extremes", i.e., pure altruists and pure egoists among Nordic young volunteers.

Methods and Data

The Volunteer Functions Inventory

The data used in this study is part of the Comparative Nordic Research Project on Volunteer Motives (referred as the Nordic study) from which some national results are already published (Andersen 1996; Júlíúsdóttir and Sigurðardóttir 1997; Lorentzen and Rogstad 1994). In this Nordic study, an American *Volunteer Functions Inventory* developed and tested by Clary, Snyder and Ridge (1992) was used to explore volunteers' motives through thirty statements. As a result of a factor analysis, the original study produced six motive factors, each of them consisting of five statements: value, understanding, esteem, social, career, and protective.

According to Clary, Snyder and Ridge (1992, 335-338), the value motive, also referred to as altruism, includes the importance of helping others or serving as an advocate for a group or a cause. The understanding motive is associated with satisfying the desire to "learn for the sake of learning", for example or "to understand the people whom one serves, the organisation for which one volunteers, or oneself" (Clary et al. 1992, 337). Volunteering is not only for helping others or learning something new. It can also be a way of strengthening one's self-esteem. Self-esteem is defined as strengthening one's self-identity and increasing the feeling of belonging to a community (Lorentzen and Rogstad 1994, 44; Susag 1999). The esteem motive makes "one feel better about oneself", feel needed, and feel important (Clary et al. 1992, 338). The career motive is "satisfied when people volunteer to learn particular skills", for example to explore career options or "introduce them to potential career contacts" (Clary et al. 1992, 338). Finally, some people volunteer to satisfy a social function; "for them volunteering is a reflection of the normative influence of friends, family, or a social group whom they hold in esteem" (Clary et al. 1992, 338). In this chapter, I refer to the value motive as an altruistic motive, and to the learning, esteem, career, and social motives as egoistic motives (see Lorentzen and Rogstad 1994, 70).

A factor analysis was utilised to test whether theoretical functions (motives) found in Clary et al. (1992) would also apply to Nordic volunteers. The statements assumed to be protective did not make a factor in a Norwegian pre-study (Lorentzen and Rogstad 1994).[2] Therefore, these statements were excluded from the comparative part, leaving 25 statements for the final analysis. Volunteers should score statements in a seven-point scale from "not at all important" (1, 2) and "somewhat important" (3, 4, 5) to "extremely important" (6, 7). The data were analysed with a factor analysis (varimax rotation), and resulted in a five-factor model similar to that of Clary et al. (1992): value, learning,[3] esteem, social, and career.[4] The results are presented using the highest scores 6 and 7 (extremely important). In addition to the statements already mentioned, the Finnish questionnaire included an open-ended question asking about the three most important reasons for volunteering.

Young Nordic Volunteers

In the Nordic study, we wanted to study voluntary activity which provided social interaction and personal help. We focused on people who were already volunteers in a voluntary social welfare organisation. Therefore, this study was not a survey in which questionnaires are sent to a representative population of a certain age group. The questionnaires were mailed or delivered personally to a number of voluntary organisations without knowing how many volunteers they had or in what age categories they fell. In order to receive comparable data, the Red Cross was selected on account of its similarities in all five countries. The activities of young people at the Red Cross were most often connected with first aid training, help offered at accidents, leading groups, and visitor services. In order to locate a greater variety of volunteers, the following organisations were also included: organisations for retired people, child welfare and associations for unemployed people.[5] In addition, volunteer centres were selected from Finland, Denmark, and Norway. These new types of centres are run by municipalities or by local voluntary organisations, and they recruit volunteers for various social and health institutions (e.g. hospitals,

94

residential homes for older people) or for work in individual homes (Brekke 1994; Suutarla and Hakkarainen 1997). The selected voluntary organisations and centres represent a wide geographical region, including both rural and urban areas, in all five countries.

The data were collected in 1994 and 1995, and consist of all age groups. In this study, I concentrate just upon the young people between 15 and 25 years. The proportion of all young people (n = 664) is the following: 6 % from Finland, 12 % from Denmark, 10 % from Iceland, 59 % from Norway, and 13 % from Sweden (Table 7.1). The data are nationally biased with half of the volunteers coming from Norway. The majority of volunteers are females over 20 years.

Table 7.1 Demographic characteristics of young volunteers (%)*

Characteristics (n = 664)	%
Country	
Iceland	10
Denmark	12
Finland	6
Norway	59
Sweden	13
Sex	
Female	63
Male	37
Age	
15-19	36
20-25	64
Labour status (missing n = 46; 6 %)	
Employed	30
Unemployed	7
Student	43
On pension	2
Other (pupils, homemakers)	12
Education (after compulsory school; missing n = 104; 15 %)	
0 years	11
1-3 years	36
4-6 years	30
7 or more years	8

* All categories do not total 100 % because of missing values.

One third of volunteers had from one to three years of education after basic (compulsory) school, another one third had from four to six years, and 8 % more than seven years. 11 % did not have any education after compulsory schooling (some of them were still attending the basic school), and 15 % did not reply. One third of all young volunteers were employed, and 30 % of them were in a part-time job. The majority of volunteers were students (43 %), and only 7 % were unemployed, and 2 % were on a pension.[6] The remaining 12 % were pupils attending an elementary school or homemakers (p. 95, Table 7.1).[7] There were differences among young volunteers in each country. For example, almost half of the Danish volunteers were in a paid job compared to Finland, Iceland, Norway, and Sweden where the majority were students or pupils. Denmark and Sweden had most unemployed volunteers.

Table 7.2 Voluntary organisations and activity of young volunteers

Voluntary organisation	(%)*
Red Cross	82
Volunteer Centre	17
Child Welfare association	0.4
Seniors' associations	0.1
Associations for unemployed	0.5
Earlier volunteer experience	
Yes	54
No	46
Active at other voluntary organisations	
Yes	29
No	71
Volunteer hours previous month	
(missing n = 102; 15 %)	
0 hours	18
1-10 hours	30
11 hours or more	37

* All categories do not total 100 % because of missing values.

The majority of young people volunteered at the Red Cross, and less than one fifth at volunteer centres (see p. 96, Table 7.2). Only a few volunteered at organisations for retired people, child welfare and associations for the unemployed. Half of the volunteers had earlier volunteer experience, and one third were volunteering at another voluntary organisation simultaneously. One third had volunteered one to ten hours the previous month, another one third more than ten hours a month and some up to 350 hours (that would be 11 hours a day!). Information about volunteer activity reveals that volunteers who replied to this study were active volunteers, many of them having previous volunteer experience and had been volunteering on a regular basis.

Results: Young Volunteers' Motives

Young people regard the value motive as their most important motive of all 25 statements (68 %). The learning motive was scored almost as high as the value motive (66 %), and the third most important motive was esteem (46 %). The career motive (22 %) and the social motive (13 %) did not receive very high scores (Table 7.3). Half of volunteers scored combinations of the value and learning motives (55 %), or the value and esteem motives (40 %) as extremely important.

Table 7.3 Motives by country (%)[a]

	Value	Learning	Esteem	Career	Social	n
Finland	75	85	75	36	7	40
Denmark	71	72	51	22	1	79
Iceland	82	87	61	18	9	69
Norway	63	60	36	20	18	391
Sweden	85	74	61	32	7	85
Average[b]	**68**	**66**	**46**	**22**	**13**	664
Mean[c]	2.7	2.6	2.3	1.8	1.6	

[a] Only the highest scores (extremely important).

[b] Missing cases 10-21.

[c] 1 = not at all important, 2 = somewhat important, 3 = extremely important.

The statement "*I feel it is important to help others*" received the highest scores (79 %) from all five value statements (Table 7.4). Although the value motive was scored highest of all motives, there are some differences among single statements and countries. For example, the statement "*I am concerned about those less fortunate than myself*" was highest among Icelanders (77 %), and lowest among Finns (35 %). Also Danes, Swedes, and Norwegians scored significantly higher than Finns. On the other hand, the statement, "*I can do something for a cause that is important to me*" was scored higher by Finns than Norwegians.[8] Do these results indicate that Finns are more selfish than other Scandinavians? Helve (1998) has found that Finnish young people's attitudes towards poor people and foreigners have sharpened during recession. Also an international study from 1995 states that only half of young Finns considered solidarity towards "less fortunate" people important for themselves (Ahonen 1997). Therefore, it is no great surprise that volunteers in social welfare are not too concerned about others. This result might be connected to the recession and the high unemployment rate in the early 1990s.

Table 7.4 Most important altruistic and egoistic motives to volunteer

Altruism	Egoism / personal needs			
Value[a]	**Learning**[a]	**Esteem**[a]	**Career**[c]	**Social**[c]
• important to help others • concern about less fortunate • compassion for others • cause is important to me	• learn how to deal with variety of people • learn more about the cause • learn through "hands on" experience • gain new perspective on things	• makes me feel needed • way to make new friends[b]	• helps me to get paid job	• my friends volun-teer

[a] Statements that received over 50 % of all replies in rank-order from most important to least important.

[b] This statement loaded only .35 in factor analysis for esteem factor.

[c] Statements that scored highest in this category.

Egoistic Motives

Learning how to deal with different people and problems provides practical experience "with real life" helps to widen a person's world perspective. These learning motives seem to be especially important for Finns and Icelanders (Table 7.3). The feeling of being important and needed in the society was also meaningful for Finnish volunteers (75 %). It could be attributed to a "desire to belong", and "not to be left outside of society".[9] The esteem motive scored rather high also for Icelanders (61 %), Swedes (61 %) and Danes (51 %) but much lower for Norwegians (36 %). It is not only young Norwegians but also adult volunteers who do not consider this motive so important (Andersen 1996, 49-53). The most important statement in the career motive was "*volunteering experience is helpful when I seek for a paid job*" (40 %). Otherwise young volunteers did not score the career motive very high, although this was assumed by young British volunteers to be an important motive (Gaskin 1998). The social motive was scored even lower than the career motive, the highest statement being "*my friends volunteer*" (31 %). It seems that young people do not feel socially obliged to volunteer. However, for Norwegians (18 %) this motive was somewhat more important compared to other nationalities (1 % - 9 %). Maybe this has to do with the social environment and whether friends and relatives are accepting and supporting your volunteering effort or not. Egoistic motives need not be understood only as negative; they can also be called "healthy egoism" or individualistic motives.

Background Characteristics and Motives

There are only a few demographic and background characteristics that explain why young people have different motives (see p. 100, Table 7.5). Here, I analyse the five different motives according to the background variables that are crosstabulated with motive factors. (Significance levels at 5 % level, $p < 0.05$ or less are reported.[10]) These are sex, unemployment, working part-time, volunteer hours, and volunteer experience that are significant at the 5 % level ($p < 0.05$). Only education and country were significant at the 1 % level ($p < 0.01$). Norwegians scored lowest on all except the social motive. Women scored both the value and the learning motive higher than men. This might indicate that women are able to combine learning with compassion for other people. Girls often learn communication and self-reflection skills among their friends. In addition, they are empathic, responsible, and altruistic in relation to other people (Näre and Lähteenmaa 1992, 329-330). Do male volunteers also have these characteristics? Some Finnish male volunteers mentioned that self-development, and learning human relations are important motives to volunteer.[11] Some considered volunteering satisfying activity where you meet and interact with others. Being useful for others makes you feel needed. Consequently, volunteering can be used as a "tool" to change self-image and self-identity, but also increase self-awareness and reflexivity (Matthies 1994, 57; referring to Jakob 1993).

Table 7.5 Summary of motives by background variables

	Value	Learning	Esteem	Social	Career
Women vs. men	*	*			
Working full-time vs. part-time				*	
Unemployed vs. student			*	*		*
No education vs. high education					**
Active earlier vs. not active	*				
Zero volunteer hours vs. more than 10 hours	*	*	*	*	*

*p < 0.05, **p < 0.01 (only highest scores are significance tested).

Another significant difference concerning motives was found among unemployed volunteers and students. Egoistic motives, learning, esteem, and career had more importance for unemployed volunteers than for students. Also volunteers with no education considered the career motive higher than others (see Andersen 1996, 58-59). Those working part-time considered the social motive higher than those working full-time. There were no statistically significant differences among volunteers in paid work and those not in paid work (i.e. pupils, students, unemployed). Even so, Lorentzen and Rogstad explain (1994, 60) that it is more important for the unemployed to "strengthen one's self-identity" than for those in a paid job. It seems reasonable that people without a job or education are interested in finding qualifications for themselves through volunteering.

Volunteers who have volunteered before scored higher on the value motives compared to those who have not volunteered previously. This might indicate that those who have volunteered previously already know what drives them to volunteer, for example, a compassion for others. Volunteers who volunteer more than ten hours a month are not only altruists, because all motives were scored higher by them than those who volunteer less. Active volunteers seem to be more committed to their tasks than others who volunteer less than ten hours. To sum up, female volunteers favour altruistic motives, and unemployed volunteers are more interested in egoistic motives.[12]

Mixed Motives of Helping, Learning and Feeling Needed

The majority of the respondents had both altruistic and egoistic motives. Young people ranked altruistic values as high as other age groups. However, they had higher scores for learning and career motives than older people (Andersen 1996; Frisch and Gerrard 1981, 572-574; Nylund 1998). In addition to analysing the "average volunteer", I looked at the "extremes". These are volunteers who replied either with "extremely important" or "not at all important" for all five motives. However, I found only a small proportion of young people who were "extremes". Table 7.6 (see p. 102) shows that 35 young volunteers scored highly on both the value motive and all egoistic motives (learning, esteem, social, and career). Avrahami and Dar (1993, 712) call these types of volunteers "vital experimenters" who are strongly motivated by all orientations but I prefer to call them "individualistic altruists" (see Näre and Lähteenmaa 1992, 330).

Those who scored high on the value motives but low on the egoistic motives can be called "pure altruists". However, there were only two persons in this category (Table 7.6). On the other hand, there were no "pure egoists", i.e., volunteers who scored both value motives low and all egoistic motives high (called "expressive individualists" by Avrahami and Dar 1993, 712). Indeed, it would be rather strange to find that people volunteering in social welfare would be purely egoistical, because this type of volunteering often involves helping others or promoting public good. Furthermore, there were five volunteers who scored low on all five motives. This does not mean that they are really "motiveless" (called

Table 7.6 "Extreme" volunteers

Altruistic motive: value

		High[a]	Low[b]
Egoistic motives: learning self-esteem career social	High[a]	*Individualistic altruist* n = 35	*Pure egoist* n = 0
	Low[b]	*Pure altruist* n = 2	*"Motiveless"* n = 5

[a] Only the highest scores (extremely important).
[b] Only the lowest scores (not at all important).

"indifferent" by Avrahami and Dar 1993, 707) but rather that they can consider motives other than the given statements as important. These "motiveless" youths were between 15 and 19 years old, two of them had volunteered earlier but none of them had volunteered simultaneously at another voluntary organisation. Only one of them had volunteered more than 10 hours in the previous month, and the other four, zero hours. This information tells that they were not active at the time of the study. It might also be the case that these young people were asked to volunteer by someone else. Furthermore, motives will also vary during the life course from self-esteem to altruism, and from altruism to learning (Matthies 1994, 56-58). It is difficult to find clear typologies of young volunteers from the Nordic data (Table 7.5 and Table 7.6). Perhaps it is not even possible because young people's value changes are not connected to any given ideology, and a person's ideas can change from individualism to humanism depending on the issue in question (Helve 1998; Päivärinta 1997).

Some researchers have argued that surveys and questionnaires do not reveal all the motives for volunteering in the same way as in-depth interviews do (Lähteenmaa 1998, 149), and that the selection of methodologies is not discussed properly (Puuronen 1989, 14-15). Even though this Nordic study was based solely on a questionnaire with predetermined statements, it nevertheless provides a picture of several combinations of motives. I agree that surveys will neither give the whole picture nor help to understand nuances in people's motives for volunteering (Lähteenmaa 1998; Paolicchi 1995). The statements measure often what is already known from previous studies or what researchers assume might be volunteers' motives. For example, some of the respondents commented at the end of the questionnaire that "researchers seem to assume that people volunteer only because of selfish reasons". The majority of the respondents scored at least one egoistic motive highly. However, the result of the study proved that there were no "pure egoists" among young volunteers. On the other hand, I thought that hardly anyone would rank low on all motives but there were in fact some "motiveless" young people. Though questionnaires will not reveal all motives, they still prove to be useful in comparative studies if we want to reach a larger number of respondents than is possible with in-depth interviews and other qualitative methods. In addition, there are very few studies on this topic in Nordic countries. One of the problems with questionnaires is how to use exactly the same wording because concepts have different meanings in different countries. This cannot be avoided either in in-depth or narrative interviews, although these latter methods can surely better bring out the voice of the volunteers, depending upon how the results are presented (see Paolicchi 1995).

The statements in this particular questionnaire do not reveal all varieties of motives (Avrahami and Dar 1993). For example, they do not include the motive of "enjoyment and fun" but some other studies do so (Gaskin 1998; Gillespie and King 1985, 810). Lähteenmaa (1996, 144) has combined altruistic and egoistic motives in a concept she calls "altruistic hedonism". She came to this conclusion after interviewing young people volunteering in a youth cafe. They responded that in helping others they learned something, enjoyed themselves, had fun, and "it made them feel good". It is obvious from my results (the statements and the open-ended replies) that egoistic motives are at least as important as altruistic motives for young volunteers. Egoistic motives are often connected with self-development and learning something new about yourself in interaction with others. Developing individual skills is in most cases combined with a will to help others. Therefore, altruistic and egoistic motives need not be considered as opposites (Qvarsell 1993, 29) but as motives co-existing "side by side" with each other (Puohiniemi 1996, 36-39).

Although young Finns in general have changed their values from hedonism and egoism towards more traditional and altruistic values (Puohiniemi 1996, 48), they combine these different values in voluntary work. The open ended-questions from young Finnish volunteers gave replies that can be called representative of "altruistic hedonism":[13] *"It (volunteering) is fun and it gives new friends"*; *"It is nice and fun"*; *"Fun, good friends, good atmosphere"*; *"To combine fun and usefulness"*. However, in my opinion, altruistic hedonism does not explain all the combinations of altruistic and egoistic motives. For example, altruism or the desire to help others was frequently combined with the self-esteem motive in open-ended replies: *"I feel good when I have done something special."* Instrumentally oriented motives, for example, to learn new skills, whether practical or psychological, "fit" neither with the concept of hedonism nor that of altruism. I do not think that instrumentally oriented motives (learning) or self-fulfilment (esteem) motives can always be considered as hedonism, something enjoyable, something I do for myself. Consequently, a new concept is needed beside altruistic hedonism. Fun, enjoyment, the importance of feeling needed, and being part of a community can be found in a "camaraderie" or friendship while volunteering if the atmosphere is good.[14]

The combinations of altruistic and egoistic motives indicate that volunteers do not have "either-or" motives but rather "both-and" motives (Lähteenmaa 1996, 144; Näre and Lähteenmaa 1992, 329). This describes volunteering as a "postmodern activity" where volunteers "pick out" the motives that are important for them for a particular volunteer task at a particular time. Mixed altruistic and egoistic motives can leave us with the conclusion that today's young volunteers are combining individual needs with a desire for being part of a community or among friends. Therefore, volunteering can be called "individualistic togetherness" where friendship is combined with ego-centrism (Bauman 1995, 44-49; Paakkunainen 1998 referring to Maffesoli 1995, 176), but without commitment and sacrifice (Hautamäki 1996, 36-37). Young people will be committed to voluntary work as long as they receive satisfaction from what they are doing (Gaskin 1998), and positive feedback from co-workers, other volunteers, and the group that they are helping.

Concluding Remarks

Young volunteers do not want to be left outside of society. They want to feel needed, and to be part of a community with other "like-minded" individuals. Lähteenmaa (1997) had similar findings in her research of volunteers at youth cafés, and Päivärinta (1997) with unemployed people who were satisfied with the possibility of doing subsidised jobs because of the feeling of being part of a working community. Paid work is not any more the only area where you can feel yourself to be an accepted and worthy citizen. While volunteering you are a part of a larger community where you hope to be accepted and needed with the skills that you have. In addition to positive experiences that encourage volunteers stay, some young people have also had negative experiences at some voluntary organisations where they felt that they were not needed or valued (Gaskin 1998; Lähteenmaa 1997).

MacDonald (1996, 28-29), in his article about voluntary work and unemployed people, found out that some 16 to 24 year-olds were encouraged to engage in voluntary activity for their local communities: "The project aimed to develop a variety of social and personal skills through volunteering, for example they constructed a children's playground. The aim was to develop 'active citizens' – people who would later make a greater input to their local communities." Many of these youth wanted "real" paid jobs, not volunteering. I think this has to be kept in mind while engaging young people "involuntarily" in volunteering. In this case, it should be called something other than voluntary work, for example, a skills training program or job creation (see about enforced volunteering Gaskin 1998, 8; Lähteenmaa 1997, 204). Young people want to have challenges and responsibilities in voluntary work, but at the same time it needs to be flexible and to satisfy their individual needs (Gaskin 1998, 47, 67-68). Voluntary organisations and volunteer centres face a big challenge in how to recruit volunteers, and how to keep them. If they want to have fresh ideas and enthusiastic young people among their volunteers, organisations have to be more flexible and find tasks where altruism and individual needs can be satisfied and combined in a some kind of "individualistic togetherness".[15] This approach could be called empowerment-oriented recruitment and engagement if young people can also participate in the planning and development of the voluntary organisations concerned.

Acknowledgements

I wish to thank Teppo Kröger and Aila-Leena Matthies for their helpful comments and suggestions for this article.

Notes

1. An European comparative study focused also on social welfare organisations (Gaskin and Davis Smith 1995, 121).

2. According to Clary, Snyder and Ridge (1992, 338) protective motive is characterising a "person who feels lonely or guilty and volunteers to relieve the self of these unpleasant feelings".

3. In Clary et al. (1992, 336-337) the learning motive was called "understanding". I prefer to use the term "learning" in this study, that is also used in Norwegian studies (Andersen 1996; Lorentzen and Rogstad 1994), because it better describes the five statements.

4. There were 23 statements loading over .40. According to Clary et al. (1992) the statement "volunteering is a way to make new friends" was part of the esteem motive. In my study it loaded .35 in esteem factor but .37 for learning factor. Another statement, "I am genuinely concerned about the particular group I am serving", assumed to belong to the value motive (Clary et al. 1992), loaded only .17, but .34 for learning factor. However, I included these two statements to original factors similar to a solution made in earlier Nordic studies (Andersen 1996, 71-73; Lorentzen and Rogstad 1994).

5. Finland was encouraged to include associations for unemployed because similar associations do not exist in the other Nordic countries, and the total rate of unemployment in Finland was high at the time of the study (18 %).

6. The replies did not indicate the reason for pension, but I assume these are people (n = 8) on sick pension because of a physical or a mental disability.

7. Elementary school stands for the obligatory basic schooling, usually nine or ten grades when pupils are 15 to 16 year olds.

8. This statement seems to have more egoistic characteristics than altruistic.

9. Open-ended replies (Finland).

10. For significance testing I used a "Zigne signifikans" program testing percentage differences in attitude studies. It can also be used on ordinal-scale variables (see p. 100, Table 7.5). This program was develop by Bernt Aardal and Frode Berglund, Institute for Social Research, Oslo, Norway, 1995.

11. There were only five male volunteers in the Finnish data. Therefore, I cannot generalise this to all male volunteers in social welfare associations.

12. Proportion of female unemployed (10 %) and male unemployed (12 %) were almost equal.

13. Open-ended replies have at least partly been affected with the given statements but they also revealed some new aspects of motives.

14. Frisch and Gerrard 1981, 572-573.

106

15. See Jeppson Grassman and Svedberg (1996, 424): "Activities (in voluntary organisations) are organised mainly to promote 'spirit of togetherness'."

References

Ahonen, S. (1997), 'Demokratia nuorten odotuksissa Suomessa ja muualla Euroopassa' (Aspirations of Democracy among Young People), *Hyvinvointikatsaus 4/1997*, pp. 12-17.

Airaksinen, T. (1993), *Moraalifilosofia* (Moral Philosophy*), 3rd Edition, WSOY, Juva.

Andersen, R. K. (1996), *Motiver for frivillig innsats i Norges Røde Kors* (The Norwegian Red Cross: Motives for Volunteering), Report 96:2, Institute for Social Research, Oslo.

Avrahami, A. and Dar, Y. (1993), 'Collectivistic and Individualistic Motives Among Kibbutz Youth Volunteering for Community Service', *Journal of Youth and Adolescence, 22(6)*, pp. 697-714.

Bauman, Z. (1995), *Life in Fragments: Essays in Postmodern Morality*, Blackwell, Oxford.

Brekke, J.-P. (1994), *Frivillig og lokalsamfunn: En studie av to frivillighetssentrals omgivelser* (Volunteers and Community: Two Volunteer Centres and Their Surroundings), Report 12, Institute for Social Research, Oslo.

Clary, E. G., Snyder, M. and Ridge, R. (1992), 'Volunteers' Motivations: A Functional Strategy for the Recruitment, Placement, and Retention of Volunteers', *Nonprofit Management & Leadership 2(4)*, pp. 333-350.

Clary, E. G., Snyder, M. and Stukas, A. A. (1996), 'Volunteers' Motivations: Findings From a National Survey', *Nonprofit and Voluntary Sector Quarterly, 25(4)*, pp. 485-505.

Davis Smith, J. (ed.) (1993), *Volunteering in Europe: Opportunities and Challenges for the 90s*, The Volunteer Centre UK, London.

Davis Smith, J. (1996), 'Volunteering in Europe', *Social Work in Europe 3(1)*, pp. 19-24.

Frisch, M. B. and Gerrard, M. (1981), 'Natural Helping Systems: A Survey of Red Cross Volunteers', *American Journal of Community Psychology, 9*, pp. 567-579.

Gaskin, K. (1998), *What Young People Want from Volunteering*, Institute for Volunteering Research, London.

Gaskin, K. and Davis Smith, J. (1995), *A New Civic Europe? A Study of the Extent and Role of Volunteering*, The Volunteer Centre UK, London.

Gillespie, D. F. and King, A. E. O. (1985), 'Demographic Understanding of Volunteers', *Journal of Sociology and Social Welfare, 12(4)*, pp. 798-816.

Hautamäki, A. (1996), 'Individualismi on humanismia' (Individualism is Humanism*), in A. Hautamäki, K. Lagerspetz, J. Sihvola, J. Siltala and J. Tarkki (eds.), *Yksilö modernin murroksessa* (Individual in Transition of Modernity*), Gaudeamus, Helsinki.

Helve, H. (1993), *Nuoret humanistit, individualistit ja traditionalistit: Helsinkiläisten ja pohjalaisten nuorten arvomaailmat vertailussa* (Young Humanists, Individualists and Traditionalists: The Value Worlds of Young People in Helsinki and Ostrobothnia in Comparison. English summary: A Comparative Study of the Attitudes, Attitude Structures and Values of Young People), Finnish Youth Co-operation – Allianssi and The Finnish Youth Research Society, Helsinki.

Helve, H. (1997), 'Nuorten elämäntilanne' (Summary: The Life Situation of Young People), in H. Helve, J. Lähteenmaa, T. Päivärinta, K. Päällysaho, H. Saarikoski and

P. Virtanen (eds.), *Nuorten elämänpolkuja lama Suomessa, Nuorisotutkimus 2000, 3/1997* (Life Tracks of Finnish Young People during Recession, Finnish Youth Research 2000 Programme), The Finnish Youth Research Society, Helsinki, pp. 3-12.

Helve, H. (1998), *Reflexivity and Changes in Attitudes and Value Structures*, Paper presented at the 'Youth, Citizenship and Empowerment' seminar, The Finnish Youth Research Society, December 7-8, 1998.

Inglehart, R. (1990), *Culture Shift in Advanced Industrial Society*, Princeton University Press, Oxford.

Jakob, G. (1993), *Zwischen Dienst und Selbstbezug: Eine biographieanalytische Untersuchung ehrenamtlichen Engagements*, Diss., Leske + Budrich, Opladen.

Jeppsson Grassman, E. and Svedberg, L. (1996), 'Voluntary Action in a Scandinavian Welfare Context: The Case of Sweden', *Nonprofit and Voluntary Sector Quarterly, 25(4)*, pp. 415-427.

Júliúsdóttir, S. and Sigurðardóttir, S. (1997), *Hvers vegna sjálfboðastörf? Um sjálfboðastarf, félagsmálastefnu og félagsráðgjöf* (Why Volunteering? An Icelandic Study on Volunteering, Social Policy and Social Work), Háskólaútgáfan, Reykjavik.

Júliúsdóttir, S. and Sigurðardóttir, S. (1998), *The Icelandic Part*, Unpublished manuscript for the Comparative Nordic Research Project on Volunteer Motives, May 1998.

Labour Force Statistics (1997), September 3, 1997, Statistics Finland, Helsinki.

Lähteenmaa, J. (1996), 'Youth, Voluntary Work and Postmodern Ethics', in H. Helve and J. Bynner (eds.), *Youth and Life Management: Research Perspectives*, Helsinki University Press, Helsinki, pp. 140-147.

Lähteenmaa, J. (1997), 'Nuoret vapaaehtoistyöntekijät: motiiveja ja moraalipohdintoja, Tapaustutkimus pääkaupunkiseudulta' (Young Volunteers: Motives and Moral Discussions, Case Study from the Helsinki Metropolitan Area*), in H. Helve, J. Lähteenmaa, T. Päivärinta, K. Päällysaho, H. Saarikoski and P. Virtanen (eds.), *Nuorten elämänpolkuja lama Suomessa, Nuorisotutkimus 2000, 3/1997* (Life Tracks of Finnish Young People during Recession, Finnish Youth Research 2000 Programme), The Finnish Youth Research Society, Helsinki, pp. 162-209.

Lähteenmaa, J. (1998), 'Nuoret vapaaehtoistyön tekijät ja hedonistinen altruismi' (Young Volunteers and Altruistic Hedonism*), in K. Ilmonen (ed.), *Moderniteetti ja moraali* (Modernity and Moral*), Gaudeamus, Helsinki, pp. 146-164.

Living Conditions (1994), Data collected by Statistics Finland, Unpublished material.

Lorentzen, H. and Rogstad, J. (1994), *Hvorfor frivillig? Begrunnelser for frivillig sosialt arbeid* (Why Volunteer? Motives for Voluntary Social Work), Report 11, Institute for Social Research, Oslo.

MacDonald, R. (1996), 'Labours of Love: Voluntary Working in a Depressed Local Economy', *Journal of Social Policy, 25(1)*, pp. 19-38.

Maffesoli, M. (1995), *Maailman mieli: Yhteisöllisen tyylin muodoista* (Original: La contemplation du monde – Figures du style communautaire, translated by Mika Määttänen), Gaudeamus, Tampere.

Matthies, A.-L. (1994), *Kansalaistoiminnan resurssit: Saksalaisen tutkimuksen näkökulma* (Resources of Citizen Action: Views from the German Research*), Sosiaali- ja terveysministeriön selvityksiä 1994: 8, Ministry of Social Affairs and Health, Helsinki.

Näre, S. and Lähteenmaa, J. (1992), 'Moderni suomalainen tyttöys: altruistista individualismia' (Modern Finnish Girls: Individualistic Altruism*), in S. Näre and J. Lähteenmaa (eds.), *Letit Liehumaan: Tyttökulttuuri murroksessa* (Summary: Shake

108

your Hair! Girls' Culture in the Process of Change), Finnish Literature Society, Helsinki, pp. 329-337.

Nylund, M. (1998), *Volunteering in Finland – Volunteers Involved with Caring and Learning*, Unpublished manuscript for the Comparative Nordic Research Project on Volunteer Motives.

Omoto, A. M and Snyder, M. (1993), 'AIDS Volunteers and Their Motivations: Theoretical Issues and Practical Concerns', *Nonprofit Management & Leadership, 4(2)*, pp. 157-176.

Paakkunainen, K. (1998), *The Operative Contingency and the Young Fortuna in the Risk Society*, Paper presented at the 'Youth, Citizenship and Empowerment' seminar, The Finnish Youth Research Society, December 7-8, 1998.

Päivärinta, T. (1997), 'Minä, työtön nuori' (Summary: I the Young Unemployed), in H. Helve, J. Lähteenmaa, T. Päivärinta, K. Päällysaho, H. Saarikoski and P. Virtanen (eds.), *Nuorten elämänpolkuja lama Suomessa, Nuorisotutkimus 2000, 3/1997* (Life Tracks of Finnish Young People during Recession, Finnish Youth Research 2000 Programme), The Finnish Youth Research Society, Helsinki, pp. 13-55.

Paolicchi, P. (1995), 'Narratives of Volunteering', *Journal of Moral Education, 24(2)*, pp. 159-173.

Puohiniemi, M. (1996), 'Suomalaisten arvot yhteiskunnallisessa muutostilanteessa' (Finnish Values and Social Change), in K. Ahlqvist and A. Ahola (eds.), *Elämän riskit ja valinnat – Hyvinvointia lama-Suomessa* (Risks and Choices in Life – Welfare during Economical Crisis in Finland*), Edita, Central Statistical Office of Finland, Helsinki, pp. 30-54.

Puuronen, V. (1989), *Nuorisoryhmien toiminta ja toiminnan mieli* (Summary: Action of the Youth Groups and its Meaning), Research Reports of the Faculty of Education, No. 24, University of Joensuu, Joensuu.

Qvarsell, R. (1993), 'Välgörenhet, filantropi och frivilligt socialt arbete – en historisk översikt' (Charity, Philanthropy and Voluntary Social Work – A Historical Overview*), in *Frivilligt socialt arbete: Kartläggning och kunskapsöversikt* (Voluntary Social Work: Mapping and Knowledge Overview*), Statens offentliga utredningar (SOU) 1993:82, Socialdepartementet, Socialtjänstkommittén, Stockholm, pp. 217-241.

Susag, C. (1999), *Finnish American Ethnicity as Measured by Collective Self Esteem*, Publications in Social Sciences, No. 37, University of Joensuu, Joensuu.

Suutarla, A. and Hakkarainen, P. (1997), *Suomen olotilat 1997: Vapaaehtoisten kohtaamispaikat ja työttömien toimintakeskukset* (Meeting Places in Finland in 1997: Meeting Places for Volunteers and Action Centres for Unemployed*), Kirkkohallitus/KDYK and Kansalaisareena ry. (Church Council / Centre for Diaconia and Society and The Citizen Forum), Helsinki.

Van Til, J. (1988), *Mapping the Third Sector: Voluntarism in a Changing Social Economy*, The Foundation Center, U.S.A.

*Translated by Marianne Nylund. Translations without a star (*) are translated by the author/s or a research group, and references with "summary" are already translated in the original book or the article.

8 Young Adults and Shared Household Living: Achieving Independence through the (Re)negotiation of Peer Relationships

SUE HEATH and LIZ KENYON

Introduction

Across much of Northern Europe, young adults are remaining dependent on their parents for longer periods of time and are experiencing later partnership formation than twenty years ago (Commission of the European Communities 1989; Jones 1995; European Commission 1997). An associated trend has been the growth of independent living arrangements: young people living alone or with other single young adults, without partners or dependants living in the same household. Such arrangements are most marked in Scandinavia and the Netherlands (European Commission 1997; de Jong-Gierveld and Beekink 1989), and are increasingly common in the USA (Goldscheider and Goldscheider 1993), yet increasing proportions of British young people are also living in such households (Murphy and Berrington 1993; Bynner et al. 1997). This is partly attributable to the rapid expansion of higher education over the last decade, with young adults in their late teens and early twenties increasingly likely to move away from the parental home to study. However, *non-students* – both graduates and non-graduates – are also opting for independent living arrangements. In 1991, for example, approximately 15 % of non-students in their early to mid-twenties, and between 5 and 8 % of those in their late twenties, were living in shared households (Heath 1999). These rates are higher than those identified by Penhale's analysis of comparable data from 1981 – an analysis which had included students, thus inflating the overall figures (Penhale 1990).

Whilst these overall trends and the socio-economic characteristics associated with different living arrangements have been widely noted by demographers (Jones 1995; Bynner et al. 1997), the significance of independent living to those involved remains largely uncharted. In other words, what meanings are attached to the experience of sharing with other single adults? This article draws on data from a two year study, the "Young Adults and Shared Household Living" project, in order to explore whether shared living might be considered a route to empowerment for young adults in contemporary Britain. It focuses on the role of shared households in providing a forum in which young adults can explore new ways of relating to each other as friends and partners, and on the redefinition of independence which goes hand in hand with those explorations.

Shared Household Living in Context: Towards a New Household Form?

Until relatively recently, shared household living has been most strongly associated with student status. Unlike Southern European countries such as Spain, where virtually all students study in their home town or city (Heath and Miret 1996), approximately 87 % of English and Welsh higher education students move away from home and live in some form of communal living arrangement with other students. This may be in a hall of residence with hundreds of other students, or in a house shared with student friends. Despite growing financial pressures to remain at home in order to study (Charter 1995), the rapid expansion of higher education means that in absolute terms more young people than ever before are gaining experience of shared living.

Having experienced shared living, many young people continue to share housing on graduating or, if moving to a new area, will opt for a shared household in preference to living alone or in lodgings. The link between graduate status and the propensity to live in shared housing is borne out by Bynner et al.'s analysis of the 1996 sweep of the 1970 British Cohort Study. House sharers proved to be the most highly qualified group within the cohort: over half of the young men living in shared households, and 60 % of the women, had obtained a degree or equivalent qualification. Moreover, the great majority were in full-time employment (76 % of men and 81 % of women), with two out of three sharers working in professional or managerial positions.

Graduates and students aside, a third group of young people are increasingly likely to share housing. In October 1996, a new ruling was

111

introduced affecting the level of Housing Benefit payable to under-25 year olds (Housing Benefit subsidises the full cost of housing for people on low incomes). The ruling restricted payments to a sum equivalent to the average cost of *shared accommodation* in the area in which a claimant lived, with the expectation that the claimant would move into a shared house. This change – known as the single room rent (SRR) – was introduced primarily as a cost cutting measure, but also because the Secretary of State for Social Security felt that it was unfair for Housing Benefit claimants to be able to afford better housing than non-claimants, amongst whom sharing is not at all unusual (Kemp and Rugg 1998). In this instance, then, living in a shared household was constructed very much as a "second best", and when the measure was introduced it was widely criticised by housing and welfare rights campaigners for being an unnecessarily punitive measure; it was assumed that young adults would not want to share if given the choice.

However, a recent study of the impact of this policy suggests that, far from young people feeling constrained in their choices by the introduction of the SRR, the majority of under-25 year olds expect or even want to live in shared accommodation rather than alone (Kemp and Rugg 1998). Older respondents were as likely as younger respondents to express a preference for sharing. However, the young people involved in the study stressed the importance of distinguishing between *enforced sharing*, and sharing where they had control over who their housemates would be, with considerable resistance towards the former type of shared living. The researchers conclude that "the SRR has been based on a misconception: that young people take advantage of Housing Benefit to move into self-contained accommodation" (Kemp and Rugg 1998, 37), and their research tends to support the notion that shared living is increasingly seen as an important and desirable experience.

The increased appeal of shared living may in part reflect the exposure given to such arrangements in the media. In the last five years, television programming has been saturated with images of young adults living together in shared accommodation, with *Friends, This Life, Ally McBeal* and *Men Behaving Badly* being the best known examples. Roseneil (1998) argues that such images fed an increased appetite for non-familial living amongst young people in the late 1990s, offering attractive images of happiness and stability outside of traditional heterosexual relations, particularly those linked to marriage and parenthood. It could be argued, though, that sharing with friends has long been seen as an attractive option, particularly for young women. Wallace's study of young adults growing up in the Isle of Sheppey noted, for example, the strong appeal for the young women in her sample of leaving home in order to share a flat with friends, regardless of how realistic an option this was for them (Wallace 1987).

Much previous research on household formation amongst young adults has tended to downplay or ignore the importance of shared living arrangements. Shared living has been represented – if at all – as a household form only of interest for its transitional status. Thus shared housing has been constructed as a buffer zone prior to couple formation, with household formation being presented as a linear process: parental dependency, intermediate/transitional housing, couple household. We have three specific difficulties with the assumptions underpinning this view of shared living. First, it ignores the possibility that shared living may be becoming increasingly important as a household form in its own right, and may be a very deliberate choice for many young people, reflecting changing attitudes to household and family formation. In other words, the decision to live in a shared house may not necessarily be linked to constraint and short-termism.

Second, it assumes that family formation is a once and for all event, when this is clearly not so, given the impact of divorce, remarriage and step family formation (Allan 1996; Smart and Neale 1999). As Beck has argued in the context of debates concerning individualisation and risk in late modernity, "the lifelong standard family... becomes a limiting case, and the rule becomes a movement back and forth among various familial and *non-familial* forms of living together, specific to the particular phase of life in question" (Beck 1992, 114 – emphasis added). Thus young people are increasingly likely to find themselves moving into a variety of living arrangements over the life course, and may not necessarily associate certain household forms with a sense of linear progression or regression.

A third difficulty relates to the commonly assumed links between household formation, dependency and independence. Within mainstream youth research, dependency tends to be strongly associated with living in *the family of origin*, whereas full independence tends to be equated with living in *the family of destination* (Coles 1995). This tendency is exemplified by a recent paper which operationalises the attainment of "social independence in relation to the home environment" in terms of the birth of a young person's first child (Saunders and Becker 1994). Whilst this is an extreme example, most researchers acknowledge that independence is linked to a series of interlinked key events. Jones, for example, argues that "the transition to adult independence involves status passages, such as leaving home, starting a job, the formation of partnerships, the birth of a child" (Jones 1995, 89). However, the literature does not tend to equate shared living arrangements with

113

independence in quite the same way; rather, it tends to be seen as something of a halfway house – neither fully dependent, nor fully independent.

Our own view, drawing on our current research, is that shared housing represents an important forum for exploring the social and cultural meanings of independence, and for challenging popular assumptions concerning the link between "full" independence and formation of a couple household. In particular, there is evidence to suggest that many young people regard shared arrangements as the ultimate form of independence, offering not only independence from parents, but independence from a live-in relationship with a partner and the responsibilities of family formation. This is not to say that young people who live in shared households do not want or, indeed, have partners – far from it – but that shared household living involves a complex set of (re)negotiations of the power relations implicit in traditional partnership formation. The flip side of this is a corresponding set of (re)negotiations of the ways in which young people relate to each other as friends, both within the household and on the fringes of the household. The role of shared household living in allowing young people to explore new ways of relating to each other as both friends and partners is, we argue, an important form of empowerment, allowing young people to redefine the concept of "independence". The rest of this chapter goes on to explore these themes in more detail, but firstly we outline the aims and methodology of our current research.

The "Young Adults and Shared Household Living" Project

This chapter is based on data taken from a two year research project, *Young Adults and Shared Household Living*, funded by the UK's Economic and Social Research Council (grant number R000237033). The project's principle aim is to explore the significance of the growth of shared household living amongst young adults in Britain, focusing on whether such arrangements are significant only as transitional arrangements prior to family formation, or whether they are becoming increasingly important household forms in their own right (albeit of a largely temporary nature).

The project has three broad research questions: (i) who lives in shared households? (ii) how do shared households work? and (iii) why do young people live in shared housing? The first question is concerned with developing a socio-demographic portrait of shared household living. The second is concerned with issues such as divisions of labour, divisions of time and space, décor, socialising, support for household members and non-household members, negotiating partnership formation, economic organisation, privacy and intimacy. The third question is concerned with processes of household formation, re-formation and disintegration, and the push and pull factors which lead to shared household living: in particular, how does shared household living relate to arguments concerning choice versus constraint?

The project uses a multi-method approach. The first question is based on secondary analysis of Samples of Anonymised Records from the 1991 Census of Population. The second and third questions provide the focus for the main phase of the project, which is based upon a combination of both household and individual interviews. The group interviews focus on the household members' current experiences of living together, and are structured around a series of video clips of popular images of shared household living (taken from *Friends, This Life* and the film *Shallow Grave*). Individual interviews focus on the young person's housing biography and their future aspirations. Two households have also produced photographic records of shared living. The eventual aim is to secure at least 30 household interviews, and as many individual interviews as possible with the members of those 30 households. To date we have completed twenty five "main phase" household interviews (plus three pilots) and 65 individual interviews. The majority of the household members are in their mid-twenties. Excluding the pilot interviews, seven households are all-female, five all-male, and in total they contain 41 women and 40 men. Eight of the houses are owned by a household member, the rest are in the private rented sector. The majority of household members are in employment, the exceptions being a student teacher, a PhD student, five undergraduates (four of them mature students) and two students studying English as a foreign language. Our households are all located in a southern English city, and have been largely accessed through "rooms to let" adverts in the local daily newspaper, through the co-operation of estate agents and landlords who have posted on our mailings to their tenants, and through snowballing.

Shared Household Living as a Route to Empowerment

To recap, our argument is that shared household living provides a unique forum for young adults to explore the boundaries of both friendship and partnership. Within the mainstream literature on household formation, independence is invariably linked to leaving the parental home, but its fullest expression is assumed to be linked to "settling down" with a partner and/or a child. However, the traditional linear trajectory referred to above – parental dependency, intermediate/transitional housing, couple household – could equally be represented as a movement from one state of (co)dependency to another, with only the intermediate housing forms (shared living, living alone) representing full independence. In practical terms, young people living in shared households are learning to balance the demands of friendship and partnership with the relative freedom, which comes from living independently.

We are not, of course, seeking to generalise to the experiences of all young people living in shared accommodation, not least because we are aware of the limitations of our current sample (as discussed above). We acknowledge that not all young people will experience shared household living in such a positive light, and may be extremely unhappy in their living situation. However, the evidence we have gathered so far suggests that for a very specific group of young adults – relatively affluent professionals – shared household living forms an important part of their chosen lifestyle. Indeed, several of the households contacted so far have consisted of people not only performing the same work, but also working in the same workplace. Thus work and home life are combined and merged together to an astonishing degree.

Exploring New Ways of Relating to Friends

Of the twenty five main phase households we have contacted so far, six have contained individuals whose friendship did not predate moving into the household (four of the houses were owned by one of the residents, and tenants had been sought to help with mortgage payments, whilst in the other two households new tenants were either selected by the non-resident landlord or by agreement amongst existing tenants). Of the other nineteen, the members of sixteen had *all* known each other prior to living in their current household, whilst in the remaining household two members had been friends before moving in. Nine of these prior friendship groups were based on having studied together, and in the majority of cases they had also lived together as students, for at least a year. The remainder of the prior friendship groups consisted of individuals who had not studied together (indeed, many of the individuals in this category had not studied beyond eighteen), but had known each other for varying lengths of time, in some cases going back to childhood. Three of the student-based friendship groups had not studied in the town in which the research is being conducted, but for a variety of reasons had all ended up moving to the same location, and not necessarily deliberately (for example, three physiotherapy students who had studied in the Midlands had all ended up getting jobs in the same hospital, even though they had all applied to a variety of sites; four chemists had similarly studied together at a southern university and had all got jobs in the area, three of them working for the same multinational company). So, most of the households had evolved from earlier friendships, and a decision to continue living together or deciding to move in together after a break apart was seen as the ideal solution to both their immediate housing needs, and also their *social* needs.

In households containing at least one member who was new to the friendship group, automatic access to a group of friends was seen as a key advantage of sharing. Heidi, for example, who had moved to the area with a new job, argued that:

It's a new area, that's why I wanted a shared house. I work from home, so I work on my own, so therefore the only way I'm going to meet people, initially, is to house share... I wanted to socialise, I don't like living alone.

Carl, who lived in a shared household next door to Heidi, made a similar point:

When I came here I didn't know anybody. And now I know fifty people through all of you.

One of the households contained individuals who were chosen by the non-resident landlord, and who were not usually known to each other beforehand, but even here a large network of friends had grown up around the household. A new household member had moved in shortly before the interview, and during her first week a dinner was held in her honour to which around 15 previous household members and friends of ex- and current household members were invited, and she now regularly socialises with this larger group. This highlights a strong sense of expectation that shared household living requires an element of commitment to the household. In practical terms this involves not just pulling one's weight with respect to domestic labour (vitally important), but being prepared to be part of a group of friends who enjoy spending time together, both within the house and outside of the house. Rick and Zac, for example, who had studied together in the South-West of England and who were now both working in the research town, expressed extreme disappointment that their newly acquired third housemate (not known to them previously) was hardly ever around. Ironically, she had been chosen over other potential candidates because she had expressed enthusiasm at their expectation of active involvement in the life of the house as an equal partner. In one of the households this had been a problem with a previous tenant, Roger:

Nicky   But he didn't like having, joining in on what we were doing –
Carl   No, he wasn't part.
Nicky   He was like, no don't do that.
Rob   I mean that's the thing. We all do – no, but we all do socially similar things here. Ish. And I think that's the connection.
Carl   Roger would bring cider and vodka into the house and drink in his room and stuff like this and it wasn't – it didn't feel like it was the right thing.
Rob   He'd sit in his room and get plastered on his own.
Carl   But that was his – okay, that's fine by him, but it didn't fit in with any of us.

In these households, then, there appears to be little room for "loners"; rather, household members are expected to make the effort to get on with each other and socialise together, and thus develop their relationships further. In the case of Rob and Carl's households, which are located next door to each other, they had even removed the fence dividing their gardens, and there was relatively free movement between the two houses by all household members, whether to get peace and quiet when one house got too noisy, to watch an alternative television programme, or to escape from arguments between Rob and his girlfriend.

The social side of shared household living is clearly very important, and plugs in to the popularity of media images of such living arrangements. Most of our interviewees, perhaps surprisingly, feel that there is a high degree of realism in the sense of fun portrayed in the soap representations of shared living. The following are typical responses to a question concerning the best things about sharing:

Rob   I love the buzz, the buzz of there's always something happening, you're never lonely and there's always something happening. And I really do enjoy that. And I think we've got a great group of people. So it is good.
Jane   Permanently socialising!

Di	Possibly just having a laugh, can't you? There's always people to chat to, there's always people about.
Sarah	It's just like, as I keep saying, it's just like Friends, Friends on TV. It's brilliant, I love it. It's like Neighbours. Like our own little soap opera, it's really good.

The friendship networks associated with shared living clearly extend well beyond the immediate household members, and many individuals have talked about the pleasure they derive from getting to know a very diverse group of people. In many cases, friends of friends become almost honorary household members, and come and go frequently. Lin for example, speaking of one such friend, argued that "we would just treat her like she lived here... she can just go off and make a cup of tea or whatever. Paint the dining room for us. That kind of thing."

Social aspects of shared living are, therefore, a major draw. However, shared household living is also valued for the emotional support which is readily available when life is going less well, or simply in coping with the mundanity of daily life. This was particularly noticeable where household members shared the same work, and were therefore able to discuss the nitty gritty of work-related problems without having to explain the broader context. More generally, though, all of the households listed ways in which both emotional and practical support were provided between household members on a routine basis; examples included waiting up for someone who was late coming home, cooking for each other, collecting prescriptions when someone was ill, helping each other through relationship crises, doing odd bits of grocery shopping, and generally "being there" for each other.

In discussing the degree of bonding which had occurred over time, it was clear that most of the households regard themselves as strong social units in their own right, and not just a collection of individuals who happen to live under the same roof. In many households, they liken their situation to "an alternative family", and talk of feeling as close to each other, if not closer, than siblings. We would see parallels here with work on "families of choice" of lesbian and gay people (Weston 1991; Weeks et al. 1999). Further, this strong sense of collective bonding is reflected and celebrated in visual displays around the house. Most of the households have photographs on display in their main shared living space, and these often include at least one photograph of all the household members together. Images include photographs of graduation, foreign holidays, hen nights and household parties, and invariably show some or all of the household members laughing and joking, often in close physical contact. One household even has a wall display of images of the "Mr Men" characters, with the name of a different household member attached to each one, whilst another had made a collage of photographs taken on a recent foreign holiday together.

Exploring New Ways of Relating to Partners

In addition to providing young people with opportunities to expand their friendship networks and to explore ways of living together platonically, shared household living clearly provides a forum for developing new ways of relating to partners. The shared household is very much a halfway house in this regard; it provides a space where partners can come and go with relative ease (importantly, free from the parental gaze), yet also provides a space which is a step removed from actually living together. For many, this represents the best of both worlds, and for those whose partners have also moved out of the parental home, they find themselves effectively living simultaneously in two independent households. Padfield and Proctor (1995) refer to this phenomenon as "transhabitation", whilst Murphy (1996) prefers the term "living apart together". The significance of such an arrangement is that it provides the partners in a relationship with the space to be together, yet simultaneously *the space to be apart*. This independence is highly valued: Sean's girlfriend, for example, is currently seeking a new place to live, and Sean feels pressured to ask her to move into his shared household. He is not enthusiastic about this, because he feels that not only will it affect the dynamics of his relationship with his girlfriend, but significantly will also affect the dynamics of his relationship with his housemates.

Around two thirds of the individuals in our sample are currently involved in relationships with a partner who lives in a separate household, and the roles that partners play within the household are the subject of often heated debate. In two of the five all-male households, we were struck by the way in which girlfriends were rendered peripheral to the life of the house, and almost seemed to be regarded as a diversion from the generally "laddish" lifestyles of the individuals concerned. In one such household, James's girlfriend was actually in the house during the interview, but was left sitting in the kitchen – and eventually gave up waiting and went home without saying goodbye! In contrast, the male partners of individuals living in the seven all-female households involved so far tend to be regarded as very much part of the extended household ("He's one of the girls"), and are the subject of much discussion, as well as expressions of approval or disapproval.

120

Across all the households there appear to be clear assumptions about the amount of time that a partner should spend within the household. In Huw's household this had been the subject of considerable tensions in the past:

Huw   We were quite looking forward to living with this guy (a new housemate), cos we'd known him from uni, but we never lived with him. But from the very first day (his girlfriend) was sort of – I think the first two weeks that we were here she spent more time here than we did. And then she started cooking his dinner before he got in from work and things like that...

Mindful of this experience, Huw's housemate James subsequently expressed some misgivings concerning the nature of his relationship with his current girlfriend:

James   There's more space in my house and I've got a double bed and she's just got a single bed. It's very tempting to stay at my house a lot of the time. That's not really fair for the others. But it's difficult to keep it 50:50. Because on the one hand if I'm around her house, her house is smaller so I'm more likely to be noticed by her friends, whereas here I can disappear into my room.

James's comments hint at the reverse problem: spending too much time at a partner's house. Indeed, the reason why Rick and Zac's new housemate is never around is because she has just started a new relationship and is spending all of her free time at her boyfriend's house. Whilst they understand her reason for being out of the house so much, equally they are quite disappointed that she is not playing her full part in the household. This again underlines an expectation that shared household living can only really work if household members are prepared to put something into the relationship. Julie and Cathy, two members of a household currently made up of three members, similarly complained of two previous tenants who had started going out and had become "too much of a couple" (they had even eventually moved into the same room). In most of the households, then, there was a unanimous view that it would be a bad move *for the household* if a partner were to move into the house on a permanent basis.

In some cases, previous residents who had moved out to live with a partner managed to maintain a strong link with the house. One of our households we believed was made up of six nurses, who had all trained together and now all worked in the same hospital. During the interview it transpired that Chloe had actually recently moved out to live with her fiancé, yet "I'm constantly round here". When asked whether she felt more at home in her new home, she expressed some ambivalence:

Chloe No, I'm always really confused. Say last night I said "Oh, I'm going to go home and see the girls". Whereas now when I go home, to go home I'll say I'm going home again, so I call both places home. I don't know, it's weird.

Dee And it's hard as well because we still think, you know, people say oh, who do you live with and I say five other girls, I still can't get over that there's five of us.

Laura It hasn't been that long, it's only been about eight weeks.

Dee After so many years.

Chloe I mean I still say, oh my housemates do this and my housemates do that and people, they're "well, haven't you just moved in with your boyfriend?"

In another all-female household, Helen was just about to move in with her boyfriend, yet the other three members had no intention of renting out her room to a new tenant. Rather, her room was going to be kept for her, in the hope that she would be a frequent visitor.

So far the discussion has focused around the negotiation of heterosexual relationships. Zac and Jim, who both own the houses they live in, are gay and both commented on the importance of ensuring that their shared living arrangements provide a supportive environment. They both talked about the need to ensure that any new tenants were okay about their sexual orientation, as it would clearly be intolerable to have to share one's house with someone who was even remotely homophobic. In both households, the subject had been raised with prospective new household members during the selection process. Jim said that he had never encountered any negative responses, but equally felt it was important to inform people in advance, rather than to "just let them find out". Zac recalled one slight hiccup, though, when his (female) housemate's new boyfriend had come across Zac and his boyfriend kissing in the hallway, and it was quite clear from his response that she had not told her boyfriend that Zac was gay.

This raises the question of the boundaries of privacy and intimacy in shared households. Whilst there has been a lot of good natured teasing and laughter about the problem of "unwanted noise", it is also clear that most household members respect each other's right to privacy, and their right not to be embarrassed by displays of intimate behaviour in the shared spaces of the household. Jill and Lorraine, for example, had recently moved into a two bedroom flat, having just moved out of a shared house with two other women. Commenting on Jill's relatively new relationship, Lorraine said quite explicitly that the noise of sex from Jill's room was not at all a problem, but what she had objected to was the fact that Jill and her boyfriend had gone through a phase early in their relationship of talking all night, which had been a source of considerable annoyance. In other households, the boundaries of acceptable behaviour were quite clear, with the nurse household being most explicit about this:

Dee	If they're in the lounge, as long as they're not sort of slobbering on each other it's alright. Or they'll go to their room if they want to slobber...
Jan	I don't mind someone putting their arm around their boyfriend.
Dee	Yeah, sitting and having a cuddle and that.
Rachel	Holding hands. On top of each other might be going a bit far.
Jan	Removing each other's clothes –
Dee	Kissing –
Jan	Nibbling at the ears, yeah.
Dee	Fondling breasts and things is out.
Jan	Whispering sweet nothings whilst you're trying to watch ER [a hospital drama].
Rachel	Being a bit pukey is a bit of a no no, isn't it?

Conclusion

This article has outlined some of the ways in which shared household living represents a forum in which young people are able to explore new ways of relating to each other both as friends and as partners. In both respects, living in a shared household provides young people with the freedom to relate to each other in quite different ways to how they would if they still lived with parents, or even if they lived alone. In particular, shared household living allows them the space to develop close friendships with a broad range of people and the space to be involved in intimate sexual relationships without losing a sense of independence or compromising their desire for personal space which is a step removed from their partner.

We are struck by the extent to which these patterns and expectations lend support to Giddens' arguments concerning the emergence of what he calls "the pure relationship" (Giddens 1991 and 1992). Pure relationships, he argues, are the consequence of "reflexively organised life-planning" under the conditions of late modernity. A pure relationship is "one in which external criteria have become dissolved; the relationship exists solely for whatever rewards that relationship can deliver" (Giddens 1991, 5). In other words, pure relationships are sought only for what they can give to the partners involved, whether sexual or platonic. To the extent that the households we have so far investigated are based very much on a sense of give and take and fair exchange, then shared household living would appear to be an ideal forum for developing pure relationships. A pure relationship is also characterised by a high degree of independence and the need to maintain appropriate boundaries of privacy and intimacy, and again these are features that we have found to be characteristic of the negotiations of friendship and partner relationships within shared households.

To conclude, most of the young people we have spoken with so far very much enjoy living in a shared household and regard it as integral to their sense of identity as an independent yet nonetheless responsible person. Whilst few of them intend to remain in shared housing indefinitely, at the same time they clearly do not regard it as an inferior household form, but as the ideal setting in which to develop, and explore new ways of relating to, their careers, their friendships and their partnerships.

Acknowledgements

We would like to acknowledge the support of the Economic and Social Research Council in funding this research (grant number R000237033). Thanks too to all of the household members who have generously given of their time to take part in this research.

References

Allan, G. (1996), *Kinship and Friendship in Modern Britain*, Oxford University Press, Oxford.
Beck, U. (1992), *Risk Society: Towards a New Modernity*, Sage Publications, London.
Bynner, J., Ferrie, E. and Shepherd, P. (1997), *Twenty-Something in the 1990s: Getting on, Getting by, Getting nowhere*, Ashgate Publishing Ltd., Aldershot.
Charter, D. (1995), 'Now home is where the HE is', *Times Higher, 28th July, 6.*
Coles, B. (1995), *Youth and Social Policy: Youth Citizenship and Young Careers*, UCL Press, London.
Commission of the European Communities (1989), *Young Europeans in 1987*, Luxembourg Office for Official Publications of the European Communities, Luxembourg.
de Jong-Gierveld, J. and Beekink, E. (1989), *Young Adults Leaving Home in Search of Independence and Freedom*, Paper presented at the IUSSP Conference, New Delhi.

European Commission (1997), *Youth in the European Union: From Education to Working Life*, Eurostat.

Giddens, A. (1991), *Modernity and Self-Identity: Self and Society in the Late Modern Age*, Polity Press, Cambridge.

Giddens, A. (1992), *The Transformation of Intimacy: Sexuality, Love and Eroticism in Modern Societies*, Polity Press, Cambridge.

Goldscheider, F. and Goldscheider, C. (1993), *Leaving Home before Marriage: Ethnicity, Familism and Generational Relationships*, University of Wisconsin Press.

Heath, S. (1999), 'Young Adults and Household Formation in the 1990s', *British Journal of Sociology of Education, 20, 4*, pp. 545-61.

Heath, S. and Miret, P. (1996), 'Living in and out of the Parental Home in Spain and Great Britain: A Comparative Approach', *Cambridge Group for the History of Population and Social Structure: Working Paper Series, No. 2*, The Cambridge Group, Cambridge.

Jones, G. (1995), *Leaving Home*, Open University Press, Buckingham.

Kemp, P. and Rugg, J. (1998), *The Single Room Rent: Its Impact on Young People*, Centre for Housing Policy, York.

Murphy, M. (1996), 'Family and Household Issues', in A. Dale (ed.), *Looking Towards the 2001 Census*, OPCS Occasional Paper 46, OPCS, London.

Murphy, M. and Berrington, A. (1993), 'Household Change in the 1980s: A Review', *Population Trends 73*, pp. 18-26.

Padfield, M. and Proctor, I. (1995), *Transhabitation: A Variation on the Trend to Cohabitation*, Paper presented to 'Youth 2000 Conference', University of Teesside, July 1995.

Penhale, B. (1990), *Living Arrangements of Young Adults in France and England and Wales*, Longitudinal Study Working Paper 68, SSRU, City University, London.

Roseneil, S. (1998), *Queer Tendencies: Sexual and Gender Transformations of Postmodernity*, Paper presented at 'Gender, Sexuality and Law Conference', Keele University, June 19-21, 1998.

Saunders, K. and Becker, H. (1994), 'The Transition from Education to Work and Social Independence: A Comparison between the United States, The Netherlands, West Germany and the United Kingdom', *European Sociological Review, 10, 2*, pp. 135-54.

Silva, E. and Smart, C. (eds.) (1999), *The New Family?*, Sage Publications, London.

Smart, C. and Neale, B. (1999), *Family Fragments*, Polity Press, Cambridge.

Wallace, C. (1987), *For Richer, for Poorer: Growing up in and out of Work*, Tavistock, London.

Weeks, J., Donovan, C. and Heaphy, B. (1999), 'Everyday Experiments: Narratives of non Heterosexual Relationships', in E. Silva and C. Smart (eds.), *The New Family?*, Sage Publications, London, pp. 83-99.

Weston, K. (1991), *Families We Choose: Lesbians, Gays, Kinship*, Colombia University Press, New York.

PART 4

CITIZENSHIP AND MARGINALITY

9 Critical Discussion: From the Margins – The Darker Side of Empowerment

LYNNE CHISHOLM[1]

The term empowerment enjoys an almost unassailably positive connotation amongst the politically correct of our times – a group into which the pundits would undoubtedly place all the contributors to this volume, one might add. For at least two decades, empowerment has served as a banner under which radical educators, social reformers and political liberals have gathered to express the belief and the hope that all members of a given society should and could have equal rights and equivalent opportunities to express and assert themselves as distinctive voices and communities.

Empowerment emphasises personal agency and human dignity in the search to take one's life into one's own hands, in the confidence that one has the knowledge and skills to do so and against a background of respect for difference and diversity. The practice of active citizenship inevitably presupposes empowerment – the capacity and the will to take up distinctive position, to claim cultural identity and to enter into the life of the polity – *la vie de la cité* – on equal terms with those who share the same patch of the playing-field.

Critical pedagogic practice – whether inside mainstream schooling, on the terrain of the intercultural youth educators or out on the youth workers' city streets – continues to struggle with how to do it: how to make empowerment a reality, and most especially for those young people on the margins of any kind of citizenship at all. How is it possible to bring them in from those margins, given the objective circumstances of social marginalisation and the personal damage with which this process is all too frequently accompanied, if not quite likely to have caused?

The answers are various and the outcomes sometimes inspiring, but often discouraging. Certainly it helps to gain the confidence to assert one's rights, but when one's rights are formally restricted – as in the case of migrant workers and refugee groups – empowerment must remain partially elusive. And it is hardly a straightforward affair for young women to maintain a positive self-image and build high aspirations when – to take a crude but symbolically significant example – the family photographs taken at European Council Summits still present an unrelieved panorama of ageing men in grey suits.

By and large, individual and social silence and withdrawal accompany lack of empowerment. Those who remain or who become disempowered may be caught in a psychological trap of self-blame – as in the case of women who are raped by their partners, discussed by Sari Näre. Caught within an intense field of the economy of emotions, whose division of labour accords the task of managing emotional processes to women alone, they themselves take the responsibility and feel guilty for what has happened to them. Alternatively, in Leena Suurpää's analysis of the social construction of the foreigner, partial benign acceptance by the host society is exchanged for the willingness to assimilate silently and invisibly. Where foreigners accede to the boundaries set for their expression and participation, they are accepted as a community-within-a-community, which can then practice an "indoor ethnicity" defined and controlled by the maintenance of strict boundaries between the private and the public spheres of social life.

The margins, however, are themselves populated by a diversity of marginalised identities and social circumstances. Not all these voices remain silent, and their search for empowerment can go badly wrong, not only for themselves but also for those who stray onto their paths. The four chapters in this section each provide examples of dysfunctional and counterproductive empowerment strategies, in that they address physical and symbolic violence channelled into gendered or racialised forms of expression. In these contributions, it is young men who populate the territory of physical violence, whereas both sexes exercise symbolic violence. These studies cannot be charged with distorting social reality: physical violence may not be an exclusively male phenomenon, but it is undeniably overwhelmingly so.

Whatever the gender of the perpetrator, it is reasonable to argue that the exercise of physical and symbolic violence indicates at least a felt lack of individual or social empowerment and the search to achieve it by inappropriate means. Boys who join violent skinhead gangs may well be doing so, according to Tarja Hilden, essentially to prove their masculinity to themselves, the fragile process of the construction of gender identity having been unseated by teasing and bullying at school for not exhibiting the appropriate physical and behavioural markers. But the origin and the expression of lack of empowerment can equally take more abstract and symbolic forms, engendered by the cultural anxieties that may result when macro-social change leaves people feeling economically and psychically unprepared for a more uncertain future. This is the underlying message of Leena Suurpää's analysis, in which Finland stands at the crossroads between continuity and change following a decade of economic, social and political turbulence.

These studies, then, explore individual and collective, physical and symbolic violence within the context of the challenges and pressures of contemporary modernisation processes in Finland. Since 1989, Finland's objective circumstances have changed, prompting destabilisation of its established sense of cultural and social self. The political break-up of the Eastern European bloc and the deregulation of established economic relations in the region were probably more significant for Finland than for any other Western European country with the exception of the Federal Republic of Germany. From a long history of struggle for national independence, post-war Finland had managed to build and maintain a delicate formula that combined political neutrality with trading relations both east and west, securing along the way a high standard of living for a small and scattered population.

This population also maintained a culturally homogeneous and highly cohesive self-image, supported by the realities of a distinctive language and, in pan-European terms, an isolated geographical location. In no small sense, Finland took on the image, for Europeans, of a rather curious and almost exotic, but essentially tame, snow-laden fairyland clinging to the edge of the world. The Finns were certainly not the "tame victims" that Leena Suurpää describes as the most powerless and pitiable category of foreigners in today's Finland. They may have taken the role of the benign cultural oddity, but in the eyes of other Europeans the Finns were indisputably civilised and enjoyed a high standard of living – not quite like us, perhaps, but near enough to be tantalising rather than fear-provoking.

Just how culturally homogeneous Finnish society has actually been is another question altogether – the Sami people are the formally celebrated national minority, but regional differences are also well-contoured; not surprising, perhaps, in a part of the world where long-range mobility was a tortuous affair. The social construction of cultural and ethnic homogeneity is equally as theoretically interesting as the social construction of cultural and ethnic difference, and although this is not the chosen focus of the chapters that follow, it is one that deserves more sustained attention. If the chosen interpretation of the tensions and contradictions that are accompanying contemporary modernisation in Finland hinges on an analysis of the shift from homogeneity to heterogeneity and from stability to unpredictability, then the objective and ideological basis of the former as well as the latter requires critical assessment. Certainly, the close attention paid inside and outside Finland to research into the origins of the people and the language suggests that the construction of homogeneity founded in uniqueness is itself an ideology of considerable symbolic force. This may also help explain why it is that young Finns evidently consider that it is virtually impossible to become a "real" member of the culture. The quotation from Leena Suurpää's group discussions is particularly striking in this context:

> "I think it's terrible for someone to have to become Finnish. If you come from another country and you ought to ..."
> "I think that they can adopt some Finnish characteristics, whatever they want, but they can't undergo a total metamorphosis, and I think it's a good thing that's impossible."

It is, presumably, a good thing not only because – as politically correct assessments would argue – this ensures the maintenance of cultural and ethnic diversity in that the "foreignness" will not be wholly lost, and that is to be welcomed. It is equally a good thing because the boundaries between insiders and outsiders become defined as immovable, unassailable – and it is exactly this that serves to maintain the sanctity of cultural and ethnic homogeneity amongst Finns themselves. It is also in this more disturbing sense that Leena Suurpää understands the socially constructed hierarchy of difference between Finns and Others to have a constitutive and political impact. The hierarchy of difference delineates and controls the status and position of cultural strangers. The Other must be defined as deficient in order to sustain the legitimacy of control by the dominant culture and its statutory equivalents, even where the deficiency is as much imagined as real.

Leena Suurpää's young respondents defined this deficiency in the first instance as linguistic deficiency: the inability to speak Finnish ("properly", one assumes) is the key marker of social exclusion. For young Finns, a common culture presupposes a common language, functioning as a symbolic and political boundary line between "us" and "them". It is this kind of ideological construction that leaves room for symbolic violence – not the aesthetically symbolic violence that "foreigners" may be seen to do to the Finnish language, but the culturally symbolic violence that marks people as outsiders because they do not, and cannot necessarily, fall within the continuum of linguistic – and by extension cultural – acceptability.

The objective changes in Finland's economic and geo-political circumstances that took place after 1989 were accompanied by the cultural pluralisation occasioned by immigration. This was evidenced most visibly by the admission of refugees from Northern and Eastern Africa, especially Somalis, but more generally by the adaptation of immigration and mobility legislation and practice to the EU *acquis* as a corollary of accession in 1995. In addition, after the collapse of the Soviet Union, the Finnish government enabled Russian citizens of Finnish ethnic origin, who come in particular from Russian Karelia and Ingria (near St. Petersburg), to re-settle inside Finland. This has brought similar integration problems as those arising in Germany following significant return migration of ethnic Germans, most of whom had been resident in Russia and neighbouring countries for generations.

These mainly rural farming groups had retained distinctive cultural identities and, until the changes brought by industrialisation, urbanisation and the spread of universal mass education, distinctive languages. Many also experienced ostracisation and exclusion by the majority society, partly simply because they were distinctive and chose to remain so, but also, in the case of ethnic Germans, as a consequence of the bitterness engendered by German military and fascist aggression in the first half of last century. This included, in the case of the Soviet Union, forced migration to isolated and harsh regions, with families having to leave everything they owned and loved behind them. In the case of Karelia, part of the region had formerly belonged to Finland, but Finland lost it during the second world war and practically all residents of the lost territory left their homes and moved to the Finnish side of the border. However outside that lost part of Karelia, there were still people of Finnish ethnic origin.

The histories and cultures of such groups are little known and appreciated in much of Europe, but it is not difficult to understand why they would want to take up the offer to return to the country to whose majority language and culture they had maintained a feeling of belonging, however attenuated this had become over the decades and centuries. The reality of return has often dashed their hopes of a better quality of life and their expectations of full acceptance. These groups discover that they are no less distinctive, culturally and linguistically, than they were in their regions of immediate origin. They frequently experience a new round of disempowerment, which has all the more impact because they arrive as legally full citizens with their ethnic membership having been formally recognised by the receiving state. The decision to return has typically been taken by parents and grandparents, whereas young people themselves are not necessarily so enthusiastic about leaving their friends and a social environment from which they draw confidence and a sense of self-identity. Whilst younger children are likely to adapt quickly to the new context, young people in their teenage years face more objective difficulties (negotiating the transition from school to work, for example) and identity conflicts (in the process of gaining acceptability with peers, for example).

Language can indeed be a serious barrier: whilst grandparents may speak the "old-new" language well (if often in an antiquated dialect), parents may only speak it as a second language and much less fluently than Russian, whereas their teenage children are likely only to understand it partially, if at all. In such circumstances, language takes on a heightened symbolic significance as a boundary marker between groups, and in both directions. When the new arrivals speak what they thought was their own language, they find themselves marked as linguistically deficient; when they speak Russian (or perhaps Romanian), they are likely to be labelled as culturally deficient. The experience of disempowerment and marginalisation follows. One way to resist this process and, instead, gain more power and control is to turn the tables, using Russian as a new distinctive boundary marker. As one of Leena Suurpää's respondents described:

> "Some minority youth groups hang around at Kamppi (a shopping centre in the heart of Helsinki). It seems to me like they behave more or less like they own the place, or with an attitude like, 'come on, you have to learn Russian if you want to talk to me' ..."

The choice of the shopping centre as the youth clique's territory is equally symbolic, for it represents an attempt to claim the consumer citizenship rights from which these young people and their families are typically excluded – they simply do not usually have enough money to participate in this dimension of modern Finnish culture – and which, ironically enough, was precisely one of the most attractive features of the societies they assumed they were joining as full members.

Young people seeking a degree of re-empowerment by distinctive group public presence are using the classic strategies of demonstrative youth cultural power in much the same way as do indigenous cliques and gangs everywhere. But in the context of the social construction of "foreignness" as a hierarchy of difference founded in power relations between majority and minority groups, the use of these strategies can intensify the risk of escalation towards inter-group violence. The public boundary-setting used by minority youth cliques as an initially defensive re-empowerment strategy is likely to be interpreted as a potential threat by indigenous youth cliques, especially those whose members have themselves experienced relative weakness and marginalisation in the mainstream society. Regaining control over those defined as outsiders attempting to transgress the normative code regulating insider/outsider relations is likely to involve "putting them in their rightful place", including, ultimately, by violent means. Timo Virtanen's account of the racialisation of youth gangs in 1990s Finland provides examples of such spiralling into cycles of inter-ethnic violence, largely involving skinhead attacks on minority youth but also developing into violent conflicts between different minority groups themselves (such as Somalis and Albanians).

The conjuncture between economic destabilisation and cultural pluralisation in today's Finland has therefore produced a new volatility in social relations, not least amongst young people. Physical violence may be the most extreme expression of the resulting tensions, but the underlying issue addressed in these chapters is the capacity – or perhaps the relative incapacity – of Finnish society and culture to respond positively to difference. Young people are caught in a tension between, on the one hand, attachment to traditional and convergent identities and ways of life and, on the other hand, the desire to embrace diversity and divergence as sources of enrichment and variety in what they also feel to be a rather "grey and monotonous" society.

The researchers conducting the studies reported here are spurred, amongst other things, by the search to answer the unsettling question of how far Finland, a modern European democracy, is really capable of making the transition to an open and multi-ethnic society. As part of that search, they are striving to develop adequate interpretative frameworks to explain how and why minority groups are kept out at the social margins of citizenship and empowerment. In the course of this search, they are uncovering and describing the ideological and practical strategies used by majority Finnish society to contain what is experienced and understood to be a potential threat to established identity and cultural stability: the visible presence of unfamiliar cultural, linguistic and ethnic diversity.

The distance and lack of empathy between the Finnish majority and the new minorities certainly means that all sides routinely misconstrue each other. Overt antipathy is not the central problem here, certainly amongst the overwhelming majority of young people. However, contacts between Finns and the new minorities remain essentially fragmentary and, in rural areas, quite possibly wholly hypothetical. Even young Finns in Helsinki seem unlikely, as a rule, to have much to do with minority youth except as features of the music scene, at multicultural festivals or as distinctive artefacts of urban street life. This lack of direct and everyday experience of living within diversity provides an only too fertile soil for right-wing political interests to feed collective anxiety and distrust, as well as lending apparent justification for tighter security measures to control people's movements within and across national borders and public spheres of activity.

It can also lead to categorically undesirable outcomes, such as the "date rape" phenomenon described by Sari Näre as a specifically Finnish problem. In her study, two-fifths of the perpetrators of this kind of sexual assault were men of non-Finnish origin, i.e. they are over-represented in this type of rape case. The problem arises, it seems, because these men are not familiar with Finnish patterns of making acquaintance with someone of the opposite sex. They cannot recognise the intended meaning of the encounter and do not register the messages conveyed by Finnish women to men they are just getting to know about the possibilities and limits of the interaction between them. Lack of cultural knowledge is not the only factor, of course, since evidently Finnish men may be prone not to read the signs correctly either.

Rape is above all a violent assertion of power and control which places the needs and desires of the perpetrator above those of the victim; it is perhaps the crudest strategy of personal empowerment achieved by the disempowerment of another human being. It also quintessentially represents the darker side of empowerment as oppression and suppression of other people's individual and collective human and social rights. Dysfunctional and counterproductive empowerment strategies are negative feedback loops fed by attempts to assert strength and control over individuals and groups socially and culturally defined as weak or deficient. Asserting control, by whatever means, acts as a compensation for felt weakness.

Tarja Hilden describes exactly this kind of negative feedback loop in the case of violent male youth gangs, whose members seek the protection of an intimidating group to prove their masculinity to themselves by exercising physical violence as a mechanism of control over others. The assertion of such control provides evidence of their own strength over others' weakness – and the objectively weaker or disadvantaged the victim, the easier it is to feel individually and collectively stronger. This kind of dysfunctional empowerment strategy is not only oppressive of the victim, but it is ultimately counterproductive as well – for the perpetrator is gradually disempowered by the strategy itself exerting control over the user. Proof of one's masculinity through violent action, argues Tarja Hilden, can be effectively maintained only when continually re-enacted. And the collective witnessing of each other's violence by the gang members traps them into a mutual dependence from which it can be difficult to escape.

It seems banal to recall that the negotiation of sustainable social life necessarily incorporates the recognition of and respect for others' rights as well as one's own, and that this necessarily requires compromise and control on both sides. Where these kinds of boundaries are transgressed, and where there is too little understanding and practice of negotiated compromise as the foundation of democratic life, then the door is open to the darker side of empowerment, including the use of violence. Empowerment is charged with risk when the contextual values and norms within which empowerment may be legitimately sought and exercised are not firmly anchored in people's hearts and minds. Empowerment can too easily become oppression when the capacity for critical reflection of the dialectic between self and society is individually and socially underdeveloped.

This returns us to the beginning of the discussion: we still need to find more effective ways to educate for constructive empowerment and to learn for active citizenship. Education, formal and informal, is not a panacea, but it remains the only rational strategy at our disposal with which to sustain democratic and humanitarian principles and practices as integral elements of identity and expression. Whether we ourselves deserve the dignity and benefits of citizenship in all its contemporary dimensions is, after all, less a question of our capacity for self-empowerment and more a matter of the extent to which we can recognise and live positively with the empowered Other within ourselves and our societies. The capacity of Finnish society and culture to meet that challenge may be the underlying concern of the chapters that follow, but there is no particular reason to suppose that this should be more of a concern in Finland than elsewhere in Europe.

Note

[1] This contribution represents the professional and personal views of the author, does not necessarily present official policy positions of the European Commission, nor does it implicate the European Commission in any field of its activities.

10 Skinheads – Masculinity and Violent Action

TARJA HILDEN[1]

Introduction

Skinhead gangs perpetrating racial violence have emerged in recent years in Finland. Various explanations have been advanced for the attraction of these gangs and activities for young people including the role of masculinity, childhood experiences and economic marginalisation. Here I consider these explanations in the context of a study of skinheads and police reports about them in the region of Joensuu where skinhead gangs have been noticeable.

Background of the Study

Joensuu is a town of approximately 51 000 inhabitants in Eastern Finland, near the Russian border. In the 1990s Finland's economic depression had a serious effect on this area and some of its major industrial enterprises went out of business. Unemployment levels rose sharply and the standard of living declined (see Puuronen 1996). This lead in turn to many forms of deprivation and marginalisation, especially among young people.

The economic crisis was felt most concretely in the suburb of Penttilä, a residential area close to the industrial centres that were hardest hit. At the time when unemployment was mushrooming in this area, close to a hundred Somali refugees were brought into the Joensuu area. People saw not only their standard of living falling, but their comfortably homogeneous population structure collapsing as well. Young people from families so affected, particularly in the Penttilä area, started to react to the situation with vandalism and violent action. Soon they adopted the "skinhead" look, with pseudo army uniforms and shaved heads.

Puuronen (1996) has argued that that there is a causal connection between the effect of the economic depression on people's standard of living, the assumption of refugees having a luxurious life and young people becoming skinheads. This would seem to be correct in the sense that most of the so-called original skinheads of Joensuu came from the Penttilä suburb. However, I believe there have been other strong influences on these young people as well. Young people of 15-20 years old, like the skinheads, tend not to be extremely concerned for their future economic prospects. They live for the "here and now", doing what they think is "cool", seeking the support of like-minded friends in order to reinforce their personal sense of power (see Bjorgo 1997). All this makes it easy for them to become "skins". Thus, I would argue that violent, racist acts by skinheads would need to be seen in the context of these situationally specific elements of youth sub-cultures and the group dynamics associated with male-bonding and masculinity.

Setting of the Study

The object of this study is the 15 to 20 year-old youngsters who belong to skinhead gangs and have committed criminal acts in Joensuu and the surrounding area. The setting for the problem then is related to the crimes committed by these youngsters. My aim is to analyse and interpret the explanations these youngsters have given for their crimes. These explanations also seem to represent the young criminals' attempts to understand and justify their own actions (see Perelman 1996).

The crimes committed by skinheads mostly consist of violent assaults and vandalism, though there are also a variety of other types of crimes among them. Violent assaults take the form of attacks on people where the victim is hit and kicked repeatedly, whilst vandalism is directed against property with the intent to cause damage. The empirical material for my study includes the interviews with the youngsters who have committed these crimes and police reports of the preliminary investigations, as well as statements made to the police by witnesses and the perpetrators themselves and transcripts of the resulting criminal trials. These in turn include information about the gangs themselves and other participants in the crimes. The analysis is based upon approximately 350 police reports from years 1995-1996 concerning 10 to 15 active members of the skinhead gangs. This analysis is only at an early stage, so the observations and interpretations offered here are tentative. However, it does offer insights into the reasons given for joining the skinhead gangs which challenge both the individual-centred and societal-centred explanations.

Vandalism and Violent Action in a Finnish Town

There are estimated to be about 150 skinheads in the Joensuu area, although exact information is rather difficult to come by (Puuronen 1996). Police reports show that young people between 15 and 20 years old are most active in committing crimes and participating in criminal activities. These young people tend to band together in groups or gangs of 10 to 20 members. These gangs are as a rule all male. The crimes typically committed by skinheads are, as mentioned above, violent assaults and vandalism, with property crimes also playing a part. The kind of crimes committed by the individual seems to depend upon the position in the gang. Some individuals commit mostly violent crimes and assaults and others more property crimes and vandalism. The more involved in the group and the ideology of the group, the higher is the amount of violent crimes and assaults.

The most common scene of these crimes is the centre of the town, usually near the market-place. Many crimes take place in restaurants. Friday, Saturday and Wednesday nights are the most frequent times for these crimes to occur. Alcohol plays quite an important role in these crimes, with both the perpetrators and the victim having usually been drunk. As acts, the crimes are often defined with situationality. They are connected with hectic hedonism: in such a situation the perpetrator (actor) acts hectically and impulsively, satisfying what he perceives to be his immediate direct needs without considering the consequences (see Kuure 1996). These needs involve establishing and proving one's own masculinity through violent action.

Approximately one out of eight crimes committed by skinheads is explicitly racist, meaning that the victim's ethnic background or race was a stated motivational factor in committing the crime in question (see Miles 1994). The selection of victims along racial lines tells us about the racist ideas in the ideology of skinheads. However, this does not necessarily mean that racist assaults are premeditated: the members of a skinhead gang may notice a person of an ethnic minority and spontaneously assault him or her for this reason. This is "accidental" in the sense that the victim might

141

have avoided the assault by not happening to be in that given place at that given time. Crimes of vandalism, on the other hand, are usually premeditated. The main motivational factor in such crimes is a sense of revenge. Often the victim has been a witness against some gang member in court. Another, less clearly defined, revenge motive involves the assumption that by collecting welfare subsidies the foreigners and refugees are impoverishing the Finnish families in need of social assistance.

Explanations for Becoming Skins: Individual-Centred and Societal-Centred Perspectives

A range of explanations have been put forward for the motivations for participation in skinhead gangs. These can be divided into societal-centred perspectives and individual-centred perspectives. Societal-centred explanations have focused upon changing social structure. The style of skinheads and the symbolic meanings of their outlook has been interpreted as an answer or protest to the growing power of the middle class and the diminishing of the significance of manual work. For example, at the end of 1960s skinheads protested against the hippy-movement, which was known for despising the traditional work ethic. The decreasing significance of the working class and the political left has been seen as another factor in the spreading of the skinhead subculture (see Clarke 1976). The subculture has also been seen as a sort of imaginary answer to social problems including the decline of traditional working class neighbourhoods through urban restructuring and the influx of immigrant groups (Cohen 1997). Furthermore, we could say that the image of masculine supremacy is expressed as a protest against the changing status of traditional aspects of gender. Globalisation and growing trends towards internationality are also seen as a threat. Skinheads respond to these phenomena through hostility towards foreigners and violent action (Lähteenmaa 1991). Furthermore, the participation of working class, lower educated young men is often explained in terms of the marginalisation of this group by modernisation processes generally which has tended to leave this group disadvantaged and unemployed (Heitmeyer 1992). Thus, the societal-centred perspectives include changes in social structure, in globalisation, in modernisation and in gender regimes as an explanation for participation in xenophobic gangs. Economic crisis of various kinds is often invoked in the societal-centred perspective.

More individual-centred explanations can be found in the psychoanalytical investigation of how these youngsters came to get involved in the skinhead sub-culture. Such explanations stress individual features of personality and personal identity (Smith 1996; see also Puuronen 1997). Some have claimed for example, that childhood experiences such as teasing and bullying at school can lead young people search for shelter in a strong male-bonded group, where one's own subjective weakness is hidden by a tough appearance and violent action (see Siltala 1995). However, we could say that both the societal-centred and individual-centred traditions are significant in the sense that both the individual's subjective experiences and their social situation have an influence on the motivations for entering this subculture.

However, whilst both societal-centred and individual-centred explanations for participation in skinhead gangs are important contributory factors, they do not explain why given gangs emerge in particular contexts and why some people become involved and not others. Many young people are economically disadvantaged or bullied in the playground; why does this only lead some of them to join skinhead gangs and not others? Furthermore, such arguments tend to be deterministic essentialist in nature. They do not provide scope for the shifting social constructions of meaning based upon social interaction in particular contexts (Back 1994).

To understand this, I would argue, we need to turn more to the group dynamics of the skinhead gang, its reproduction through spontaneous acts of violence and especially how these are reinforced through a concept of masculinity. The group participation and social reward structure involved in these crimes demonstrate the skinheads' ideological basis in racism and their group dynamics. The group stresses concrete action and pushes the individual towards action, rewarding him with admiration after a successful act of aggression (Bjorgo 1997). Actions are defined by the excitement of the moment. However, this kind of situational peer group pressure is not usually recognised in accounts of reasons for joining skinhead gangs (see Christensen 1994).

From Masculinity to Power and Violence

Skinheads band together in aggressive gangs which stress manly, masculine ideas and values. Skinheads have taken certain objects, ideas and symbols from mainstream culture and adopted them for their own use, giving them new meanings and significance (Cohen 1955). Their self-constructed image is intensively masculine: military-style jackets, jeans, Doc Marten boots, shaved heads or extremely short hair and tattoos are intended to display manly strength and power (see Knight 1982; see also Christensen 1994). The gang can be taken as "a culture within a culture", with new symbolic meanings being given to its objects of identification (Cohen 1955).

The gang is bonded by violent acts and by objectification of the "other" as an enemy (the role given, for example, to Somali refugees). Juha Siltala examines the issue of entrance into the skinhead subculture in his article "Violence as guarantee of the capability of action". His opinion is that the individual exchanges his/her feeling of powerlessness and insecurity for one of power by joining an intimidating group (Siltala 1995). Tore Bjorgo identifies similar factors in Norway. He describes the feeling of weakness as a factor pushing some young people towards the skinhead group and the fact that one of the reasons for joining the group is a sense of being powerless and weak in the eyes of others. These young people search for a sense of masculine power in such groups and find it in the gang by means of masculine dominance and violence (see Bjorgo 1997). This thesis finds further reinforcement in the work of Loren Christensen (1994) who found that together with the other members of the gang it is easier to find and establish a gender-specific identity. Gender-building is an interactive process, very much influenced by the opinions of others (see Vesivalo 1998). According to Harris (1995) gender-identity is a social construction which deals with person's own conceptions of self in interaction with others and we can analyse the skinhead gangs using this perspective.

Masculinity can be determined from gender or from the relation to its margins (Brod and Kaufman 1994). Stereotypical models tend to rely upon gender as an essentialist concept, but it is difficult to define the margins of masculinity. Skinheads define certain aspects of male-behaviour as defining the boundaries of masculinity: men must act aggressively and violently. These conceptions encourage to strive for a strong masculine identity. Skinheads have chosen violence as a mean by which to attain and maintain masculinity and aggression comes with it. Masculinity is both constructed and expressed in action. From their perspective, "you need a good fight once in a while to vent your feelings and to stay in control of the situation" (Siltala 1995). In this way they see their criminal actions as not only acceptable, but even necessary within the group. However, they also use other elements to construct their masculinity and here we can identify bodybuilding, family authority and patriotism.

144

Part of skinhead culture is to develop masculine identity through bodybuilding. Big muscles give the young person a sense of masculine power and this type of training is one means of building aggression (see Puuronen 1996). Both bodybuilding and violent action have been considered to be signs of masculinity. Though studies have shown that women too are quite capable of violent and criminal action (see Campbell 1993) and are of course also present in the bodybuilding culture, these two elements are not combined by women in the same way. "Real men" are still considered to be violent and aggressive as well as tough physically, always ready for action (see Bowker 1998).

Skinheads are continuously seeking for justification for their ideology, together with its principles and values. They claim to admire the traditional patriarchal model of the man as the head of the family (Lähteenmaa 1991). The patriotic defence of homeland is another basic value which they latch onto. In this way they take up and transform more socially approved values in their own way. Values become principles to be defended – even by violent means.

Other members of the group have a key position in each skinhead's search for approval. They very seldom act alone; most of their crimes are committed in groups or gangs of 2 to 10 persons (Bjorgo 1997). Group discipline and solidarity make each member perform a certain amount of violent action. The idea of to "Hit or be hit" gives a licence to use power and avoid passiveness. But still "having fun" is one of the justifications the skinheads give for their criminal actions. The evening has not been successful without a good fight, and this feeling is enhanced through the use of alcohol and narcotics (Moore 1994). Shared secrets and group-solidarity drive skinhead-youngsters to defend their friends in violent acts and also give grounds for the control of group members by one another, backed up by revenge or retributive violence if necessary. Defence is masculine when using violence, and defence also justifies the crime committed. Thus, the group-dynamic of skinheads seems to be one reason for their masculine, violent action and for its further escalation in the context of the gang. This dynamic is also one reason why it is difficult for young men to leave the gang.

Conclusion

This chapter has considered the explanations for participation in criminal youth groups through an empirical study of skinhead gangs in a small town in Finland. Both societal-centred and individual-centred perspectives are shown to be inadequate explanations in themselves for this kind of activity. Instead, I have argued for an explanation that takes into account the spontaneous excitement of gang violence/action and the role of masculinity in helping to bond relations between gang members. This kind of self-empowerment of young men to take action against foreigners and to defend what they perceive as their culture and economic resources could be seen as a negative aspect of youth empowerment and citizenship. The growing autonomous power of youth sub-cultures and youth groups can be channelled in anti-social ways as well as progressive ones.

Note

[1.] This article comes from my own contribution to a project currently underway, financed by the Finnish Academy of Arts and Sciences, entitled, "The Skinheads of Joensuu – Product of a Community?".

References

Back, L. (1994), *New Ethnicities and Urban Culture: Racisms and Multiculture in Young Lives, Race and Representation 2*, UCL Press, London.

Bjorgo, T. (1997), *Racist and Right-Wing Violence in Scandinavia: Patterns, Perpetrators and Responses*, Doctoral dissertation, University of Leiden.

Bowker, L. H. (ed.) (1998), *Masculinities and Violence*, Sage Publications, London.

Brod, H. and Kaufman, M. (ed.) (1994), *Theorising Masculinities*, Sage Publications, London.

Campbell, A. (1993), *Out of Control: Men, Women and Aggression*, Pandora, London.

Christensen, L. (1994), *Skinhead Street Gangs*, Paladin Press, Colorado.

Clarke, J. (1976), 'The Skinheads and the Magical Recovery of Community', in S. Hall and T. Jefferson (eds.), *Resistance through Rituals*, Hutchinson, London.

Cohen, A. (1955), *Delinquent Boys: The Culture of the Gang*, Macmillan, London.

Cohen, P. (1997), *Rethinking the Youth Question: Education, Labour and Cultural Studies*, Macmillan, London.

Harris, I. M. (ed.) (1995), *Messages Men Hear: Constructing Masculinities*, Taylor & Francis, London.

Heitmeyer, W. (1992), *Rechtextremistische Orientierung bei Jugendlichen: Empirische Ergebnisse und Erklärungsmuster einer Untersuchung zur politischen Sozialisation,*

Juventa, Weinheim.

Knight, N. (1982), *Spirit of '69: A Skinhead Bible*, William Clowes Ltd., Beccies and London.

Kuure, T. (1996), *Marginaalin politiikkaa: Marginaalista murtautumisen vaihtoehtoiset strategiat* (Marginal Politics – Alternative Strategies of Breaking from the Margins), Doctoral dissertation, University of Tampere, Department of Political Science.

Lähteenmaa, J. (1991), *Hip-hoppareita, lähiöläisiä ja kultturelleja: Nuorisoryhmistä 1980-luvun lopun Helsingissä* (Hip-hoppers, Local Kids and Culturalists: Youth Groups of the late 1980s in Helsinki), Youth Centre publication No. 1, The City of Helsinki.

Miles, R. (1994), *Rasismi (Racism)*, Vastapaino, Tampere (originally published in 1989 by Routledge, London).

Moore, D. (1994), *The Lads in Action: Social Process in an Urban Youth Sub-Culture*, Addition Studies Unit, School of Psychology, Curin University.

Perelman, C. H. (1996), *The Idea of Justice and the Problem of Argument*, Routledge, London and Henley.

Puuronen, V. (1996), 'Skineys ideologiana ja toimintakulttuurina' (The Skinhead Movement as an Ideology and Action Culture), *Nuorisotutkimus 3/96* (The Finnish Journal of Youth Research), pp. 12-18.

Puuronen, V. (1997), *Johdatus nuorisotutkimukseen* (Introduction to Youth Research), Finnish Youth Research 2000 Programme, The Finnish Youth Research Society, Vastapaino, Tampere.

Siltala, J. (1995), 'Väkivalta toimintakyvyn takeena' (Violence as Guarantee of the Capability of Action), *Nuorisotutkimus 1/95* (The Finnish Journal of Youth Research), pp. 23-31.

Smith, P. (ed.) (1996), *Boys – Masculinities on Contemporary Culture*, Westview Press.

Suoninen, E. (1997), 'Selonteot ja oman toiminnan ymmärettäväksi tekeminen' (Explanations and Making One's Own Actions Understandable), *Sosiologia 1/1997*, pp. 26-38.

Vesivalo, O. (1998), 'Mie miehenä: Poikien elämästä Etelä-Karjalassa' (Me as a Man: Boys' Life in Southern Karelia), in H. Helve (ed.), *Nuorten arki ja muuttuvat rakenteet, Nuorisotutkimus 2000, 5/98* (Everyday Life of Young People and Changing Structures, Finnish Youth Research 2000 Programme), pp. 116-158.

147

11 The Racialisation of Youth Gangs: When Violence Turns into a Fight over a Turf

TIMO VIRTANEN

In the 1990s, the issues of "race" and "ethnicity" have emerged as new concepts among young people in Finland. The new migration movements which characterise this period have introduced new citizens, non-citizens and partial citizens into Finnish society in the form of EU migrants, refugees and asylum seekers. Some of these have been additionally subject to a process of racialisation. During this period, the racialisation of youth gangs has taken place, either through the staking out of the claims by native youths such as skinheads to keep away from "niggers" and "black heads", or through ethnic gangs distancing themselves from native youth. In countering this, a range of anti-racist actions are offered by a variety of agencies and actors. In the present article the issue of racist violence is considered with respect to violent brawls between skinheads and Somali youngsters, and actions taken by the police to alleviate the situation.

Racist violence may take many forms and consist of attacks on property as well as on people on account of perceived factors such as colour, race, nationality and ethnic or national origins. This can be considered racist if the victim believes that the act takes place on racial grounds and/or there is evidence of racism (Commission for Racial Equality 1987). Moreover, the concept of racism is considered to include popular and institutional sites (Back 1994). While popular racism refers to the experiences of racism in daily contexts, some forms of racism operate within institutions and organisations, constructing racialised subjects, issues and discourses which can disadvantage groups at which they are directed. However, it has become increasingly evident that these forms of

148

racism may be intertwined, acting as a complex process stretching from individual racist acts to more elaborated forms of racism.

In Finland, Black Africans and Arabs have been typified as the targets and skinheads as the perpetrators of racist violence and harassment (Virtanen 1996). Thus, the risk of victimisation seems to be aggravated in case of groups defined as "non-white" by their skin colour and this is aggravated if they are further defined as not being full citizens of the society. Nevertheless, violence is not only directed against immigrants and ethnic minorities, but also against anti-racists and the native-born friends of immigrants. Young immigrant men, in particular, seem to fall victims of racist violence in the streets and other public places. They may also be less inclined to report racist incidents to the police. Giddens (1994) refers to multiple discrimination, and here we can see that young people may fall victims of three-fold discrimination: that based upon ethnicity, social class, and race. The more recent influx of asylum seekers and refugees as well as illegal immigrants who do not have full citizen status creates a further dimension of discrimination, one that can intersect with these more classical forms of discrimination in complex ways.

In Finland, there have been a number of cases when immigrants have been beaten by local skinheads (Virtanen 1998). Typically, skinhead violence has become entrenched in some local communities. In some cases it has taken forms which have been pervasive in everyday life among certain youth groups but then faded away later. In Finland, the first skinhead generation marched out at the beginning of the 1970s (Luukka and Muukkonen 1997). The "skin" ideology became conspicuous by opposing the culture of those favouring money, consumerism and "Americanism". The skins, by contrast, cherished the "fatherland", the army and the idea of a strong leader which was embodied in the most famous Finnish neo-Nazi, Pekka Siitoin. For example, a subculture of violence and "white power" music emerged in Naantali, which, however, lost much of its attraction towards the end of the 1990s.

In the 1980s, the antipathies of skinheads were raised by other youth sub-cultures, notably, hip hoppers and rappers which were seen to be sympathetic to "Negro" and "black" music, leading to gang brawls. The Somali refugees who came to Finland at the beginning of the 1990s then became the objects for more organised skinhead violence. Skinhead violence has ranged from threats of violence to serious assaults with knives and other weapons towards victims who are alone or in a small group, often targeted at anybody "in the wrong place at the wrong time" (Virtanen 1998). Thus, skinheads have been quick to adopt a message that asylum seekers constitute the greatest threat.

In the context of this escalation of youth problems and racist incidents, local communities seem to differ as to how alert they are to the dangers of violence and harassment. Some communities seem to allow the emergence of these problems, while others are more effective in taking action against them through legal, social or cultural channels. For example, in Joensuu, the emergence of the skinhead problem may perhaps be connected with sinking economic conditions and in this community it was a long time before counteracting activities were initiated. In Mikkeli, the skinhead issue was placed on the public agenda as a problem only in 1997, two years or more after the problem first appeared. Due to the fear of being labelled as a hotbed of racism, counter actions were initiated by the police and city officials, to curb the problem of racist violence. In Turku, racist violence on the part of skinheads evident in the early 1990s declined considerably by the mid-1990s, perhaps because of the rising number of immigrants in the city. However, Black Africans, in particular, still run the risk of falling victims of racist violence in the city of Turku (Forsten-Lindman 1998).

In some Finnish communities, the violent settlings of accounts between the skinheads and the Somalis have represented a persistent cycle of attacks: the skinheads have worked in an organised manner, pursuing victims and assaulting them in some suitable place. This is consistent with conventional definitions of social terrorism denoting an attempt to create fear and terror among a special population (Gurr 1989). In Helsinki, more organised skinhead activities evolved at the beginning of 1997. In one highly publicised case, a mob of 40 skinheads from Konala attacked 25 to 30 Somalis during a football match, with baseball bats and hammers. The police were called to the place, but were unable to prevent the fight. Some of the skins told the court that they were under the influence of alcohol and narcotics. According to the skins, the aim of the attack was retaliation for events that took place the Friday before. The attack lead to a counter attack by the Somalis, in which two skins were assaulted, one with a knife.

Although the Konala incident represents a rare occurrence, it may be interpreted as evidence of the "racialisation" of social relations (Willis 1978). Young men have taken over the policing of the area to keep it "clean" of "niggers" and "black heads". Nevertheless, skinheads should not be categorically regarded as natural allies or potential members of neo-fascist groups in Finland, which seems to be more typical of an organised form of behaviour linked to far right groups in other Nordic countries (Bjorgo 1997).

In Helsinki, Somali youngsters resorted to a gang attack against skinheads, other immigrant youths, and the police in summer 1998. The incident started with minor quarrelling. Later on, a civil-clothed policeman was wounded with a knife, and Albanian youngsters were attacked by about 50 Somalis. Thus, while ethnic gangs may offer protection to their members in urban environments, they may also contribute to learning crime-prone attitudes and skills as well (Spergel 1995). This then unfortunately often leads to labelling ethnic minority youths in general as violence-prone. The incident in Helsinki started public discussion on the possibilities and limitations of youth work to combat cycles of violence. However, despite the fact that such measures were begun by a coalition of city youth offices and by voluntary organisations, no youth clubs were opened for ethnic minority youth.

Ethnic conflicts are often considered as a threat to civil society due to their potential for escalation. Traditionally, violence has more commonly occurred at the instigation of small and close-knit groups than by mobs. Once violence has begun, it legitimates repression by the state authorities, polarises the public and binds groups of militants together more cohesively (Tarrow 1994). So far, outbreaks of ethnic rioting have been a rare occurrence in Finland. Nevertheless, it is a challenge to devise ways to deal with emerging demographic and ethnic diversity. For example, it is of great importance that the breakdown of relations between immigrant youths and the police can be prevented. In Helsinki, immigrant young people with a history of violence have been successfully attracted to the activities of the counteractive Non-Violence Team, helping to reduce potential violence by decreasing the availability of guns and other weapons.

During the 1990s, anti-racist activities evolved in Finland, ranging from peaceful demonstrations to actions against racist rock events (Virtanen 2000). So far, racist music events have not turned into mini-riots between anti-racists and police in Finland, as has been the case in many other European countries. Unfortunately, some incidents indicate that the Finnish police also have a tendency to wield their power repressively with respect to ethnic minorities and members of the counterculture. As identified by Reiss (1968), behaviours that are most likely viewed by the public as police brutality may include, for example, the use of abusive language, stopping people on the street as well as the actual use of physical force or violence. Clearly, the issue of confidence in the police is important because there is still the potential to offer an opportunity for combating the emergence of ethnic conflicts on the Finnish scene, if police power is used appropriately. Police actions could start by monitoring and reporting racist incidents in order to shed light on the multi-faceted issue of crime and victimisation among young people, in particular. Moreover, the training of police officers should provide new opportunities for developing more professional policing and more creative strategies for responding to racist violence.

References

Back, L. (1994), *New Ethnicities and Urban Culture: Racisms and Multiculture in Young Lives, Race and Representation 2*, UCL Press, London.

Bjorgo, T. (1997), *Racist and Right-Wing Violence in Scandinavia: Patterns, Perpetrators, and Responses*, Tano Achsehoug, Oslo.

Brah, A. (1996), *Cartographies of Diaspora: Contesting Identities. Gender, Racism and Ethnicity Series*, Routledge, London and New York.

Commission for Racial Equality (1987), *Living in Terror: A Report on Racial Violence and Harassment in Housing*, London.

Forsten-Lindman, N. (1998), *Psycho-Social Adjustment among Somali Refugees in Finland*, Paper presented at 'Variations on the Theme of Somaliness, International Congress of Somali Studies', Turku, Finland, August 6-9, 1998.

Giddens, A. (1984), *The Constitution of the Society*, Polity Press, Cambridge.

Gurr, T. R. (1989), 'Political Terrorism: Historical Antecedents and Contemporary Trends', in T. R. Gurr (ed.), *Violence in America: Protest, Rebellion, Reform, Vol. 2*, Sage Publications, Newbury Park, CA, pp. 201-230.

Luukka, P. and Muukkonen, M. (1997), 'Erään helsinkiläisen skinijengin synty ja elämäntapa' (The Lifestyle of a Skinhead Gang in Helsinki), *Nuorisotutkimus 15, 4* (The Finnish Journal of Youth Research), pp. 31-48.

Reiss, A. J. Jr (1968), 'Police Brutality: Answers to Key Questions', *Society 5, 8*, pp. 10-19.

Spergel, I. A. (1995), *The Youth Gang Problem: A Community Approach*, Oxford University Press, New York.

Tarrow, S. (1994), *Power in Movement: Social Movements, Collective Action and Politics*, Cambridge University Press, Cambridge.

Virtanen, T. (1996), 'Oh They Say It's a Foreigner Who Made Trouble', *Siirtolaisuus-Migration 2*, pp. 10-17.

Virtanen, T. (1998), 'Racist Violence from the Part of Skinheads: The Expression of Hate in Finland', in H. Helve (ed.), *Unification and Marginalisation of Young People*, Finnish Youth Research 2000 Programme, The Finnish Youth Research Society, Helsinki, pp. 172-184.

Virtanen, T. (ed.) (2000), *Youth, Racist Violence and Anti-Racist Responses in the Nordic Countries*, The Finnish Youth Research Society, Helsinki, http://www.alli.fi/nuorisotutkimus/julkaisut/virtanen/index.html.

Willis, P. (1978), *The Profane Culture*, Routledge and Kegan Paul Ltd., London.

12 Economy of Emotions and Sexual Violence against Adolescent Girls

SARI NÄRE

Introduction

The constitution of citizenship is subject to constant challenge and change according to shifts in the definition of public problems and the activities of social movements. Arguably in the early 21st century, sexuality and sexual integrity should be seen as an aspect of citizenship as young people or children have right to pursue and define different sexualities but also the right to be protected from sexual abuse. Thus the sexuality of young people and children needs to be both recognised and protected. This applies especially to young women who are most likely to be the victims of sexual abuse. In the following chapter, the problems of recognising and protecting sexual rights are addressed.

During the 1990s, the commercial influences in Finnish gender culture strengthened. Partly because of spreading sex trade, young girls and women meet sexual and verbal aggression (see Saarikoski 1998; 1999) more than before. Children's right to be safe and secure (on children's rights e.g. Calam and Franchi 1989) is not guaranteed in a society where a libertarian ethos of sexuality prevails (Näre 1995; 1998). According to some researchers (Kelly 1988; Stanko 1990) violence against women is an ordinary part of life, but sexual violence can be shown to have some new contemporary elements as well as some culturally specific ones.

This chapter deals with sexual violence against pubescent and adolescent girls aged 10 to 20 years. The observations are based upon the interpretation of phone call reports in a help centre for raped women in Helsinki. The place is called "Raiskauskriisikeskus Tukinainen", and the data presented here is selected from a total of 2791 reports which have been coded for research purposes. The quantity of phone calls from girls and young women is 299, and when the phone calls which are not very specific or which are concerned more with professional consultation have been excluded, the number of phone calls interpreted here falls to 261.

There are some problems associated with using this kind of material. Because of the therapeutic character of the phone contact between the caller and person on call, the information is not collected very systematically. The person on call cannot start to ask questions very directly, she can only record the information that the customer is willing to provide and on this basis she fills out a form after the phone call. Therefore, enumerating very exact percentages is not relevant, but we can nevertheless make some general remarks about how girls and young women face sexual violence.

The Economy of Emotions

In my doctoral dissertation (Näre 1995) I have used the concept of the economy of emotions as a part of a given gender system. According to my thesis, the gender system has four levels: the biological, psychological, social and cultural levels. The economy of emotions is connected with the psychological level of the gender system. The psychological level of the gender system is a kind of intermediator or connecting link between the biological and social levels of the gender system. It is produced and developed in the economy of emotions and feelings. This kind of economy includes intimate and personal relations. The more contacts and communication a person has, the more intensive the economy of emotions. The most intensive economy of emotions of all is usually developed in the family, and the family can be the place of violence as well as love. A very important factor in the economy of emotions is the degree of personal confidence.

Gender segregation – especially in the division of labour – may lead to a gender division in the economy of emotions. Emotional divisions can lead towards the power of care on the one hand but also to violence, on the other. In some more traditional family cultures, the woman may represent the power of care and the man may represent the potential to use violence as part of a stereotypical and essentialist dichotomy. In late modern societies, this kind of division has started to collapse and is even becoming

155

dysfunctional. The lack of emotional skills in societies which increasingly value communication and negotiation in the workplace and in personal life, leads to a risk of social marginalisation and this seems to happen more among young men than among young women. Young women, by contrast, develop emotional skills very effectively as part of their informal girls' culture (Näre and Lähteenmaa 1992).

The economy of emotions includes the interpersonal relations between individuals as well the intrapersonal relations of each individual. This means that the economy of emotions consists of the psychohistory of the person as well as their contemporary set of relationships. Emotional problems (e.g. in work places) have their psychohistorical origins. In the same way, sexual violence can be caused by emotional marginalisation and isolation. In this presentation, I use the concept of economy of emotions as a psychosocial rather than cultural concept consisting of personal interaction.

The economy of emotions is my starting point when making classifications and interpretations of rape. I have categorised six basic types of rape according to the intensity of the economy of emotions where the rape happens. Below I present this rape typology and also some preparatory observations of the characteristics of each type of rape in terms of the economy of emotions. In order to preserve confidentiality, I do not refer to specific cases.

1. Sexual Violence in the Family

The economy of emotions is most tight and intensive inside the family. This is where we find the largest number of cases of sexual abuse, 77 cases altogether. Almost every third case, 30 %, belongs to this kind of sexual violence. In these cases, the abusers are fathers, step fathers, mothers' boy friends, cousins and brothers of the victims. In a couple of cases, the abuser is the girlfriend of the father and in one case girls' mother.

Sexual violence inside the family seems to have the most damaging effect on the victim out of all the different kinds of sexual abuse. On account of the intensity of the emotions it seems to be most difficult to survive mentally after incest. In the psychodynamics of incest, the child is required to keep the secret of her/his family silent. This destroys the transitional sphere where the child can play in his/her fantasy life in order to practice adult life (see Kajamaa 1994; Varilo and Linna 1993).

The typical emotional symptoms girls suffer after abuse and rape in the family are different kinds of fears, shame, guilt, nightmares, insomnia, anxiety and depression. Depression can result in self-destructiveness and suicide attempts on the one hand, or aggression and anger towards others, on the other hand. There are several cases where the girl spent time in a psychiatric hospital after the rape – in some cases even 2 to 3 years. Incest can be a factor behind eating disorders and alcohol and drug abuse as well.

The offence of incest is less often reported to the police than other kinds of sexual violence. In my data, only ten cases were reported. However, in the court system, the incest cases seem to be almost unrecognised. Thus, sexual violence in the family is still invisible violence in our society, even though probably about 1 % of Finnish children encounter such kinds of sexual abuse (see Sariola 1993).

2. Sexual Violence in Intimate Relationships

Intimate relationships are exceptional compared with other relationships because they include also a sexual relationship. Intimate violence belongs to the kind of violence which takes place inside the economy of emotions as well. This means rape by boyfriends and husbands. There were 6 %, 15 cases of this kind in my data. According to Sue Lees (1989, 32) a woman's duty has been to take on the responsibility for male sexuality. Girls and women are seen as sexual gatekeepers (Koss and Cleveland 1997; Bateman 1991). This is one reason why women tend to hide sexual violence which they encounter in an intimate relationship – women feel guilt and shame on account of the men's behaviour. In fact, it is a point of honour for women to take care of the economy of emotions (Näre 2000).

Children suffer from the intimate violence between their parents as well (see e.g. Sundholm 1993). They are invisible victims who may have difficulties in creating partnerships in their later life. Young women tend to meet intimate violence more often than older women (Heiskanen and Piispa 1998). Typically, women are taken by surprise in this kind of case and at first they think that the (sexual) violence is just a temporary disorder. Unfortunately, it usually gets worse with time (see Näre 1994; Husso 1994; Viano 1995; Dutton 1995).

Intimate violence may start when the young girl or woman is leaving her boyfriend or husband. Usually she leaves her boyfriend because he is violent and in many cases he tries to take revenge by raping her. In this kind of case it is easier for the girl to report to the police than when violence takes place actually during the partnership. Hence, offences of intimate sexual violence are not usually reported. It is difficult for the girl to make a report to the police if she lives together in the economy of emotions with the partner.

3. Sexual Violence by Misusing Professional Position

There were 8 % or 21 cases of sexual violence by different kinds of authority figures who are in similar kinds of positions to parents in relation to the children or young people in their care. That means, the rape also happens inside the economy of emotions: the younger the girl is the more the abuse damages her.

The abusers of this kind misuse their professional or economical position. They can be teachers, youth workers, doctors, masseurs, nurses, employers, landlords and landladies. The intensity of abuse increases according to the spent time: there is a continuum from full-time parenting and residential care to day care and occasional care (see Ward 1989). The risk for abuse is higher in occasional care. Also, rape can be seen as one end of a continuum of abusive (male) sexuality beginning from verbal harassment (Kelly 1988).

The abusers misuse the emotions of friendship and trust when pursuing their purpose. Perpetrators in confidential relations tend to break the borders of the emotional trust of their victims in ways that the victim is hardly conscious of. Living in abusive and incestuous relations in childhood and adolescence excludes young women from the innocent fantasies which are shared in girls' informal culture (Sundholm 1989, 66) in a similar way that the stigmatisation as a whore can exclude them from love (Saarikoski 1999).

Some young women are willing to report such offences, but usually only many years after the crime has happened. This may occur during therapy later in life.

4. Sexual Violence Made by Familiar People

There were 52 cases – 20 % – of sexual violence carried out by familiar people like friends, neighbours and fellow workers. This kind of sexual violence happens on the borders of the economy of emotions. Often the rapists of the girls are boys of the same age, e.g. from the same neighbourhood or school. There were a couple of cases where the rape was carried out at, or near the school by the boys whom the girl knew from school.

Every seventh rape against young girls seems to be group or gang rape and in a proportion of them, the rapists are in some way familiar to the victim. This incidence of group rape was higher than expected. This type of rape is experienced most often by young girls who are still virgins. Group rape has a very traumatic and isolating effects on the victim's emotional life. Gang rapes often involve male fraternities (Martin and Hummer 1993).

Unfortunately, it is sometimes the case that older, familiar men rape adolescent girls as well. This always comes as a surprise for the girl and may damage her confidence in people. Informal girls' culture is generally orientated to support the economy of emotions: girls learn many emotional skills in their culture (Näre and Lähteenmaa 1992), and their tendency to trust and not to hurt others is misused by adult rapists.

The familiar, like the unfamiliar rapist, may take the initiative when the girl is drunk or asleep. Sometimes rapists (especially unknown ones) use weapons like guns, knives and dope. A typical way to rape is to use physical force and surprise attack from behind, including strangling, cutting and sometimes blackmailing the victim.

5. Sexual Violence in Making Acquaintance

There were 32 cases (12 %), belonging also on the borders of the economy of emotions, which represent a very special characteristic of Finnish gender culture. These rapes happen in the process of making acquaintance: a young girl meets a man and on the same day or evening joins his company in order to get to know him better, or in some cases because she or he does not have another place to go. Most typically she goes to his place after a restaurant or sometimes she has joined his company from the street, or other public place.

This kind of directness is not typical of every culture. Actually, it may be based on confidence, a kind of trust that men are able to control their drives and desires. Making acquaintance on the first evening means getting to know the person as well as sometimes (but not always) the possibility of making love. Before joining the man's company, the young girl or woman may tell him that she is not willing to have sex with him, she just wants to get to know him better or just to come to stay with him overnight (or take the man to stay with her overnight if he has missed the last bus or train). In some – much more rare – cases, the girl was even orientated to have sex but did not like the way the man behaved.

Therefore, many of these kinds of rapes happen when the man does not listen the woman's wish not to make love; he does not take into account her wish but forces her to have sex. In most of the cases this means the cancellation of a tacit agreement by the man or in some cases it results from girl's inability to negotiate and solve agreements. The man may start to be aggressive and use force and violence when the girl rejects him. The verbal "no" is forced to become "yes" by physical violence.

Negotiating and solving agreements seems to be especially difficult with foreign men from cultures with a different gender system: 40 % of the rapes in making acquaintance are made by foreigners. Most of them are from cultures of gender segregation, mainly from Islamic cultures where women and men are in a complementary relation with each other. In complementary gender cultures the meanings of intentions are strongly structured by time and place, and that's why for men, the meaning of time and place can be more important than the expressed wish of the woman (see Näre 1995). However, it is interesting to note that in my data this kind of sexual violence is not reported as so called "date rape" (see Levy 1999).

6. Sexual Violence by Strangers

In 24 % – 64 cases altogether – of sexual violence this takes place outside of the economy of emotions. That means sexual violence is carried out by unknown attackers and strangers. Sexual violence outside the economy of emotions is directed towards pubescent and adolescent girls more often than towards older women (Honkatukia 2000). Typically these cases happen somewhere publicly and the victim is attacked from behind. Surprise attacks can also happen inside confined spaces such as a restaurant, in telephone cabins, in toilets and so on.

This kind of sexual violence, rapes and harassment (harassment was not actually mentioned in my material as it was too common an experience) happens normally in public places more often than in private places. In the so called geography of fear, women and young girls avoid walking alone in empty places (Koskela and Tuominen 1995). Public places can be forests, parks, streets, beaches, but also schools, restaurants, cars and ferries. Cars and cabins in ferries could be private places also, but the way to get the girl into the car or cabin is to take her by force – by taking her from the public place into the private place.

Half of the cases where the attacker is unknown – as well as in the cases where the attack happens in making acquaintance – have been reported to the police. These kinds of cases are the ones most easily recognised by the criminal justice system. Even though the most damaging form of sexual violence for the victim is sexual violence in the family, because it intrudes into the deepest level of the emotional economy, the official interpretation of rape seems to be that it usually happens outside the economy of emotions, by strangers.

The police and court believe victims better if they have proof of sexual violence, secured through a medical examination and if they did not know the person before. Thus, the girl has to be very strong and rational in order to get justice. After being raped she should not shower (which could be the first, spontaneous reaction) and "destroy the proof" but immediately go to be investigated. However, given the risk of HIV/AIDS, it can actually be more risky to keep the liquids inside and on the skin or mucous for investigation and the investigation itself can damage the mucous in some cases too. Thus, it is difficult for the young woman to present physical proof of sexual abuse and there are many risks involved.

After Rape

The typical fear after sexual abuse and rape is that of catching venereal disease and some girls did get a disease from the rapist. The time to waiting for the results of the HIV tests is very risky period for suicide attempts. In these data, a couple of girls also became pregnant from the rape.

In the cases of incest, permanent mental disorders, suicide attempts, alcoholism and drug abuse are more typical outcomes than among the other types of sexual violence. Post-traumatic stress disorders, shame, guilt and fear are long standing, often life-long wounds among the adolescent girls who have experiences of sexual violence. It is also difficult to concentrate at school when having been abused or raped. If the girl has tried to forget the abuse and violence, it easily comes into her mind when having sex with future boyfriend(s). Rape can also break up the relationship with a partner who cannot support or understand the girl's way of handling the trauma.

The most important person to help in managing after sexual violence seems to be the mother of the girl. Many of those who call the help centre are the mothers of raped girls and they need help themselves too. The daughter's rape activates the mother's own experiences of sexual violence and if she has had this kind of experience, she needs to try to work through the trauma in order to help her daughter. Therefore, a mother is a very important resource in coping with this kind of trauma.

The most damaging situation for the girl is if her mother (and sometimes father as well) blames the victim or does not believe her. This is the case especially in many incest cases. The mother thus makes her daughter's sexual abuse by her own partner invisible. If the girl does not trust her mother, she will not tell her about her experience and may remain alone with her trauma. She has to work through the trauma perhaps for her whole life, in the worst cases in hospital or in prison.

Conclusion

Therefore, we can look at the different kinds of sexual violence in terms of their relationship to the economy of emotions. The likelihood of reporting the abuse, its reception by the police and the courts and the therapeutic assistance appropriate after the experience, all depend upon their relationship to the economy of emotions. Here, the awareness of sexual abuse depends upon the empowering of girls and young women to report and deal with it. Sexual citizenship can only have meaning if girls and young women are also empowered to assert their needs against those of their abusers.

References

Antikainen, J. (1994), *Lasten seksuaalinen hyväksikäyttö: Ammatilliset haasteet ja työorientaatiot* (Sexual Abuse of Children: Professional Challenges and Work Orientations), STAKES research 46 (National Research and Development Centre for Welfare and Health), Helsinki.
Bateman, P. (1991), 'The Context of Date Rape', in B. Levy (ed.), *Dating Violence, Young Women in Danger*, The Seal Press, Englewood.

Calam, R. and Franchi, C. (1989), 'Setting Basic Standards', in W. Stainton Rogers, D. Hevey and E. Ash (eds.), *Child Abuse and Neglect: Facing the Challenge*, The Open University Press, London.

Dutton, D. G. (1995), *The Domestic Assault of Women: Psychological Profile*, Basic Books, New York.

Heiskanen, M. and Piispa, M. (1998), *Usko, toivo, hakkaus: Kyselytutkimus miesten naisille tekemästä väkivallasta* (Faith, Hope, Beating: Questionnaire about Men's Violence towards Women), Statistics Finland and Council for Equality, Helsinki.

Honkatukia, P. (2000), 'Tytöt ja seksuaalisen väkivallan jatkumo' (Girls and Sexual Violence), in P. Honkatukia, J. Niemi-Kiesiläinen and S. Näre (2000), *Nuoriin tyttöihin kohdistuva seksuaalinen lähentely ja väkivalta* (Sexual Harassment and Violence towards Young Girls), The Finnish Youth Research Network, Helsinki.

Husso, M. (1994), 'Parisuhdeväkivalta ja pahoinpidelty ruumis' (Violence in Intimate Relationships and a Manhandled Body), in S. Heinämaa and S. Näre (eds.), *Pahan tyttäret: Sukupuolitettu pelko, viha ja valta* (The Daughters of Evil: Gendered Fear, Anger and Power), Gaudeamus, Helsinki.

Kajamaa, R. (1994), '"Kaikesta hyvästä joutuu maksamaan:" Insestin psykodynamiikkaa' ("You Have to Pay for Something Good:" The Psychodynamics of Incest), in S. Heinämaa and S. Näre (eds.), *Pahan tyttäret: Sukupuolitettu pelko, viha ja valta* (The Daughters of Evil: Gendered Fear, Anger and Power), Gaudeamus, Helsinki.

Kelly, L. (1988), *Surviving Sexual Violence*, Polity, London.

Koskela, H. and Tuominen, M. (1995), 'Yökaupunki – pelon kaupunki' (Nighttown – The Town of Fear), in J. Lähteenmaa and L. Mäkelä (eds.), *Helsingin yö* (Helsinki by Night), City of Helsinki Urban Facts, Helsinki.

Koss, M. P. and Cleveland, H. H. (1997), 'Stepping on Toes: Social Roots of Rape Lead to Intractability and Politicization', in M. D. Schwartz (ed.), *Researching Sexual Violence against Women: Methodological and Personal Perspectives*, Sage Publications, London.

Lees, S. (1989), *Growing up Good: Policing the Behaviour of Girls in Europe*, Sage Publications, London.

Levy, B. (ed.) (1991), *Dating Violence, Young Women in Danger*, The Seal Press, Englewood.

Martin, P. Y. and Hummer, R. A. (1993), 'Fraternities and Rapes on Campus', in P. B. Bart and E. G. Moran (eds.), *Violence against Women: The Bloody Footprints*, Sage Publications, London.

Näre, S. (1994), 'Pakenevat prinssit: Naisvihaajan muotokuvia' (Escaping Princes: Portraits of a Womanhater), in S. Heinämaa and S. Näre (eds.), *Pahan tyttäret: Sukupuolitettu pelko, viha ja valta* (The Daughters of Evil: Gendered Fear, Anger and Power), Gaudeamus, Helsinki.

Näre, S. (1995), *Etnopsykoanalyyttisia näkökulmia sukupuolikulttuuriin, Sosiologian laitoksen tutkimusraportteja 229* (Ethnopsychoanalytical Perspectives on Sex Culture, Research Reports of the Department of Sociology 229), Helsinki University Press, Helsinki.

Näre, S. (1998), 'Seksuaalipoliittinen libertarianismi ja egalitarismi' (Sexual Political Libertarianism and Egalitarianism), in K. Ilmonen (ed.), *Moderniteetti ja moraali* (Modernity and Moral), Gaudeamus, Helsinki.

Näre, S. and Lähteenmaa, J. (eds.) (1992), *Letit liehumaan! Tyttökulttuuri murroksessa* (Shake Your Hair! Girls' Culture in the Process of Change), Finnish Literature Society, Helsinki.

Saarikoski, H. (1998), 'Tytön maineen käsite ja huoraksi leimaamisen kansantapa' (The Concept of Girl's Reputation and a Folkhabit to Stigmatise Someone as a Whore), in T. Koskinen (ed.), *Kurtisaaneista kunnian naisiin* (From Courtesans to Women of Honour), Helsinki University Press, Helsinki.

Saarikoski, H. (1999), 'Tytön rakkaus ja häpeä huoran maineen sääteleminä' (Girl's Love and Shame Controlled by the Reputation of Whore), in S. Näre (ed.), *Tunteiden sosiologiaa I: Elämyksiä ja läheisyyttä* (The Sociology of Emotions I: Experiences and Intimacy), Finnish Literature Society, Helsinki.

Sariola, E. (1993), 'Seksuaalinen hyväksikäyttö ja väkivalta kodeissa' (Sexual Abuse and Violence at Home), in *Miten auttaa lasta: Lapsen fyysisen ja seksuaalisen pahoinpitelyn tutkimus ja hoito* (How to Help a Child: The Research and Cure of Physical and Sexual Violence of Childen), Lastensuojelun keskusliiton julkaisuja 89 (Central Union for Child Welfare), Helsinki.

Stanko, E. (1990), *Everyday Violence: How Women and Men Experience Sexual and Physical Danger*, HarperCollins, London.

Sundholm, S. (1989), *Insesti* (Incest), Gaudeamus, Helsinki.

Sundholm, S. (1993), 'Seksuaalisen hyväksikäytön kohtaaminen' (Facing Sexual Abuse), in *Miten auttaa lasta: Lapsen fyysisen ja seksuaalisen pahoinpitelyn tutkimus ja hoito* (How to Help a Child: The Research and Cure of Physical and Sexual Violence of Childen), Lastensuojelun keskusliiton julkaisuja 89 (Central Union for Child Welfare), Helsinki.

Varilo, E. and Linna, L. (1993), 'Lasten seksuaalinen väärinkäyttö' (Sexual Abuse of Children), in *Miten auttaa lasta: Lapsen fyysisen ja seksuaalisen pahoinpitelyn tutkimus ja hoito* (How to Help a Child: The Research and Cure of Physical and Sexual Violence of Childen), Lastensuojelun keskusliiton julkaisuja 89 (Central Union for Child Welfare), Helsinki.

Viano, E. (ed.) (1995), *Intimate Violence: Interdisciplinary Perspectives*, Hemisphere, London.

Ward, A. (1989), 'Caring for Other People's Children', in W. Stainton Rogers, D. Hevey and E. Ash (eds.), *Child Abuse and Neglect: Facing the Challenge*, The Open University Press, London.

13 Foreigners as a Strategic Construction: Finnish Young People's Accounts of Immigrants

LEENA SUURPÄÄ

Everybody is somebody, not just a victim (Modood 1990, 95).

Introduction

Finland, as a country with rather little experience of immigration, does not have any long established immigration policy; nor do Finns have any clearly articulated general understanding of how to live together with cultural differences. This country finds itself caught in a web of different narratives of the everyday lives of its foreign residents along with different policy positions and collective images related to them. During the 1990s Finland has faced a situation where its immigration policy as well as immigrants' position in the country have required serious reconsideration. This is also the case with everyday attitudes towards, and encounters with, immigrants.

What kinds of interpretative perspectives can we use to conceptualise this socially, culturally and politically challenging theme? What sort of images of immigrants are being formed as a result? How can we best analyse the rather ambiguous, diverse, confused and uncertain reports we hear about immigrants? These are the questions I address in this article.

The empirical research on which this chapter is based consists of interviews conducted in the winter of 1997 among Finnish young people, from 17 to 19 years old, living in Helsinki.[1] On account of my particular research interest – young people's representations of immigrants – and due to the value-laden, normative nature of the research topic, I have applied an open group discussion model where no structured set of predetermined questions was used. This is not to say that the interviews were totally "spontaneous"; I influenced the discussions by providing starting points and presented key questions. In this way I could analyse how concepts of immigrants and related issues were formed in the young people's reflections, ideas and experiences. These concepts cannot be distinguished as either individual or collective: it is the dialogue between the two which is at the centre of my interest. The interpretation process takes place in an interplay between a certain social environment, the concrete interaction in the interview and the individual life world.

This chapter is divided into four parts. The first part examines the concepts about immigrants held by the interviewed young people. The focus here is on the encounter process, whereby immigrants are put into a conceptual framework in order to make sense of them. In the second part, I examine the application of these concepts in the social and cultural spheres by analysing young people's accounts of immigrants as social actors.[2] The emphasis here is on the dynamic interplay between public and private spheres: the diverse living spaces and positions conceptually assigned to immigrants. In the third part, young people's ideas of social and cultural inclusion and/or exclusion are analysed. Here the emphasis is on the process of integrating immigrants, or the images projected onto them, to established societal norms. The fourth section then contains concluding reflections based on the functions that the categorisation of immigrants seems to have for the young interviewees. In this way, I hope to clarify how the central concepts discussed here acquire a "meaning-in-everyday-use" (D'hondt, Blommaert and Verschueren 1995, 105).

The Process of Categorisation – A Tool for Understanding and Control

To speak of foreigners means to construct categories.[3] To construct categories is a means of controlling the persons, groups, cultures, appearances and identities behind the labels. Moreover, categorisation is a particular way of recognising one's own collective identity in relation to the categories being formed. As soon as particular characteristics are connected to a certain group of people – based on such characteristics as their being black, women, young or non-western – the criteria for those who are doing the categorising are also chosen; as Robert Miles points out, the definers themselves "are being represented" in a specific way (Miles 1989, 38).

In addition, categories make strangers more familiar: we all recognise the labels even if we do not know the people behind them. Categorisation processes are always historical and context-bound – as are the criteria and definitions of immigrants. The more ambivalent the images of immigrants are, the more conceptual control these images demand and the more they challenge social and cultural predictability in general. This in turn leads to a perceived need to identify and control immigrants (Tabboni 1996, 247-250).

Finns are well aware of the multiethnic societies existing in many European countries. But in Finland, especially in rural areas, immigrants exist still mainly as a possibility, a potential neighbour or a passer-by; genuine personal contact with immigrants is not part of people's everyday experience. A stranger is often presented by his/her absence, as Danilo Martucelli points out in describing the case in Italy (Martucelli 1994, 279). Of the young people from Helsinki, however, nearly every one interviewed had contacts with immigrants, although usually more or less fragmentary. It can be seen in these interviews that there is an evident need to construct more experience-based images of immigrants, or at least to create a certain relation between real and imagined communities. In addition, the interviewed young people strive to present themselves as liberal, claiming a certain individualistic ideal, when immigrants are discussed. According to them, immigrants should be treated as individuals rather than as faceless representatives of a particular culture; as prisoners of their origin. In concrete interview discussions, however, immigrants are often portrayed as a group or in an even more abstract manner, as a set of characteristics. Moreover, they are often valued according to certain norms of political and cultural traditions. These implicit norms function as a hidden horizon for standpoints claiming to seek neutrality and individuality.

I have elsewhere (Suurpää 1998) constructed an analytical hierarchy of difference based on young people's representations of diversity. Here I will elaborate on this idea and apply it more concretely to young people's accounts of immigrants. This hierarchy is formed around two axes. For the first axis, difference is represented as a matter of individual or social resources. At one end we find the idea of difference seen as a positive resource, forming an empowering basis for coping in a new environment. At the other end we find the idea of difference as deviance, representing deprivation and lack of requisite means for coping in a new landscape. The other axis is based on two integrated dimensions: firstly on the degree of familiarity (based on a collective image of immigrants) and secondly on the degree of social controllability of these immigrants, whether they be imagined or real. This axis presents a continuum ranging from conceptually unfamiliar and socially uncontrollable to the more familiar and controllable forms of difference. When these two axes are combined, they give rise to four image types for immigrants, enabling us to examine these young people's accounts of immigrants in an analytical way (Figure 13.1).[4]

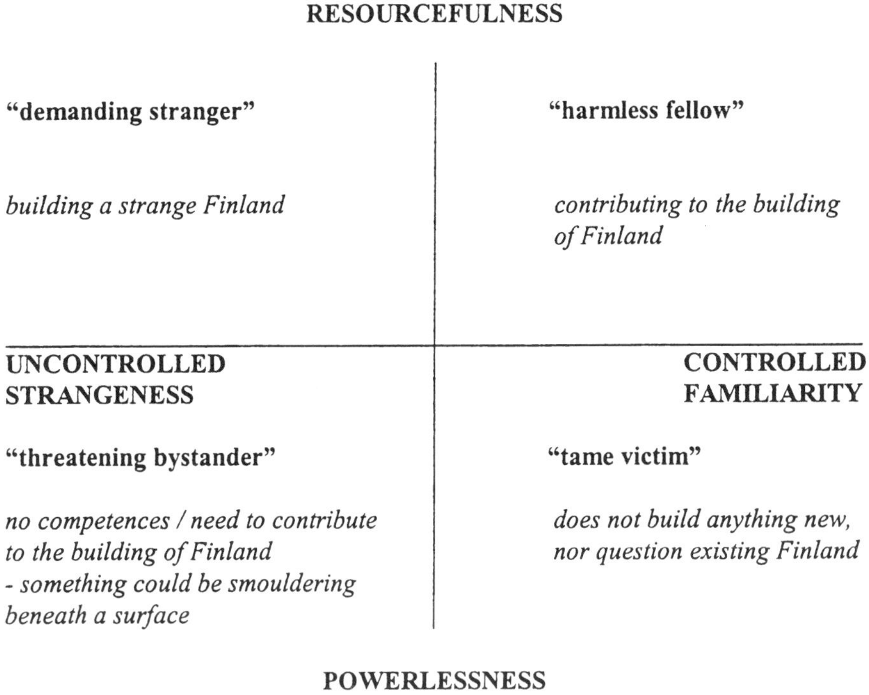

RESOURCEFULNESS

"demanding stranger"	**"harmless fellow"**
building a strange Finland	*contributing to the building of Finland*

UNCONTROLLED STRANGENESS	**CONTROLLED FAMILIARITY**
"threatening bystander"	**"tame victim"**
no competences / need to contribute to the building of Finland - something could be smouldering beneath a surface	*does not build anything new, nor question existing Finland*

POWERLESSNESS

Figure 13.1 Hierarchy of difference

168

Though I will analyse these image types separately, it should be emphasised that in the empirical data they often overlap: young people might describe the same person or group differently depending on the context in which the person discussed is placed. The young people's simultaneous use of different styles of description of immigrants – varying both according the particular situations and particular groups in question – demonstrates the strategic function of these descriptions. They help to create a relationship between the supposed cultural and historical backgrounds of immigrants and the present social status assigned to them.

The Tame Victim

The young people's accounts of immigrants, as diverse as this group may be even in Finland, often end up referring mainly to refugees. Or, to put it in another way, regardless of their real background or status in Finland, immigrants, especially if they are dark skinned, are frequently labelled as refugees coming from tragic circumstances. They are further depicted as coming from outside Europe, from non-western societies and from developing countries. This reflects Finland's official discourse on immigration, which overemphasises refugees, regardless of the fact that they form a rather low percentage of the immigrants living in Finland (Halonen 1997, 93).

> Most of the people of other cultures that we meet are refugees, no migrants move here, well, some returnees from the east... The image which has been impressed on our minds is that if someone is from a foreign culture, then he is a refugee and then he is in excess (boy, 18 years).

In the young people's accounts, the primary characteristic of a refugee is a lack: he/she is both economically poor and politically and socially powerless.[5] What is essential is not only the image of poor people but the way this conception is elaborated by the interviewees. Poverty is not primarily described as a consequence of present circumstances, but rather as a collective characteristic detached from the concrete conditions of particular immigrants. Thus, the poverty of these people is seen as more or less inevitable: it is an integral, natural element of their being refugees. It is at the same time an ahistorical fact – something without any history and rooted in the past, a matter of heritage. The most significant thing refugees are believed to have is their cultural heritage. But in this form of "ethnic absolutism" (Gilroy 1987, 16), their heritage is seen as a supplementary factor which can isolate these people from the rest of the society, rather than as an empowering resource that could facilitate their living in Finland in a new social milieu. Being culturally different in this context implies a political weakness with few resources suitable for societal participation (Gianni 1997).

> If you come from somewhere in Africa – if you're sent as a refugee to another country – of course you come with your head hanging down in a "sorry that I'm here" style. After all, you've been pushed to this country and been given the label of a refugee. It's totally different from deciding on your own that you want to go abroad. You've been thrown to the other side of the world and you have to start a new life there (girl, 18 years).

The young people interviewed adopt a rather reflexive attitude toward their own collective past which is described in diverse ways, ranging from appreciated festive traditions and institutional structures to everyday habits which they consider changeable over the course of time. In contrast, when talking about refugees, their background is pictured as a permanent state of affairs. In this context the idea of "roots politics", normally described as an empowering element for the minority group, has a different meaning (Hewitt 1996). This idea of refugees' inevitable burden concerns not only their culture but also their appearance, especially their dark skin colour:

> I don't think it's easy for some Somalis to adapt in Finland. When you see them on the street, for example, they seem like they could be decent citizens. I just feel sorry for them because they can't do anything about their own skin colour (girl, 17 years).

Refugee is no longer just a word – it has become a concept, a symbol of deprivation. A refugee is a person who is to be pitied from a distance, but not necessarily with great empathy.

> I think that once we have taken them in to Finland, we sort of have to take care of them. It's the same as if you take home a stray dog; obviously you have to go all the way in taking care of it or else the animal protection person comes and wrings your neck for it (girl, 18 years).

Empathy here implies a sympathetic understanding of someone's life situation. It demands a willingness to break, to a certain extent, cultural or personal boundaries between you and I: an emotional insight into another person's life conditions and feelings, or at least a respect for his/her life. In contrast, one can pity a person from a distance, in both emotional and cultural terms, without necessarily disturbing the hierarchy between the deprived and powerful. In this respect one ought to ask, what are the implications of feelings of pity? Is the idea that we (the powerful representatives of the majority) ought to be morally committed to pity and/or tolerate these people because of their lack of resources? Or do these sentiments implicitly victimise the people labelled as refugees? In the sense of the latter question, pity can be seen as a means by which we can show who is weak and who is in charge. Besides this, the question being asked is whether a person can be seen solely as a victim of his/her origins without making a crude generalisation about the relationship between past and present, and without strengthening the existing hierarchy of power.

The Demanding Stranger

The image of a refugee presented above is a familiar concept; the idea of a non-western background and socio-political silence in the host country can be neatly combined. In contrast, the concept of a demanding stranger defies these firmly established characteristics. To speak about uncontrolled strangers refers to the ambivalence which is formed between a traditional image of a powerless refugee and an active social actor. These people are not what the concept of a tame victim would demand them to be: they are therefore not within the framework of conceptual control. The interviewees seem to have difficulties in seeing demanding strangers as fulfilling their normative expectations of a refugee. In this case poverty and victimisation, linked with the concept of the refugee coexist with quite different characteristics of active social and cultural participation.

The tension between the potential power connected with this image and the idea of immigrants as aliens, both in social and in normative terms, brings such immigrants under suspicion. They are no longer conceptually unproblematic people having problems in their new social life, but rather may be seen as people creating potential problems. Here the essential question is not only whether immigrants are difficult to conceptualise or whether their traditions and habits are peculiar. It is also whether their intentions are understandable or acceptable from a normative point of view, and whether they are assimilable from a more social perspective.

171

The immigrant, still seen as refugee, has thus entered into the public sphere, where he/she does not conceptually belong.

> 1. Some minority youth groups hang around at Kamppi (a shopping centre in the heart of Helsinki). It seems to me like they behave more or less like they own the place, or with an attitude like, "come on, you have to learn Russian if you want to talk to me". They must think that...
> 2. That's because they're such big groups of them in that one particular area.
> 1. Yeah, I guess they're looking for a place where they can get by in their own language (1: boy, 17 years; 2: boy, 18 years).

As soon as an immigrant is connected with the public arena, multiple suspicions and restrictions are placed on him/her that do not apply to the image of a deprived refugee. The more ambiguous the power relation between "us" and "them" becomes, and the more difficult the concept is to control, the more limited the social space for "them" seems to be. At least this is the case with regard to people considered strangers but not entirely without resources: seen on the one hand as potentially powerful, on the other hand as socially deprived or risky because of the stereotypes attached to their background.

To illustrate, let me take the example of Somalis, a group which has been given a lot of attention in the Finnish media and also by the interviewed young people.[6] Most of the Somalis in Finland have come as asylum seekers, and are for the most part regarded as refugees in the interviews. Given their cultural and geographical background, as well as their present formal status in Finland, these people are conceptually ambiguous. They do not fit well with the stereotype of a poor immigrant – of a tame victim.

> ... those who look like foreigners and who express their foreignness or behave even a little arrogantly. – I don't know, but it's...odd when you look at Somalis or other black skinned people, if they're walking around with the fine gold watches on their hand and the latest designer clothing... they really don't look at all like poor people. – (I am ready to receive) those in need from the countries in war or from the developing countries, not welfare refugees or those kinds of people (girl, 17 years).

The significant transgressions here concern the relation between the image of the origin of Somalis and the social aspirations of some of them. The interpretation of their background as an obstacle to successful social

172

participation makes their concrete attempts to gain some social status difficult for the interviewees to grasp. The concept of political refugees, which is often translated at an everyday level into the pejorative concept of "welfare refugees", is often connected to Somalis, with an implicit disapproval of their active social role: they cannot be easily conceptualised as refugees without social resources because of their socially active appearance.[7] One way to solve this cognitive problem is to use the well-known concept of welfare refugees and thus to make them intelligible in that way. Their activities are treated as dubious because of their Somalian origin and their status as not having full legal citizenship, but nevertheless seeking "social citizenship" – striving for a right to participate in Finnish socio-political and cultural life.

These kinds of negative arguments, which may be seen as a part of Finnish everyday folklore, are not very familiar from the interviews. In fact, as I will discuss later in this chapter, there seems to be an ambivalence between the need for the young people to control those immigrants who seem unfamiliar to them and a wish to somehow give more space for the immigrants and thus create a more heterogeneous Finnish cultural landscape, a landscape which many young people consider "monotonous".

The Threatening Bystander

From the point of view of the young people's discussions, the image of a threatening bystander is quite rare and rather ambivalent. To the extent that this concept is seen as applicable to some people, they are portrayed as a potential menace or as a hidden risk for the maintenance of conceptual and social harmony. In such cases the young people seem to wonder whether there is something going on under the surface somewhere, beyond the grasp of the majority – outside their control. Some groups representing seemingly tame victims may threaten to develop towards becoming more critical or demanding. In many accounts this relates to Russian immigrants, as well as to Russian-speaking Ingrian "returnees",[8] whose number in the Helsinki area has increased remarkably during the 1990s. On the one hand, they can be considered more or less like us, since the returnees' ethnic roots are Finnish. On the other hand, their lifestyle, language and habits do not resemble those of the interviewed young people. Contacts with them are thus superficial and they are accused of being socially too closed off. Thus, the conceptual ambiguity makes this category oppressive and uncontrollable.

Harmless fellows are in many ways the easiest category to conceptualise. They have become a part of our society in social and cultural terms. They are under control, not believed to be hiding something, like the threatening bystanders. They seem to have learned the prevailing ways of behaving and thinking accepted in Finland – or they do not question too radically these models. However, this category shows how restricted the social and cultural space for even "good" immigrants can be in Finland. Immigrants and their activities can be intelligible and even welcome, but in controlled and predictable circumstances: as presenters of their ethnic origin in multicultural events, or in the typical roles of restaurateurs, kebab sellers, etc. These restrictions concern particularly more unfamiliar people coming from non-European societies. Regardless of the real strangeness of immigrants, they are conceptually familiar to us as ethnic-musicians, or as humorous media personalities in sitcom series – or as "local colour" around the centre of Helsinki (Koskenniemi 1997; Essed 1991; Ålund 1997). This kind of ethnicisation of social roles which makes immigrants familiar is not only taken for granted but also criticised by the interviewees, especially when it concerns people nearer to the dominant culture, such as Finland's more traditional minorities:

> If we take the Sami people for example, okay, we might organise a great festival in Helsinki's market square – some kind of a Lapland-week. Then people living in Helsinki visit there and think like, "well that's great. We must protect this cultural heritage. This is something valuable." But then we go back to everyday life and things don't work that way (girl, 18 years).

The second type of immigrant classified as a harmless fellow is someone with whom the interviewed young people may easily find connections – cultural, generational or geographical. People coming from other European countries, or those referred to as westerners, with historical and cultural similarities, are evidently considered more or less like us. No conceptual problem seems to arise in their case. Their probable differences do not count; rather, the diversity which they bring with them is seen as an enriching element of social interaction. The young people talked easily, without ambiguity, about persons such as exchange students, due to their similar social status as school pupils and as members of the same age-group.

Quite often (immigrants) are pretty decent looking. I guess a lot of those are maybe students or something. In our school we also had dark skinned girls or women who wore veils over their faces. They seemed harmless enough though; they didn't bother you at all (girl, 17 years).

Good and Bad Immigrants – A Struggle for Participation

As can be seen above, the hierarchy of difference not only describes immigrants' characteristics; it also has a more constitutive – even political – impact: it outlines and controls the status and position of immigrants, both in social and in spatial terms. The primary issue here is the social and cultural space for immigrants in Finnish public and private spheres. That is, the conceptions of immigrants' societal positions as well as the degree of social visibility or invisibility in varying social contexts. In order to elaborate on this conception of an immigrant as a cultural and social actor, I will add one supplementary conceptual pair to the scheme presented above – the good immigrant and the bad immigrant. The distinction of a good vs. a bad immigrant refers here particularly to the young people's views of immigrants' suitable and acceptable vs. doubtful and rejected societal roles and positions.

Tame victims can be seen as good immigrants. They do not challenge Finland's supposed political continuity, nor the country's dominant cultural traditions. They are supposed to remain as observers regardless of what their real position is, both in socio-cultural and in legal terms. They are politically silent with a certain willingness to display a minimum of more or less externally demanded loyalty towards social practices and cultural values described as "common" or "dominant", whether Finnish or Western.

The interviewees' accounts of language illustrate this reasoning. Because a tame victim is not supposed to be able to speak Finnish, he/she has difficulties in interpreting the Finnish socio-cultural atmosphere, and consequently he/she lacks one of the most central tools for a successful public presence. This assumption of the fundamental problem of language deficiency was taken up in almost every interview, which implies the great significance attached to the language when a certain "Finnishness" is outlined. Most of the interviewees share the idea that a common culture presupposes a common language and that the most influential political decision-makers should be fluent in Finnish. Language can be seen as a symbolic as well as a political boundary marker, a particular criterion for access to cultural and political communities. Moreover, it functions as a justification for the low proportion of immigrants in influential positions in Finnish society, their high unemployment rates etc. (Dieckhoff 1996; Essed 1991; Hjerm 1998).

Provided that good immigrants accept often rather invisible social or cultural borders outlined for them, they are accepted as a more or less controlled community, even if their living habits or cultural traditions may not always be understood, nor necessarily even greatly respected.

> If they (the drummers) would just present their culture by way of some kind of concert tour of Finland,[9] then they would be gladly accepted, but then if they decide to stay and live somewhere in Puistola (a residential area on the outskirts of Helsinki with a bad reputation) for example, then... (boy, 18 years).

> When you see a group like that beating their drums somewhere in the central station you automatically think, "get out of here!" But when you see them in some event in a market nearby and it's like, cool (girl, 18 years).

As these arguments imply, the drummers can be seen as good immigrants. They take on the character of harmless fellows. They construct a colourful Finland, but mostly on Finnish conditions – in certain restricted spaces, in certain familiar and predictable ways. If they escape this public role, attitudes toward them change as well. They become perceived as bad immigrants, as demanding strangers, who do not sufficiently accept the idea of an "indoor ethnicity", which implies the maintenance of strict boundaries between private and public spheres. In that case, their presence may put Finland's cultural or social sovereignty to risk – the symbolic order at a deeper level, which is not evident even to the interviewees themselves.

The need to privatise ethnic and cultural sides of immigrants' collective identity reveals the political significance which it holds. Collective identity can indeed be seen as "an act of power" (Laclau and Zac 1994) which symbolises diverse resources and competencies. This kind of power, and an effort to achieve an active public position as its concrete manifestation, is not easily legitimised, at least not if immigrants are supposed to remain silent or are seen as representing a menacing counter culture (Cahen 1994).

176

The case of the conceptually problematic Somalian group presented above could also serve as an example in this context. The interviewees' representations of even traditional, familiar minorities in Finland, especially of the Roma people, also show how difficult it can be to accept an active public presence of people who are not ready to restrict their particular cultural values and social practises in order to be entitled to social participation. Thus, they are often portrayed as bad aliens, as demanding strangers, even if they are Finnish citizens and not newcomers, nor legally immigrants. How can this paradox be explained? Roma are thought to challenge the idea of cultural assimilation as a prerequisite for social participation (see Huttunen 1997, 10-12). Consequently, their formal status does not guarantee a political voice for them. On the contrary, the ambiguity between Roma's alternative public appearance and their social and political rights – formally equal to those of every Finnish citizen – makes the interviewees suspicious of Roma culture. Only a partial citizenship is readily recognised for them.[10]

When you think about Gypsies, obviously some of them have got rid of that culture, as individuals, and have been able to change themselves in some way. I knew one girl who until 6 years old she was just like one of our gang, behaving like any other Finnish kid. But after that she changed totally; her mother has turned her to a real little gypsy girl, and after that you can't hang around with them any more. All those introvert... if the groups are large enough they can find all the contact they need from inside (boy, 17 years).

According to recent Finnish immigrant policy statements (Sisäasiainministeriö 1997; Act number 493/1999), the integration of the immigrants into the majority culture relies upon the idea of the public recognition of ethnic and cultural differences as a basis for integration. However, there seems to be a gap between the supposedly recognised cultural rights of minorities and concrete encounters on the everyday level in which these rights are to be recognised in practice. This is not only a phenomenon limited to Finland by any means; it is also found in countries with much longer histories of immigration such as in Britain. As John Solomos and Les Back argue (1996, 215):

There is a growing awareness of the gap between formal citizenship and the de facto restriction of economic and social rights of minorities as a result of discrimination, economic restructuring and the decline of the welfare states.

However, it can be read from the interviews that the accepted social positions of a given ethnic group and their assigned cultural space are not unchangeable. The same group can be portrayed as the good or the bad immigrants, depending on the context. The accounts given of Rastafarian groups may serve as an illustration here. One can interpret from the interviewees' reasoning, that even if the Rasta image shows some elements of powerlessness (especially their skin colour), their urban appearance – associated by many with Western traditions – makes their difference easier to handle and their acceptable social and cultural space larger. It is assumed that this group is capable of abiding by Western social and cultural rules seen as necessary for coping in a modern urban environment. In fact, Rastafarians seem to young people to represent a certain myth of modern sojourners; nomads whose cultural and social home moves with them, regardless of their outward circumstances. Their position symbolises a certain freedom and flexibility. In addition, Rastafarians are closely connected with youth culture – particularly regarding the styles associated with reggae culture – which makes their difference less important in the minds of those interviewed. Thus, in a way the Rastafarians fall into the category of harmless fellows as well.

In contrast, the African tribal drummers, more often connected with rural milieus, are seen as non-western and thus believed to have difficulties in adapting to urban or European milieus. According to interviewees' accounts, two conditions have to be met, at least symbolically, before these people can be recognised as powerful social actors: first, they have to find their way from the traditional world to the modern world, and secondly, they must abandon rural life in order to be able to live in the city (Lapeyronnie 1996).

> Well, those Rasta guys, in principle that culture was born in the cities. ...These guys have their own touch. They have what we call exoticism; they look like different (boy, 18 years).

> These guys (Rastafarians) are certainly from USA or from Canada... they are like blacks from industrial countries and the others (drummers) are blacks from developing countries. – These guys (Rastafarians) have certainly found it easier to come (to Finland) from the point of view of attitudes. – Their cultural difference is certainly smaller (girl, 18 years).

> Those (the drummers) don't have a kind of frightening image – they are certainly the persons who have to experience the heaviest insults and the like.

178

They don't look as frightening and that's why people are brave enough to go and say whatever straight to their faces (boy, 18 years).

Thus, diverse background elements can be regarded as a resource or as a handicap depending on what kind of geographical, social or cultural heritage one is dealing with. Or both aspects can be connected with the same group, as demonstrated by the case of the Rastafarians: they can be considered as both good and bad immigrants, representing some elements of all four of the above categories. In other words, there is no standard social or cultural space and position reserved for any given group of immigrants. Whether they are regarded as more or less powerful social actors and more or less acceptable cultural actors depends on the particular group being examined and the particular conditions with which this group is identified.

Integration – The Interplay Between Inclusion and Exclusion

In the previous section the focus was on how immigrants are perceived as social actors in Finnish society. As has been highlighted, the real position of any given immigrant is often socially and culturally reformulated through the process of representation. When examining the empirical data it seems evident that a black-and-white view of a social actor as either included in Finnish society or excluded from it is a gross simplification of the multifaceted perceptions of immigrants. As these young people's accounts show, immigrants may be considered to be both inside the society and at its margins; inside the political or at least the geographic frontiers, but often beyond the symbolic, cultural boundaries.

As has been pointed out earlier, these data were collected during an interesting period in Finland's history. The lively official debate about immigrants' social and political space is rather novel. Regardless of the rather recent presence of immigrants in the Finnish politico-cultural milieu, or perhaps due to it, the discussion of immigrants' lives in Finland is a useful framework for considering the political and cultural dynamics of the country. Immigrants can be taken as a central symbol facilitating a certain Finnish self-understanding and giving a form to its future trajectory. They can help to emphasise cultural reform moving towards a more modern, cosmopolitan self-image on the one hand, or the maintenance of the traditional order with a more conformist image on the other. Finland has woken up to the discrepancy between the country's political and symbolic landscape, based until recently on the idea of the public homogeneity, and the concrete conditions of European migration and cross-cultural encounters – a development which Finland is no longer able to ignore. Consequently, the question to be asked is not only how immigrants will be able to get by in this new environment, but especially how strong are Finland's and the Finns' political and cultural reception skills?

The question is centrally embedded in the tension between the concepts of participation and that of integration of immigrants. The interviews referred to here reflect the idea of integration as a functional matter. It is an exchange, whereby immigrants can become entitled to a particular status, with civic rights and responsibilities, after having been in a new country for at least a certain period of time.[11] They can, at least in principle, have access to the social and civic dimensions of societal participation. By way of payment for this, immigrants are indirectly required to keep their cultural traditions mostly in the private sphere – or to present them within controlled contexts. Furthermore, they are asked to show a certain willingness to act according to existing rules and agreements in their new country, in both cultural and judicial terms.

This kind of idea of integration resembles the process of socialisation, which here refers to the technical process of learning the principles of social life and some minimum cultural norms. An immigrant is seen in this context as a special kind of pupil (Lapeyronnie 1996, 256). This image is often linked with the discussions to tame victims, who are assumed to be keen on learning how to live in Finland, or to harmless fellows, who have already been socialised into the Finnish social and cultural landscape. Rather paradoxically, the young people still regret that the Finnish cultural outlook is so "grey and uninteresting": they believe that "it is only a matter of time before we will be able to see true cultural variety in our daily lives", and wonder if "Finnish culture could be and could always have been a mixture of different influences or pressures from the West and the East, so that there is no such thing as Finnish culture". These examples manifest a tension between the need for a reformulation of Finland's rather homogenous cultural milieu and a subjective uncertainty when real or imagined societal changes are confronted.

This tension can be analysed from another point of view. Despite the emphasis on the technical side of integration, the respondents' accounts reflect an idea presented by Alain Touraine, among others, that integration cannot be seen solely as an objective contribution to the production of society. It also entails an awareness of belonging to a common social, political and cultural milieu (Touraine 1992). Thus, it is difficult to reduce the idea of integration to the idea of functional co-existence or to the silent assimilation of immigrants (Rea 1995). Integration always means participation in a particular social and cultural environment as well. As such, it implies an identity investment, an idea of the participant who is at the same time political and personal, civic and cultural (Schnapper 1998; Touraine 1997).

This tension is often handled by a certain discursive turn. In the interviews, the emphasis is often put on the idea of immigrants who cannot or do not want to integrate into society, rather than on those who do not have access to societal action, who are excluded from it (Martiniello 1993, 128-131). Here the focus is especially on "problematic immigrants": on demanding strangers and/or threatening bystanders. This is not to say that the young people's accounts of integration would correspond with the idea of a cultural and social melting pot. Rather, it refers to functional, formal integration. However, there is no clear idea of how integration should be applied in practice, as the following discussion shows:

1. I think it's terrible for someone to have to become Finnish. If you come from another country and you ought to...
2. I think that they can adopt some Finnish characteristics, whatever they want, but they can't undergo a total metamorphosis, and I think it's a good thing that that's impossible.
3. Not like in the United States where this adaptation...
2. That's not real adaptation. They've got huge conflicts there; different areas for different people and so on.
3. I think it's very wrong to attack other people, but everybody has to live within the limits of law. In a way it's like when you're in Finland, do as the Finns do. But it's true that if I had to move to some other country I would still try to hang onto something unique... I wouldn't want to just blend into the crowd.
1. I don't think it's easy to immigrate to Finland, because like the Finns... start pointing you out and...
2. ... labelling you.
1. Yeah, in a way.
2. I think the problem is that we don't show them what our own cultural values are, really, in the sense of teaching them step by step... or in a sense we undervalue our own traditions. Then we see these folk and think that, well that

guy comes from abroad, so he doesn't do things the way everybody else does
(1: girl, 18 years; 2: boy, 18 years; 3: boy, 19 years).

It is crucial to distinguish between the different levels of argument used in this context: first, on an individual level, where the emphasis is particularly on immigrants' individual capacities and willingness to be part of Finnish society. Second, at a more structural, collective level where one also deals with the political implications and societal disposition of the receiving country, whether seen as a capacity or as a willingness to absorb other cultures. This relates to the question of responsibility as well: when the issue is described as an individual matter, it is easy to treat possible problems and failures as individual responsibilities, resulting from wrong individual choices or individual faults. In contrast, when emphasis is put on structural elements of cross-cultural encounters, the ultimate responsibility for immigrants' living conditions is more collective by nature.

Reflections – A Functional Hierarchy of Difference

As this article has shown, categories can have symbolic, instrumental and political functions. The categorisation of immigrants can be seen as an interpretative process in the course of which a social and conceptual significance is attached to immigrants. Consequently, it gives a framework for reflecting upon oneself as well. Benedict Anderson's (1991) rather frequently used concept of an "imagined community" relates in an interesting way to the hierarchy of difference described here. According to Anderson, the imagined community is normally supposed to have distinct boundaries (whether political, cultural or symbolic) which give it a certain sense of coherence regardless of possible internal heterogeneity. To imagine often rather various or distant groups of immigrants as distinctive communities is a way to capture diversity and render it more intelligible. The characteristics of a particular historical group are seen as a more or less unchangeable destiny. In this kind of reasoning, culture is defined as a heritage which helps or hinders immigrants in a new environment, rather than as an ongoing process which is constantly changing in response to the environment (Wetherell and Potter 1992, 129).

In terms of the conceptual scheme with which we began, it seems that the young people often attempt to move immigrants from categories on the left side of the horizontal axis to those on the right, that is, towards a familiar and controllable sphere (see p. 168, Figure 13.1). The aim seems to be that an immigrant should be detached from those features, whether real or imaginary, which are incomprehensible and threatening. This is done, for example, by focusing on the well-known features of immigrants as the Rastafarian case demonstrates: they are interpreted within the conceptual framework of youth culture and thus moved towards the familiar category of harmless fellows. Their strangeness is something to be appreciated rather than feared. In this way, their difference is construed as intelligible and more or less familiar and thus Rastafarians' specificity is understood. Then they fall more easily into a decent category, or into a welcome group in Finland.

This example shows that the categories also function as tools that help the young people to attach a meaning to the immigrants who otherwise threaten to remain unintelligible. In the interviewees' representations of African drummers both the aspects of intelligibility in a conceptual sense and control in a societal sense are present. In order to make sense of the drummers, they are conceptualised as black and non-western, and often regarded as refugees who fall for the most part into the category of a tame victim. They can also be seen as harmless fellows in a societal sense, provided that they stay within the familiar social space outlined for them: as ethnic-musicians, as restaurant owners, as asylum seekers.[12] In some cases, however, the level of conceptual intelligibility and that of social control do not overlap. Let me illustrate this with the same group of African drummers: if they escape from the suitable social space in the public sphere, they may be considered socially uncontrollable. However, in conceptual terms it can be argued that familiar myths of dark-skinned foreign criminals, welfare abusers and violent suburban gangs beyond social control make them intelligible. These labels are a part of a popular folklore which is easy to grasp.

In conclusion, the representations of immigrants cannot be analysed solely as the personal concepts of the interviewed young people. They are constructed in a dialogue with the overall environment, with its cultural, normative and rhetorical dimensions. Thus, every category analysed here has a specific relation to collective discourses on immigrants found in the various fields of Finnish society. To give some examples in closing: the category of the tame victim can be found in certain immigration policy texts where immigrants are often treated as objects for political action, people to be integrated into Finnish society. One of the aims seems to be to transform tame victims into harmless fellows. This is done with the help of institutional measures ranging from welfare policy to educational arrangements and other policy steps. The demanding stranger and the threatening bystander are frequently portrayed in the Finnish media. More recently, the prominence of these categories has been challenged by more nuanced accounts of immigrants. The interviewed young people's relationship to the information spread by the media, and often reproduced by everyday folklore, seems to be somewhat ambivalent, the same person's accounts containing both a sharp criticism of the media along with a certain maintenance of media discourses. When the topic of discussion is something which cannot be explored without revealing rather sensitive sides of oneself as a human being – his/her values, attitudes, feelings and fears – a certain ambivalence among the respondents is not surprising. It is rather inevitable.

Notes

[1.] The interviewed young people (19 boys and 20 girls) live in three districts of Helsinki, chosen because of their social and cultural structure as well as their geographical locations. In all of these districts the number of foreign inhabitants is proportionally higher than in Helsinki on average. The interviewees are all secondary school students with variable family backgrounds ranging from academic to more working class. Neither socio-economic nor socio-cultural background was used as a strict criterion when the empirical data was collected.

[2.] Even if the individual level is emphasised here, accounts cannot be regarded solely as personal stories, as purely individual attitudes or descriptions. Rather, they should be seen as an element of multidimensional knowledge which combines both daily experiences and influences with more general, collectively shared conceptions of social reality (Essed 1991, 54-65). A few words will suffice concerning the relation between accounts and representations: when talking about representations the specific process of understanding and of forming interpretations of social reality is emphasised, whereas account refers here rather to the description and evaluation of this reality. To put it more concretely: a process of representation forms social images of immigrants, which are then expressed in accounts (Bonneau 1994; Hall 1997; Moliner 1996).

[3.] The interviewed young people often use the concept of "foreigner" when talking about immigrants or people whom they do not consider as being a part of "Finnish people" or "Finland" – regardless of what this "Finnishness" more concretely means. This ambiguous term has also been used as a general concept in the Finnish public debate before the question of immigration became a politically acute issue in the 1990s. Today, more exact concepts, such as immigrant, refugee, asylum seeker, ethnic minority, population with migrant origin, have been increasingly used in the official discussion. The etymology of the Finnish word of "foreigner", "*ulkomaalainen*", gives a framework of its common use. The term means literally a person who is, or who belongs, outside the country; and as such, it can be compared with a German equivalent term "Ausländer" (see Räthzel 1994, 84).

4. These categories as well as the very hierarchy of difference must be understood as generalisations and stereotypes: the use of alternative concepts of immigrants allows the young people to examine and discuss the issue from several perspectives (Thomas 1993).

5. This image is not a recent construction; it can already be found, for example, in Alfred Schütz's (1976) definition of a stranger: the stranger is uprooted from his/her social, cultural and geographical home, from his/her origins, and he/she is an invalid in creating a new life in a new socio-cultural milieu.

6. During the 1990s, Finland has received a proportionally large number of Somalian people; most of whom are rather young (under 30 years old) and living in the area of Helsinki (Hautaniemi 1997, 18-19).

7. Somalian municipal officials were elected to the Helsinki city council for the first time in the 1996 municipal elections. In the 1999 Euro parliamentary elections Finnish candidates included Somalian representatives.

8. Ingria is the name given to the area in Russia surrounding what is now St. Petersburg. Before this major city was built at the mouth of the Baltic Sea the area was inhabited by people of close ethnic relation to Finns. Together with the "ethnic Finns" living in Russian Karelia, these people are legally entitled to "return" to Finland. This portion of Finland's immigration laws shares many features (and problems) with Germany's policy of receiving "ethnic Germans" back from Eastern Europe.

9. In order to get a complete picture of the informants' representations of immigrants I have used a method by which verbal discussion is partly combined with the interviewees' responses to photographic images of different foreign groups, presented by a researcher. In this article, four of the six photos utilised in the interviews are discussed: Sami people, African drummers, a Rastafarian group and two Roma women with their children. This method has been discussed and evaluated elsewhere (Suurpää 1999).

10. The ambivalent status of the Roma people is not a Finnish phenomenon; in fact, the social position of Finnish Romas is considered quite good in comparison with many European countries.

11. In Finland a person is eligible for Finnish citizenship after being a resident of the country for five years.

12. Ethnicised roles and contested participation are not however stable or inevitable. This year, on International Women's Day, one Somali woman was publicly rewarded for her work as a midwife in Finland.

References

Act (493/1999), on the Integration of Immigrants and Reception of Asylum Seekers.

Ålund, A. (1997), 'The Quest for Identity: Modern Strangers and New/Old Ethnicities in Europe', in H.-R. Wicker (ed.), *Rethinking Nationalism and Ethnicity: The Struggle for Meaning and Order in Europe*, Berg, Oxford, New York, pp. 91-109.

Anderson, B. (1991), *Imagined Communities: Reflections on the Origin and Spread of Nationalism*, 2nd Edition, Verso, London.

Bonneau, M. (1994), 'Jeux et enjeux identitaires autour des représentations de la région', in K. Fall, D. Simeoni and G. Vignaux (eds.), *Mots, représentations: Enjeux dans les contacts interethniques et interculturels*, Les Presses de l'Université, Ottawa, pp. 323-339.

Cahen, M. (1994), *Ethnicité politique: pour une lecture réaliste de l'identité*, L'Harmattan, Paris.

D'hondt, S., Blommaert, J. and Verschueren, J. (1995), 'Constructing Ethnicity in Discourse: A View from Below', in M. Martiniello (ed.), *Migration, Citizenship and Ethno-National Identities in the European Union: Research in Ethnic Relations Series*, Avebury, Aldershot, pp. 105-119.

Dieckhoff, A. (1996), 'La deconstruction d'une illusion: L'introucable opposition entre nationalisme politique et nationalisme culturel', *Année Sociologique Vol. 46, No. 1*, pp. 43-55.

Essed, P. (1991), *Understanding Everyday Racism: An Interdisciplinary Theory*, Sage Publications, London.

Gianni, M. (1997), 'Multiculturalism and Political Integration: The Need for a Differentiated Citizenship?', in H.-R. Wicker (ed.), *Rethinking Nationalism and Ethnicity: The Struggle for Meaning and Order in Europe*, Berg, Oxford, New York, pp. 127-142.

Gilroy, P. (1987), *There Ain't No Black in the Union Jack*, Hutchinson, London.

Hall, S. (1997), 'The Work of Representation', in S. Hall (ed.), *Representation: Cultural Representation and Signifying Practices*, Sage Publications, London, Thousand Oaks, New Delhi.

Halonen, T. (1997), 'Suomen ulkopolitiikka ja ulkomaalaiskysymys' (Finnish Foreign Policy and the Debate of Foreigners), in *Muukalaiset: Juridiikasta ja asenteista kansojen kohdatessa* (Aliens: Jurisprudence and Attitudes in the Era of National Encounters), Edita, Helsinki, pp. 92-99.

Hautaniemi, P. (1997), 'Pääkaupunkiseurun nuorten somalialaispoikien aikuistuminen kahden kulttuurin välissä' (Somali Adolescents in the Helsinki Area: Growing Up between Two Cultures), *Nuorisotutkimus Vol. 15, No. 4* (The Finnish Journal of Youth Research), pp. 16-24.

Hewitt, R. (1996), 'Us and Them in the Late Space Age', *Young – Nordic Journal of Youth Research Vol. 3, No. 2*, pp. 23-33.

Hjerm, M. (1998), 'National Identities, National Pride and Xenophobia: A Comparison of Four Western Countries', *Acta Sociologica Vol. 41, No. 4*, pp. 335-347.

Huttunen, L. (1997), 'Romanit suomalaisina ja vähemmistöidentiteettinsä rakentajina' (Gypsies as Finnish Citizens and Builders of a Minority Identity), *Nuorisotutkimus*

Vol. 15, No. 4 (The Finnish Journal of Youth Research), pp. 4-15.

Koskenniemi, M. (1997), 'Muukalaisuus ja kansainvälinen järjestelmä' (Strangeness and an International Structure), in *Muukalaiset: Juridiikasta ja asenteista kansojen kohdatessa* (Aliens: Jurisprudence and Attitudes in the Era of National Encounters), Edita, Helsinki, pp. 99-198.

Laclau, E. and Zac, L. (1994), 'Minding the Map: The Subject of Politics', in E. Laclau (ed.), *The Making of Political Identities*, Verso, London, New York.

Lapeyronnie, D. (1996), 'Les deux figures de l'immigré', in M. Wieviorka (ed.), *Une société fragmentée? Le multiculturalisme en debat*, Editions La Découverte, Paris, pp. 251-266.

Martiniello, M. (1993), 'Dynamique et pluralisme culturels dans l'ensemble bruxellois', in R. Gallissot (ed.), *Pluralisme culturel en Europe: Culture(s) européeenne(s) et culture(s) des diasporas*, Editions L'Harmattan, Paris, pp. 121-143.

Martucelli, D. (1994), 'L'expérience italienne', in M. Wieviorka (ed.), *Racisme et xénophobie en Europe: Une comparaison internationale*, Editions La Découverte, Paris, pp. 215-283.

Miles, R. (1989), *Racism*, Open University Press, London and New York.

Moliner, P. (1996), *Images et représentations sociales: De la théorie des représentations à l'étude des images sociales*, Presses Universitaires de Grenoble, Grenoble.

Räthzel, N. (1994), 'Harmonious "Heimat" and Disturbing "Ausländer"', in K. K. Bhavnani and A. Phoenix (eds.), *Shifting Identities, Shifting Racisms*, Sage Publications, London, New Delhi, pp. 81-98.

Rea, A. (1995), 'Social Citizenship and Ethnic Minorities in the European Union', in M. Martinello (ed.), *Migration, Citizenship and Ethno-National Identities in the European Union: Research in Ethnic Relations Series*, Avebury, Aldershot, pp. 179-198.

Schnapper, D. (1998), *La relation à l'autre: Au cœur de la pensée sociologique*, Gallimard, Paris.

Schütz, A. (1976), 'The Stranger: An Essay in Social Psychology', in A. Brodensen (ed.), *Collected Papers II*, Martinus Nijhoff, The Hague, pp. 91-106.

Sisäasiainministeriö (1997), *Hallittu maahanmuutto ja tehokas kotouttaminen: Ehdotus hallituksen maahanmuutto- ja pakolaispoliittiseksi ohjelmaksi: Maahanmuutto- ja pakolaispoliittisen toimikunnan mietintö* (Controlled Migration and Efficient Integration: A Proposal for a Governmental Programme for Migration and Refugee Policy: A Report of a Committee for Migration and Refugee Policy), Sisäasiainministeriön julkaisu (The Ministry of Interior), Helsinki.

Solomos, J. and Back, L. (1996), *Racism and Society*, Macmillan Press, London.

Suurpää, L. (1998), *Politics of Difference and Finnish Young People*, An unpublished paper presented in the 'Nordic Youth Research Symposium', Reykjavik, Iceland, 5.6.1998.

Suurpää, L. (1999), 'Kulttuurinen katse ulkomaalaisiin: kuvia, kertomuksia, käsityksiä' (A Cultural View to Foreigners: Images, Narrations, Conceptions), in P. Houni and P. Paavolainen (eds.), *Taide, kertomus, identiteetti* (Art, Narration, Identity), Acta Scenica, Helsinki, pp. 70-99.

Tabboni, S. (1996), 'Le multiculturalisme et l'ambivalence de l'étranger', in M. Wieviorka (ed.), *Une société fragmentée? Le multiculturalisme en debat*, Editions La Découverte,

Paris, pp. 227-250.

Thomas, J. (1993), *Doing Critical Ethnography*, Qualitative Research Methods Series 26, Sage Publications, Newbury Park, London, New Delhi.

Touraine, A. (1992), *Critique de la modernité*, Fayard, Paris.

Touraine, A. (1997), *Pourrons-nous vivre ensemble? Egaux et différents*, Fayard, Paris.

Wetherell, M. and Potter, J. (1992), *Mapping the Language of Racism: Discourse and the Legitimation of Exploitation*, Harvester Wheatsheaf, New York, London.

PART 5

CITIZENSHIP, VALUES AND ATTITUDES

14 Critical Discussion: Modern or Postmodern Youth?

GILL JONES

We always expect that new generations will challenge the values and beliefs that they find and will seek to develop their own ways, unconstrained by what has gone before. Indeed, the social world depends on the emergence of new ideas from new generations as one of the forces for social change (Mannheim 1927). At the same time, however, the established adult society can easily hold a fear, usually an irrational fear, of the younger generation. Thus we have the notion of "generation conflict" as the differences between the values of the young and those of older people are exposed through research and highlighted in the media (e.g. Wilkinson and Mulgan 1995). The values of the younger generation may change and become more normative as they get older, and are thus likely in their turn to be challenged by an even newer generation. The danger is that each cohort of young people, the younger generation, will be seen as a unitary, homogeneous group, where in practice they have been unified and homogenised by political commentators, the media and even researchers into constructed "phenomena". We find this in references to "Generation X", or the "lost generation". Where Mannheim referred to generations as consisting of "generation-units" of people who shared a socio-temporal location, it sometimes seems that we have lost the ability to differentiate young people by social class, gender or ethnicity.

Over the last few years, the UK has seen increasing concerns with the breakdown of normative moral values, and a new emphasis on the need to rediscover the values associated with "citizenship". In the UK, the career of the concept of citizenship has closely followed the fortunes of the welfare state (Jones and Wallace 1992). In the post-war era, with a universalist welfare state, citizenship was unconditionally available to all;

191

following the impact of recession, unemployment and increased dependency, the Thatcher welfare reforms resulted arguably in a distinction between the deserving and undeserving, as welfare was increasingly targeted; the arrival of "Third Way" politics under Blair, has continued Thatcher reforms under the mantle of "social justice". Citizenship is now perceived in the UK as a package of rights and responsibilities, in which the two are balanced. Welfare citizenship is conditional upon some normative definition of "good behaviour". On the basis that it is "feckless" and socially irresponsible to draw on the welfare state without contributing to it, good citizens are rewarded, while bad citizens are not. This simple attempt at social control represents an apparent return to the days of the deserving and undeserving poor, and is clearly identifiable in government policies for young people in the UK today: increasingly, access to state benefits is becoming conditional on promises of good behaviour, as shown in the UK equivalent of US "workfare" policies, and young people are having to show their willingness to contract into the welfare state. It is, however, difficult for young people to prove themselves as good citizens, since they may not have had the chance to pay taxes, vote, or visibly serve their communities.

Attention has thus turned to the values and attitudes of young people amid establishment concerns that the UK is in need of a re-assertion of normative moral values. Concerns that young people are being "irresponsible" and need to be brought into line as citizens thus not only fit within the requirements of a trimmed new welfare state, but also reflect concerns that moral values are breaking down. We have a new focus in the UK on "citizenship education" in schools. Based perhaps on an assumption that young people will not contribute to society unless either they have to or that they are socialised into doing so, and based also on an assumption that citizenship education can no longer be provided by parents, formal education in being a good citizen is now provided in secondary schools. There have been a number of government initiatives developing the notion of "citizenship education", focusing on social and moral responsibility, community involvement and political literacy (Jones and Bell 2000). The UK Education Secretary David Blunkett described the aims of education thus:

> We want a literate, numerate, but also civilised society in which actively contributing to the well-being of others is seen as a natural part of a strong and caring community (DfEE press release 104/99).

192

In the UK then, the values and attitudes of young people are a cause for concern, and the concepts of community participation and belonging have come to the fore. This is particularly seen in a context where there is also concern over the ability of a parent generation prone to marital breakdown to provide adequate socialisation in the home, and where the kind of secondary socialisation in schools was also apparently in need of reform, leaving young people "at the mercy" of socialisation by their peers. Fears about generation conflict during the 1960s and 1970s were eventually laid to rest by research which indicated that youth cultures were largely a reflection of parent cultures rather than oppositional. It is ironic that now, in an era when youth cultures are largely a construction of the consumer markets, we have renewed fears that moral values have been lost. Lacking a firm framework of family life in a society where marital breakdown continues to increase, politicians seek solace in the concept of community. The rhetoric stressing the need for a return to "traditional family values" is being replaced under New Labour by a new emphasis on "community values", whatever they may be.

To what extent do the values and attitudes of young people reflect their own generation, or the values and attitudes of a cultural grouping within the wider society? Or are they the response to global influences of labour and consumer markets? Theories of reflexive modernisation (e.g. Giddens 1991) suggest that there may be a greater interplay between structure and agency than ever before.

In this section we turn to the values and attitudes held by young people in present day Europe. Contributors from the Ukraine and Finland describe their recent research. All three chapters address the questions of whether young people constitute a distinct social grouping, and explore the extent to which they vary both within their own age cohort and with other age groups. First Helve examines whether as a result of wider socio-economic trends, there has been a universal shift in values among young people in Finland towards a "post-materialist" culture. The hypothesis is further tested by Karvonen and Rahkonen, who reflect further (also from a Finnish perspective) on the nature and source of new value orientations. Finally, Svynarenko draws on his research in post-soviet Ukraine to explore the differential impact of political and social transformations on self-identity and whether there are generational differences in concepts of citizenship and belonging.

Helve examines values from the perspective of reflexive modernity.

193

She tests Inglehart's (1997; 1998) hypothesis that economic, cultural and political change are changing people's world views away from a concern with basic needs (associated with recession) to "post-materialistic" values (associated with greater affluence). In other words, with greater affluence and a higher standard of living, people can afford to be more altruistic. This interpretation implies both homogeneity and linearity, the latter in contrast to the central precept of reflexivity in theories of reflexive modernisation, and Helve's analysis concludes with a rejection of Inglehart's hypothesis.

Helve seeks to explore the sources of young people's world views, in particular the ways in which there may be variation according to their education, gender and family beliefs. This raises the question of whether young people's beliefs arise spontaneously out of the generation itself, or are the result of socialisation. Her study finds that satisfaction with life is mainly associated with economic and political security, that political and community participation is associated with higher educational level, and that a hardening of attitudes to disadvantaged groups appears to be associated with the personal impact of recession. She identifies and describes a typology, indicating variation in values among the young. Thus: "Humanist – Egalitarian", is closely associated with feminism, and contrasts with "Traditionalist – Conservative", which is more associated with rural young people and males. In another continuum, she finds "Environmentalist – Green", mainly among females in upper secondary schools, and contrasting with an emphasis on technological and economic values, which is mainly held by males. "Cynics – Passives" are mainly urban females in vocational schools. The last category is "Internationalist – Globalist", which contrasts with those holding racist views, who are mainly males in vocational schools. Young people's values appear then to be differentiated according to gender, educational level, and spatial location. Helve also finds that they are situational, in other words that in different circumstances young people may choose to identify with different values and ideologies, thus holding and managing multiple value identifications. Alongside this finding, which supports the postmodernist approach, the main findings suggest that it is not by chance or entirely by choice that young people have particular value systems, and that the effects of wider social, political and economic trends on young people's values vary according to individual circumstances. In other words, young people's reflexive ability varies according to their position in society.

194

Helve's argument that post-materialist views are held by Humanists, Environmentalists and Internationalists suggests to me that post-materialism is the domain of the educated middle class. Poorer working class young people are less altruistic, but perhaps this is because they can recognise their own needs and may need to pay priority to meeting these. So does economic scarcity cause an increase in materialistic values, or is it rather that the disadvantaged lack the resources to be "post-materialistic" – but would be if they could? If the latter, then the way to increase levels of altruism in a society would be to improve the economic situation of the disadvantaged within that society. The lesson for the UK, or any other, government seeking to encourage citizenship values would therefore be to tackle poverty. How far, though, do disadvantaged groups develop and perpetuate cultures of self-survival, or altruism only towards others belonging to the same group?

Karvonen and Rahkonen pick up these themes. They point out that Inglehart was arguing that greater affluence produced changes in attitude, and quote Giddens' (1991) proposition that the emancipatory politics of high modernity were being replaced by "politics of self-actualisation" in which the individual biography becomes the principal agenda. Their own study, which explores the relationship between the value orientations of fifteen-year-olds, and their lifestyles, social class and gender, contrasts somewhat with that of Helve. They find that many values were shared within the age group, rather than varying by social class, gender and "lifestyle", but there was strong support for the work ethic, patriotism, and other mainstream values, indicating inter-generational continuity rather than inter-generational change and conflict. This, as they suggest, is not necessarily a "good thing", if societies depend on younger generations for innovation and renewal. Indeed Karvonen and Rahkonen describe this as "value stagnation". The study thus only partly supports the findings of Helve, and the emphasis is perhaps more on intra-generational similarity than on intra-generational difference.

Age thus clearly affected values. However, gender and social class were also seen to affect attitudes towards traditional gender roles and towards "societal cynicism". Far from identifying the younger generation as homogeneous, Karvonen and Rahkonen identify young working class males as more likely to hold values which are both more gendered and more disaffected. Among a small minority of working class males, they find a rejection of the normative values of gender equality and greater liberalism found in Finland. Gender differences surface in attitudes to work and leisure, too. These findings indicate resonances of the defiant hegemonic masculinity described by Mac an Ghaill (1994). The findings of Willis (1977), as indicated in the chapter, are still relevant to understanding the values of some working class males, even though, or especially because, the opportunities for asserting their masculinity in the ways described by Willis no longer exist (with the demise of manufacturing and loss of jobs in the youth labour market). As other observers have indicated (e.g. Connell 1987), what has happened has been a defensive re-assertion of traditional masculinity in a new caricature, typified by intolerance to challenges to hegemonic masculinity (from feminism and homosexuality) and difference, and providing fodder for right-wing sexist and racist groups. This current form of anti-school peer culture (Willis 1977) is associated with drinking and aggression (Canaan 1996), perhaps even an underclass culture (Macdonald 1997). The implication is that while young people's values may be changing overall, they may also be becoming more polarised (as is the case with wealth).

How far are values and attitudes the consequence of structural constraint or choice? Do young people have equality of opportunity to choose lifestyles and values? A great deal must depend on their educational level and attainment. In my view, "lifestyle", like attitudes, is likely to be structured by social class and/or education, and thus does not lend itself to treatment as an independent variable. Social class (if not gender) still affects access to higher education, and may thus still structure value options. Karvonen and Rahkonen's conclusion is that there is little evidence to support Giddens' (1991) hypothesis that there has been a shift away from more altruistic emancipatory politics towards life-politics with a greater focus on self. Though standards of living may be higher, they are not universally higher, and we find a polarisation of wealth even within the younger generation in the UK, for example (Jones and Martin 1999). This means that some young people have even less access than previously to the new frameworks for opportunity and choice. Nevertheless, the prevailing rhetoric about choice seems to blind postmodernist thinkers to the fact the that mechanisms of social reproduction still operate. In a "real" world of poverty and social exclusion, is not surprising if the poor retain a preoccupation with their own basic needs, and if those living in inner city estates do not participate in community activities, and if the disaffected do not vote. The chapter shows that in terms of their values, as in terms of their positions in the social structure, young people do vary, and that we can only speak of generational values in a limited way.

With the chapter by Svynarenko, the context moves to Ukraine, which has experienced dramatic recent social, political and economic shifts. Here we can test the hypothesis that individual values change with overall social, economic and political change (i.e. are structurally produced). The chapter is about constructions of national and ethnic identity.

"Communities" are essentially relational (as Cohen 1985 indicates), sources of both *inclusion* and *exclusion*, with spatial, social and symbolic boundaries. One of the main internal sources of division is "ethnicity" with distinction between locals and incomers (Crow and Allan 1994). This insider/outsider distinction associated with belonging to a society or being on the margins of it, can also be applied respectively to the older and younger generations (the latter being outsiders to the adult society). In practice, someone describing herself as a citizen or belonging to a particular social group may not be seen by others as such. This was apparent from a recent qualitative study of young people's perceptions of belonging to a rural community in Scotland (Jones 1999). According to Jenkins (1996, 20), social identity is the result of "the internal-external dialectic of identification", and thus at the heart of the relationship between agency and structure. However, following Giddens' terminology, how reflexive can a person's identity be without coming under threat?

In this chapter identity is defined (like other levels of socio-spatial identity) by identification of insiders in relation to outsiders, through the drawing of boundaries. Far from being a fixed state, national identity can change in relation to societal and political change as the boundaries of belonging get drawn and re-drawn. In the case of Ukraine, change was rapid and fundamental, and, as the study indicates, its effect on national/ethnic identity significant. Svynarenko explores the concept of "citizenship" – ranging from the local to the global (e.g. "Citizen of Ukraine", "Citizen of the World", etc.) on the basis of *self-identification*. This is, in a sense only half the picture.

Svynarenko finds that self-identity is defined by negative reference to others, so that young people were clearer about who they were not, than about who they were. They had, however, drawn the boundaries more narrowly around themselves. Thus, there was a strong reaction against identification with the Soviet system, the USSR or Russia in all age groups, and identification as a "Citizen of Europe or of the World" was

197

also weak. In all age groups, it was the feeling of ethnic identity that was strongest, though Ukrainian identity appeared stronger among the older age groups. Svynarenko suggests, then that young people were less likely to hold mainstream values of patriotism than older people, and he reasonably questions whether this represents a generation difference or simply an age difference. He comments that inter-generational transmission of culture and ideas may be indirect, and that a cohort effect may be more immediate and significant. The study did not differentiate between young people, only between them and other age cohorts, so we cannot tell whether their ideas were widely held within their own generation, or varying by social group. The study suggests that people who had been subject to imperialism in which ethnicity was repressed reacted to the collapse of the Soviet imperialist structure by focusing on the local and constructing a safer local identity. The need to do this may have suppressed internal differences within the age cohort.

These studies are interesting, but leave many questions unanswered. The structure versus agency question is not an either/or, and the interest to social scientists lies in identifying *change* and *continuity* in the structures of inequality, and in the different ways in which structure and agency interact, according to context (time and space). Young people's lives are heavily structured by the expectations of governments, parents and even peers, opportunities for individual choice may be different. Pre-materialism could be mistaken for post-materialism if the inequalities and differences between and within societies are not taken into account.

Karvonen and Rahkonen quote Furlong and Cartmel (1997, 5), who refer to a prevailing postmodernist "epistemological fallacy", an illusion of greater equality and individualisation. In practice, structures of solidarity are continuing to affect young people's lives. Risk, like wealth, may be more prevalent, but this does not mean that it is equally shared. Trends can be countervailing and appear contradictory. Bauman (1995) has indicated that alongside the trend towards globalisation, there is an increasing focus on the local, and he refers to this as "glocalisation". Giddens (1994) similarly comments on the ways in which in an age of high modernity people increasingly draw reference from, and if necessary construct, "tradition". These countervailing trends are reflected in the findings in the following chapters, where return to hegemonic masculinity and ethnic identification can be seen on the one hand, and more modern (post-materialist?) value orientations of egalitarianism, environmentalism and internationalism on the other. Seemingly contradictory trends can thus co-exist and even be mutually dependent. Value shifts among the mass may be accompanied by a move towards extremism at both ends. The difficulty may be to see the continuities of social reproduction when a parallel tendency may be more visible and more amenable to study. Faced with a real ambivalence, there may be a gravitational pull on those sitting on the fence to come down on one side or the other. Ultimately, the interpretation depends on the researcher's own values.

I am not a postmodernist. In my own research on young people in the UK, I see that whatever globalising influences are at work, the structures of patriarchy, capitalism and imperialism are still visibly structuring the life chances of young people. Their values, attitudes and identities vary at least in part as a response to these continuities.

References

Bauman, Z. (1995), *Life in Fragments: Essays in Postmodern Morality*, Blackwell Publishers, Oxford.

Canaan, J. E. (1996), 'One Thing Leads to Another: Drinking, Fighting and Working Class Masculinities', in M. Mac an Ghaill (ed.), *Understanding Masculinities: Social Relations and Cultural Arenas*, Open University Press, Buckingham.

Cohen, A. (1985), *The Symbolic Construction of Community*, Tavistock, London.

Connell, R. W. (1987), *Gender and Power*, Polity Press, Cambridge.

Crow, G. and Allan, G. (1994), *Community Life: An Introduction to Community Relations*, Harvester Wheatsheaf, London.

Furlong, A. and Cartmel, F. (1997), *Young People and Social Change: Individualization and Risk in Late Modernity*, Open University Press, Guildford and King's Lynn.

Giddens, A. (1991), *Modernity and Self-Identity: Self and Society in the Late Modern Age*, Polity Press, Cambridge.

Giddens, A. (1994), 'Living in a Post-Traditional Society', in U. Beck, A. Giddens and S. Lash (eds.), *Reflexive Modernization: Politics, Tradition and Aesthetics in the Modern Social Order*, Polity Press, Cambridge, pp. 56-109.

Inglehart, R. (1997), *Modernization and Postmodernization: Cultural, Economic and Political Change in 43 Societies*, Princeton University Press, Princeton, New Jersey.

Inglehart, R. (1998), *Clash of Civilizations or Global Cultural Modernization? Empirical Evidence from 61 Societies*, Unpublished paper presented at the 1998 meeting of the International Sociological Association, Montreal, August 27 - 31, 1998.

Jenkins, R. (1996), *Social Identity*, Routledge, London.

Jones, G. (1995), *Leaving Home*, Open University Press, Buckingham.

Jones, G. (1999), 'The Same People in the Same Places? Socio-spatial Identities and Migration in Youth', *Sociology, 33(1)*, pp. 1-22.

Jones, G. and Bell, R. (2000), *Balancing Acts? Youth, Parenting and Public Policy*, York

Publishing, York.

Jones, G. and Martin, C. D. (1999), 'The "Young Consumer" at Home: Dependence, Resistance and Autonomy', in J. Hearn and S. Roseneil (eds.), *Consuming Cultures: Power and Resistance*, Macmillan, Basingstoke.

Jones, G. and Wallace, C. (1992), *Youth, Family and Citizenship*, Open University Press, Buckingham. Japanese edition (trans. M. Miyamoto), Shinhyouron, Tokyo.

Mac an Ghaill, M. (1994), *The Making of Men: Masculinities, Sexualities and Schooling*, Open University Press, Buckingham.

Macdonald, R. (ed.) (1997), *Youth, the "Underclass" and Exclusion*, Routledge, London.

Mannheim, K. (1927), 'The Problem of Generations', in P. Kecskemeti (ed./trans. 1952), *Essays on the Sociology of Knowledge*, Routledge and Kegan Paul, London.

Wilkinson, H. and Mulgan, G. (1995), *Freedom's Children*, Demos, London.

Willis, P. (1977), *Learning to Labour: How Working Class Kids Get Working Class Jobs*, Saxon House, Farnbourgh.

15 Reflexivity and Changes in Attitudes and Value Structures

HELENA HELVE

Introduction

Max Weber postulated that societies are characterised by religions which have an important influence on the societies' political and economic life (Weber 1989). Ronald Inglehart (1997; 1998, 1) argues that Western Christianity, the Orthodox world, the Islamic world, and the Confucian, Japanese, Hindu, Buddhist, African and Latin American cultural and religious traditions are still powerful in spite of modernisation. He has argued in his book "Modernization and Postmodernization: Cultural, Economic, and Political Change in 43 societies" that economic, cultural and political shifts are changing people's values and world views.[1] Inglehart (1997) presents empirical evidence that economic development is linked to changes in values and behaviour. He finds that the most basic shift is towards a secular-rational world view. His study shows that all of the Nordic countries rank very highly in the list of societies with the most postmaterialist values (Inglehart 1997, 151).

Within the discipline of sociology, scholars such as Ulrich Beck, Anthony Giddens and Scott Lash have suggested that we live in the time of reflexive modernity (Beck, Giddens and Lash 1994). Giddens (1991, 2-3), for his part, describes this type of modernity as a post-traditional order. Now we live in a world which he calls "high" or "late" modernity, where our present day world is reflexively constructed. We live in a world of uncertainty and multiple choices. Our future is overshadowed by the risks of ecological catastrophes, the collapse of global economic mechanisms, etc. (see also Beck 1992). This can also be seen in the values of young Europeans in 1990 (Les Jeunes Européens 1991, 20).

201

The active hypothesis of my article here is that the risks of late modernity, such as economic recession, which happened in Finland during 1990s, are changing the attitudes, values and value structures of young people, but these changes are also dependent on education, gender and ideological/religious backgrounds.

My research interest has arisen from a curiosity about certain questions, inspired by a sort of multi-disciplinary approach: How do people's beliefs, concepts of the world, attitudes and values form the "lenses" through which they view the world? How, for example, do age, gender and education effect world views? What other influences on the world views of contemporary young people can we find?[2] My starting premise in this research has been that everyday world views are socialised into people by their own culture during their childhood. Thus I began my world view research project, in 1975, with field research work in my own home environment, collecting both qualitative and quantitative data from Finland's first generation of suburban children and their parents (Helve 1987; 1991; 1993a; 1995 and 2000).

This article is based on a comparative follow-up study of attitudes and values which started in 1989 (Helve 1993b; 1993c; 1994; 1996; 1997a; 1997b and 1999). This second the study covered 240 young people, age 16-19, who lived in the capital of Finland, Helsinki, and in rural Ostrobothnia in the middle of Finland's west coast (cf. Banks et al. 1991).[3] Some of the young people attended upper secondary schools or vocational institutions, and the rest were either employed or officially seeking for employment. In 1992, 70 % of these same young people took part in the next follow-up study. Comparative data were collected again in 1995-1996 among 457 young people living in Helsinki and Ostrobothnia who went to upper secondary schools, vocational institutions and business colleges. Research methods included interviews, questionnaires, projective tests and attitude measures developed by the Centre for Finnish Business and Policy Studies (EVA 1991). Sources also include international comparative studies (see p. 214, Appendix 1, Table 15.3).

This chapter firstly compares young people's attitudes and values in different European countries and secondly analyses the changes in the values of Finnish young people which have happened during the economic recession in the framework of education, gender and ideological/religious backgrounds (cf. Jowell et al. 1996; Friesl et al. 1993; Young Europeans 1993; The Young Europeans 1997).[4]

Satisfaction with Life

A European comparative study (Friesl, Richter and Zulehner 1993) shows that young people's sense of satisfaction with life is linked to their economic situation; the exception here being the Irish, who show a higher level of satisfaction than, e.g., the Western Germans though the latter were more than twice as rich in terms of their per capita GNP in 1991 (Inglehart 1997, 62).[5] But overall, young people from rich and secure societies such as in Denmark, Iceland, Sweden, the Netherlands and Norway are more satisfied with their lives than those living in societies where economic and political life has been insecure, such as in the former Communist countries of Estonia, Latvia, Lithuania, Hungary and Eastern Germany (see p. 204, Table 15.1).

Young people's subjective feelings of freedom and their level of influence in matters concerning them are interrelated.[6] Nordic young people (like their US and Canadian counterparts) appear to be very content in their individual freedom. They also have a strong confidence in people (Table 15.1, p. 204).

Subjective feelings of freedom and satisfaction with life seem to be higher among young people from advanced welfare states than among young people who live in insecure political and economic situations (see also Inglehart 1997, 62-63).

Young People as Citizens

The participation of young Europeans in community life is generally poor (see p. 205, Table 15.2; cf. Spannring et al., this volume). In the Eurobarometer survey of 1997 nearly every other respondent from the fifteen EU-countries said that he or she did not belong to any organisation or association of any sort whatsoever. Of the organisational options proposed, sport clubs were the most popular (27.6 %). Sport clubs had the most attraction for young people from Sweden (50.7 %), the Netherlands (50.2 %), Denmark (44.4 %) and Luxembourg (40 %). In a distant second place came religious organisations (8.7 %), followed by youth recreational organisations such as scouting (7.4 %). Religious and church organisations had their strongest popularity among young people in Italy (18.3 %) and the Netherlands (17.6 %), both with over twice the average European rate

**Table 15.1 Overall satisfaction with life and subjective feeling
of freedom: youth and young adults aged 17-30**

Overall satisfaction with life	Mean value	Subjective feeling of freedom	Mean value
Total	7.31	Total	7.11
Denmark	8.29	Finland	7.98
Iceland	7.99	U.S.A.	7.81
Sweden	7.90	Canada	7.72
Netherlands	7.86	Sweden	7.69
Norway	7.85	Norway	7.69
Austria	7.84	Northern Ireland	7.59
Ireland	7.84	Austria	7.54
Canada	7.76	Iceland	7.49
Belgium	7.73	Ireland	7.34
Finland	7.73	Denmark	7.34
U.S.A.	7.66	Great Britain	7.19
Northern Ireland	7.62	Western Germany	7.18
Western Germany	7.41	Czech Republic	7.17
Great Britain	7.40	Slovak Republic	7.17
Italy	7.37	Italy	7.05
Spain	7.19	Lithuania	7.00
Portugal	7.13	Portugal	6.71
Czech Republic	7.04	Latvia	6.69
Slovak Republic	6.94	Spain	6.67
Poland	6.93	Slovenia	6.61
France	6.79	Hungary	6.58
Eastern Germany	6.76	Estonia	6.53
Slovenia	6.72	Eastern Germany	6.53
Hungary	6.40	Poland	6.42
Estonia	6.31		
Lithuania	6.19		
Latvia	5.74		

1 = not happy at all; 10 = very happy (Friesl et al. 1993, 7 and 8).

of participation. Only 4.4 % of all respondents were members of trade unions or political parties. The most active young people in this sense came from Nordic countries: every fourth Swedish young person (25.8 %), and almost as many Danish young people (22.4 %) said that they were members of trade unions or political parties. The Finnish young people were the Nordic exception: only 12 % belonged to these types of organisations. The Eurobarometer showed that the organisations with the lowest average participation rates among young people in EU countries were human rights movements (1.5 %) and consumer organisations (0.9 %).

The general trend is for young people to join neutral organisations of a general nature (e.g. scouts) rather than those with a more specific purpose such as trade unions, political parties, etc. In general the more educated the young people were, the more active they were in participating in organisations and community life (The Young Europeans 1997). This also explains why young people from the Northern welfare states seem to be more active in community life (see also Helve 1997b, 228-233).

Table 15.2 Participation in community life of young Europeans (%)

From the following list, could you tell me which organisations you are a member of or whose activities you participate in?

1. Social welfare or charitable organisations
2. Religious or parish/church organisations
3. Cultural or artistic associations
4. Trade unions or political parties
5. Human rights movements or organisations
6. Organisations for the protection of nature, animals, the environment
7. Youth organisations (scouts, youth clubs, etc.)
8. Consumer organisations
9. Sports clubs, associations
10. Hobby or special interest clubs/associations (collectors, fan clubs, computer clubs, etc.)
11. Other clubs or organisations (SPONTANEOUS)
12. No club or organisation (SPONTANEOUS)

Country	1	2	3	4	5	6	7	8	9	10	11	12
B	4.0	2.3	6.1	6.3	2.2	3.7	12.9	0.1	23.5	4.1	3.1	52.9
DK	6.0	5.4	8.5	22.4	3.5	9.0	17.6	1.3	44.4	14.1	3.0	22.8
WD	2.2	7.9	4.2	4.6	2.5	6.7	6.5	1.0	38.8	9.6	6.8	38.2
D	2.0	7.1	4.1	4.4	2.2	6.4	6.2	0.9	35.6	9.7	6.5	41.7
OD	1.0	3.8	3.8	3.5	1.0	5.1	4.8	0.5	22.6	10.3	5.0	56.4
GR	3.5	2.4	5.5	1.5	0.7	4.4	2.9	0.8	15.5	1.8	4.1	64.4
E	3.3	6.4	5.4	2.2	1.0	3.0	8.3	0.2	11.8	2.1	6.1	62.3
F	5.4	3.0	7.7	1.3	0.6	5.0	6.7	1.2	28.2	3.9	3.2	51.0
IRL	4.8	7.1	3.7	3.5	2.5	1.3	11.6	0.5	43.7	7.1	5.3	38.8
I	8.2	18.3	5.8	2.9	0.7	4.8	6.8	1.2	23.1	2.8	2.3	45.6
L	2.7	5.7	6.7	5.3	2.0	7.4	25.8	2.8	40.0	7.1	1.7	33.9
NL	9.5	17.6	4.5	6.1	3.2	11.2	7.9	2.5	50.2	9.1	6.1	23.3
A	4.9	12.1	4.6	5.7	2.7	12.0	9.1	2.9	27.0	7.5	2.4	39.8
P	2.5	8.1	4.9	4.0	0.7	2.5	5.4	0.3	21.1	2.5	1.7	59.6
FIN	5.9	12.1	5.2	12.0	2.2	7.7	11.3	0.3	26.6	15.5	2.8	32.9
S	4.9	13.3	7.9	25.8	4.5	9.2	9.4	2.1	50.7	13.8	3.8	17.8
UK	3.6	7.4	2.1	5.9	2.1	5.6	7.8	0.4	28.0	10.7	1.7	50.1
EU15	4.7	8.7	5.1	4.4	1.5	5.5	7.4	0.9	27.6	6.3	3.9	47.6

B = Belgium; DK = Denmark; WD = West Germany; D = Germany; OD = East Germany; GR = Greece; E = Spain; F = France; IRL = Ireland; I = Italy; L = Luxembourg; NL = Netherlands; A = Austria; P = Portugal; FIN = Finland; S = Sweden; UK = United Kingdom; EU15 = mean value in EU countries (The Young Europeans: Eurobarometer 47.2 1997, 21).

Impact of Recession

The deteriorating economic situation in Finland was reflected in young people's more rigid attitudes regarding, for instance, refugees and development aid. Whereas in 1989, during the economic boom, when Finland's GNP per capita was the third highest in the world, every other boy and every fifth girl were of the opinion that development aid should not be increased as long as people in Finland needed help, three years later during the recession (1992) almost every second girl (40 %) and a clear majority of boys (66 %) thought so. Nor have these figures gone back down as the Finnish economy has recovered: in 1995-1996 41 % of girls and 57 % of boys were against increases in development aid as long as there is need in Finland (see p. 215, Appendix 2, Table 15.4.1 "Development aid...").

In 1989 young people (84 % of girls and 73 % of boys) considered the standard of living in Finland to be high enough that the country could afford to take better care of the unemployed and other disadvantaged population groups. This supportive attitude weakened during the recession, but well over half (78 % of girls and 59 % of boys) were still of the same opinion in 1992.

This shows the impact that a decrease in standard of living has on young people's attitudes. Although in 1995-1996 the majority of the nation's young people still considered Finland's standard of living to be high enough that it could take better care of the unemployed and the disadvantaged, the overall figures of support for this initiative had gone down yet again (68 % of girls and 51 % of boys were of this opinion; see p. 215, Appendix 2, Table 15.4.2 "Our standard of living...").

In 1989 most young people (66 % of girls and 77 % of boys) thought that Finland was too indulgent with regard to people who abuse the social welfare system – the lazy and other "spongers". The attitudes of the same girls had become more adamant three years later when Finland was in the deepest recession (70 %), whereas the attitudes of the boys had stayed the same (77 %). The most uncompromising attitudes in this respect were found among the young working population. In the comparative study in 1995-96 the girls (69 %) gave still more strict answers regarding those who abuse social welfare than the girls had given in 1989. Instead the attitudes of the boys had become more lenient in 1995-96 (67 %) (see p. 215, Appendix 2, Table 15.4.3 "People who take unfair advantage...").

Value Structures, Gender, Schooling and Local Differences

According to my findings from the data of 1989-1992, it is possible to divide young people into three different groups with regard to their values, which are *"Humanists"*, *"Individualists"* and *"Traditionalists"* (Helve 1993b; 1994).[7] In the analysis of the new data from 1995-96 the young people are divided into five value groups.[8]

"Humanists – Egalitarians" are those whose values stress gender equality, e.g., in working life. They have no objections to working for a woman boss and in their opinion work is no less important for a woman than for a man. Men and women both need to earn money and take care of the home and the family. In their opinion there should be more women in leadership and other important jobs and it is very important to live according to one's conscience. They would not mind if their children went to school where half of the children were of another race (see p. 216, "Humanists – Egalitarians" factor and loadings, Appendix 3, Table 15.5.1).

"Traditionalists – Conservatives" supported such statements as, "Couples who have children should not divorce", "Marriage is for life", and "Young people today don't respect the traditional values enough". These young people agreed with the opinion, "Our country needs strong leaders who can restore order and discipline and the respect of right values" (see p. 216, "Traditionalists – Conservatives" factor and loadings, Appendix 3, Table 15.5.2).

"Environmentalists – Greens" stressed the opinion that the development of economic welfare should not be taken any further. Nuclear energy should be given up, even if it would result in a decrease in standard of living. They believed that a continued rise in economic well-being only increases mental suffering, and science and technology are beginning to control people instead of serving them. They were willing to lower their standard of living in order to decrease pollution and environmental problems. They also believed that "Even young people can promote world peace by participating in peace work" (see p. 217, "Environmentalists – Greens" factor and loadings, Appendix 3, Table 15.5.3).

"Cynics – Political Passives" agreed with the statements, "Citizens' opinions don't have much influence on the decisions made in society", "The political parties have become estranged from ordinary people and their problems" and "None of the existing political parties advocate things that are important for me" (see p. 217, "Cynics – Political Passives" factor and

loadings, Appendix 3, Table 15.5.4).

One significant new group of values was the global (cf. Watson 1997, "Generation Global"). *"Internationalists – Globalists"* thought that if more foreign people came to Finland, these contacts would be mutually beneficial. In their opinion it was not a privilege to be Finnish and "East, west, home is best", was an obsolete phrase (see p. 218, "Internationalists – Globalists" factor and loadings, Appendix 3, Table 15.5.5).

In the variance analysis, significant differences in these values of boys and girls were found. Girls more than boys valued environmental issues; secondary school urban girls most of all. Boys valued technology and science more than girls (urban upper secondary school boys in particular). Vocational school urban girls were most politically passive and critical of politics. The most active in politics were urban upper secondary school girls. Business school students valued technology and economic welfare most heavily, whereas secondary school students were most critical of them. Green values were given as an alternative to technological and economic values. On the other end of the spectrum from the *"Internationalists – Globalists"* were *"Racists,"* who were more often boys, the majority of whom studied in vocational or business schools and colleges. Most traditionalist conservative values were found among secondary school boys and most urban girls were against these values. The most humanistic values were found among secondary school girls (cf. Brown 1996). In general rural young people valued family values more than urban young people. With respect to gender differences girls valued humanism and equality more than boys, who valued technology and economic welfare more (cf. the next article of Karvonen and Rahkonen, this volume).

Some Critical Afterthoughts

Inglehart's comparative value study describes the changes in contemporary values using the categorical designations of "materialist" and "postmaterialist" (Inglehart 1977, 27-28; 1990; 1997). He presents a hypothesis of scarcity, according to which people generally consider whatever resources are scarce to be important. Thus people's basic needs and values reflect the socio-economic situation in society (Inglehart 1977; 1990; 1997). He claims that the postmodern period is connected with the postmaterialist value world, which criticises the modern and materialist value world. My findings indicate that postmaterialist values are to be found among Finnish young people as well. They are found especially among "humanists" supporting gender and racial equality and among international "globalists" with their cosmopolitan value worlds. The "greens" also expressed postmaterialist ideas in criticising the raising of the material standard of living, and in being willing to lower their standard of living in order to eliminate nuclear power (cf. Inglehart 1997, 104).

People's multiple needs, attitudes and values, however, form a more conflictory value world than Inglehart's typology suggests. A person may have very different needs, attitudes and values, a portion of which are materialist and a portion of which are postmaterialist. For example my follow-up study of young people's value systems indicates a decline in postmaterialist values among young people during the recent period of economic recession. Although a portion of young people can be described as humanists, attitudes towards poor people and foreigners became sharper among them as the result of the recession just as they did among the individualists (Helve 1993b). Economic scarcity can thus be seen in the increase in materialistic values. The same young people, however, also valued things other than material goods. Most of these young people were ready to compromise their own standard of living in order to protect, among other things, the environment and help those less fortunate (Helve 1997a and 1999).

According to Inglehart, those who are postmaterialists in their value world are more ready to give economic help to poor countries and they are also more concerned about women's rights (Inglehart 1977, 30). Young people's values are generally postmaterialistic (Inglehart 1977; 1990, 76). Recent research, however, has indicated that traditional attitudes are still wide-spread in modern societies (Inglehart 1990, 3; Vinken and Ester 1992, 411). All of the new national political movements within Europe – with such diverse concerns as environmental issues, peace, human and animal rights, fighting poverty and promoting equal rights for developing countries and between genders – cannot necessarily be taken as expressions of postmaterialist values. Inglehart's theory oversimplifies this; in the light of my research, the value worlds of young people appear to be far more complex than anything that he describes as part of the category of postmaterialist values.

Discussion

The comparative follow-up study shows that although different value structures can be found, only a few young people clearly belonged to just one category. Because young people are not tied to the values of any given ideology, they choose different values according to the situations in which they find themselves (cf. Bourdieu 1987; Frazer and Nicholson 1991; Lyotard 1984 and 1985). Thus the same young person may be an individualist in some areas, a humanist in others and a racist in others. It is worth asking though, are these young people, with their floating values and their variety of sub-cultures, better adapted to the uncertainty of the "risk society" and changing world than we older folk are (cf. Beck 1992; Giddens 1994 and 1995)? Is it a rational or a reflexive response to postmodern uncertainty?

We are at a historical turning point. The break up of the modernist paradigm of Marxism and centralised economic planning in the former Communist countries have been radical changes. There is, however, also a strong modernist backlash against postmodernism (Jencks 1996, 477). For example, many physicists do not want to accept the uncertainty principle, chaos theory and other manifestations of postmodern thought.[9] And yet there are phenomena which lead one to believe that the world is facing a genuine paradigm shift as we begin the new millennium, affected, for example, by ecological crises such as the greenhouse effect. One of the key shifts taking place in the postmodern world is a change in epistemology, the understanding of knowledge (Jencks 1996, 478). It is coming to emphasise the continuity of nature and the developmental nature of science. This does not mean complete scepticism and an end to all master narratives and beliefs (cf. the concept of "metanarrative", Lyotard 1996, 481-513), but it rather means support for relative absolutism and the idea that propositions of truth are time- and context-sensitive. This, in turn, is bringing about a fundamental change in people's values.

Notes

[1] Ingleharts's research is a part of the series of World Values surveys which began in 1981, and it is also tied to the Eurobarometer surveys of Commission of the European Union.

[2] In my doctoral dissertation (Helve 1987; 1993a) I examined the development of the world views of the same group of young people from childhood into adulthood, after which I

continued on as a researcher with the Finnish Academy comparing the attitudes and values of 16- and 19-year-old young people from Helsinki with those of the same ages in rural Ostrobothnia (the region around the centre of Finland's west coast) in the years 1989 and 1992 (Helve 1993b). This has been further expanded as a project of the Finnish Academy into a study of values and world views, as well as gender ideologies, on the basis of empirical research data collected in the years 1992, 1995, 1996 and 1997 (see Helve 1995; 1996; 1997a; 1999 and 2000).

3. The Ostrobothnia is an area which has always had many particularly strong political and religious movements.

4. Finland's per capita GNP in 1989 was the third highest in the world, after Japan and Switzerland, but after that Finland experienced an economic recession and the unemployment rate rose very quickly. The GNP recovered again, and in 1997 it reached higher levels than in 1989-90, but with the difference that unemployment has still remained much higher than ten years ago. Employment has not grown in proportion to GNP per capita.

5. Inglehart argues that subjective well-being rises with rising levels of economic development (1997, 62-63).

6. According to my data from the 1995-1996 study, the Finnish young people rated individual freedom third in their hierarchies of personal values, alongside peace, after health and close personal relationships.

7. The differences in attitudes and values were investigated using factor analysis. From the 19 variables used to measure attitudes, principal components followed by varimax rotation produced a three-factor result in the two phases of the study (see more Helve 1994, 84-90).

8. In the factor and variance analysis of the new data from 1995-1996 I tried to get more information about the value systems of young people. In this analysis I enlarged the framework from the original 19 to 31 variables, using more variables than in the previous phases of the study for considering issues of politics, environment, science and technology, economics, nationalism, gender equality, human rights, participation, work and family values (see also the three-factor analysis Helve 1999, 53-56).

9. Cf. genetic cloning.

References

Banks, M. et al. (1991), *Careers and Identities*, Open University Press, Taylor & Francis, Milton Keynes.

Beck, U. (1992), *Risk Society: Towards a New Modernity*, Sage Publications, London.

Beck, U., Giddens, A. and Lash, S. (1994), *Reflexive Modernization: Politics, Tradition and Aesthetics in the Modern Social Order*, Polity Press, Cambridge.

Bourdieu, P. (1987), *Outline of a Theory of Practise*, Cambridge University Press, Cambridge.

Brown, P. (1996), 'Cultural Capital and Social Exclusion: Some Observations on Recent Trends in Education, Employment and the Labour Market', in H. Helve and J. Bynner (eds.), *Youth and Life Management: Research Perspectives*, Helsinki University Press, Helsinki, pp. 17-43.

EVA (1991), *Suomi etsii itseään: Raportti suomalaisten asenteista 1991* (Finland Searching for Itself: Report about the Attitudes of Finnish People 1991), Elinkeinoelämän valtuuskunta (Centre for Finnish Business and Policy Studies), Helsinki.

Fraser, N. and Nicholson, L. (1991), 'Social Criticism without Philosophy', *Theory, Culture & Society, 5. (2-3)*, Sage Publications, London.

Friesl, C., Richter, M. and Zulehner, P. M. (1993), *Values and Lifestyles of Young People in Europe*, Report, Vienna.

Giddens, A. (1991), *Modernity and Self-Identity: Self and Society in the Late Modern Age*, Polity Press, Cambridge.

Giddens, A. (1994), 'Living in a Post-Traditional Society', in U. Beck, A. Giddens and S. Lash (eds.), *Reflexive Modernization: Politics, Tradition and Aesthetics in the Modern Social Order*, Polity Press, Cambridge, pp. 56-109.

Giddens, A. (1995), 'Elämää jälkitraditionaalisessa yhteiskunnassa', in U. Beck, A. Giddens and S. Lash (eds.), *Nykyajan jäljillä: Refleksiivinen modernisaatio*, Vastapaino, Tampere, pp. 83-152.

Helve, H. (1987), *Nuorten maailmankuva: Seurantatutkimus pääkaupunkiseudun erään lähiön nuorista* (English summary: The World View of Young People: A Follow-Up Study among Finnish Youth Living in a Suburb of Metropolitan Helsinki), Doctoral dissertation, Helsinki University Press, Helsinki.

Helve, H. (1991), 'The Formation of Religious Attitudes and World Views: A Longitudinal Study of Young Finns', *Social Compass, International Review of Sociology and Religion, Vol. 38, No. 4*, pp. 373-392.

Helve, H. (1993a), *The World View of Young People: A Longitudinal Study of Finnish Youth Living in a Suburb of Metropolitan Helsinki*, Annales Academia Scientiarum Fennica, Gummerus, Jyväskylä.

Helve, H. (1993b), *Nuoret humanistit, individualistit ja traditionalistit: Helsinkiläisten ja pohjalaisten nuorten arvomaailmat vertailussa* (Young Humanists, Individualists and Traditionalists: The Value Worlds of Young People in Helsinki and Ostrobothnia in Comparison. English summary: A Comparative Study of the Attitudes, Attitude Structures and Values of Young People), Finnish Youth Co-operation – Allianssi, The Finnish Youth Research Society, Helsinki.

Helve, H. (1993c), 'Socialisation of Attitudes and Values among Young People in Finland', *Young – Nordic Journal of Youth Research, Vol. 1, 3*, Swedish Science Press, Stockholm, pp. 27-39.

Helve, H. (1994), 'The Role of Religion in Postmodern Society: A Longitudinal Study of the Values of Contemporary Young Finns', *Temenos, 30*, Åbo Akademi University Printing Press, Turku, pp. 81-93.

Helve, H. (1995), 'Religion, World Views and Gender Ideology', *Temenos, 31*, Åbo Akademi University Printing Press, Turku, pp. 77-92.

Helve, H. (1996), 'Values, World Views and Gender Differences among Young People', in H. Helve and J. Bynner (eds.), *Youth and Life Management: Research Perspectives*, Helsinki University Press, Helsinki, pp. 171-187.

Helve, H. (1997a), *Arvot, maailmankuvat, sukupuoli* (Values, World Views, Gender), Helsinki University Press, Helsinki.

Helve, H. (1997b), 'Perspectives on Social Exclusion, Citizenship and Youth', in J. Bynner, L. Chisholm and A. Furlong (eds.), *Youth, Citizenship and Social Change in a European Context*, Ashgate Publishing Ltd., Aldershot, pp. 228-233.

Helve, H. (1999), 'What Happened to Young "Humanists", "Individualists", and "Traditionalists"?, A Comparative Study of Changing Value-worlds of Young People in the Framework of Postmodernity', in V. Puuronen (ed.), *Youth in Everyday Life Contexts, Psychological Reports, No. 20*, University of Joensuu, pp. 48-66.

Helve, H. (2000), 'The Formation of Gendered World Views and Gender Ideology', in A. Geertz and R. McCutcheon (eds.), *Perspectives on Method and Theory in the Study of Religion*, Brill, Leiden, Boston, Köln, pp. 245-259.

Inglehart, R. (1977), *The Silent Revolution: Changing Values and Political Styles among Western Publics*, Princeton University Press, Oxford.

Inglehart, R. (1990), *Culture Shift in Advanced Industrial Society*, Princeton University Press, Oxford.

Inglehart, R. (1997), *Modernization and Postmodernization: Cultural, Economic and Political Change in 43 Societies*, Princeton University Press, Princeton, New Jersey.

Inglehart, R. (1998), *Clash of Civilizations or Global Cultural Modernization? Empirical Evidence from 61 Societies*, Unpublished paper presented at the 1998 meeting of the International Sociological Association, Montreal, August 27 - 31, 1998.

Jencks, C. (1996), 'The Death of Modern Architecture: From What is Post-Modernism?', in L. Cahoone (ed.), *From Modernism to Postmodernism: An Anthology*, Blackwell Publishers, Oxford, pp. 469-480.

Jowell, R., Curtice, A., Park, A., Brook, L. and Thomson, K. (eds.) (1996), *British Social Attitudes, The 13th Report, Social and Community Planning Research*, Dartmouth Publishing Company, England and USA.

Les Jeunes Européens en 1990: Eurobarometre 34.2 (1991), Commission des Communautés européennes, Bruxelles, Luxembourg.

Lyotard, J-F. (1984), *The Postmodern Condition: A Report on Knowledge*, Manchester University Press, Manchester.

Lyotard, J-F. (1985), *Tieto postmodernissa yhteiskunnassa*, Vastapaino, Tampere.

Lyotard, J-F. (1996), 'From the Postmodern Condition: A Report on Knowledge', in L. Cahoone (ed.), *From Modernism to Postmodernism: An Anthology*, Blackwell Publishers, Cambridge and Oxford, pp. 481-513.

The Young Europeans: Eurobarometer 47.2 (1997), European Commission, Brussels.

Vinken, H. and Ester, P. (1992), 'Modernisation and Value Shifts: A Cross Cultural and Longitudinal Analysis of Adolescents' Basic Values', in W. Meeus, M. De Goede, W. Kox and K. Hurrelman (eds.), *Adolescence, Careers and Cultures*, Walter de Gruyter, Berlin and New York, pp. 409-428.

Watson, R. (1997), 'Do it, Be it, Live it', *Newsweek, October 6, 1997*, pp. 28-35.

Weber, M. (1989), *Maailmanuskonnot ja moderni länsimainen rationaalisuus: Kirjoituksia uskonnonsosiologiasta* (Original Print: Gesammelte Aufsätze zur Religionssoziologie [1920]), Vastapaino, Tampere.

Young Europeans in 1990 (1993), Commission of the European Communities, Luxembourg.

Appendix 1

Table 15.3 The phases and methods of the research

1989	Phase 1. 16-19 year olds 123 girls, 117 boys (n = 240)	Methods · Questionnaires · Word association and sentence completion tests · Individual and group focused interviews (video taped) · Attitude scales
1992	Phase 2. Follow-up study 19-22 year olds 93 girls, 72 boys (n = 165)	Methods · Questionnaires · Word association and sentence completion tests · Attitude scales
1995-1996	Phase 3. Comparative study 16-19 year olds 228 female, 229 male (n = 457)	Methods · Questionnaires · Word association and sentence completion tests · Attitude scales

The attitude scales used were taken from the survey of economic, political and social attitudes conducted by the Centre for Finnish Business and Policy Studies (EVA). The study also makes use of direct and projective questions, word association and sentence completion tests and focused interviews which were used in my original longitudinal study of the world views of young people (1993a). This study has followed the same young people, who lived in a suburb of Metropolitan Helsinki, for over 20 years, from their childhood to adulthood.

Appendix 2

Table 15.4.1 "Development aid to foreign countries should not be increased as long as there are people in need of help in Finland." Comparison of 1989, 1992 and 1995-1996, %

Year			1989	1992	1995-96
Total	Agree		35.2	51.2	48.5
	Difficult to say		16.7	15.4	19.0
	Disagree		48.1	33.3	32.5
Sex	Agree	Girls	21.4	40.2	40.5
		Boys	50.0	65.7	57.1
	Difficult to say	Girls	15.7	17.4	16.4
		Boys	17.9	12.9	21.7
	Disagree	Girls	62.9	42.4	43.1
		Boys	32.1	21.4	21.2

Table 15.4.2 "Our standard of living is so high that we must have the means to care for the sick and other people who are badly off." Comparison of 1989, 1992 and 1995-1996, %

Year			1989	1992	1995-96
Total	Agree		79.0	69.8	59.8
	Difficult to say		12.4	17.9	27.4
	Disagree		8.6	12.3	12.8
Sex	Agree	Girls	84.3	78.3	67.5
		Boys	73.2	58.5	51.4
	Difficult to say	Girls	10.7	14.1	22.7
		Boys	14.3	22.9	32.4
	Disagree	Girls	5.0	7.6	9.8
		Boys	12.5	18.5	16.2

Table 15.4.3 "People who take unfair advantage of the social services, idlers and spongers are treated far too well." Comparison of 1989, 1992 and 1995-1996, %

Year			1989	1992	1995-96
Total	Agree		71.2	73.3	67.9
	Difficult to say		20.6	16.8	21.8
	Disagree		8.2	9.9	10.3
Sex	Agree	Girls	66.1	70.4	69.2
		Boys	76.8	77.2	66.5
	Difficult to say	Girls	24.8	17.6	22.8
		Boys	16.1	15.7	20.8
	Disagree	Girls	9.1	12.1	8.0
		Boys	7.1	7.2	12.7

Appendix 3 Factors and Loadings

Table 15.5.1 Factor 1. Humanists – Egalitarians

	F 1	F 2	F 3	F 4	F 5
I would not want a woman to be my boss.	-.62				
It is less important for a woman to go to work than it is for a man.	-.60				
A man's job is to earn money and a woman's job is to take care of the home and the family.	-.58				
It's very important to me to live according to my conscience.	.51				
There should be more women bosses in important jobs in business and industry.	.51				
I would not mind if my child went to a school where half of the children were of another race.	.40				(.39)
There is too much talk about gender equality.	-.40				
Saving is an obsolete virtue.	-.39				
Everyone should have the freedom to live as one likes.	.37				
Individual person's acts have no mentionable effect on the state of nature.	-.36				
I am willing to lower my standard of living in order to decrease pollution and environmental problems.	.30	(.44)			
The building of a fifth nuclear power plant in Finland is to be supported.	-.30	(-.40)			
There are situations where military action is allowed, e.g. when a country defends its independence.	.30				

Table 15.5.2 Factor 2. Traditionalists – Conservatives

	F 1	**F 2**	F 3	F 4	F 5
Couples who have children should not divorce.		.61			
Marriage is for life.		.55			
Young people today don't respect the traditional values enough.		.51			
Divorce is too easy to get these days.		.50			
Our country needs strong leaders who can restore order and discipline and the respect of right values.		.44			

216

Table 15.5.3 Factor 3. Environmentalists – Greens

	F 1	F 2	**F 3**	F 4	F 5
Further development of economic welfare should not be carried out.			.56		
Nuclear energy should be abandoned even if it would cause a decrease in the standard of living.			.54		
The continued development of economic well-being only increases mental ill-being.			.53		
Science and technology are beginning to control people instead of serving them.			.48		
I am willing to lower my standard of living in order to decrease pollution and environmental problems.		(.30)	.44		
Even young people can promote world peace by participating in peace work.			.40		
The building of a fifth nuclear power plant in Finland is to be supported.		(-.30)	-.40		
Economic growth is the only possible basis for continuous social welfare.			-.39		
Development aid to foreign countries should not be increased as long as there are people in need of help in Finland.			-.35		
We should have more respect for the conviction of a conscientious objector.			.32		(.39)
Our standard of living is so high that we must have the means to care for the unemployed, the sick, the disabled and other people who are badly off.			.31		

Table 15.5.4 Factor 4. Cynics – Political Passives

	F 1	F 2	F 3	**F 4**	F 5
Citizens' opinions don't have much influence on the decisions made in society.				.65	
The political parties have become estranged from ordinary people and their problems.				.59	
None of the existing political parties advocate things that are important for me.				.49	

Table 15.5.5 Factor 5. Internationalists – Globalists

	F 1	F 2	F 3	F 4	F 5
If more foreign people came to Finland, we would benefit from useful international influence.					.49
It is a privilege to be Finnish.					-.46
"East, west, home is best" is an obsolete phrase.					.44
I wouldn't mind if my child went to a school where half of the children were of another race.	(.40)				.39
We should have more respect for the conviction of a conscientious objector.			(.32)		.39

218

16 Young People's Values and Their Lifestyles

SAKARI KARVONEN and OSSI RAHKONEN

Introduction

Recently there has been an ongoing debate about the value changes in present-day societies. In the popular literature, the structural and political developments over the past ten years have been suggested to have left large groups of people ideologically "homeless" (e.g. Blair 1996). In sociological and philosophical studies analysing these changes, different, even contrasting positions have been taken largely depending on the more general frame of reference in relation to societal change (e.g. Lyotard 1984; Featherstone 1991).

Ronald Inglehart (1977; 1990) represents the position of a radical break and argues that there has been a shift in the advanced industrialised societies from "materialist" to "post-materialist" values. According to Inglehart, the increasingly materialistic standard of living has meant that people place more and more emphasis on orientations that stress values like self-actualisation, quality of life and belonging instead of the earlier concern for basic needs and safety.

The idea of a clear-cut value shift has been challenged, among others by Anthony Giddens (1991) who claims that instead of the radical break that the advocates of the postmodern theory suggest, we are experiencing an intensifying of a societal development already apparent during the earlier phases of modernity. This period is characterised by "post-traditional order" and it establishes "high" or "late" modernity typified by emancipatory politics – which refers to the politics against oppression or inequality – being replaced by life politics. Life politics is, according to Giddens, a "politics of self-actualisation": fulfilling in this way modernity's central organising principle, namely reflexivity on the level of personal lifestyle and therefore also value orientations.

Giddens seems to imply that at the level of value orientations increased reflexivity produces more contextuality, less rigid patterns of values and more sensitivity to the societal changes or "risks" of modernity (also Beck 1992; Noro 1991). Youth can be expected to be particularly prone to adopting newly developed reactivity into their value systems as the transitions of the youth phase of life involve gaining more independence from the parents and through identity work the formation of a personalised system of values (Ziehe 1992).

Earlier Finnish studies give some support to the idea of reactivity to societal changes. Helena Helve (1998; see Helve's article in this volume) found that among 16- and 19-year-olds materialistic ideas related to subsistence gained more resonance during the recession of the early 1990s. Similarly, Tytti Solantaus et al. (1991) showed that young people's hopes and worries reflect themes apparent elsewhere in society, such as the fear of war or AIDS. Recent youth barometers have also reported that young people are becoming more and more conservative in their orientation towards society. According to these studies, governmental institutions, the police and the army were trusted more towards the end of nineties than in the mid-1990s. Other studies have, however, suggested youth to be increasingly segmented with both extreme right-wing and left-wing orientations receiving support among them (Paakkunainen 1998).

Helve separates young people into five groups according to their value orientations: humanists, traditionalists, environmentalists, internationalists and politically cynical young people. Two groups which arise from these orientations have recently been visible in the media due to their radical actions: the animal rights activists claim to base their efforts on an environmental ideology, whereas the skinheads seem to be recruited mainly from those politically most cynical. However, even though it is clear that youth are demarcated by the extent to which they stress particular values, less is known of the size of the groups attracted by the more extreme orientations.

Furthermore, factors patterning value orientations are also less well known. In Helve's study, values were related both to gender and the level of education among the 16- and 19-year-olds roughly so that humanistic and environmental values were most stressed by girls having the highest education (upper secondary school). Upper secondary school boys were the most conservative ("traditionalists") whereas political cynicism was, perhaps somewhat surprisingly, the highest among urban girls studying at vocational schools.

Those proposing a complete erosion of traditions could be seen to imply the vanishing of gender patterning as sex roles were among the factors producing sharp divisions in traditional society. Late modern theorists stress, however, that gender may still determine access to forms of self-actualisation and empowerment that are the core of (late) modern reflexivity. In addition to gender, also social class has been suggested to give way to lifestyles as important signifiers and producers of social distinctions (Giddens 1991). David Chaney (1996, 15), for instance, sees particularly consumeristic lifestyles representing the more fundamental cultural values of our society. Cockerham, Rütten and Abel (1997, 321) suggest the following:

> Given the massive social, economic, technological and political changes that have taken place in the late 20th century, lifestyles have gained particular significance as individual and collective expressions of differences and similarities.

The subtle distinctions associated with lifestyles are seen to be the primary source of differentiation, which is assumed to have increased the complexity of modern life even more (Bourdieu 1983; Furlong and Cartmel 1997). According to Patrick West (1997), this is particularly typical for youth as the (comprehensive) school effectively equalises all other social divisions, at least in relative terms, denoting that the influences on individual biographies are first and foremost facilitated by lifestyles. West analyses, however, mainly health differentials (for Finland, see Rahkonen and Lahelma 1992). The role of lifestyle and its relationship with gender in other spheres of life is documented poorer.

The purpose of this study is to explore the relationship between value orientations and lifestyles, social class and gender among 15-year-old young people. This age group has been chosen since in Finland these young people are still within the compulsory school system allowing us to analyse the possible equalising effect of the lifestyle. Yet, they also start spending more and more leisure time with peers which further stresses the importance of lifestyles and peer influences. Leisure involving mainly peer-related activities can be hypothesised to create more extreme or less traditional values and that the value sets of those who orient more towards their family and the home tend to be more "conservative" in the sense that they correspond with the cultural values apparent elsewhere in Finnish society (see Suhonen 1988).

More specifically, the study has three aims: first, we aim to discover the relative size of each particular value set by analysing the extreme groups. Secondly, we analyse the relationship between lifestyles (denoted by leisure styles) and values, and, finally, the extent to which social class, gender and leisure styles account for each of the value orientations established in the analysis.

Data Sources

The material for the study comes from a collaborative study project comparing 15-year-olds from Helsinki and Glasgow. Here, we use the Helsinki data only that were collected from a 75 % sample of local schools (35 schools) with young people in their final year of comprehensive school. Three schools refused to participate while the other 32 schools carried out the survey during two school hours in the last two weeks of April 1998 (n = 2392, response rate 77 %).

The survey included a range of questions about the health, well-being, lifestyles and social background of the young people. Questions were especially focused on the final year of statutory education allowing the exploration of the young people's circumstances and experiences before their entry into the labour market or other adult roles.

In the survey 32 statements that were derived mainly from earlier studies (Macintyre et al. 1989; Helve 1993; Bynner et al. 1997) were asked. These were hypothesised to measure certain core *value dimensions*, such as values related to the environment, gender roles or the work ethos. Bearing our general framework of cultural comparison in mind, culturally sensitive items were selected.

In an oblimin rotated oblique factor analysis, eight value factors were found. Two of them, however, contributed hardly more than a single item to the variance explained and were excluded. The complete six factor solution is presented in Table 16.1 (see p. 223). Based on the factors simple sum scores of the original items were first constructed and their reliabilities tested. This analysis reduced the number of items further. The final dimensions were as follows:

Table 16.1 Oblimin rotated factor matrix describing the value dimensions among 15-year-olds (n = 1940)

	1	2	3	4	5	6
Any job is better than unemployment...	**0.62**			0.26		-0.19
If I didn't like my job, I'd pack it in...	**-0.60**		0.19	0.14		-0.41
Even if I didn't like my job, I'd try my best	**0.54**	0.20	0.15	0.27		
Once you find a job, hang on to it...	**0.51**	-0.30	0.11	-0.11		-0.29
You need to have job to feel like a member of society	**0.44**			0.18	0.14	-0.18
You can get satisfaction out of life without a job	**-0.38**	0.15	0.33	0.28		-0.26
Some equality is ok, but...		**-0.79**		0.20		
Men earn money, women look after children		**-0.78**	0.13			-0.16
Same jobs around the house		**0.70**	0.21	0.12		-0.27
Women should look after relatives		**-0.68**		0.12		-0.24
Equal opportunities		**0.63**	0.17	0.23	0.12	-0.16
If you live with your parents they can decide...	0.16	**-0.35**	0.28		0.11	
Restrictions on cars...			**0.77**			0.18
No increase on the material standard of living		0.13	**0.64**	-0.12		-0.20
People should accept a lower standard...			**0.63**	-0.10	0.24	0.12
The young do not respect traditional values	0.10	-0.25	**0.46**	0.23		
People depend too much on the welfare state			**0.45**	0.12	0.18	
Nothing wrong in owning a big house		0.14	-0.19	**0.66**		-0.21
If you try hard enough, you'll find a job			0.14	**0.61**		
I am proud to be Finnish	0.13	-0.11		**0.53**	0.17	0.15
People should feel part of society	0.15	0.19	0.11	**0.52**	0.20	
It is better to live here than elsewhere...		-0.18	-0.17	**0.47**	0.30	
The government should help people where they are					**0.68**	-0.16
People should be loyal to their family				0.34	**0.54**	
The police help and are friendly to young people			0.14	0.14	**0.48**	
To help the poor, the rich should be taxed	-0.12		0.38	-0.22	**0.44**	
It doesn't really matter which party rules						**-0.64**
Too much environment in the media		-0.29	-0.33	0.11	0.13	**-0.54**
A personalised numberplate on your car is a good way to show...	0.12	-0.32	-0.10			**-0.50**
Most problems are due to people being excluded		0.13			0.25	**-0.47**
The church is the best authority		-0.39	0.18	-0.29		**-0.47**
The idea that society owes you a living is outdated		-0.16	0.14	0.33	-0.33	**-0.34**

Loadings below 0.1 have been omitted.

1. The Protestant work ethos (including four items describing work commitment and belief in work as a value in itself; Cronbach's alpha for the reliability of the score: 0.65),
2. traditional gender roles (five items relating to traditional gender roles or equality, such as sharing domestic tasks. The last items were reversed for the final score; alpha for the score: 0.80),
3. environment (four items relating to pollution, anti-materialism and traditional values plus a fifth, antiwelfare state one; alpha: 0.65),
4. patriotic individualism (five items, describing determination to get work and showing off one's success. There were also two items representing patriotism and a third one where belonging society was valued, probably referring to Finnish society; alpha: 0.61),
5. citizenship (three items each referring to a sense of belonging to a collective [society, family]; the score had the poorest alpha: 0.57), and
6. societal cynicism (five items, representing political cynicism [parties, media, society], materialism and trust of the conservative authority of the Church; alpha: 0.63).

The dimensions find some support from the earlier studies even though direct comparison is difficult due to variation in scales and settings. Bynner et al. (1997) report the work ethic and sex equality dimensions in a sample of British young adults that correspond to our protestant work ethos and traditional sex role dimensions. Interestingly, in the Bynner et al. study there was a separate dimension measuring support for traditional marital values. Further, Helve's environmentalists and politically cynical young people appear to share similar value orientation to our respective groups (see Helve, this volume).

The oblimin rotation was selected to allow for the values to correlate with each other as there was no theoretical reason why the dimensions should be uncorrelated. The work ethos correlated positively with all other value sets suggesting that this dimension is shared widely among young people. It correlated the strongest with societal cynicism (Pearson $r = 0.39$) and individualism (0.44). Traditional gender roles were associated particularly with societal cynicism (0.48). Environmentalists tended to support citizenship (0.36).

There were 15 questions about the frequency with which *leisure time activities* were pursued. The list incorporated two dimensions of leisure time activity: a) basically passive activities, such as listening to music, vs. more active pursuits (playing an instrument) and b) the context of the activity, whether indoors (reading) or outdoors (hanging out with friends). In a varimax-rotated factor analysis conducted separately by gender (data not shown), six leisure styles were identified. Two of them were clearly home-based: 1) reading and 2) computer-centred leisure. The other styles involved either passive outdoors activities, 3) the street-oriented leisure or more active outdoors leisure, such as 4) the traditional conservative hobbies (scouts, going to church), 5) music (playing and listening to, more typical for boys) and 6) commercial youth culture (such as going to the cinema, more typical for girls).

Four variables were included to measure social divisions among young people. These were as follows: gender (48 % girls, 52 % boys); social class denoted by the educational level of the father (f) and mother (m) both classified into four groups: highest (i.e. university degree; f: 35 %, m: 36 %), high (i.e. matriculation; f: 25 %, m: 16 %), low (i.e. compulsory education plus some vocational studies; f: 23 %, m: 30 %), and lowest (i.e. basic, compulsory education only; f: 18 %, m: 18 %). The fourth measure described the family type of the young people (standard, two-parent family, 72 %; two-parent family with a stepmother/father, 9 % and single-parent family or some other type, 19 %). That was included as especially values related to gender roles were expected to derive partly from own experiences in the family.

The relationship between leisure dimensions and social class was studied first by correlating them with each other, and in the final step of the analysis by means of a series of regression analyses where each value measure was taken as the dependent variable and gender, social class, family type and leisure time as independent variables.

Results

The relative size of the groups of the young people attached to the value orientations was assessed by dividing responses into the value "extremists", i.e. by summing up those who agreed or fully agreed (or, respectively disagreed or fully disagreed) with all the items of the value set. As the groups were not mutually exclusive, there may be considerable overlap with each set (see p. 226, Table 16.2).

Table 16.2 The frequency of the value "extremists" (total number of cases between 1642 and 1823; varies by value set)

Value set (total n)	Affirmative,[1] %	Negative,[2] %
1. The Protestant work ethos (1700)	10.6	1.9
2. Traditional gender roles (1680)	0.8	33.8
3. Environment (1666)	6.5	1.5
4. Patriotic individualism (1693)	19.1	0.6
5. Citizenship (1823)	25.2	1.3
6. Societal cynicism (1642)	2.7	4.9

[1] Agrees or fully agrees with all the statements of the dimension.
[2] Disagrees or fully disagrees with all the statements of the dimension.

A core of values traditionally apparent in Finnish society appeared among young people, too. Roughly one in ten agreed with all the statements concerning work commitment, one in four with citizenship statements and one in five with patriotic individualism. Also environmental issues were highly valued by a sizeable group of young people. One in twenty resented the societal cynicism statements. The most disregarded were, however, the statements about traditional gender roles. Every one in three disagreed with all of these five items.

Table 16.3 Pearson correlations between leisure styles and value dimensions among 15-year-olds (n = 1485)

Values	Computer-oriented	Reading	Consumer	Traditional	Street-based	Music
Protestant work ethos	-0.03	-0.01	0.14	0.02	0.07	-0.02
Traditional gender roles	0.12	-0.08	0.19	0.01	0.06	-0.13
Environment	-0.06	0.06	0.04	0.06	-0.02	0.12
Patriotic individualism	0.04	0.06	0.09	-0.02	0.05	-0.02
Citizenship	0.03	0.04	0.07	-0.03	0.01	0.00
Societal cynicism	0.10	-0.09	0.28	0.11	0.19	-0.05

Correlations higher than 0.10 have been underlined (correlations higher than 0.05 are statistically significant at the 0.05 level [2-tailed]).

Most value dimensions showed moderate *correlation with leisure styles* (see p. 226, Table 16.3). Traditional gender roles were appreciated by those, whose leisure mostly involved computers, and by the consumer-oriented young people. The environment was valued by those involved with music during their leisure, while traditional gender roles were not. The work ethos was associated with consumeristic leisure style only. Societal cynicism, instead, was related to most leisure styles so that those with a consumer-oriented, computer-oriented, traditionally conservative or street-oriented leisure style valued this dimension, while those who mostly read during their leisure were more critical towards these values. Citizenship was not associated with any particular leisure style.

Factors relating to value dimensions were analysed by means of multivariate linear regression models. Most of the models accounted only for a negligible share of variance in values among young people (p. 228, Table 16.4). In other words, citizenship, work ethos, environmentalistic or individualistic values could not be described adequately on the basis of young people's leisure styles, social class, family type or gender. Still, leisure styles did relate significantly to values in each model but their factual influence remained small.

Two value dimensions could, however, be described on the basis of these factors. Both the appreciation of traditional gender roles and societal cynicism were more typical for boys than girls and for those from the lower social classes than for those whose parents had had higher education. Furthermore, valuing traditional gender roles and societal cynicism were related to the street-based leisure style and the consumer-oriented leisure style. These values were less typical for those whose leisure activities included reading and, for traditional gender roles, also music.

Gender was the only social characteristic that related to most of the value dimensions. Only citizenship did not show gender patterning whereas protestant work ethos, traditional gender roles, societally cynical and individualistic values were all valued more by boys than girls. Girls favoured environmentalist values more which is in accordance with Helve's earlier study (1998; and Helve in this volume) as well. Further, in the final models gender was the strongest single determinant of three value orientations: societal cynicism, individualism and, not surprisingly, traditional gender roles.

Table 16.4 Factors related to value. Parameter estimates and the t-test significance of the variables measuring social background and lifestyles

	Protestant work ethos	Traditional gender roles	Environment	Societal cynicism	Patriotic individualism	Citizenship
	Stand. beta (t-test sig.)	Stand. beta (t-test sig.)	Stand. beta (t-test sig.)	Stand. beta (t-test sig.)	Stand. beta (t-test sig.)	Stand. beta (t-test sig.)
Gender (⇒ girls)	-0.10 (<0.001)	-0.58 (<0.001)	0.07 (0.01)	-0.23 (<0.001)	-0.09 (0.001)	-0.03 (0.29)
Mother's education (⇒ high)	ns.	-0.05 (0.04)	ns.	ns.	ns.	ns.
Father's education (⇒ high)	ns.	-0.06 (0.02)	0.08 (0.003)	-0.09 (<0.001)	ns.	ns.
Computer-oriented	-0.08 (0.004)	ns.	ns.	ns.	ns.	ns.
Reading	ns.	-0.07 (0.001)	ns.	-0.13 (<0.001)	ns.	ns.
Consumer	0.13 (<0.001)	0.06 (0.02)	ns.	0.20 (<0.001)	0.09 (0.002)	0.09 (0.01)
Traditional	ns.	ns.	ns.	ns.	-0.06 (0.05)	-0.07 (0.01)
Street-based	ns.	0.08 (<0.001)	ns.	0.14 (<0.001)	ns.	ns.
Music	ns.	-0.05 (0.02)	0.11 (<0.001)	ns.	ns.	ns.
Adjusted R^2	0.029	0.362	0.022	0.161	0.024	0.008

Also tested: family, interactions between gender and significant main effects.

For the gender role dimension interaction between gender and street-oriented leisure, for the individualistic dimension, gender and consumerist and for the cynical dimension, gender and street-oriented leisure became significant but they contributed negligibly to the variance explained.

Discussion

An exploration of value dimensions and factors associated with them showed that there is a group of values that are shared by many young people and that characteristics such as gender, social class or lifestyle were associated with these values only to a small extent. The 15-year-olds almost totally regardless of their background or leisure style appreciated work, stressed individualism, patriotism (being a Finn) and citizenship. All these values have been traditionally present in Finnish society (Suhonen 1988). Even among present-day youth roughly one in ten agreed with all the statements concerning work by taking a position which we denoted as value extremism. One in five showed individualistic and patriotic extremism and one in four extremism in terms of citizenship. The high frequency of such extremists supporting traditional values challenges the notion of a radical value shift in late modern society. Even though the dynamics of value trends cannot be assessed in a cross-sectional study, our findings suggest continuity rather than change. A survey may, however, produce more conservative picture of young people's value orientations as values tend to be normative so that the respondents usually prefer the options they perceive as the most desired ones (Suhonen 1988). Our main aim was not to estimate the "true" prevalence of these preferences and this type of bias should not distort the analyses of the relationships between leisure, class and value orientations.

Instead, criticism towards pollution and to an extent also to the modern way of life in general could be regarded as a sign of late modern reflexivity. According to this view, these values would represent a sensitivity to societal problems created by the very "risk" society itself (Beck 1992). Ecological criticism highly apparent in young people's world view is also in accordance with the earlier studies (Helve, this volume). The fact that environmental values were only to a small degree dependent on social class or lifestyle, however, suggests that the environment is appreciated by all youth. That these values do not divide young people might also signify their being supported only in principle and they would not produce any practical consequences in the form of political or other action. For the majority of young people ecological support would, then, comprise environmental "Sunday culture" to apply Orvar Löfgren's (1985) concept of describing the discrepancy between orientations and everyday behaviour.

The lack of social and lifestyle divisions in the values of youth does not necessarily imply that there are no distinctions among young people. As the study was conducted in Helsinki, differences that are associated with area of residence or school might still be highly significant which would also support the argument of the equalising tendencies of the comprehensive school system (West 1997).

Contrary to these tendencies, however, two of the value dimensions were clearly related to gender and social class, but also to the leisure styles of young people. Interestingly, they were also the values that were disliked most by the respondents, namely traditional gender roles and societal cynicism. In studies comparing the welfare systems of different states, Finnish society has been characterised as one of relative equality between the genders (Hernes 1988; Esping-Andersen and Kolberg 1992) where gender equality could be considered as norm. For instance, in a study conducted among members of a manual workers union (SAK) fifth of the respondents included gender equality among the three most important values (Kehälinna and Melin 1985; cited by Suhonen 1988). Diverting from this norm is, then, likely to comprise a truly distinct value orientation.

Susan Faludi (1991) suggests that from the late 1980s there has been a "backlash" of gender equality which is characterised by increasing misogyny and a desire for traditional male dominance. The "backlash" was originally identified in popular culture and was seen to be represented by such cultural products as the film *Top Gun*. The cultural backlash in Britain was soon seen to be echoed in the behaviour of young males, "the new lads", again represented e.g. in the TV-sitcom *Men Behaving Badly* (Thomas 1997). This group of young, working class boys is likely to comprise the essence of the proponents of the traditional gender roles. According to our findings, frustration towards the media and political parties, complying with materialistic arrogance and granting religion its conventional authority also find resonance in this group.

Societal cynicism and traditional gender roles were also related to leisure that involved basically passive and informal leisure spent with friends out in the streets, thus comprising probably the most visible part of the city youth. This also supports the hypothesis that leisure spent predominantly among peers facilitates value systems that divert from the cultural norm. Future studies should, however, analyse closer whether the values of these young people correspond to their structural position similarly to Paul Willis' (1977) early study on working class males. The cynical and frustrated youth may also react to their marginal position by recruiting to militant right-wing groupings, as Kari Paakkunainen (1998) seems to suggest. According to this study, however, these values are supported by a small minority. At the same time they are also the most likely to be non-respondents, so a questionnaire study may not constitute the best methodology when assessing the size of these more extreme value groups.

Earlier studies have shown that leisure is heavily gendered with boys involving more in outdoors activities, while the leisure space of girls tends to be more limited to indoors. The range of leisure activities, however, seems to be narrower for boys than girls so that when all activities and the frequency of their participation is taken into account, the girls' overall activity is higher than that of the boys' (Furlong and Cartmel 1997, 54-59). Our findings suggest that gender divisions in youth culture extend from leisure to young people's values, too. "Feminine" sets of values included environmentalism, gender equality, low work ethos and little support for societal cynicism, while boys tended to support hard work and disregarded green values. Especially traditional gender roles and societal cynicism were "masculine" value orientations, which could reflect the marginalised position of the less educated boys both in the face of the societal changes and the transformation of the gender roles.

Leisure that involved reading, music or other cultural hobbies was associated with less extreme gender-related values and supporting societal affiliation even after social class and gender were controlled. Active involvement with hobbies, such as playing in a band, seems to facilitate more egalitarian values as well as acquiring information actively by reading newspapers and magazines. Reading appears also to channel frustration to more societally acceptable goals.

In addition to reading, there was another mainly home-based leisure style, namely involving computers. It was associated with a decreased work ethos, which diverts from the cultural norm of praising the value of work as a means in itself. This opposes to our hypothesis that "deviant" values would arise from youth spending their leisure mainly among peers. Even though home computers offer an additional source of information and potential for interaction and peer relations from which to ground one's own value orientation apart from the influences of the family.

On a more theoretical note, the strong postmodern thesis suggesting the dominance of lifestyle over the life course of individuals and a radical break in the value systems should be rejected according to our study. Even though leisure clearly patterned value orientations among the Helsinki youth, social class also played a significant role in affecting young people's values. Andy Furlong and Fred Cartmel (1997) have conceptualised the seemingly controversial observation showing that the range of options available to young people have widened at the same time as the societal structures have remained untouched, or in some cases, even strengthened. They refer to "the epistemological fallacy" of late modernity which implies that although structures continue to pattern young people's lives, the structures become increasingly obscured with the weakening of collectivist traditions.

Individualism along with the Protestant work ethos were here among the core of values supported by a sizeable group of young people. Striving for success by means of one's own efforts and hard work remain in the heart of the Finnish work ethos according to the sociological literature (Kortteinen 1992). It is no surprise, then, that individualism included a note of patriotism in young people's responses. One would have, however, expected more signs of "post-materialist" values, particularly as the Helsinki youth should comprise the most "postmodern" youth in Finland. Indeed, Helve (1994) found the Helsinki youth to be less traditional and to show more value diversity than young people from rural Ostrobothnia. Our picture is more of a value stagnation but as we lack regional comparison it may well be that youth from the other parts of the country are even more traditional in their orientation. The study shows, however, that the conclusions concerning changes in and the content of young people's values should be made carefully. For instance, although parts of the youth have been active in themes high in the life politics agenda (such as animal rights), there is clearly room for emancipatory politics as well. The traditional emancipatory themes, such as gender roles or employment, are still well represented in the values of the present Helsinki youth.

References

Beck, U. (1992), *Risk Society: Towards a New Modernity*, Sage Publications, London.
Blair, T. (1996), *New Britain: My Vision of a Young Country*, Fourth Estate, London.
Bourdieu, P. (1983), *Die feinen Unterschiede: Kritik der gesellschaftlichen Urteilskraft* (The Fine Differences: A Social Critique of the Judgement of Taste), 2nd edition, Suhrkamp, Frankfurt am Main.
Bynner, J., Ferri, E. and Shephard, P. (1997), *Twenty-something in the 1990s*, Ashgate, Gateshead, Tyne and Wear.
Chaney, D. (1996), *Lifestyle*, Routledge, St Ives.
Cockerham, W. C., Rütten, A. and Abel, T. (1997), 'Conceptualizing Contemporary Health Lifestyles: Moving beyond Weber', *Sociological Quarterly, 38 (2)*, pp. 321-342.
Esping-Andersen, G. and Kolberg, J. E. (1992), 'Welfare States and Employment Regimes', in J. E. Kolberg (ed.), *Between Work and Social Citizenship*, Sharpe, Armonk, NY.
Faludi, S. (1991), *Backlash: The Undeclared War against American Women*, Crown Publishers, New York.
Featherstone, M. (1991), *Consume Culture and Postmodernism*, Sage Publications, London.
Furlong, A. and Cartmel, F. (1997), *Young People and Social Change: Individualization*

and *Risk in Late Modernity*, Open University Press, Guildford and King's Lynn.

Giddens, A. (1991), *Modernity and Self-Identity: Self and Society in the Late Modern Age*, Polity Press, Cambridge.

Helve, H. (1993), *Nuoret humanistit, individualistit ja traditionalistit: Helsinkiläisten ja pohjalaisten nuorten arvomaailmat vertailussa* (Young Humanists, Individualists and Traditionalists: The Value Worlds of Young People in Helsinki and Ostrobothnia in Comparison. English summary: A Comparative Study of the Attitudes, Attitude Structures and Values of Young People), Finnish Youth Co-operation – Allianssi, The Finnish Youth Research Society, Helsinki.

Helve, H. (1994), 'The Role of Religion in Postmodern Society: A Longitudinal Study of the Values of Contemporary Young Finns', *Temenos, 30*, pp. 81-93.

Helve, H. (1998), *Reflexivity and Changes in Attitudes and Value Structures*, Paper presented at the conference 'Youth, Citizenship and Empowerment', Helsinki, December 7-8, 1998.

Hernes, H. (1988), 'The Welfare State Citizenship of Scandinavian Women', in K. B. Jones and A. G. Jonasdottir (eds.), *The Political Interests of Gender: Developing Theory and Research with a Feminist Face*, Sage Publications, London.

Inglehart, R. (1977), *The Silent Revolution: Changing Values and Political Styles among Western Publics*, Princeton University Press, Princeton, N.J.

Inglehart, R. (1990), *Culture Shift in Advanced Industrial Society*, Princeton University Press, Princeton, N.J.

Kehälinna, H. and Melin, H. (1985), *Työtä työlle: Tutkimus SAK:n jäsenistön sosiaalisesta koostumuksesta ja suhteesta työhön* (Work for Work: A Study on the Social Composition and Attitudes towards Work among the Members of SAK), SAK (Central Organisation of Finnish Trade Unions), Helsinki.

Kortteinen, M. (1992), *Kunnian kenttä: Suomalainen palkkatyö kulttuurisena muotona* (The Field of Honour: Finnish Wage Labour as a Cultural Form), Hanki ja Jää, Helsinki.

Löfgren, O. (1985), 'Vardagsliv, Söndagstankar' (Everyday Life, Sunday Thoughts), in D. Gaunt and O. Löfgren (eds.), *Myter om svensken* (Myths of the Swedes), Liber Förlag, Stockholm.

Lyotard, J.-F. (1984), *The Postmodern Condition: A Report on Knowledge*, Manchester University Press, Manchester.

Macintyre, S., Annandale, E., et al. (1989), 'The West of Scotland Twenty-07 Study: Health in the Community', in C. Martin and D. McQueen (eds.), *Readings for a New Public Health*, Edinburgh University Press, Edinburgh.

Noro, A. (1991), *Muoto, moderniteetti ja "kolmas": Tutkielma Georg Simmelin sosiologiasta* (Form, Modernity and "the Third": A Thesis on Georg Simmel's Sociology), Tutkijaliitto (The Finnish Association for Academic Researchers), Helsinki.

Paakkunainen, K. (1998), 'Ääriryhmät valmiita väkivaltaan' (Extreme Groups are Ready for Violence), *Helsingin Sanomat, Vieraskynä*, February 10, 1998.

Rahkonen, O. and Lahelma, E. (1992), 'Gender, Social Class and Illness among Young People', *Social Science & Medicine, 34*, pp. 649-656.

Solantaus, T., Rimpelä, M. and Rimpelä, A. (1991), *Finnish Young People's Hopes and Worries 1983-91*, Poster presented at the 9th Congress of the European Society of Child and Adolescent Psychiatry, London, September 1991.

233

Suhonen, P. (1988), *Suomalaisten arvot ja politiikka* (The Values of Finns and Politics), WSOY, Juva.

Thomas, A. M. (1997), 'Men Behaving Badly? A Psychosocial Exploration of the Cultural Context of Sexual Harassment', in A. M. Thomas and C. Kitzinger (eds.), *Sexual Harassment: Contemporary Feminist Perspectives*, Open University Press, Guildford and King's Lynn.

West, P. (1997), 'Health Inequalities in the Early Years: Is There an Equalisation in Youth?', *Social Science & Medicine, 44*, pp. 833-858.

Willis, P. (1977), *Learning to Labour*, Saxon House, Farnbourgh.

Ziehe, T. (1992), 'Nuoriso kulttuurisessa modernisaatiossa' (Youth in Cultural Modernisation), in T. Aittola and E. Sironen (eds.), *"Miksi piiriin?" Thomas Ziehe koulusta, nuorisosta ja itsestäänselvyyksien murenemisesta* ("A Circle – What for?" Thomas Ziehe on School, Youth and Breaking down of Self-Evidences), Publications of the Department of Education, University of Jyväskylä, Jyväskylä.

17 National, Political and Cultural Identities of Youth: Tendencies in Post-Soviet Ukraine

ARSENIY SVYNARENKO

Introduction

In recent ten years the Ukrainian state and Ukrainian society have been experiencing fundamental political, economic and social transformations. The political and economic crisis in Ukraine has a crucial impact on the values, lifestyles, and attitudes of various social groups in the Ukraine. It is the younger generation of Ukrainians who will experience the repercussions of today's reforms and therefore we concentrate upon them in our analysis.

The main goal of this chapter is to present the major tendencies within a limited set of socio-cultural identities of young people in Ukraine. Explanations will be based upon the idea of the succession of generations, which indicates the links between generations and cultural continuity in a rapidly changing society.

The following discussion about youth in Ukraine is based upon empirical data from two surveys conducted by the stuff of the Sociology Department at the Odessa Mechnikov University. The first was conducted in the end of 1996/beginning of 1997 in the Southern Ukrainian cities of Odessa, Belgorod-Dnestrovsk, Izmail, Bolgrad, and in seven surrounding villages. Altogether, 575 standardised interviews were collected.[1] The sample was representative of basic demographic categories and reflects the gender/age/education structure of population in each area. Respondents were asked 80 questions aimed to disclose a variety of ethno-cultural processes, among people aged 18 and upwards. The second survey was conducted in schools in Odessa, Belgorod-Dnestrovsk, Izmail and some other towns in Southern Ukraine in 1997. Standardised interviews were collected from 400 pupils between 15 to 17 years old.

Background

Young people have both their own unique values and also some common values linking this group to other generations. In this respect, social identities can indicate both the diversity between age groups and the succession of generations. There are many definitions of the term "identity" in social sciences. In this particular case, we define it as a feeling of belonging to a community. This feeling is shaped by a common historical past and present (the so-called "historical memory") and by the prospects of a common future (Smith 1991; Jadov 1994). The background for this feeling generally lies in a similarity of lifestyles, traditions, values and world-views, generated at a certain time and reflecting the "spirit" of the time. Thus we are using "identity" here in the sense mentioned in the work of Benedict Anderson (1983): identity is a socio-cognitive construct, which is both spatially and temporally inclusive, both enabled and shaped by broader social forces. Anderson suggests that there are some key moments in identity construction – that is, times during which cultural (language, values, etc.) and social factors (capitalism, socialism, state, etc.) convene in a particular historical moment, effectively remaking collective images of the *national* self.

Anthony Smith adopts a more moderate approach to national identity. He defines national identity as a product of both "natural continuity" and conscious manipulation. Natural continuity emerges from the pre-existing ethnic identity and community; whilst conscious manipulation is achieved by commemorations, citing a "need for community" as integral to identity work (Smith 1995). In Smith's view, this two-part combination is the basic feature of *national identity*, making it the most fundamental and inclusive type of collective identity. This approach can be well applied to our study of transitional societies.

Identity is formed in the process of comparing the group of "us" with "them, the aliens". A person's identity is affected by how "others" perceive it. In that moment of perception, identity can be enforced or transformed. The transformation of the "us" identity may happen if some of its attributes do not correspond to the expectations of group members at a certain time and in a certain environment. As a result the "us" identity can be reinforced, or weaken and join to a stronger identity, or it can be transformed into a new identity. The loss of identity may cause psychological problems, a decline of values and it cannot be allowed to go on for too long.

This stage of transforming identities can be called marginality. Abnormally fast social changes in Ukraine inevitably creates uncertainty for young people in political, economical, and social spheres. New identities appear, for example, "citizen of independent Ukraine", but the meanings of these identities are not always clear. The Ukrainian State is a new structure, which previously only existed for a very short time at the beginning of twentieth century. That means there are no traditional norms on which to draw for life in a new state. There are no historical memories and original political traditions of Ukrainian citizenship to apply to the modern system.

The marginality for Ukrainian youth in this respect could be seen as an outcome of the evolutionary process of interaction between different cultures. In our case we have a traditional Soviet culture (e.g. the political culture of former Soviet Ukrainian Republic) and an emergent new political environment, which brings a certain diversity to the current political culture.

The Political and Cultural Identities of Young Ukrainians

In order to analyse political and socio-cultural identities we used a special scale in our questionnaire, different from the one used by Eurobarometer of the European Commission. We did not suggest that respondents make clear and distinct choices between various types of identities: *National only*, *National plus European*, *European plus National*, *European only*. We expected and provided more freedom of choice. We assumed that for a particular individual his/her identity is not always clear (and in the field we find that it is often unclear). Even expert scholars have a wide range of ideas about what identity is. Compared with the set of questions concerning identity used in the Eurobarometer, our questions give us more information about the significance of being a representative of a certain community.

We analysed the following identities:

1. *Citizen of Ukraine* – national identity;
2. *Soviet Person, Citizen of USSR* – former national identity (which is now only hypothetically existent);
3. *Citizen of Russia* – national identification with the neighbour state which is taken to be both the official and unofficial successor of the Soviet Union;
4. *Member of a Certain Ethnic Group* – local ethnic, mainly cultural identity;
5. *Citizen of Europe* – cosmopolitan, transnational identity;
6. *Citizen of the World* – cosmopolitan global identity.

There are a couple of points to be clarified before the explanation of the data. The first is that in this context the term "citizen" is mainly relating to the phenomenon of citizenship in the sense of meaning membership of a social community, rather than a legally constituted form of citizenship. For this reason, we shall term it "social citizenship". Secondly, there is often no clear margin between the political and cultural content of each identity. This is probably the main problem for these kinds of studies, since people might attribute various meanings to the identities they are asked about.

Citizen of Ukraine

This identity has a formal/legal aspect as well as a non-formal one. Some respondents in Ukraine may say that it is written in their passports that they are citizens of Ukraine and there cannot be any discussion about it. However, "Ukraine" also means the territory, culture, tradition, place of birth and/or life. As we shall see below, the cultural understanding of contemporary Ukrainian identity can be either understood in terms of national culture or in terms of Soviet culture. That means there still might be some people who live in a non-existing hypothetical space, the world of the non-existent Soviet Republic of Ukraine.

Soviet Person

The background for this identity lies in the Soviet state. In the USSR, many Soviet scholars wrote numerous books and articles about the "Soviet lifestyle" and "Soviet values". Being "Soviet" ("Sovietness") is a very complicated phenomenon which existed for many years, involving several generations and many millions of people, as well as many national-ethnic groups. Briefly, the Soviet nation can be described as a product of ideology as well as an outcome of economic, administrative, and social policy. For many people in the past, Soviet identity came to replace or supersede local ethnic identity.

Citizen of Russia

The construct of this identity is more or less similar to the "Ukrainian" one. There are two main differences between this and the Ukrainian identity. The first difference is spatial: Russia is a different nation-state with its own territory and separate political, economic and legal systems. The second difference is that consciously and subconsciously, people accept Russia as the successor of the USSR. That is why for a certain group of people, Russia is associated with the Soviet Union.

Ethnic Identity

This too is a mainly cultural phenomenon. In our particular context, it has a clear meaning and is associated mainly with a particular ethnic community, ethnic origins, traditions, and language. The only problem appears to be that over the years there have been more and more frequent interethnic marriages, especially since the culture of modernity has eliminated the traditional patronymic means of ethnic succession. Hence, ethnic identity has a clear meaning but in practice it's a rather muddy concept.

In the transition period, the strength of Ukrainian and Russian national identities are probably linked to the economic situation and the strength of the welfare system in these countries. The successful organisation of everyday life along with the economic and administrative environment give a person more reasons for identification with the community which provides these advantages. Some may argue that there are many historical examples in different states and times of economic and political problems being accompanied by a growth in national identity. There is a set of possible explanations for this. First we should look at the content of national-ethnic identity in each particular situation and specific context. What are the major constructs in these identities? What is stressed?

In some cases, we are faced with very strong ethnic identity. The main source of this may be a clear opposition to a group of "aliens" or "them". These aliens in turn are blamed for all of the economic and other problems. (The classic example of this is the way in which, for many centuries, the Jewish community was treated as such an "alien" group in many European societies.) In other cases, however, the "alien" group is not such a significant factor in the construction of the "us" identity.

We should also here deal with temporary identities. The construction of identities might be mainly influenced by *retrospective* thinking, *present day* thinking, or *future* thinking. *Retrospective identity* is based first on the historical memories of people in a community. This seems to have become a significant factor in the Ukrainian educational system, in that the subject "The History of Ukraine" has come to be of national importance. The *present day identity* definitely requires economic and social stability in the state, so this identity tends not to be stressed, nor does it have a crucial influence on people's actions. Compared with retrospective and future perspective identities, the present day sort has relatively little influence on attitudes towards the social, economic, and political environments. The *future identity* is based upon a hypothetically existent social reality made up of expectations, judgements, and assumptions about the future of this community. Identity of this sort can be demolished and weakened if the everyday reality strongly conflicts with people's thoughts and expectations about their own future inside this state. The scenario can be entirely different for the development of future perspective identity in the conditions of crises. National-ethnic groups inside a certain state may believe in national-ethnic consolidation as the way to solve (or at least weaken the impact of) economic and/or other problems affecting the territory of this community.

Citizen of Europe/Citizen of the World

Our theoretical speculations about these types of identity are mainly derived from the definition given to the term identity by the prominent Russian sociologist, Jadov (1994). It is also important to mention that each of these types of identity plays a significant role in our study, in terms of describing the specifics of the identity structures of different generations in the transition society, where it is important to see which type is most emphasised in each generation.

In the modern state and society, the cultural unification of everyday life is rapidly increasing. The idea of a succession of national-ethnic traditions has been largely superseded by an urban-utilitarian concept of culture. The strongest cultural distinctions in terms of national mentality seem to be under increasing pressure from the forces of universal business philosophy (Weber 1978). One of the things which makes it extremely interesting to analyse the identities of young people in the transition countries is that they still have multiple choices between traditional and new identities; some of which would probably not be significant for young people in other European countries, others of which could be even more important elsewhere. Youth identities are also an object of sociological interest because this is the period in human life when the cultural and political identities are in the process of construction. That is not to say that in adulthood identities are consistent, but youth is the period when certain aspects of the background for all later identities are formed.

For the reasons stated above, regional and global identities are the main feature of many modern societies. Cosmopolitan identity is particularly important for young people in Ukraine today. This is the generation which has gained access to the means of global communication and global culture. To be cosmopolitan is to participate in a wider order, beyond the national culture; be it universal humanity, European culture or Western civilisation (Delanty 1995). Cosmopolitan identities are based mainly on some universal trends in modern culture. Applying Habermas's (1996) theory of the process of globalisation, it might be suggested that the emergence of global discourses of law and order provide radical democracy with an institutional space in which to bring about increased democratisation by granting a central place for new definitions of citizenship. Essential to this is the notion of collective actors. Soysal (1994) also has drawn attention to the emergence of new forms of citizenship on the global level, where a discourse on human rights has usurped the sovereignty of national citizenship. Gerald Delanty (1998) suggests that cosmopolitanism can also be seen as a real force in the world manifested in people's multiple allegiances and identities.

The Main Trends in Youth Identities in Ukrainian Society

In our research we used a nine-degree scale for each of the above mentioned forms of identity. Respondents were asked to estimate the strength/weakness of their own identity in terms of their agreement with the statement: "Since the decline of the USSR I feel myself to be a...<title of category>..." A score of "9" meant that respondent identifies himself/herself very strongly as, for instance, a citizen of the Ukraine; "1" would indicate that he/she completely disagrees with the statement and does not feel at all attached to this form of community.

As a matter of convenience in the secondary data analysis, an integrated index of identity was adopted. The index (i) contains values from -1 to +1 ($-1 \leq I \leq +1$) using a formula of:

$$i = (\Sigma A - \Sigma B)/\Sigma C$$

ΣA = the sum of those respondents who have chosen degrees 7, 8, 9.
ΣB = the sum of those who have chosen degrees 1, 2, 3.
ΣC = the total number of all responses.

The strongest type of identity in Ukrainian society as a whole appears to be the ethnic. As a general rule the importance of ethnic identity seems to increase with age: for 15-17 year old respondents, the index value is +0.29. For young people from 18-22 and 23-30 years old the values are +0.46 and +0.56 respectively. The exception here is that the 31-45 year-old cohort showed a relative decrease in ethnic identity, with a value index comparable with that of the 18-22 year-olds (i = +0.47). But then the 46-55 year-old respondents again showed a stronger sense of ethnic identity, almost matching that of the 23-30 year-old respondents (i = +0.55). This seems to hint at intergenerational succession having some significance. In a certain sense, these age cohorts can be interpreted as generations of "parents" and "children". It is tempting to label these generations relative to certain periods in history or to given events in the past. In this research, however, we will resist this temptation, since it would engage us in a broader discussion of the life-courses and deep cultural specifics of the generations. The cohort of 23-30 year-old respondents (i = +0.56) can be roughly estimated to be the children of those in the cohort just over 46 years old, which almost shares their index value in this area (i = +0.55).

Likewise the cohorts just below each of these in age could be considered to represent succeeding generations: those age 18-22 being the "children" ($i = +0.46$) and 31-45 years, the "parents" ($i = +0.47$) (see p. 250, Appendix, Table 17.1).

For young people, the process of interaction with older cohorts is the main source of information about the Soviet Union and life in the Soviet system. This interaction is not limited to direct communication within families and sharing their experiences, it also involves the wider effects of education and socialisation. The primary sources of such information are the mass media and school teachers (the majority of whom are over 30 years old). This information, accompanied by other minor sources, creates a sufficient background for clarifying each young person's own position and attitudes toward the community of "Soviet Persons". For young people aged 15-17 and 18-22, the index value here is -0.34. Not surprisingly the level of acceptance of Soviet identity increases proportionately to the age of the respondents (e.g. 46-55 year-olds $i = -0.24$, over 56 years old $i = -0.11$).

For respondents of age 15-17, the index of Russian identity is -0.51; among 18-22 and 46-55 year-olds $i = -0.70$. For the cohorts of 23-30 and 31-45 years old $i = -0.72$. The oldest cohort was also strongly negative towards Russian identity ($i = -0.71$).

Cosmopolitan identity is rather contradictory within various cohorts. For teenagers (15-17 years old) world citizenship was rated $i = +0.16$, with a weaker showing still among young people of the 18-22 year-old group ($i = +0.12$). The 23-30 and 31-45 year-old cohorts are more decisively negative in this respect ($i = -0.27$ and -0.35). It is also quite significant that among young people of 15-17 years old European identity ($i = +0.11$) is stronger than Ukrainian identity ($i = +0.094$). This speaks of teenagers' increasing tendency to seek self-realisation in the context of modern Europe. The European identity is slightly more attractive. This does not mean, however, that Ukrainian identity has been discarded. Nowhere are there negative index values for Ukrainian identity and Ukrainian social citizenship in our research. Nowadays, Ukrainian citizenship is regarded as being on par with that of any other European society, in the European discourse.

243

The Internal Structure of Social Identities

As mentioned above, while we can measure the relative strength or weakness of some forms of identity, this measurement tends to be rather abstract in terms of the meaning and content of these identities. The best way to discover and clarify the "meaning" of identity is to conduct qualitative interviews. If we use quantitative research, through standardised interviews there are two major alternatives as how to obtain the needed information: first, by asking questions about identities suitable for advanced statistical analyses (correlation analyses, factor and cluster analyses) and second, to ask a set of indirect and in-depth questions (which must, however, still generate responses suitable for complicated mathematical analyses as well). Taking the limitations of the length of this chapter into account, let it suffice now for us to present only some results of the first methodology. Table 17.2 (see p. 250, Appendix) presents matrixes of correlation between measured identities. The strongest correlation is between "Ukrainian" and "ethnic" identities (r = 0.329). On the one hand, this relates to the ethnic identities of many ethnic groups interviewed in the field and these are primarily cultural phenomena. On the other hand, there is a Ukrainian identity which relates mainly to the idea of social citizenship, which is a socio-political phenomenon. Our assumption about the strong correlation between these two identities is that ethnic groups in Ukraine are not opposed to a Ukrainian State and society in which they are perceived and treated as equals. This promotes the development of tolerant ethnic relations. In other words, this correlation coefficient means that for most of the ethnic groups in Ukraine, the state is accepted as a multiethnic community which does not prefer an ethnic majority to ethnic minorities: the stronger the ethnic identity, the stronger the Ukrainian national identity. It is commonly accepted that the Ukrainian nation is a community of many ethnic groups.

Another strong correlation exists between Ukrainian national identity and the Russian identity (r = -0.356). These two identities are mutually exclusive for most of the people. The coefficient (r = 0.444) of correlation between "Russian" and "Soviet" identities gives us a reason to suggest that there is a tendency towards recognition of Russian identity, Russian state and society in terms of "Soviet" state and society. Russia is thus expected to be a successor to the Soviet Union in political and cultural respects.

The coefficient of correlation (r = 0.154) between National and

European identities means that European identity (European space, discourse) is involved in the process of the construction of the Ukrainian identity. People rethink Ukrainian identity in the context of current European processes, the European community, and European culture.

At the same time ethnic identity is somewhat related to both national and European identity (r = 0.160). This means that the particular ethnic group see themselves as recognised within the (mainly cultural) space of what they identify as Europe. This also means that the European citizenship involves ethnic and national identities as its main constructs. In this respect the concept of Europe as a region is confirmed. The main trend is the shaping of the uniqueness of each national-cultural group, not their unification and homogenisation. Meanwhile the European identity is closely related to the global cosmopolitan identity – World citizenship (r = 0.611).

We base the following statement on the idea that the origin of social identity lies in subjective knowledge about the main target of the particular identity, which also involves participation in the structure of social relations within this community, following its norms and values.

The indexes of national identity for 15-17 and 18-22 year old age groups are 0.094 and 0.14 respectively (see p. 250, Appendix, Table 17.1). The increase in age is accompanied by an increasing sense of the inclusion of the individual into the wider system of the social relations represented by Ukrainian state institutions. This is linked with the feeling of historical unity of the individual life-course with the "life-course" of the system. In each case the national identity corresponds with the main features of the social structures in which it was constructed. The national identity of older generations was built during the period of the stability of the Soviet state. Today, this generation translates its identity to the Ukraine. As a result, this generation's Ukrainian citizenship is associated with the Soviet citizenship.

The Social Marginality of Youth

The data described above also give us some indication that young people's identities built upon a scheme of "not-me" are more clear and emphatic than affirmative identities of "I am". For instance, Russian identity contrasts with Ukrainian identity, but young people are far more certain about not being Russian than they are about being fully Ukrainian.

245

The social identities of young Ukrainians have some very important and recently developed characteristics. To describe this trend we must refer to identities as being "positive" or "negative" (or "constructive" vs. "destructive"). This categorisation is rather simplified, but we believe that it is sufficient for further explanations.

The model we apply includes two types of identity constructs:
Type 1. The scheme of identity construction built upon the acceptance of a group "us": "I AM ..."
Type 2. The scheme of rejection of a group: "I am NOT ... (one of them)..."

Let us analyse the identities of the youngest age group – 15-17 year-olds – teenagers. The positive identities of this group are presented in Table 17.3 (see p. 251, Appendix) and negative in Table 17.4 (see p. 251, Appendix).

The index value for negative identity vastly exceeds the index for positive identity. This fact confirms the suggestion that being able to distance oneself from certain social structures is particularly important to Ukrainian teenagers. We might suggest that the construction of the "positive" identity is based upon the reflexivity of the contemporary social, political and economic environment. The "negative" identity is based mainly upon the historical memory and cultural succession from elder generations to younger ones. For teenagers the contemporary social system is not well-known and not particularly attractive. Compared to older people, teenagers are not so fully involved in the functions of the existing political and socio-economic system. They have strong ethnic identities which in some respects can be considered as "pre-existing", less dependent on personal choice. The uncertainty of the situation is a temporal feature faced by all teenagers. The further inclusion of young people into the functions of wider communities and into the networks of social relations in terms of social citizenship (as part of the ageing process) stimulates an increase in the significance of self-recognition within these political, economic and cultural structures. Thus, we could conjecture that identities within communities may increase with time.

We must take into account the assumption that during the present period of transition, new political and social systems are not well-known nor clearly understood even by the older cohorts, to say nothing of the younger ones. The main peculiarity of the older generations is that in the process of identity construction, they may use their own experience and knowledge gained from their life in the previous state of the society. They may apply their own attitudes, systems of values and norms to construct and regulate social relations within the new system. This is a reconstruction of reality, but also the creation of new reality. The problem is that their previous experience is not fully appropriate for the new environment. Moreover, older generations are prone to treat the new structure as though it has the characteristics of its predecessor.

Conclusions

Young people in the transition society are on the verge of two cultural systems (cultural in the wide sense of being political, economic, and traditional systems). These cultural systems are:

- the former Soviet state;
- the new Ukrainian state (or if you like, the revived Ukrainian state).

Young people are involved in social participation in both systems. This causes a certain marginality among young Ukrainians. While the global transformation of the Ukrainian society continues, the phenomenon of cultural marginality may exist because of the predominance of negative social identities over positive ones.

Anthony D. Smith claims global culture to be memoryless and lacking conviction. In his understanding, the main forces that shape modern collective identities are ethnic ties and ethnic history (Smith 1991). The analysis of survey data presented here reveals the internal tendencies of national and ethnic identities. Ethnic identity seems to be the strongest identity in the set of collective identities presented here. Analysing ethnic identity we show that there are certain ways (or what we may call "technologies") for the construction of ethnic identities: one of them is dominated by *"collectivist"* values and orientations (for instance respondents who were young adults in mid 1990s), another by *"individualist"* (the youngest generation). Furthermore, we suggest that generational differences influence the construction of one's ethnic identity. Different methods of statistical analysis indicate the existence of at least four distinct generations of Ukrainian citizens.

247

Furthermore, if we take Ukrainian national identity to be a sign of Ukrainian patriotism, the most patriotic cohort at the end of 1990s were those over 56 years old. In these terms, young people are much less "patriotic". Is this true? What can we expect to happen in Ukrainian society in the future? Young people have not yet become fully involved in the public and political systems, and that is why political and national self-identification is not so significant for them. There is a clear tendency for older people to see the contemporary state of Ukraine in the context of former USSR: Ukraine for them is still mainly a "Soviet Ukrainian Republic". Young people have very different ideas about the Ukrainian state and citizenship. They see it in a European cultural and political context. The national identity of young people is therefore weakened by the economic and social problems of the transition period.

In transitional society, the intergenerational succession of values, norms, and attitudes from elder generations to younger ones has an indirect, mediating nature. When young people confront the problem of forming their own attitudes, positions, values and norms, they cannot apply the heritage of older generations (which does not relate to the changes which have taken place in society) directly. This could have the effect of making young people more independent and self-sufficient (in each new generation). But in fact the phenomenon seems to be more complicated than that, since parental mediation continues to be of great significance for the formation of worldviews of young people under conditions of intensive social change.

Note

[1] It was often discussed at the conferences of Ukrainian sociologists in Kiev and Kharkiv that survey data from Southern region of Ukraine coincides with the main tendencies of the general Ukrainian population, in the topics concerning political and ethno-cultural processes.

References

Anderson, B. (1983), *Imaginary Communities: Reflections on the Origin and Spread of Nationalism*, Verso, London.

Delanty, G. (1995), *Inventing Europe: Idea, Identity, Reality*, Macmillan, London.

Delanty, G. and Cutler, R. (1998), *Nations without Nationalism: Concepts of Cosmopolitanism*, Paper presented to the Tampere Peace Research Institute, University of Tampere, Finland.

Habermas, J. (1996), *Between Facts and Norms: Contributions to a Discursive Theory of Law and Democracy*, Polity Press, Cambridge.

Jadov, V. (1994), 'Sotsialnie Identificatsii Lichnosti v Usloviah Bystryh Sotsialnyh Peremen' (Social Identities of Personality in the Conditions of Rapid Social Changes), in V. Jadov (ed.), *Sotsialnaya Identificatsia Lichnosti* (Social Identity of Personality), Institute of Sociology Press, Moscow.

Smith A. (1991), *National Identity*, Penguin Books, London.

Smith, A. (1995), *Nations and Nationalism in the Global Era*, Polity Press, Cambridge.

Soysal, Y. (1994), *The Limits of Citizenship: Migrants and Post-National Membership in Europe*, Chicago University Press, Chicago.

Weber, M. (1978), *The Protestant Ethic and the Spirit of Capitalism*, 2nd ed., George Allen and Unwin, London.

Appendix

Table 17.1 Macro-social identities of various age groups

I feel myself as ...	Age					
	15-17 years	18-22	23-30	31-45	46-55	56- and more
1. ...*Citizen of Ukraine*	0.094	0.14	0.23	0.26	0.25	0.49
2. ...*Soviet Person, Citizen of USSR*	-0.34	-0.34	-0.27	-0.27	-0.24	-0.11
3. ...*Citizen of Russia*	-0.51	-0.70	-0.72	-0.72	-0.70	-0.71
4. ...*Member of my Ethnic Group*	0.29	0.46	0.56	0.47	0.55	0.57
5. ...*Citizen of Europe*	0.11	-	-	-	-	-
6. ...*Citizen of the World*	0.16	0.12	-0.27	-0.35	-0.16	0.05

Table 17.2 Matrixes of correlation between identities

I feel myself as ...	Citizen of Ukraine	Soviet Person, Citizen of USSR	Citizen of Russia	Member of my Ethnic Group	Out of any Ethnic or National Group, Member of my Local Community	Citizen of Europe	Citizen of the World
Citizen of Ukraine	1	-0.066	-0.356**	0.329**	0.048	0.154**	0.092
Soviet Person, Citizen of USSR	-0.066	1	0.444**	-0.039	0.059	-0.032	-0.058
Citizen of Russia	-0.356**	0.444**	1	-0.105	-0.071	-0.018	-0.046
Member of my Ethnic Group	0.329**	-0.039	-0.105	1	-0.155**	0.160**	0.095
Out of any Ethnic or National Group, Member of my Local Community	0.048	0.059	-0.071	-0.155**	1	0.061	0.057
Citizen of Europe	0.154**	-0.032	-0.018	0.160**	0.061	1	0.611**
Citizen of the World	0.092	-0.058	-0.046	0.095	0.057	0.611**	1

Table 17.3 Type 1. "I AM a ... ."

Identity	Index
... *Member of my Ethnic Group*	0.29
... *Citizen of the World*	0.16
... *Citizen of Europe*	0.11
... *Citizen of Ukraine*	0.094

Table 17.4 Type 2. "I am NOT a ... (one of them)... ."

Identity	Index
... *Soviet Person, Citizen of USSR*	- 0.34
... *Citizen of Russia*	- 0.51

PART 6

NEW ACTORS, NETWORKS AND EMPOWERMENT

18 Critical Discussion: Globalisation and Empowerment

PAT ALLATT

The world summit on education was heading for a confrontation between governments and powerful coalitions of Non-Governmental Organisations (NGOs) on its opening day over who pays for the education of the poorest people on earth in the next 15 years (J. Vidal, The Guardian, 26 April, 2000).

The chapters in this section of the book are deeply political, taking up the issue of young people's empowerment and setting it within a public landscape stalked by three sets of actors. The first comprises the young people themselves, located here in two realms – the exploited and marginalised children in developing countries and young people's political activism in societies undergoing political change. The second set of players consists of the societies in which the young people live, for the subtext of these chapters is how societies and their powerful elites position themselves with regard to their young. In the cases described here, such positioning specifically includes the extent of social protection afforded the young, perceptions of young people's place in their society, and the roles and attitudes that are expected of them, allowed or desired. These two sets of players are joined by a third. These are the Non-Governmental Organisations (NGOs), in all their variety, which seek to bring about change with regard to the young and which may be active both within and external to any particular society. Such groups and groupings, whose presence extends from local initiatives to the arenas of national and international debate and policy, are becoming increasingly vocal and impatient with the failure of governments and global bodies to address the needs of young people, especially in the face of gross deprivation. It could

255

not be more apposite that, as I write, the World Education Forum opens in Dakar, and that in his formal opening address the UN secretary general, Kofi Annan, "accused politicians of failing children and ignoring human rights" (J. Vidal, The Guardian, 17 April, 2000). With such a mix of players, all operating in conditions of change, it is not surprising to find tension and difficulties surrounding what amounts to the redistribution of power.

Within this matrix, the chapters are diverse, focussing on different phenomena in different societies, each society differing in its political and economic cultures. Moreover, the age range covered by studies is wide, extending from children as young as five to the official definition of youth in South Africa, which extends to age 35. Thus, Rahman addresses the situation of street children and child labour in the developing countries of the southern hemisphere characterised by the divorce between economic and social policies, and where children have neither a voice nor institutional support from their own states or societies; Everatt, focussing on youth NGOs, follows the political role of urban, black, South African youth from the turbulence of the movement towards and arrival at an anti-apartheid society into the 1990s, and the supersession of these young political activists by those who are seemingly dominated by the consumerist lifestyles which accompany the liberalised economic policies of this transforming society; and Macháček analyses the political mobilisation of the young people of Slovakia in 1989 and, particularly since 1993 with the shift from a centralised state and command economy, their civic or public participation in a post-communist society and the role of NGOs in nurturing a democracy.

This apparent diversity is situated at the confluence of several strands of contemporary discourse. It is set in a globalising world which touches all our lives, and the studies cohere in their themes of youth empowerment, its societal implications and the emergence and role of NGOs in the field of youth. In addition, conceptually, the studies bring to the fore the issue of youth as a category, highlighting in particular problems in the definition of youth *per se,* the idea of children's and young people's rights, and the notion of youth transitions. They point to the fact that political involvement of the young (and indeed adults) is an ambiguous and contested concept, but most importantly that the form involvement takes, and its absence or apparent absence, is critically linked to people's circumstances and the changes through which they are living. Thus the matters raised by these writers resonate with debates beyond the particular societies and young people considered here.

The context in which the authors write is that of globalisation and a narrowing world. Rahman firmly identifies the exploitation and marginalisation of children and young people in the Third World as a global problem. In this connected world, especially in societies where power is personalised rather than institutionalised, the exploitative conditions of young workers are exacerbated by untrammelled world market liberalisation, the burgeoning of tourism, for example, extending the forms of children's exploitation as sexual commodities. The technology which furthers global markets, however, is a potential factor in its control, enhancing communication and the possibilities for co-operation amongst those who would moderate or reshape it. Thus for NGOs, especially those concerned with developing countries, the connectedness and transparency flowing from technological change not only increases the availability and amount of information but also broadens and deepens the opportunities for networking. Together these offer a base for collaborative organised representation and protest. Rahman notes the extensive networking of NGOs which focus on the exploited child. More recent examples of such public protest have been seen on the streets of Seattle during the December 1999 meeting of the World Trade Organisation.

The issue of children and young people's rights has been richly debated. Within the childhood literature Brannen and O'Brien (1996, 4) argue the duality of these rights, that the young have a right to protection and that these might conflict with those which confer self-determination. They suggest that the individualising language which presupposes an autonomous, unsupported, self-determining adult clouds other aspects of children's and young people's needs and what they might rightly expect from adults. The NGOs noted by Rahman take up this protective position, and he himself argues for the provision of basic rights to education, health (particularly with regard to HIV/AIDS) and indeed the protection of childhood itself. He sees these as the necessary grounding of empowerment, the foundation for what he refers to as "global citizenship". Ultimately, he argues, such social protection is in the interests of the state, since exploited and marginalised children may become disaffected and damaged adults, and hence a costly threat to the stability of the society. Yet there is still an echo of children's voices, and the rights lodged in the conventional understanding of citizenship, in a child's plea to be listened

257

to. The responsibilities carried by some of these working children also throws open to question the notion age related adulthood, along with transitions to adulthood, particularly the issue of extended transitions, so prominent in the current youth literature of the West. Any notion protective of rights, however, must be tempered by an understanding of the local economic and cultural systems which shape daily lives and practices. The prohibition of child employment, for example, imposed by distant edict, can exacerbate local poverty and distress.

Globalisation is implicit in the case of Slovakia, lodged in the economic and political changes which have opened up the society to external influences. However, like C. Wright Mills (1956) writing some fifty years ago, Macháček points to the democratic significance of civil society – that complex of organisations and groupings which spontaneously arise out of individual's interests. NGOs in this civic sense both form and nurture those critical aspects of citizenship which curb the power of the state over the individual. Such intermediary associations, however, are characterised by both fragility and power; and Macháček notes the difficulty in establishing and legitimating them as components of public life in a post-communist society where competing ideologies and practices are still battling for control.

The problem lies in the role of youth in this transformation. Paradoxically, whilst the children of the southern hemisphere have been brought onto the stage of public discourse, the fall of Communism has served to push Slovakian youth off stage. Not only have they lost their institutionalised role in the former regime as political actors and carriers of the future, but also lost are the facilities and rights that accompanied this role. They are, moreover, victims of rising unemployment and job insecurity, though the latter appears to be moderated by what could be called self-responsibilitisation, the notion that they are responsible for their own progression. Concern about the deeper integration of the young into civic activity is perhaps misplaced if this is solely seen in terms of political and social movements – NGOs such as environmental groups extending across national borders. These play a part, and the evidence suggests that many of the young are politically aware if not politically active. Civil society, however, as Macháček notes, is not comprised solely of activities which can be denoted purely as civic, that is, directly related to the obligations and rights of the citizen. Civil society crosses that hazy boundary to include membership of "a citizen community" (The Pocket

Oxford Dictionary), built out of the kind of association which some might see as lesser or trivial, and which implies positive engagement in public space. It is out of such engagement that the tools of citizenship are forged, based upon the mechanisms and skills lodged in the practices of association itself.

A theme running through all these chapters is that of generation, manifest here in the interplay between young people and their societies as succeeding cohorts move through historical time. The young are cast as the bearers of the future. Thus whilst the material and social conditions of the exploited children of the Third World harbour future problems for their societies as they enter and move through adulthood, the young people of Slovakia are seen as the potential carriers of a democratised society founded in their integration into civil society. In Everatt's chapter this theme is developed further, comparing the political activism of one generation, and the depressing legacy left with them, with the consumption-dominated culture of its successor.

Typically, the political activity of young people tends to be seen in a positive light, as something to be encouraged. Yet Everatt shows how political activism may unwittingly lead to a marginalisation. Describing the turbulence of social change which led to the overthrow of apartheid, he notes how the deep engagement of black, urban youth in the protest which "convulsed South Africa from 1976 to 1990", coupled with the disruptive and violent lifestyles of some, resulted in the sacrifice of any educational grounding, however inadequate this might have been. Concern over their ensuing marginalistion, however, both stimulated activity on the part of national NGOs and fuelled political debate. Yet, despite the contribution of the political activity in which young people had been engaged, there was a failure to find a constructive role for youth within the new order, a failure in policy and a failure to see youth (16-30 year olds comprising a quarter of the population) as a political constituency with its own needs. Nonetheless, there was a plethora of activity on the part of NGOs. Amongst these, some differed from those noted earlier. In line with the view that youth organisations should be staffed by the young, they were run and organised by young people themselves (although it will be recalled that the official definition of youth in South Africa extends to the mid 30s). But whilst those NGOs which had a local focus and were locally based were successful, those at national level failed, becoming the subject of much contention. They were variously seen as too distant from the young they were supposed to serve, and their staff in pursuit of personal careers. The question raised, however, and which is echoed where there are pressures to involve young people in the management and conduct of matters which affect them, is the extent to which this aim is possible. Everatt, for example, questions the adequacy of the level of young people's expertise and experience to meet the requirements of such positions.

Against this historical political background the South African young of today present a different set of problems, provoking dismay and nostalgia among some of their predecessors. Growing up within a society which Everatt sees as one which has reproduced the old inegalitarian values, he sees today's youth sharing the consumer values of South Africa's wealthy classes. Young people, in fact, are shaped just as were the earlier generation by the society of which they are part. Nonetheless, though hostile to adults and their rules, surveys suggest that young people are politically aware and are optimistic about the future of South Africa.

In none of these societies, discussed in this part of the book, are young people at the heart of social policy, yet the young are the future. Their rights of whatever kind, and any empowerment that flows from these, wax and wane or remain invisible according to the instrumental needs of the groups or governments in power. Indeed, collectively, these three chapters suggest that the interests of young people are promoted not by their governments but rather by Non-Governmental Organisations in all their various forms, both within and external to their society. In this regard, whilst globalisation may have devastating effects as capital relentlessly seeks the cheapest labour, and political elites may use or discard the young seemingly at will, the communication technology inherent in globalisation, and the opening to a wider gaze of formerly closed societies as they strive to restructure their economies, offers opportunities which strengthen the political role of NGOs. In this ever shrinking world, these actors, whilst not necessarily new, are certainly able to draw upon new forms of power – fed by the cultural capital of accessible information and the social capital of accessible world-wide networks. The strength, endurance and effectiveness of these bonds in the face of governments and dominant world organisations remain to be tested.

References

Brannen, J. and O'Brien, M. (1996), *Children in Families: Research and Policy*, The Falmer Press, London.

Mills, C. W. (1956), *The Power Elite*, Oxford University Press, London.

Vidal, J. (2000a), ' "Girls Will not be Forgotten, Annan Pledges", Aid Agencies Furious as World Leaders Shun Launch of Education Summit', *The Guardian, 17 April, 2000*, p. 15.

Vidal, J. (2000b), 'World Summit Clash on Education of Poor, Read the World: The Right to Education', *The Guardian, 26 April, 2000*, p. 2.

19 The Globalisation of Childhood and Youth: New Actors and Networks in Protecting Street Children and Working Children in the South

MOJIBUR RAHMAN

Background

Protecting street children and working children is a serious challenge for the national governments of the South and the international community's struggle towards peace, equity and justice. The number of working children between the ages of 5 and 14 in the developing countries is 250 million, of whom 120 million work full time. Approximately 61 % of child workers are in Asia, 32 % in Africa and 7 % in Latin America.[1] Millions of children and youth are living in appalling living conditions without education and health care in the South. The separation between economic and social policies in the South is creating a cycle of exploitation for the children from marginalised families and street children. Children in that situation find themselves in a deprivation trap of poverty, isolation, physical weakness, powerlessness and exploitation. They have to take on adult responsibilities very young losing their childhood and youth. The vulnerability of street children and working children is a problem for their very survival. They have to take responsibility for themselves in the absence of any institutional support of the state or society. The children and youth of today are the future citizens of the world. If they are not protected and empowered, their societies may face high crime rates, juvenile delinquency, violence and many other kinds of social pathology. The world is going to face a lack of socio-economic security rather than military security in the new millennium if proper institutional steps are not taken to protect children from marginalisation.

With the failure of both state and market to address the issue, Non-Governmental Organisations (NGOs) have become as gap-fillers for protecting underprivileged children of the South. A global "associational revolution" is taking place, whereby NGOs or development oriented peoples movements around the globe are facing the development problems of the South. They are providing services for underprivileged children and undertaking advocacy and social mobilisation work. Northern NGOs are developing partnerships with Southern NGOs in Third World development. Southern NGOs are creating innovative solutions to the problems such as child labour in collaboration with Northern NGOs. Northern NGOs are helping their Southern partners in strengthening the institutional capacities to provide local solutions to local problems. Bilateral and multilateral international agencies also understand the importance of the network of NGOs in development work and are increasing their support for their initiatives. Poverty reduction strategies increasingly include recognising the survival, well-being and empowerment of children and youth (Fowler 1997, 4).

NGOs are leading in the response to the vulnerable children world-wide. Their efforts have helped to put the issue on the global agenda and the international community is now more aware of the issue. In 1987, UNICEF published a landmark publication "Adjustment with a Human Face" putting rates of child labour and number of street children as important indicators of underdevelopment (Jolly 1987, 261-262). Donors are increasingly aware of problems such as child labour in the South. Yet only a very small portion of development aid in the South is spent on human priorities such as saving underprivileged children. According to UNDP, only 15 % of aid goes to education and health and less than half of this is spent on human priority issues (Smillie 1995, 19).

This chapter will discuss the problem of street children and working children in the South as a problem of development and look at how global NGO networks are working to fight the problem. Development co-operation is discussed as a channel for international relations and the promotion of the rights of children and youth as global citizens.

Why are Children/Youth Vulnerable in the South?

State-society relations in the South are undergoing a constant change in which states are weak and societies are strong. States have to depend on the local elites for their political survival. The relationship between state and society in developing countries is "three-dimensional" including security, development and participation (Samudavanija 1991, 18-19). The relative importance of security on the one hand and development and participation on the other hand determines the regimes' objectives. Political, economic and social development depends on the effective functioning of democracy and democratic institutions. However, this is hindered by the fact that power in the Third World countries is personalised rather than institutionalised. Central and local government institutions are major sources of delay in the implementation of governmental projects and programmes because of cumbersome system of procedures and controls. Thus, local politics becomes fraught with corruption and patronage. This phenomenon explains the continuing marginalisation and social exclusion of the poor in the South. Due to the lack of social capital of the poor, social cohesion is threatened in many poor regions, something which nation states themselves are unable to tackle.

Another problem is that the education system in the South is not open enough to make it possible for the children of poor families to get an education instead of going to work for their own or their families' survival. Education can build children's positive self-image and later determines the scope of self-development of the child. It also determines the circulation of knowledge, skills and capacities in societies. Even though many Southern countries are able to offer universal primary education, there is nevertheless a high drop out rate from basic education and many children do not enrol in the education system, or think that education would be no use to them. Schools in developing countries create memorising students who can become civil servants and other professionals connected to money, power and social prestige (Rahman 1998). However, students' needs are very different to what they can get from the formal public education. Thus, the massive investment in basic education failed to integrate street children and working children into the system. When there is no social capital to assist them in their education, children have to move to the urban areas to find a way of living in the streets or slums and working in the informal and formal sectors in hazardous conditions. However, there are some examples of NGOs providing Non-Formal Education to fit the needs of street children and working children as we shall see later.

Donor countries have leverage in the policy planning of recipient countries because of the aid dependence of the latter. Northern countries are more vocal in respect to human rights than to civil and political rights and often do not see social, cultural, economic and solidarity rights as human rights at all. The realisation of this latter set of rights can strengthen the overall human rights within a society. Investment in the child is the best way to save the future adults in disastrous conditions and the rights of children and youth are therefore important.

The situation of children and youth in the South is part of a global problem. Unfettered market liberalisation has greatly increased the difficulties of vulnerable people including working children in the South. This also has other repercussions. With the deterioration of conditions of life and social cohesion, there is a rise in conflict and lawlessness. Civil war or war creates the problem of refugees or migration which is a big issue of political debate in Europe. The spread of drug dependency and HIV/AIDS is also something which ultimately affects all societies in the world and not just children and young people in the South.

The Situation of Street Children and Working Children in the South

The problem of street children and working children lies in poverty, social exclusion, inequality and injustice. If we consider first the problem of working children, the majority of children involved in child labour are from the most excluded and exploited groups – migrants and refugees, the internally displaced, ethnic minorities and the poorest of the poor. They usually come from families and environments where there is no choice, no possibility of alternatives and no respect for human rights. Yet children and young people are a major resource for progress and the prime movers of innovation. Their imagination, idealism and collective energies form the creative impulse for the future of any nation. Their exclusion and exploitation creates a very big hurdle to the development of a country both in the present and in the future. The causes of child labour are mainly:

- poverty;
- socio-cultural factors;
- the low quality and irrelevance of education;
- limited access to and inadequate infrastructure of education;
- an inadequate and unsupportive policy environment;
- the lack of institutional pluralism;
- problems in the implementation of the law.

Children work in formal sectors such as the garment, tobacco and carpet industries and in the informal sectors which cover a wide range of activities such as collecting garbage, working in plantations, rock breaking, street trading, rag picking, portering, working in hotels/restaurants, tanneries, small workshops, domestic services, as bonded labourers and prostitutes. There is a myth in the North that children are engaged in export industries in a large scale. Yet it is estimated that children employed in export industries in the world represent a small fraction of the total problem of child labour in the world (estimated less than 5 %).[2] Girls are massively present in domestic services and prostitution. Work done by children is often hazardous as they work too young, long hours, with little pay and they have no chance of receiving education and/or leisure. Most of the employment exposes children to health and safety hazards and some is close to slavery. In South Asia for example, the age of child workers ranges from 5 to 14 years old. About 125 million school-aged children in SAARC countries are not in primary or secondary education (Wignaraja and Srinivardana 1998, 16).[3] According to the World Education Report 1991, there were 130 million children aged 6 to 11 who did not attend school; the figure for 12-17 age group was 227 million (Ministry of Foreign Affairs 1994, 50). Below we consider children in some fairly common situations.

Street Children

The number of street children in the world is on the rise, especially in Asia, Africa and Latin America. Street children live without any family and shelter on urban streets or slums, working on streets in informal sectors. Children are engaged in asocial activities such as pickpocketing, robbing stores, selling drugs and working as prostitutes. They live in a stressful environment where their survival chances and ability to improve their position are low. A systematic estimate undertaken by the Anti-Slavery Society in 1985 calculated around 31 million street children world-wide, of whom 71 % were child workers who had families but were not living with them, 23 % kept occasional family contacts and 8 % were entirely separated from their families (Black 1995, 9). In Bangladesh alone, in 1991, the number of street children was estimated to be 1.8 million (Cederroth 1997, 13). NGOs working with street children in Kenya reported that street girls especially go into prostitution to earn money, for affection and protection from violence on the street. The rising numbers of street children is related to the fact that the number of teenage pregnancies and suicides is rising in developing countries whilst drugs and AIDS claim more victims. Furthermore, street children are vulnerable to many different kinds of victimisation and exploitation.

The Sexual Exploitation of Children

The commercial sexual exploitation of children is on the rise globally. Poor girls are trafficked and sold into prostitution and are forced to work as sexual slaves in most parts of the South. Trafficked girls are subjected to rape and other forms of physical and psychological abuse and held in bondage from which escape is virtually impossible. There is also a financial lure for poor street children and working children to go into dangerous occupations such as prostitution. It is estimated that the number of child prostitutes in Philippines, India and Thailand are 60 000, 400 000 and 800 000.[4] Sri Lanka, the Philippines and Thailand have been placed firmly on the map of sex-related tourism. Half of Manila's prostitutes are now young boys, and their starting age can be as low as six years. In Sri Lanka there are an estimated 2000 boys engaged in child prostitution (Fyfe 1988, 77). In Thailand 30 000 million Bahts are made out of the sex industry every year, but the statistics does not distinguish whether it is adult or child prostitution (Arcahvanitkul and Havanon 1990). The flow of sex tourists into developing countries is mainly from the economically developed countries (Western Europe, Nordic countries, North America, Australasia and the Gulf states). Nepal, Bangladesh and Myanmar have serious problems with the trafficking of young girls to work in the sex trade in India, Pakistan, Thailand, Hong Kong, the Middle East and even in Europe. An estimated 4000 to 5000 Nepali girls, of an average age of 10-14 are consigned to India annually (Crawford 1994, 4). According to a study conducted by Human Rights Watch/Asia, 20 % of Bombay's Nepali brothel population of 100 000 consists of girls under 18 years old, and over half of the population there are infected with HIV (Human Rights Watch/ Asia 1995, 14). There are also over 200 000 Bangladeshi women and girls, which have been sent to Pakistan (UBINIG 1997, 3-9).

Bonded Labour and Slavery

The term refers to the phenomenon of children working in conditions of servitude in order to pay off their families' burden of debt. Many children in Nepal work as bonded labourers. Children working under the system are considered as the property of the landlord. According to Anti-Slavery International there are more than 200 000 such bonded labourers in Nepal including children. Another example is that about 19 000 children from South Asia have been sold into a horrific form of child labour to work as jockeys in the royal sport of camel racing in the United Arab Emirates (UBINIG 1997, 4).

Domestic Service

Children from poor families work as domestic servants in South Asia and they mainly work as maids or cooks. Girls are largely present in this service. There is no defined role in their work and they do not get time for study or play. In many cases, employers and their family members abuse them physically and sexually. Abuses and deaths of many domestic helpers go unpunished and according to Bangladesh Human Rights Commission report,[5] 86 % of domestic workers surveyed have faced abuse. Out of the 123 domestic workers in the study, 72 were kept locked in the house when employers went outside.

Hazardous Occupations

In South Asia generally, children can still be found working in urban areas in hazardous industries and occupations and are exposed to chemical and biological poisoning. Children work in glass factories, brick factories, tanneries, engineering workshops, slate factories, carpet weaving and many other hazardous forms of employment. An ILO study in Bangladesh discovered that more than 40 types of economic activities conducted by children were hazardous.[6] A recent study of child labour in bidi factories in Bangladesh by Terese Blanchet and her team members found that there are 270 000 children and women, who work in bidi (tobacco) factories and 8 % of the workers are below the age of 15.[7] According to a CWIN study in Nepal, 65 % of the transport helpers were below the age of 14 and the remaining 35 % between the ages of 14 and 18 years. Altogether 855 of the child transport workers in the study were suffering from eye diseases, 82 % from headache and nausea. Furthermore, a considerable number of those children were found to be addicted to alcohol and smoking (CWIN 1998, 38). In the warring parts of Asia, Africa and Latin America, children are also forced to work as soldiers and very often they are exposed to cruelty and death.

New Actors and Networks in Protecting Children

NGOs are the leading actors in protecting child rights world-wide. Their work has become very important in world affairs. New ties and relations among the peoples and institutions of the North and South are mushrooming through NGOs, often bypassing governments. They also have alliances or networks in their common goal of the protection of children world-wide. The term NGO means that it is an organisation established and governed by a group of private citizens for a stated philanthropic purpose and supported by voluntary individual contribution. However, increasingly international governmental aid is also channelled through NGOs. The term also includes broad spectrum of organisations and their networks both non-profit and non-governmental, based in the North and South that do development work with service provisions or advocacy in Third World development. Grass-root organisations or co-operatives that seek profits are not included here as NGOs. NGOs can be community-based, nationally-based or internationally-based.

The NGO movement has gone through a process of transformation and evolution. David Korten has described the idea of NGO generations (Korten 1990, 115-125). The first generation was concerned with relief and welfare, the second generation was community-based and the third generation was based upon building sustainable systems. The present generation of NGOs are examples of the people's initiatives around the world in creating local solutions to the problems which the international

269

community seeks to solve. Apart from the emergency and relief sector, most NGOs are moving away from pure delivery of services to the area of capacity building and lobbying. They are exploring the possibility and potentiality of partnership between different actors in society to promote the rights of children. This is a general indicator of the emerging perspectives of NGOs in Third World development. The general strengths of NGOs are:

- strong grass-root links;
- field based innovation and adaptiveness;
- a process oriented approach to development;
- participatory methods and tools;
- a long term commitment to sustainability;
- cost effectiveness
  (J. Clark as quoted in C. Malena 1995, 15).

Because of comparative advantages of NGOs, the World Bank and many multilateral organisations and bilateral donors have recognised the important role of NGOs in world development so that aid channelled through NGOs is a significant component of development co-operation of donor countries.

In recent years, the mobilisation efforts of NGOs have helped to develop a public debate on child labour in South Asia, the home of the world's largest concentration of working children. Most of the governments of the world have signed Convention on the Rights of the Child (CRC) and this was mainly initiated by NGOs. The present state of awareness concerning child labour in the South and North is the contribution of NGOs. For example, to help Bangladesh to protect child rights, a World Bank-led consortium involving a number of bilateral donors as well as the multilateral donors including UNICEF, UNDP and UNFPA is supporting a five-year (1996-2000) $310 million General Education Project to strengthen basic education along with an integrated Non-Formal Education (NFE) programme. The project is supported by a number of UNICEF National Committees. The project draws on a number of selected NGOs which have diverse experience at grass-root level in basic education (UNICEF 1995, 78). UNICEF in 1996 changed its mission statement expressly to include the protection of child rights guided by the UN Convention on the Rights of the Child.

270

However, the effects of international aid often has unintended consequences. For example under the pressure from the US, the government of Bangladesh dismissed 100 000 children from the garments industry. The result was disastrous for the children themselves. The dismissal of child workers, mostly girls, forced some to turn to prostitution for survival. To tackle the situation, UNICEF, ILO and Bangladesh Garments Manufacturers and Exporting Association (BGMEA) initiated a NFE programme for the dismissed children. The Bangladesh Rural Advancement Committee (BRAC) and Gonoshahajjo Sangstha (GSS), two prominent Bangladeshi NGOs were given the responsibility to operate an education programme for the children. BRAC is operating 256 schools for child workers in the area of Dhaka, Nayaranganj, Chittagong and Gazipur,[8] and GSS is running over 750 schools mostly in rural areas of Bangladesh and 3000 Adolescent Learning Centres offering education for 300 000 children.

At the beginning of 1995, BRAC was running 35 000 primary schools with Non-Formal Education. The schools had 5 % drop out rate compared to an 80 % drop out rate in government schools (Smillie 1995, 63). One of the striking points of BRAC education is that 75 % of the enrolment in these schools are girls. Under this education system, there is an attempt to deal with drop-outs and non-starters; the school timetable is adapted to family needs and the curriculum is need-based. After completion of BRAC's three-year Non-Formal Education, children can be successfully integrated into public schools. The work of BRAC is therefore an example of how supporting local initiatives through NGOs can be more effective than direct intervention which might have unintended consequences.

BRAC's success in Non-Formal Education for children has created interest among bilateral and multilateral donor agencies for supporting government education projects in Bangladesh. UBINIG, a Bangladeshi NGO is working with other South Asian NGOs to co-operate on the cross-border trafficking of children. It has formed a network of South Asian NGOs named "Resistance". Norwegian Save the Children published a landmark report "The Sexual Exploitation of Children in Developing countries" in 1989. It also produced widely distributed brochure against AIDS and child prostitution in co-operation with Den Norske Reisebransjeforeningen. Swedish Save the Children is providing courses for training of staff of the International Save the Children Alliance, police officers, and trainers for Police Academy concerning child rights in

271

Bangladesh (Rädda Barnen 1996, 3). This Northern NGO is supporting local NGOs such as Bangladesh Shishu Adhikar Forum (BSAF) and National Forum of Organisations Working with the Disabled (NFOWD).

In Nepal, the government has established a Task Force for the elimination of child labour under the National Planning Commission. The Task Force, in co-operation with UNICEF, has identified child prostitution and bonded labour as areas which need urgent action. NGOs in Nepal have been effective in raising public awareness about the problem of child labour – including the trafficking of girls. A coalition of NGOs, carpet manufacturing organisations, government and international agencies called the National Society for Protection of Environment and Children (NASPEC) was established in 1993. Advocacy for child rights in Nepal has seen some success. A 150-member NGO Child Rights advocacy network has been established. The Prevention of Child Exploitation Project in Nepal is run by both local and international NGOs. Local NGOs like CWIN and Nepal Children's Organisation (NCO) are in the forefront in the action. The project is supported by Norwegian Save the Children, Australian Agency for International Development, Save the Children - UK and the UNICEF National Committees of Finland, Germany, and the Netherlands. ILO's International Programme on the Elimination of Child Labour (IPEC) is working in developing countries in co-operation with local NGOs. By March 1997, the number of IPEC donors had increased to 14. At present there are 11 countries participating in the programme including Bangladesh, Brazil, India, Indonesia, Kenya, Nepal, Pakistan, Philippines, Thailand, Tanzania and Turkey. IPEC has collaboration with local NGOs in the implementation of programmes.

Pelastakaa Lapset ry. (Finnish Child Welfare Association) has programmes for the protection of children in developing countries. SASK has a programme in Pakistan concerning child labour.[9] Child Rights Information Network (UK), Childwatch International – Network for Child Research (Norway), UNICEF and UNESCO have jointly published the "Directory of European Research and Documentation Institutions". The NGO *End Child Prostitution in Asian Tourism* (ECPAT), which is based in Thailand, is working with national and international NGOs to fight against the exploitation of children in the sex industry world-wide since 1990. Due to the efforts of ECPAT, a First World Congress Against the Commercial Sexual Exploitation of Children was held in Stockholm in 1996. Finnish NGOs such as the Taksvärkki and Mannerheim League for Child Welfare,

are collaborating with ECPAT. Terre des Hommes drew attention to paedophile tourism in Sri Lanka in 1981 and CWIN has published a booklet for the awareness of tourists "The child and the tourist". In recent years laws to cover the commercial sexual abuse of children in tourism have been passed in Germany, Austria, France, Australia, the United States, Belgium and New Zealand with several other countries considering similar measures.

In protecting street children, the Undugu Society of Kenya is following a "Child-to-Child" approach. Rehabilitated street children in the NGO are used as educators for their peer street children. They accompany social workers to the streets or to the schools. They advise their peers on the streets and their colleagues in the schools who have not fully rehabilitated on how to build self-esteem and keep away from the streets. They talk about issues such as health, family planning and the use of contraceptives. This approach is proving very effective because it appears that the children, especially girls, tend to listen and trust each other and are able to discuss certain issues much more freely with those of their own age.

After national governments had taken the policy decision to protect children's rights in South Asia, a regional initiative to stop the exploitation of children under the forum of SAARC was also initiated.[10] The fifth SAARC summit held in Male in 1990 declared 1990 as the "SAARC Year of the Girl Child" and 1990s as the "Decade of the Girl Child" highlighting the multiple problems and discrimination faced by girl children in South Asia. In the 1993 summit, heads of states and governments endorsed the 1992 Colombo Resolution on Children, which pursued the goal of the progressive and accelerated elimination of child labour. In the 9th summit in 1997, the forum reaffirmed its commitment to take urgent action to alleviate the situation of the Girl Children in Especially Difficult Circumstances (GCEDC) including orphaned, disabled and exploited girls. Understanding the need for the promotion of rights in South Asia, the summit proposed launching the "SAARC Decade of the Rights of the Child" for the years 2001 to 2010.

Conclusion

It is evident that the need to tackle the exploitation and exclusion of children and youth in developing countries is a global problem. The presence of millions of vulnerable children living on the streets, working in exploited conditions or in the sex industry is a product of global economic developments. The repercussions are also global, affecting both more developed Northern countries and less developed Southern ones. At the same time, the recognition of the rights of children and youth has been a product of transnational co-operation and global institutions, so that in this respect citizenship is increasingly global.

The response to this problem has been a wide network of NGOs and local initiatives which can work together in partnership with international NGOs and ones from Northern countries. These NGOs are able to by-pass governments and to deal directly with the problems of children and young people. Many examples have been described in this chapter. NGOs are increasingly the form through which international aid is channelled and their role has evolved from one of straightforward relief and service delivery to that of advocacy, promotion and developing sustainable solutions in co-operation with local communities and the target populations. The empowerment of target populations has formed an important part of this strategy.

However, it is increasingly recognised that developed countries cannot implement the human rights of children in the Southern countries directly, but can rather play a supportive role to boost the efforts of local organisations. Thus, strategies of regional aid should incorporate child rights issue into the mainstream sectors of development co-operation and support initiatives by NGOs. Whatever policies or programmes taken to protect children from vulnerability or exploitation, the best interests of the children should be taken in consideration first. There should be a "First Call for Children". In the words of Antonie de Saint-Expuery's Little Prince: "Adults do not understand anything, and as a child you get tired of always having to explain to them." From this point of view, empowering children and youth points the way towards improving some of the problems described in this chapter. It has been demonstrated that child-to-child, youth-to-child or youth-to-youth contact between North and South can help to create greater understanding among the children and youth of the world, to promote cultural understanding and to make the globe a more secure place for future generations.

Notes

1. ILO (1997), 'New Weapons against Child Trafficking in Asia', *World of Work, No. 19, March 1997.*
2. Document presented by ILO and UNICEF in International Conference on Child Labour in Oslo, October 27-30, 1997.
3. South Asian Association for Regional Co-operation (SAARC) which includes seven countries Bangladesh, Bhutan, India, Maledives, Nepal, Pakistan and Sri Lanka.
4. Sachs, A. (1994), 'The Last Commodity: Child Prostitution in the Developing World', *World Watch 7 (4).*
5. Bangladesh Human Rights Commission Survey Report, 14th October, 1993.
6. See ILO (1997), Child Labour in Asia.
7. The study is supported by Solidarite Mondiale and Rädda Barnen. See The Daily Star, 16th November, 1998, Bangladesh.
8. Information sent from BRAC's NFE programme, Dhaka, Bangladesh on 29th March, 1998.
9. SASK is the Trade Union Solidarity Centre of Finland.
10. South Asian Association for Regional Co-operation.

References

Arcahvanitkul, K. and Havanon, N. (1990), *Situation, Opportunities and Problems Encountered by Young Girls in Thai Society*, Terre des Hommes, Bangkok.

Black, M. (1995), *In the Twilight Zone: Child Workers in the Hotel, Tourism and Catering Industry*, ILO, Geneva.

Cederroth, S. (1997), *Basket Case or Poverty Alleviation: Bangladesh Approaches the Twenty-First Century*, Nordic Institute of Asian Studies, Copenhagen.

Crawford, S. (1994), *Child Labour in South Asia: A Review of the Literature*, UNICEF Regional Office for South Asia, Princeton.

CWIN (1998), *State of the Rights of the Child in Nepal: Country Report Released by CWIN*, Child Workers in Nepal (CWIN) Concerned Centre, Kathmandu.

Fowler, A. (1997), *Striking a Balance: A Guide to Enhancing the Effectiveness of Non-Governmental Organizations in International Development*, Earthscan, London.

Fyfe, A. (1988), *All Work and no Play: Child Labour Today*, Trade Union Congress/ UNICEF, London.

Human Rights Watch Asia (1995), *Rape for Profit: Trafficking of Nepali Girls and Women to India's Brothels*, Human Rights Watch, New York.

ILO (1997), 'New Weapons against Child Trafficking in Asia', *World of Work, No. 19, March 1997.*

Jolly, R. (1987), 'Education', in G. A. Cornia, R. Jolly and F. Stewart (eds.), *Adjustment with a Human Face: Volume 1, Protecting the Vulnerable and Promoting Growth*, Clarendon Press, Oxford.

Korten, D. (1990), *Getting to the 21st Century – Voluntary Action and Global Agenda*, Kumarian Press, West Hartford (CT).

Laakso, L. (1996), *Nordic Development Cooperation and the Promotion of Democracy: In Search for Strategies, Working Paper 7/96*, Institute of Development Studies, Helsinki.

Malena, C. (1995), *Working with NGOs: A Practical Guide to Operational Collaboration between the World Bank and Non-Governmental Organizations*, World Bank Operational Policy Department, Washington, DC.

Ministry of Foreign Affairs (1994), *First Steps: Policy Memorandum on Children in Developing Countries*, Development Cooperation Information Department, The Hague.

Rädda Barnen (1996), *Annual Report 1996*, Swedish Save the Children, Dhaka.

Rahman, M. (1998), *Globalisation, Development Cooperation and Human Rights of Children in Least Developed Countries: South Asia in Context*, Paper presented in the Annual Conference of the Norwegian Association for Development Research – NFU, University of Oslo, June 5-6, 1998.

Sachs, A. (1994), 'The Last Commodity: Child Prostitution in the Developing World', *World Watch 7 (4)*.

Samudavanija, C. (1991), 'The Three Dimensional State', in J. Manor (ed.), *Rethinking Third World Politics*, Longman, London.

Smillie, I. (1995), *The Alms Bazaar: Altruism under Fire – Non-Profit Organizations and International Development*, IT Publications, London.

UBINIG (1997), *Resistance against Trafficking in Women and Children in South Asia*, Policy Research for Development Alternative, Dhaka.

UNICEF (1995), *Protecting Children, Protecting the Future: The Story of UNICEF in Bangladesh*, UNICEF, Dhaka.

Wignaraja, P. and Srinivardana, S. (1998), *Readings on Pro-Poor Planning through Social Mobilisation in South Asia, Vol. 1*, Vikas Publishing (Pvt.) Ltd., New Delhi.

20 Youth and Creation of Civil Society in Slovakia

LADISLAV MACHÁČEK

Introduction

In September 1998 the authoritarian populist Prime Minister of Slovakia, Vladimir Meciar, who had helped to isolate Slovakia internationally and to ensure that Slovakia was not in the first round of "European enlargement" along with its neighbours (Czech Republic, Poland and Hungary), was voted out of office. The campaign to create an electoral alternative involved the widespread mobilisation of civil society and especially of youth. Youth have been consistently the strongest supporters of democratisation and of social change throughout post-communist Europe. Hence, the involvement of youth as active citizens and agents of change is crucial in the shaping of societies after Communism. Empowering youth can have important consequences. This article reports the results of a research project by the Slovak Academy of Sciences to investigate the creation of civil society in Slovakia and the role of youth within it.

The Construction of Civil Society

The "velvet" revolution in the former Czechoslovakia and the subsequent split of the federated republic into two sovereign states in 1993 created the Slovak Republic as an independent democratic state after many centuries of struggle for national recognition. The need to build a civil society, after its destruction by the Communist regime and in the context of a newly created state, was an important challenge. However, as in all transitory periods, this one contains a dynamic mixture of fragments of the old and the new reality, of the world of the future and the world of the past. It is an intrinsically contradictory, contentious mixture. In Slovakia, the struggle

277

between the Prime Minister, Vladimir Meciar and the President of State, Michal Kovac and their respective followers between 1994 and 1998 as to the direction that Slovak society should take is representative of these tendencies.[1] Whilst Kovac emphasised again and again the need to renovate civil society, Meciar tried to crush or control the Third Sector of civil society by use of central and local state power.

The former Communist regime followed the ideas of Marx and Engels's in the German Ideology (Marx and Engels 1977, 123-4) that "civil society" was the same as "bourgeois" society and consequently "capitalist". That is why it could not set itself the goal of establishing civil society. On the contrary, Communism tried to uproot it. Uprooting civil society, meant above all the destruction of the institution of private property as the economic and legal foundation of civil society. Instead, the idea of "citizen" was seen as disagreeable, used only for describing traffic offences and most people were labelled instead as "working people", "the masses" and so on. The idea of the citizen embodies a notion of the individual manifestation of freedom and democracy which was incompatible with this version of socialism. Hence it was necessary to recreate the idea of the "citizen" after 1989.

However, after the fall of Communism, the restoration of civil society was no simple matter either. The idea of the restoration of civil society touches upon both the sphere of economics (e.g. privatisation, return to the system of contract relations between free economic entities, etc.) and the sphere of politics and the state (e.g. the civil source of the state authority, political pluralism, the rule of law etc.). But the restoration of civil society through economic or legal foundations is not enough. According to Roško, it also has to be established in the subjective thoughts, feelings and forms of association of the citizens themselves. In this respect there is always the struggle between the progressive notions of citizenship/civil society and ones which are backward looking. On the one hand there is the desire to create a self-conscious citizenship and on the other hand a tendency towards passive resignation from self-conscious citizenship (Roško 1996a).

Hence, we can define a more active definition of citizenship than that implied by T. H. Marshall (1950) in his discussion of citizenship as a set of political, juridical and welfare rights bestowed by the state. We can also invoke a non-economic sense of citizenship that is not just reliant on the institution of private property. In the words of Ján Stena, citizenship as an element of civil society could be seen as: "The grouping of people around

278

particular interests, the process of horizontal organisation, the autonomous creation of structures based on the co-ordination of people's activities embodying the free will of every individual. It must be understood as a self-contained 'layer' of social life that generates self-regulation mechanisms influencing the development of society. Civil society is very important for articulating and defending the different interests of citizens and in controlling state power" (Stena, et al. 1990, 1).

One of the tragedies of the social development of Slovak society was that the constant regeneration of associational life, party associations, clubs, interest groups, social corporations, citizens' initiatives and other movements was seen as being linked with bourgeois forms of social life, rather than an important element of the development of civilisation more generally. The mechanisms and tools of civil society enable social problems in various spheres of everyday life to be addressed or solved in ways that could not possibly be managed by central state power.

In order to better analyse the developments in citizenship in Slovak society, we have developed the concept of "citizenry" alongside that of democracy. This concept reflects the revolutionary rise of an activist, non-party layer of citizens within civil society which co-operated actively with the opposition parties in the elections of 1998. The reasons for the creation of this broad social movement of citizenry are described in the next section.

Civil Society and the Growth of the Third Sector

Civil society represents the sphere of the spontaneous association of people on the basis of their partial, mostly non-political interests; the sphere of self-organisation and self-regulation. The articulation of various interests in this sphere is possible through the membership in voluntary organisations, associations, movements and social organisations (Macháček 1996). The state does not interfere in this sphere and can only create favourable conditions for its existence. In this sphere many conflicts of interest by different actors are peacefully resolved. Hence, the basis of social transformation should not only be seen as the introduction of a market economy through the return of private property, but also the return of a variety of activities, which had previously been dominated by the state, to civil society. Even this is not a one-way process of handing over tasks to voluntary organisations and NGOs (Non-Governmental Organisations). It also involves a process of decentralisation, regionalisation and local self-government. However, civil society should be protected by law from state interference. That is, the citizen is permitted to do anything except what is explicitly forbidden, and the state bodies are permitted to do only what they are allowed by law. Thus, the state limits its own power by law in order to create from civil society a society of responsible subjects who take over substantial parts of state activity which were usurped by the totalitarian state.

The development of civil society and the citizenry can be divided into four stages. In the first phase, under Communism, there were pockets of citizens who opposed the dominant state, but generally speaking, civil society was crushed. During the second phase 1989-1994 there was the gradual re-establishment of civil society, often with the help of dissidents from the earlier stage and assistance from international organisations, along with state sponsorship of various kinds. In the third phase, 1994-1998, under the domination of Meciar, intellectuals and activists who had been active in establishing the new civil society, left government positions (or were kicked out) and moved instead to the Third Sector. During this period the regime tried to undermine civil society and reinstate state control. During the phase after 1998, when Meciar was ousted, the intellectuals and activists have once more moved from the Third Sector into public life.

The foundations of civil society can be found even under Communism. As Les has pointed out, the voluntary sector in Central and Eastern Europe is not only a product of the breakthroughs of 1989. Foundations and associations have a long history in the region (Les 1994). Moreover, the stagnation and moral crisis of Communism in the 1970s and 1980s lead to the creation of the "alternative", "parallel" or "second" society. One example of these "small circles of freedom" was the ecological movement known as the "Bratislava-nahlas" (translated as: Bratislava – say it aloud), which was very important for the Slovak anti-communist movement before 1989.

The formal establishment of civil society in the Slovak Republic had to wait until after 1989. However, after that it expanded rapidly. According to the data of May 1995, which we obtained from SAIA-SCTS (Slovak Academies Information Agency-Service Centre for the Third Sector), there were about 9800 NGOs in Slovakia. Among these were 481 foundations,

1084 civic associations, associations with 3543 experts and 380386 volunteers who registered their names on the mailing list of the Third Sector.[2] According to sociological research carried out by the Focus Agency in December 1994, approximately 15 % of citizens were members of various associations and clubs. The empirical research of Institute of Sociology of Slovak Academy of Sciences in summer 1995 (Macháček 1996) confirmed that 12.6 % of citizens participated in various corporations and associations and 2.5 % in civic movements and initiatives. In Slovakia, the overlap between membership of a hobby club and civic associations with other forms of associations such as political parties, trade unions, local councils, consumption and production co-operatives, etc., is typical. By 1996, 17 000 non-profit associations had been set up and comparative data show that the people of Slovakia were more active as citizens than were those of most other countries. Hence whilst in Slovakia 9.7 % of the population were active in working in areas of citizen and human rights, this was the case for only 6.1 % of people in Europe and 3.1 % of people in the world (Wolekova and Salamon 2000). The remarkable mobilisation of the citizenry can be explained by the rather dramatically changing political situation and power struggles during the 1990s.

A dominant cause of the changing situation of the Third Sector after 1994, during the third phase identified above, was the polarisation of the political scene in Slovakia. M. Bútora shows (1997, 18-19) how during this time the position of the government coalition was strengthened and how the state began once more to take over control of larger and larger areas of social life. It was only a question of time before the Third Sector would be once more subject to state control. One reason why this was possible is explained by Z. Fialová who maintains that: "Many intellectuals and leaders of the (reform) movements (after 1989) left their organisational activities and committed themselves to a party and government to be able to build up basic democratic structures in the country (during the period 1989-1994). This to a certain extent weakened the potential of the emerging Third Sector. However, after the 1992 elections, and in the following years, an important part of this political elite 'withdrew' itself back into the sphere of a non-government sector – as a result of electoral failures and disappointments – where they could make use of their abilities in building up democracy from 'below' " (Bútora and Fialová 1995, 33).

In my opinion, the reason for the threat to the Third Sector was that its leading members after 1994 were those who had been active in political life during the second phase of transition and who were struggling against representatives of Meciar's ruling coalition, such as M. Bútora, P. Demeš and H. Wolekova. After 1994 we can observe many attempts by the ruling coalition to undermine and control the Third Sector. For example, members of the Slovak National Party (SNS) spoke against the activities of the Open Society Fund of George Soros (pledged to fighting against totalitarian regimes of whatever kind). Another example, is when the Members of Parliament for the Movement for Democratic Slovakia (MfDS/HZDS) party discussed the issue of NGOs in the Parliament, which led to the central organs of the state administration (the Ministry of Education) cancelling the contract for the leasing of a building to the SAIA (Slovak Academies Information Agency) which provided services and a consulting centre for the Third Sector. From then on, economic controls over foundations were increased and state supervision of the Bill on Foundations was increased. I would not explain this as M. Bútora does (1997, 22): "Generally it should be noted that some voluntary associations due to their disposition get into conflict with any government team (as is often the case with environmental activists)." In fact there was not any straightforward conflict between the state and civic movements, but rather it was the case that opposition forces were transferred into the sphere of the Third Sector. This was then an oppositional political struggle against the ruling regime of the state and that is one reason why the ruling coalition was so keen on crushing the emergent Third Sector.

M. Bútora concludes his essay as follows: "It is not out of question that the Third Sector in Slovakia will be put to hard tests in the immediate period. Those ones that will hold out will harden their 'civil health'. It will not serve their purposes only it will serve the whole society on its strenuous way toward betterment of the quality of life" (Bútora 1997, 23). The problem lies only in the fact that the high moral and civil potential of Slovaks who may wish to help their fellow citizens through voluntary work requires a social climate in which they will experience praise for such initiatives, not existential distress. This is especially the case because we were not in a situation like in the West where volunteerism is often a kind of hobby and effectively a way of spending time. Voluntary work does not enjoy such high social esteem in Slovakia. It will be dependent on financial state subsidies for a long time, and thus be in the hands of government coalitions. Civic participation in various spheres of public life will remain for some time in the same condition. The ejection of representatives of the opposition from any posts in the state sector, from institutions of research and education, from diplomacy and the mass media has the consequence of helping to construct an oppositional civil society, as described by Z. Fialová. It seems that this was also the case after the electoral defeat of the former regime in Slovakia in 1994. In this case the experienced politicians and organisers moved into civil society and Third Sector organisations as a form of opposition. This was a real situation (1994-1998) in which the Third Sector, lying somewhere between the state and market, played an active role in the struggle for legislative reform.

The legal status of non-profit organisations is still rather ambiguous. Legislation between 1994 and 1998 repealed many of the advantages of civic associations in taxation and other such areas, and the whole voluntary sector was put in a position similar to that of private business. Despite that interviews confirm that citizens have the attitude that voluntary work has qualities and benefits which can neither be met nor substituted by hired labour (Bútora and Fialová 1995, 72-73). Thus, there is a problem as to where legislatively the Third Sector should belong.

Young People as Citizens: Promoters and Victims of Change

Promoters of Change

It was emphasised in the 5th meeting of European Ministers responsible for Youth in Bucharest (1998), that building a democratic Europe depends on the participation of all young people. But we can ask ourselves: are young people really in the front line of changes?

Certainly, youth have been consistently among the strongest supporters of democratic and market changes. Here we can draw upon a cross national survey carried out in 1994, 1996 and 1998 in Slovakia, the New Democracies Barometer (NDB). This study showed that young people are generally those most in favour of political and economic changes (Haerpfer forthcoming). This is also the case in Slovakia. However, in Slovakia we can see a tendency for youth to become more democratic over time. Using an index of democratisation to measure support for democracy involving a range of different variables developed by C. Haerpfer, we can see that there is a development of democracy amongst young people between 1994 and 1998. Whilst they started as less democratic than the older age group in 1994, by 1998 they were 9 % more democratic than the older age cohort (Table 20.1). In the NDB studies, it was also consistently the case that the higher educated and more urban citizens were most in favour of democracy (Tables 20.2 and 20.3). Thus, we could say that the young, urbanised and highly educated are at the forefront of change (tables taken from Haerpfer forthcoming, chapter 4).

Table 20.1 Age by per cent who are democrats according to the democratisation index, 1994-1998

	1994	1996	1998
18-29	56	53	55
30-59	53	53	57
60 plus	60	52	46

Table 20.2 Education by per cent who are democrats according to the democratisation index, 1994-1998

	1994	1996	1998
Primary	46	42	48
Secondary	59	53	55
Tertiary	58	72	72

Table 20.3 Town size by per cent who are democrats according to the democratisation index, 1994-1998

	1994	1996	1998
Villages < 6000	42	50	49
Towns 7000-100 000	64	53	55
Cities > 100 000	74	68	73

These tendencies were also visible in voting results. First time voters in Slovakia made up approximately 10 % of the electorate in the parliamentary elections in 1998 and also in the parliamentary elections in 1994. Young people, despite opposing the regime, tended not to vote in elections. Participation was very small in 1994 (25 %) when the HZDS/MfDS won.

Table 20.4 Party support by socio-demographic categories

FOCUS, September 25th - 26th, 1998[3]

Row % n = 4516		AGE				
For which party/movement have you voted?	ENTIRE SAMPLE	18-24	25-34	35-44	45-54	More than 55
HZDS (Meciar)	23	12	14	23	28	37
SDK (Dzurinda)	28	32	34	28	27	23
SDL (Migaš)	15	18	17	16	17	11
SMK (Bugar)	9	8	8	8	9	12
SNS (Slota)	9	11	11	9	7	7
SOP (Schuster)	8	13	11	9	7	4
Other parties	6	5	5	6	6	6
No answer	1	0	1	0	0	1

HZDS – Movement for Democratic Slovakia; SDK – Slovak Democracy Coalition; SDL – Party of Democratic Left; SMK – Magyar Coalition Party; SNS – Slovak National Party; SOP – Party for Citizens Understanding.

However, the election campaign in 1998 concentrated upon mobilising these young, urban and educated voters with the result that the turnout by them in 1998 was very high (80 %) when the alternative coalition won. Moreover (Table 20.4), over two-thirds (69 %) of first time voters in 1998 supported opposition parties (Dzurinda, Migaš, Schuster, Bugar) and only 23 % voted Movement for Democratic Slovakia (Meciar) and Slovak National Party (Slota) (see Focus Agency Report 1998). The main supporters of the MfDS were among people over 55 years old (37 %). The outcome of the election in which the authoritarian populist regime of Vladimir Meciar was defeated can also be seen as a result of the OK '98 campaign to mobilise citizens to become more active as voters.

In the summer months of 1998 it was clear enough that all attempts to put the voluntary civil sphere under state control had failed. The Donors Forum in Slovakia, out of which the Open Society Foundation and

Foundation for Development of Civil Society especially supported a wide range of projects of civic initiatives, focused upon the activation of citizens in the election process, especially upon the participation of first time voters.

The specific form that the campaign took can be seen in the activities of the Slovak Youth Council called "My Future" which involved distributing 250 000 postcards urging young people to vote. Others distributed T-shirts, stickers and mobile phones in order to more easily organise rallies, demonstrations and meetings in a very short time among young people. This was fast, effective and de-centralised as a method of organisation and thus difficult for the regime to control. Our sociological hypothesis on the inevitability of turning "democracy" into "citizenracy" materialised in the nation-wide civil movement as it became clear that civil passivity, apathy and indifference will not lead to the desirable social change.[4]

An important factor in maintaining this burst of activity in civil society has been the affiliation of Slovak Republic with the European Union, and its membership in the Council of Europe. For young people, this means that the activities of the youth associations and notably the Youth Council of Slovakia are of considerable importance in view of Slovakia's integration into the new Europe, all the more so since many initiatives encouraging this process are realised precisely through the help of the emerging European youth policy and its current emphasis on education for citizenship. The development of civil society in Slovakia was greatly influenced by the civic youth associations and movements, especially the uniting of national councils and international youth organisations in Europe under the recently created Youth Forum.

It is not only in youth movements, but also in the activities of other social movements (e.g. ecology, peace, human and civil rights, women's, etc.) where young adherents are important. One might say that the higher developed, modernised societies tend to become "movement societies". Youth movements that appear in this context tend to take the form of the organised and continuous collective efforts of co-operating individuals, groups and organisations aimed at supporting and sustaining social change by means of public protest activities. Therefore, it is not enough to create a state of affluence as a material base to introduce citizenship and modern individuality to everyone. Young people grow to become citizens through the organised effort, or initiative of people of equal standing and interests who, within their rights, join forces to achieve a social change. We could point to these factors then, and the distinctive role of youth, in paving the "Slovak" road to reform and her integration into the European nexus through the European Union and the transatlantic nexus through NATO.

Victims of Change

However, young people have also been the victims of change in post-communist societies. Whilst in the former regimes they were institutionalised as a social group through various youth organisations to which most young people belonged and were seen as the bearers of the "bright new communist future", this strong recognition of youth has now disappeared (Wallace and Kovatcheva 1998). Along with the disappearance of youth as formal political actors, many of the facilities which were formerly provided for them for free or with substantial subsidies, including sports centres, summer camps, skiing hostels, travel opportunities (within the Communist block) also disappeared. Thus, we can say that many Central European post-communist countries can also be seen as *post-youth* societies. After the brief political mobilisation of youth, mainly students, youth disappeared not only from the political scene but also from public discourse in general. People in Slovakia do not talk about youth problems or children's rights, but more about how to privatise the property of the former youth movements. After 1989 youth itself is in the process of deconstruction.

Young people were among the main victims of rising unemployment. According to the research conducted by the Institute of Sociology of the Slovak Academy of Sciences in 1995, 13 % in the age group over 44 had been unemployed for at least two months, 25 % in the age group 30 to 44, 35 % in the age group 25 to 29 and 44 % in the age group 18-24. Also, the older cohorts least expected to lose their jobs (35 %), but this figure was 50 % for those under 24 and 62 % for those aged 25 to 29 (Macháček 1999).

Thus we could say, that young people as citizens are both the promoters and victims of social change: their situation in post-communist Slovakia is double-faced. On the one hand they are the people most supporting the reforms and most likely to adapt to a market economy through individualisation and entrepreneurialism. On the other hand, young people are most likely to be unemployed and have lost much status and many resources in the course of post-communist transition.

During the present historical era we should see the education of young people for citizenship as having an European dimension. The new concept of citizenship most relevant here involves not only responsibility of individual citizens for themselves and their country, but also for others within our continent. It is my opinion that this can only happen adequately through the construction of new forms of solidarity.

Solidarity is to be understood as the readiness for the redistribution of the vital resources and opportunities with respect to the environment, housing, establishing families, bringing up children, access to education and jobs, according to the various needs of different citizens. This kind of solidarity is missing in both Eastern and Western Europe where collective solutions are passed over in favour of individual ones. There is a typical tendency for the youth in Europe towards individualisation. This does not mean a growth of egoism of the individuals or their unwillingness to co-operate as a group (Macháček 1998). It is rather a movement away from the previously strictly state-planned orientation of personal objectives, as was the case in Slovakia. The adolescents must focus more on their own personal development and self-realisation, and bear responsibility for a potential failure of the consequences of their decisions. This applies as much to their professional orientation as to their choice of a partner. This process is not quite so developed in transition countries where young people continue to depend extensively on their parents, relatives, state or municipal care, but we can still discern movements in this direction since 1993. For example young people are more likely to espouse those values which are most important for the transformation to a market economy, including greater competition, greater consumer choice and less state protection (Wallace 1997). Thus, whilst before 1989 young people saw it as most important to have "an interesting job", they now see it as more important to have "a steady job with acceptable income". Being a dependable employee, achieving a high professional status and getting a respectable education and professional qualification – values consistently found in the value structure of young people – are all values relevant to the development of a market economy.

Unemployment as a social threat has been absorbed as an element of individualisation among young people. Comparison of surveys in 1993 and 1995 indicate that the initial shock of unemployment had been overcome and young people were more prepared to undertake business activity and to pursue employment in a more determined way. For young Slovaks, the passive surrender to state care as a preferred survival strategy has been losing ground in favour of an orientation towards entrepreneurial activities and self-employment (Macháček 1999). The problem is to preserve the idea of solidarity with others in these circumstances.

Citizenship has many meanings. We should bear in mind that although young people are ready to become involved in civil participation we know that "I want to be a responsible citizen" does not necessarily mean "I intend to participate in public affairs". Analysis of youth who might have "civil potential", shows that there is a difference between the "onlookers", observing social events in the media and the "activists", participating in social affairs.

Social welfare, legislation and social policies have recently begun to address young people directly as holders of citizenship rights. This gradual change, not yet completed, implies that young people become more directly integrated into the national community and are more responsible towards social and political participation. Young people become subjects with individual rights as citizens, perhaps more accurately as proto-citizens, even though the age of access to civil, political and social rights is not consistent across European states.

In Slovakia we can see how difficult it is to create active citizens from people who have been subjected of political control and state paternalistic care for many years. The idea of new political rights for young people raises the question: what does the individual give to the state, to society or to local communities? Active citizenship means not only that young people must take responsibility for the welfare of themselves and their family. To be a good citizen means to have more political responsibility for the future development of one's own nation in the processes of European integration. The opinions and voting behaviour of young Slovaks show that they are keen to become free and creative citizens. The problem now is to create structures and opportunities where this can happen in such a way that encourages solidarity with others and not just individual strategies for self-improvement.

Conclusions

The further modernisation of Slovakia will depend as much upon the creation of an active civil society as upon the process of political and economic reform. That is, it will depend upon the creation of self-aware and active citizens (Roško 1996b). In recent years we have seen a remarkable institutionalisation of civil society through the creation of a variety of Third Sector organisations. This has been greatly assisted by massive financial support of the European Union through the PHARE program and of the USA through the Democratic Network program. The support can be explained by the urgent need to strengthen the transformation processes in European post-communist countries and point them towards pluralistic democracy that is a prerequisite for their integration in the community of European democracies associated with the European Union and NATO. We should bear in mind that in the context of transitional societies, where civil society is not well established and civic participation is low, state sponsorship still plays an important part.

The volunteer and non-government sector of civil society and its development between 1993-1998 was considered to be an important factor of transformation and modernisation of the Slovak Republic. The NGOs in Slovakia "...are now much more than island of isolated idealists or the so called island of positive deviants, as the independent civil activities in late 1980s were called by Slovak sociologists. They created a vivid, vibrant and efficient 'civil archipelago', an archipelago of hope and positive action" (Bútora 1997). However, the maintenance and furtherance of citizenship will depend upon the active continuation of these non-state organisations in a situation where many of their leaders have been drawn into government or state administration or have left the country.

For example, the Youth Council of Slovakia plays an important role in presenting ideas and arguments for shifting some important political citizens' rights, if not full access to citizenship, from 18 to 17 years old, and raising the public awareness of all age groups. The problem is one of how to establish the framework by which the state does not interfere, despite considerable state sponsorship, and where different political regimes will not influence the shape of civil society. The empowering of young people as voters and as social actors can have important consequences for political change as we have seen in the 1998 elections. The challenge for the future will be to create and encourage a civil society in which young people play an active part and which can help to sustain the progress towards democratisation and the development of a market economy in this new state.

Notes

1. Ironically, the respective names represent their different positions as slashers and forgers of civil society. Meciar means literally a swordsmith whilst Kovac means a blacksmith.

2. Tretí sektor a občianska spoločnosť' (Third Sector and Civil society), in Sociológia 1996, No. 3. The round-table discussion of the editorial board of the journal Sociológia took place at the Institute of Sociology of the SAS on March 26, 1996. Scholars from the Philosophical Institute (F. Novosad), Historical Institute (E. Mannová), Institute of the State and Law (Z. Magurová) and Institute of Sociology (R. Roško) participated in it. P. Demeš, the Speaker of the Gremium of the Third Sector, was a guest. The discussion was moderated by the editor-in-chief of the journal Sociológia L. Macháček.

3. This research is an election survey carried out by the FOCUS-agency for the International Republican Institute during Slovak parliamentary elections (September 25-26, 1998). Data was collected in 99 voting precincts, which were selected by a probability method from the total number of voting precincts in the Slovak Republic. Respondents were approached when leaving the polling place and asked to complete an anonymous questionnaire. Respondents were chosen by a method of probability selection. The sample consisted of 4516 respondents. (Number of respondents: 4516; Sample: voters [age structure: from 18-24 16 %, from 25-34 19 %, from 35-44 22.2 %, from 45-54 17.5 %, from 55 and over 16.7 %, no answer 8.6 %].) Final report: Election Poll for the IRI: 1998 Slovak Parliamentary Elections, FOCUS, Bratislava, 65 pp.

4. Renaissance of Civil Society, Citizens and Citizenship in the Slovak Republic. SGA - for Social Sciences 2000-2002. Principal investigator: Prof. Ass. Ladislav Macháček, CSc. Scientific co-workers: PhD M. Čambáliková, CSc and PhD R. Roško, CSc. Institute of Sociology, Klemensova 19, Sk -813 64 Bratislava. E-mail: machacek@klemens.savba.sk or surosko@klemens.savba.sk. In the grant project Renaissance of Civil Society, Citizens and Citizenship in the Slovak Republic in the Context of Europe under Integration and Mankind in the Information Technology Processes (2000-2002), the research will be focused on conceptual aspects which have been analysed less so far of the post-November renaissance of the civil society in Slovakia, as well as on the reflection of new phenomena and trends originating in the revolutionary parliamentary elections 1998. It will make possible for us to gain a deeper insight into the contradictory development of citizenship within the classical sovereign states within the borders of integrating Europe as well as within the framework of globalisation. In particular, we shall pay attention to the stimulating capacity of modern means of communication. Deeper investigation will be focused primarily on the dialectics of society and the state, mediatory function of associated agents, and heuristic potential of the concept "citizenracy". This non-traditional concept along with the concept democracy represents to our mind an instrument which, we presume hypothetically, might contribute to a more precise view of the development phase of civil society. Our analysis will reflect the revolutionary fact of the rise of an activist non-party layer of citizen in the structure of the civil society in Slovakia, its successful pre-electoral co-operation with the political opposition, directions of its post-electoral self-reproduction.

References

Bútora, M. (1997), 'Slovakia's NGOs: A Civic Archipelago of Hope and Action', *NGOs News 7, 10.*

Bútora, M. and Fialová, Z. (1995), *Neziskový sektor a dobrovol'níctvo na Slovensku* (Non-Profit Sector and Voluntarism), Focus, SAIA, Bratislava.

Čambáliková, M. (1998), 'Slovak Social Partners in the Transformation and Integration Processes', *Sociológia - Slovak Sociological Review, 6*, pp. 623-631.

Chisholm, L. and Trnka, S. (1995), 'Growing up in Europe: Childhood and Youth Research Perspectives in 1990s Europe', in Circle for Youth Research Cooperation in Europe (ed.), *The Puzzle of Integration, European Yearbook on Youth Policy and Research, Vol. 1/1995*, Walter de Gruyter, Berlin - New York, pp. 291-293.

FOCUS Agency (1998), *Final Report: Election Poll for the IRI: 1998 Slovak Parliamentary Elections*, FOCUS, Bratislava.

Haerpfer, C. (forthcoming), *Postcommunism and Democracy*, Harwood Academic Press, London.

Les, E. (1994), *The Voluntary Sector in Post-Communist East Central Europe*, CIVICUS – World Alliance for Citizen Participation, Washington, DC, USA.

Macháček, L. (1996), 'Asociatívnost' a občianska participácia' (Citizens' Participation and Associative Life), *Sociológia 28, No. 2.*

Macháček, L. (1998), 'Citizenship Potential of Unemployed and Self-Employed Youth in East-Central Europe', *Sociológia - Slovak Sociological Review, 3*, pp. 283-296.

Macháček, L. (1999), 'Youth in the Processes of Transition and Modernisation in the Slovak Republic', *Czech Sociological Review, Vol. 6, No. 1*, pp. 103-115.

Marshall, T. H. (1950), *Citizenship and Social Class and Other Essays*, Cambridge University Press, Cambridge.

Marx, K. and Engels, F. (1977), 'Nemecká ideológia' (German ideology), in *Antológia z diel filozofov: Marxisticko-leninská filozofia*, Pravda, Bratislava.

Roško, R. (1996a), 'Postkomunistické Slovensko a obnova občianstva' (Post-Communist Slovakia and Revitalisation of Citizenship), *Sociológia 28, No. 1.*

Roško, R. (1996b), 'The Transformation-Modernisation Potential of Slovak Actors', *Sociológia - Slovak Sociological Review, Fall(2)*, pp. 146-158.

Stena, J., et al. (1990), *The Project of the Research Task: Civil Society Forming in Slovakia in the Nineties*, The Institute of Sociology, Slovak Academy of Sciences, Bratislava.

Wallace, C. (1997), *Institute for Advanced Studies: Who is for Capitalism, Who is for Communism? Attitudes to Economic Change in 10 Post-Communist Countries*, Institute for Advanced Studies, 1997, No. 44, Vienna, Austria.

Wallace, C. and Kovatcheva, S. (1998), *Youth in Society: The Construction and Deconstruction of Youth in East and West Europe*, Macmillan, London.

Wolekova, H. and Salamon, L. M. (2000), *Neziskový sektor na Slovensku-ekonomická analýza* (Non-Profit Sector in Slovakia – Economical Analysis), SPACE, Bratislava.

21 From Urban Warrior to Market Segment? Youth in South Africa 1990-2000

DAVID EVERATT[1]

Introduction

The uprisings that convulsed South Africa from 1976 until the onset of negotiations in 1990 were led by young people, who came out in ever greater numbers to take on the security forces and try to make South Africa ungovernable. By the end of the 1980s youth – black, male, urban youth at least – had come to symbolise the massive social movement that was derailing apartheid. Repeatedly photographed taking on the police and army with half bricks and petrol bombs, youth were written off as a "lost generation" for whom violence and cruelty were the norm, coupled with the destruction of their own education and prospects. Opposing this "lost generation" stereotype came a different rendering: the "Young Lions" or "comrades" of the liberation movements, which were presented as politically sophisticated, fearless warriors in the struggle for liberation. Somewhere between these two were real young people.

Following the unbanning of the liberation movements and freeing of political prisoners announced in February 1990, the entire South African situation changed dramatically. Almost immediately, youth Non-Governmental Organisations (NGOs) began a vigorous assault on the media, academics and others who so easily wrote off black youth as a "lost generation". The Joint Enrichment Project (JEP) spearheaded a strategy of organising youth around development issues, mobilising the support of churches and other key social players, commissioning sensitive research and charming the media.

As South Africa moved from confrontation to negotiation, so public opinion became more sympathetic to the young people behind the well-known images. Donors supported the National Youth Development Forum

(NYDF) where young people across the political spectrum were to situate themselves at the core of their own development initiatives. A Youth Ministry was the least that was expected from two separate (if related) negotiation processes: one between sectors within the African National Congress (ANC)-led alliance,[2] the second between it and its opponents.

By the end of the decade, however, youth were most commonly spoken of in relation to crime, HIV prevalence, poor examination results and disinterest in politics and society. A range of youth-focused NGOs had been closed. The ANC-led alliance gave youth less than two pages in the Reconstruction and Development Programme (RDP) (African National Congress 1994), and much of that comprised references to youth as possible recruits for programmes such as public works. The NYDF had collapsed due to mismanagement of people, money and politics. The National Youth Commission (NYC) has been criticised consistently since its formation for failing to deliver anything substantive. Sympathy for youth has almost entirely dissipated.

The lost generation returned, in media stories and everyday speech. And in the gung-ho capitalist rhetoric of the new South Africa, youth have to either put up or shut up. Arguing for the need to understand psycho-social enabling and disabling factors, or dealing with past trauma to unlock present potential, and include these alongside a range of measures in integrated youth development programmes, is commonly disregarded as "touchy-feely" nonsense. Blind faith in the healing power of jobs and wages is the touchstone for youth development proposals. The most frequently asked question – among former activists as well as in the media – is "what's wrong with the youth?"

The new millennium began with black youth featured in *Business Day* as "The hottest target market" for advertisers.[3] The director of the hugely successful Yfm radio station was quoted as saying: "Black youth are unpolitical and extremely materialistic." The transformation was complete. The feared foot-soldiers of the revolution had been put in their place and moulded to fit the new, consumption-driven capitalist South Africa. They may have returned to the status of a lost or violent generation but – critically – they spend. And they spend only on hip, big name, expensive brands.

But have we really gone full circle? Or are we simply failing to understand youth after the struggle for a democratic South Africa – youth as teenagers rather than cadre? What has happened to young people during the 1990s? Where are they now, economically, educationally, and socially?

What are all the youth-focused institutions – the National Youth Commission, Provincial Youth Commissions, South African Youth Council and others – actually delivering?

Every major youth-centred initiative since 1990 has collapsed. Something is clearly very wrong. It is time for a critical and careful appraisal of the decade, in the hope that the next one will offer more to youth who face threats ranging from HIV/AIDS to globalisation. In this article we review the decade which began so positively and ended so emptily for the youth sector. We also briefly analyse the socio-economic profile as well as value base of young people at the close of the decade, and offer some observations regarding youth alienation.

Overview 1990-2000

Periodising the youth development movement in the 1990s may provide a clearer understanding of how the current situation was reached, the political dynamics at play, and the opportunities missed.

A rough periodisation would break the 1990s into three phases (see Seekings 1993, for a useful analysis of the 1980s):

- 1990 to 1993: optimism and organisation;
- 1994 to 1996: disillusionment and missed opportunities;
- 1997 onwards: institutionalisation, policy formulation, and drift.

Arguably, a fourth, slightly more optimistic phase has begun, with a renewed focus on integrated development, youth services and combating the spread of HIV/AIDS. We shall return to this below.

1990-1993: Optimism and Organisation

The youth sector as a whole was at its peak in the early years of the decade. This was true of political organisations and the far broader array of structures concerned with youth development. In part, they fed off the mass mobilisation of the late 1980s, as well as the on-going calls to remain "vigilant" as negotiations and rising levels of political violence took centre stage and Self Defence Units were formed. However, there was also a broader agenda emerging, which saw youth in terms of how much distance they would have to travel to be able to take advantage of the "new South Africa" being negotiated by the political parties, and worried about provision of basic services to youth as well as their inclusion in broader policy and programme initiatives.

Youth mobilisation had grown throughout the 1980s, and by the end of the decade was spearheaded by the South African Youth Congress (SAYCO) with a claimed (if untested) membership of a million youth. SAYCO was led by the flamboyant Peter Mokaba, best known for the repeated screening on national television of his singing "Kill the farmer, kill the Boer", which reflected and recreated the confrontational politics of SAYCO and "the comrades".

Even in these early years, however, there were tensions between the returned and/or released ANC leadership and the youth. Mandela's call to "go back to school" sounded like "the old men are home and will take over now", and the response was patchy. Although political organisations remained important, their influence began diminishing as soon as negotiation replaced confrontation.

The late 1980s, in Gill Straker's words, were "a time of euphoria as well as terror". Youth "saw themselves as leading the older generation to freedom" (Straker 1992, 19). They were at the forefront of the uprisings, and conscious of it. But who were these "youth"? Seekings has argued that "the youth" – an essentially political construct in the 1980s – altered over time. A smallish group of relatively well-educated students in the late 1970s had become a far bigger and broader grouping judged more by a preparedness to engage in direct action than by age or political sophistication by the mid-1980s (Seekings 1993).

Former *tsotsis* (criminals) joined youth structures because of the opportunities for fighting and direct action, because they could provide a cover for criminal activities, and because of political conviction. As Straker has noted, many others joined because of the excitement of resistance. For them, the toyi toyi, songs, stone-throwing and taunting the police were primary reasons for participating, rather than political ideology (Straker 1992). The vicious fighting on the Reef in the early 1990s, the absence of the mass protests of the 1980s and the general demobilisation of the Mass Democratic Movement left space for the more violent individuals in youth structures and provided them with a longer-term legitimation for their own actions. Straker wrote about "Len":

Len's participation in the struggle not only provoked anger and frustration which needed an outlet, but it also taught him that his frustration could be directly expressed against others. His participation in collective resistance taught him about the power of the group, and he subsequently exploited this power for personal gain. His involvement in public violence reinforced for him the fact that violence has an instrumental value in achieving desired objectives, and it also provided him with a set of justifications for his own behaviour. He clung to the political justifications for violence originally used by the comrades ... to justify his own subsequent anti-social actions, even though these justifications now lacked any legitimation by the broader community (Straker 1992, 105).

"Len" is far from unique. Concern about the youth like him, their values, their marginalisation from mainstream society as well as their effect on the rest of society, grew steadily in the late 1980s, and peaked in the early 1990s. This was inevitable: the results of youth mobilisation were frightening as well as liberating. Participation in the struggle allowed many young (and old) people to exert some control over their lives and to assert their vision of freedom over the apartheid forces. If "Len" took away spurious justifications for his own actions, many others strengthened their moral identity through participation in a struggle internationally recognised as just. But they also paid a high price.

Sitas has argued that youth in the 1980s were rarely portrayed as people, and that when they were, it was as "young men, hungry men, with hardened features and red eyes; the myth of a primal Africa when patriarchy collapses and the age-sets run loose; a new version of barbarism" (Sitas 1991, 6). The implication that only "white South Africa" saw youth in these terms is however wrong. Concern over youth marginalisation – which also feared the "comrades" and their effects – came from their parents, religious leaders, and others in the communities where youth lived and in many cases assumed to provide political leadership (cf. the stories of youth making it: Story 1, pp. 298-299; Story 2, pp. 304-305 and Story 3, pp. 316-317).

Thousands of children and teenagers joined successive waves of school boycotts in the 1980s, damaging an already deeply flawed education. Many were exposed to violence and torture. Deeply scarring events occurred in their homes as the South African Defence Force and South African Police occupied the townships under successive states of emergency. HIV/AIDS was scarcely mentioned in the 1980s but was already spreading, helped by the prevalence of sexually transmitted diseases. Teenage pregnancies added to the list of reproductive health concerns. A deepening economic crisis saw fewer and fewer jobs becoming available in the formal economy. Substance abuse was common. Although youth were frequently resilient in the face of deep trauma, the costs were mounting.

Concerns about youth marginalisation were turned into action by the two main church bodies, the Southern African Catholic Bishops' Conference (SACBC), and the South African Council of Churches (SACC). The churches formed a joint structure, the Joint Enrichment Project (JEP), to focus on youth. At the height of the uprisings of the 1980s, JEP began with a small Soweto-based youth theatre project. In 1990, however, it changed gear and in 1991 hosted the first national conference on marginalised youth. The conference saw a wide range of political, civic, cultural, student, religious and other organisations coming together and agreeing on a process of consultation and research. Over the next few years, the JEP, under the leadership of Sheila Sisulu, was at the heart of the youth development process.

"Acne and Violence"

The JEP mounted a succession of national conferences and provincial consultations focusing on marginalised youth and youth development. These culminated in 1993 with the launch of a new structure, the National Youth Development Forum. By this time the first national baseline survey of youth had found that one in two young people (52 %) were unemployed, far higher among Africans than other groups, and highest among young black women (14 % higher than among young black men). Four in ten (43 %) young women with children had fallen pregnant while still at school.

Story 1. Youth making it: "I didn't want to end up like my Mum and Dad"

F. is a striking young man, six feet and built like an athlete. Heads turn when he arrives for the interview. F.'s childhood saw the odds stacked higher and higher against him. The youngest of six children, his parents drank too much, and died within months of each other while F. was a boy at school. He carried on living in his parents' Soweto home after they died, with his younger siblings, selling biscuits to survive. By 13, he was selling clothes and "doing OK".

Then he joined a gym and began working out – in part, working out his anger. F. tells me even now, "some days I just can't stop crying because so much pain comes in my head". But this is better than when he was a teenager:

298

then he beat another boy so badly "I really scared myself". Therapy? – a costly and culturally uncomfortable intervention. F.'s anger remains but has been dimmed over time. But how many young people retain a core of anger, pain and confusion that has not been dealt with?

F. remains a staunch PAC supporter (Pan Africanist Congress, launched in 1959). But, as a teenager dodging police in Soweto in the uprisings of the 1980s, he realised "having a funeral T-shirt of myself was not enough". Where did his drive to do more come from? F. thinks long and hard, but has no answer: "It's just who I am." Why do we know so little about the conditions that spark and nurture such drive?

As a teenager, F. hung around when TV adverts were being filmed in the township, and with the support of a white director, soon got odd jobs on set. Then he started helping out more regularly, and tried his hand at acting. Finally, without experience or expectations, he applied for a scholarship to go to film school in Europe. And against all the odds, he won. South Africa was changing around F., and suddenly opportunities were available on merit.

F. tells me the problem in South Africa is that there is "no black pride" – just a rush of black people to adopt white modes of conspicuous consumption. He talks of lonely black professional women who intimidate black men and can't get dates. He talks of intense materialism and the huge pressure men feel to provide designer label goods for women. He talks of people still living in the townships, and how they are made to feel "left behind, failures" by blacks who have moved to the suburbs. He talks of friends who are dead or in prison.

What makes him angriest is the evaporation of activists: the townships are denuded of former leaders who provided children with moral, principled role-models. In their absence are the new gods of commercialism and consumption.

Despite living the peripatetic existence of a film-maker (camera-work earns the daily bread), F. has bought a house in Soweto – much to the exasperation of those around him who see this as lacking ambition and status. "The township is who I am", says F. simply. He will not be joining the trek to the suburbs. According to F., the same women who watched him arrive would ignore him if they knew he was still a township dweller.

Structurally speaking, F. should be in prison or dead. He fits all the criteria of a member of the "lost generation": the troubled child of alcoholic working class parents who left him a young orphan, who grew up as a risk-taking, aggressive PAC activist. But he is thriving – not financially, but as a professional, doing what he wants, staying true to his roots and his politics.

When he gets up to leave, people pause to watch. What made the difference between what happened to many of his friends, and how F. turned out? Drive and ambition, says F.: "I didn't want to end up like my Mum and Dad." But do we know how to detect these psychological and social factors, and support them, in our current generation of children? Have we learned any lessons from the generation that bore the brunt of the struggle?

Three-quarters of youth (73 %) did not believe themselves at risk of HIV/AIDS. A quarter of respondents said they knew friends who had been raped and the same number knew friends suffering physical abuse. A massive 59 % did not believe they would be able to fulfil their potential as human beings (Everatt and Orkin 1993).

At a focus group held in Chatsworth (a former Indian township outside Durban) in 1992, a group of young men were asked what worried them most. One replied "acne and violence". His remark encapsulated the position of many young black South Africans in the early 1990s. In part, they were adolescents, experiencing all the painful self-consciousness of the transition from child to adult. Simultaneously, however, they were living through an increasingly violent transition from apartheid to democracy, which they had played a major part in bringing about.

Youth in the early 1990s had multiple roles. They were emerging from the thrill and fear of struggle, where some form of participation was the norm and non-participation (according to Straker) was "the exception rather than the rule" (Straker 1992, 19). They were also forming adult identities, experimenting with sex and substances. Via the struggle, many had experienced the excitement of running battles with police. Also via the struggle, many had subverted the traditional authority adults assume over younger generations; youth frequently enforced "struggle discipline" on adults.

On the positive side, youth were socially engaged: only one in ten never attended a place of worship, and one in two (56 %) young African women attended church weekly or more (statistics from Everatt and Orkin 1993). This meant that youth – especially women – could be accessed by programmes targeting them. Significantly, by 1992 the youth membership of political structures stood at 12 %, reflecting the demobilisation of the Mass Democratic Movement, the lengthy and dispirited transformation of SAYCO into the ANC Youth League (see Seekings 1993) and the generally pessimistic mood of the time as political parties jockeyed for negotiating advantage and political violence claimed more and more lives. Young people had always been involved in a range of structures such as sports clubs and choirs, but those without a political role were devalued by youthful political formations.

Despite the socio-economic situation, youth were likely to describe themselves in positive terms. A fifth (21 %) of all young people described themselves as ambitious, followed by happy (14 %), caring (6 %), confident (6 %) and honest (6 %). When second and third choice adjectives were combined, "happy" was chosen by a total of 34 % of the sample across all three choices, and "ambitious" by 30 % of youth across all three choices. There were some racial skews: a fifth of African youth chose "happy" alongside a third of white and Indian youth.

The first "negative" (or neutral) term to appear in the list of self-describing adjectives in the youth baseline study of 1992/3 was "confused", the first choice of 4 %. Other negative descriptors were "ordinary" (3 %), "frustrated" (3 %) and "depressed" (3 %). "Angry", which may reflect a natural (and not unhealthy) response to the socio-economic conditions imposed by apartheid, was the first choice of only 2 % of youth, and the second and third choice of 1 % respectively. Across first, second and third choices, these negative self-descriptors remained the choice of less than one in ten young people (Everatt and Orkin 1993). The signals were positive: youthful resilience seemed to have largely held out against apartheid.

Marginalisation

Although the national conferences focused on youth "marginalisation", and the progressive sector took up the term because it challenged "lost generation", the concept was woolly. Marginalisation comprised part alienation, part externally imposed blockage, part optimism (how to move youth from the margins to the centre?), and part uncertainty about the depth of the effects of decades of repression and resistance on young people. It also reflected the insistence of the church bodies that no-one is ever "lost", merely harder to reach than others.

The accompanying research process sought to give empirical content to the notion. Marginalisation was carefully assessed across a twelve-part index covering employment, education, attitudinal, value and other axes. When these were combined to provide an aggregate measure of marginalisation, it emerged that one in twenty (5 %) of the 11 million young people in South Africa were so damaged by their past that the only way youth programmes might reach them would be via the criminal justice system.[4] This group had suffered and/or perpetrated violence, held extreme political and social views, were deeply alienated and seemed unable to connect with mainstream society at all. Somewhat controversially, they were labelled "lost" (use of apostrophes did little to assuage the unhappiness of the churches with the term).

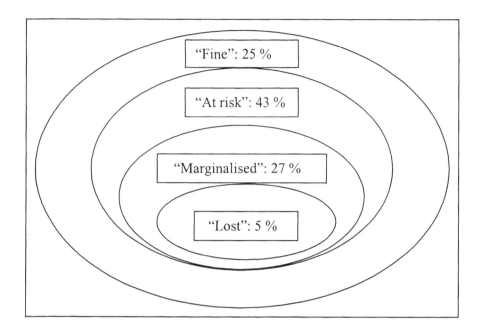

Figure 21.1 Youth marginalisation in South Africa, 1993[5]

More than a quarter (27 %) of young people were found to be "marginalised" – that is, they scored high on many but not all of the axes used in the index, and were in danger of dropping into the "lost" category. "Marginalisation" was taken to signify the extent and nature of damage coupled with the ability to reach these youth and draw them back into mainstream life. This group – the "marginalised youth" – was identified as the key audience for government and civil society interventions. They showed high levels of need combined with sufficient mainstream involvement to be accessed, a critical factor in programme design.

Beyond them, a further four in ten (43 %) were young people "at risk" – that is, they were showing worrying signs on a few of the axes, while a quarter (25 %) were "fine", showing virtually no worrying signs at all. The notion of a lost generation was empirically – if in no other way – debunked (see Figure 21.1).

African youth predominated in the "lost" and "marginalised" categories; young women were more likely to be "marginalised" while men predominated among the "lost". Reflecting the points made above about the composition of youthful political structures and the involvement of criminal elements, "lost" youth were far more likely to be found in political structures than in other organisations. The costs of participating in the struggle were considerable.

This latter finding was a bitter pill for many. During the transition, no political party wanted to admit to having delinquent youth on their books. Moreover, countering the "lost generation" notion had been premised on the argument that involvement in the struggle – even if it took for form of boycotts, civil disobedience or violence – was an indication of civil engagement, not disengagement. However, the effects of political engagement were less positive. The marginalisation index showed South Africa how much work was needed for youth to be brought into mainstream socio-economic life.

Organising the Youth Sector

The national negotiations of 1990-1993 ran parallel to the process of drawing the youth sector together around an agreed platform of key development priorities. This entailed long, difficult, see-saw negotiations with the youth wings of political movements who mimicked their parent bodies by manoeuvring for position and making progress slow and difficult. Despite the increasingly friendly-seeming national negotiations taking place in Kempton Park, the youth sector – meeting a few kilometres away – was marked by deep mistrust between the youth wings of formerly antagonistic parties, and walkouts frequently followed accusations of racial slights, bad faith negotiations and the like.

Nonetheless, the JEP (painstakingly) managed to win support for the development needs of the youth sector – training for employment, providing for missed education opportunities, sexuality and reproductive health education and service provision, HIV/AIDS education, and combating alienation. By the time of the 1993 national conference on marginalised youth, the National Youth Development Forum was ready to be launched as an implementing body, absorbing the National Youth Development Co-ordinating Committee (NYDCC) which had been formed to provide overall guidance to the youth sector.

Designed as a non-partisan body that would co-ordinate and implement interventions in the sector, the NYDF was the culmination of years of hard work, and seemed powerfully positioned to spearhead the youth sector. International donors were joined for the first time by corporate South

Africa. Mainstream media frequently discussed the issue of youth, and it seemed that the "lost generation" had been replaced by marginalised youth, and the emphasis shifted from what youth could do to what had been done to them.

The NYDF had three main tasks: to design and pilot innovative schemes such as the National Youth Service Initiative; to cohere the fractious youth sector around developmental rather than political goals; and to build on the growing sympathy for youth that had begun to emerge in the early 1990s. Tragically, it failed in all of them.

1994 to 1996: Disillusionment and Fragmentation

The mid-1990s were a period of great disillusionment for the youth sector. Mass mobilisation – including youth mobilisation – was treated as a tap that could be switched off and on as the vagaries of the negotiating process demanded. When negotiations were going smoothly, quiescence was required; when negotiations hit stumbling blocks, rolling mass action was called for. However much this reflected the needs of the time, it was difficult to maintain on-going broad-based participation, and it left youth activists in limbo. Youth began to drift away as their particular political contribution, as the footsoldiers of struggle, was increasingly seen as unnecessary. Critically, political organisations failed to develop creative means of enlisting the energy and commitment of youth in the new politics of the interregnum. Churches and political parties were the two key means of reaching youth: both failed to mount any major campaigns that gave youth a constructive role to play.

Story 2. Youth making it: "So I had to own up to my mistakes…"

J. is a highly talented researcher working in the youth sector. She consistently tops her Masters class, made it onto the Dean's list, and has a string of achievements in her CV. The same CV mentions that she has a daughter, who arrived unexpectedly while J. was a young student.

As a young, single, black mother, J. should have failed – dropped out of school, suffered from stigmatising among family and friends, battled to find work and scraped a living in a "squatter camp". All the statistics tell us of the impact pregnancy has on the lives of young women, and the subsequent burden they carry – most commonly alone. The assumption is that life on the social and economic fringes is the natural result of "teenage pregnancy". And for many

---

women, this is true. But the experience of "teenage pregnancy" is more nuanced than our current research data suggest.

J. is flourishing, defying what we know of the common experience of other young women in her situation. Having a child has affected her life. She experienced a lot at a young age – witnessing mendacity and support at close quarters. She has few friends who do not themselves have children, and some who got married have chosen to look down on her – so she ignores them. And she has no lovers who do not have children – "they see my daughter, they run" is her wry observation.

She chose not to marry the father of the child, who plays no role in his child's life. He suggested an abortion, found a phone number for J., and then left her to do everything on her own. She did nothing. As we try to learn more about the experience of teenage pregnancy, so we need to learn more about men and how to deal with their multiple roles.

When J. first told her family, she feared serious repercussions and her father indeed "went crazy" – but took it out on J.'s mother for not having informed her better. After initial anger, however, her family accepted the situation and supported J. as much as they could. By this time, J. was a local role model, performing well in exams, singing in church, keeping clean – what happens to girls/women who are not exemplars? Why is it that some families accept the situation and do the best they can, while others reject the mother and her new baby?

J.'s church – where she sang in the choir during the week and on weekends – "excommunicated me. They kicked me out for a while, then when they saw I was still on track, they slowly let me in again." Despite the flexible moral stand of her church, J. no longer attends – "I just pray by myself now".

J. is a reminder of how little we know about the phenomenon labelled "teenage pregnancies". She is a powerful reminder of the need to look behind the stereotypes. "Why did you do so well where others have not?", I asked her. "My mother has a very strict moral code", is the answer. "There's no grey. It's wrong or right. So I had to own up to my mistakes or hide away forever." When our research is able to detect the strength of moral identity behind structural factors such as "teen pregnancies", we will be able to talk with some confidence about youth.

Youth were politically demobilised, but offered no alternate channels of expression or action. Some turned to the Self-Defence Units, created in response to political violence and the sharpened ANC/Inkatha conflict. As Straker has noted (above), others turned to crime as a means of maintaining the lifestyle developed in the 1980s. Many more simply dropped out of politics.

The early years of the decade were spent countering "lost generation" pessimism. A new concept emerged, namely integrated youth development, as the programmatic counter to the "lost generation". Integrated youth development entailed designing programmes that took youth in their own context and sought to provide for various needs (such as health, education, skills training, lifeskills and so on) in a single programme. This was seen (and has subsequently been shown) to be more likely to succeed than single-focus programmes that ignored the multiple needs of participants.

But the sector was too focused on itself, spent too much time fighting over resources and political shadow boxing, and was arguably too convinced that their role in the struggle had "earned" youth special consideration from an ANC government. As a result, lacking the sense of urgency that the women's movement exhibited, for example, the youth sector failed to significantly intervene in the negotiations process.

Part of this flowed from the integrated development notion. It was widely expected that a Youth Ministry would be created to "reward" the sector – and its leaders – with an institutional base. Many inside the youth sector opposed the idea, while others supported it. Much time and effort was spent fighting over the issue, because of the fear that a Youth Ministry (if African experience were a guide) would be an unresourced junior Ministry, where youth issues would be "ghettoised" (see for example Joint Enrichment Project 1993). Moreover, integrated development required all key ministries to build the needs of youth into their programmes, not to run separate youth-only single-issue programmes. However, the youth sector fought both sides of the argument. It is scarcely surprising that youth were left to fight among themselves, and the policy formulation process moved past them.

In place of a ministry, desk officers in key ministries were proposed (see Everatt 1993; Everatt and Orkin 1993; Truscott and Milner 1994). Even here, however, it should be borne in mind that most of those proposing institutional arrangements and policy options were ill-informed about the mechanisms and modus operandi of government. The sudden shift from confrontation to negotiation after February 1990 required a massive learning curve on the part of the progressive sector as a whole. The nature of the apartheid regime and resistance to it meant that few if any in the progressive sector had had anything to do with government. Few activists knew how decisions were arrived at in government. More nuanced or appropriate proposals may have been possible, had those in the youth sector (including the author) been better informed about governance issues.

The Betrayal

The Reconstruction and Development Programme (RDP) was launched with great fanfare as the first democratic general election approached. In its own words, the RDP was "an integrated, coherent socio-economic policy framework. It seeks to mobilise all our people and our country's resources toward the final eradication of apartheid and the building of a democratic, non-racial and non-sexist future" (African National Congress 1994). The RDP was the result of intensive lobbying and horse-trading inside the ANC alliance. Sectors developed policy and programme formulations, and then had to secure support for them through the six drafts of the RDP that were circulated and debated (and fought over) inside the alliance. Youth could not make any claims based on need alone: women, people with disabilities, the homeless, rural residents and many others could make equally or more compelling arguments on such a basis. The youth sector had the advantages of detailed baseline data, agreed policy positions, and an organisational basis in the NYDF and NYDCC. The sector seemed well-positioned to secure significant commitments.

When it finally appeared, the RDP was 147 pages long, and covered an enormous range of topics from education to policing to nutrition. "Youth Development" appeared in the Human Resource Development section where it was given a total of six paragraphs, covering a page and a half. It was offered as a sub-section of "Arts and Culture" and came immediately after "Sport and Recreation". Youth had been dropped into a familiar position: give them sports fields and they'll be happy.

In 1993, there were some 11 million young people aged between 16 and 30, who were defined as youth. They comprised roughly a quarter of the South African population. Despite this enormous demographic weight, the RDP had little to say beyond citing them (along with women, farm workers, the elderly and others) as a possible target for affirmative action programmes, and as requiring economic and educational opportunities. At government level, the RDP stated merely that "appropriate government departments must more forcefully represent youth interests" (African National Congress 1994, 74).

By 1994, the shape of South Africa had been settled in terms of policy and institutional arrangements. Youth fared poorly: a national youth service initiative was the only policy proposal in the RDP, a Council, the only institution for championing youth development, and integrated youth development was entirely absent. Neither desk officers nor a Youth Ministry were proposed.

The youth sector as a whole suffered a major setback because of the failure of youth structures and leaders in the tripartite alliance to secure any significant commitment to or understanding of youth development in the RDP, despite their lobbying. This in turn reflected and led into a broader failure to develop a coherent set of sector-wide demands that were consistently championed by representatives of all parties as well as civil society, and taken into the negotiating halls where South Africa's future was being decided.

A Failure of Strategy

If the RDP showed the relative weakness of the youth sector within the tripartite alliance, the weakness of the sector as a whole was reflected in the failure to intervene in the multi-party negotiations that dominated the political scene until 1994. The contrast with the women's movement is informative. The Women's National Coalition (a multi-sectoral structure like the NYDCC) tried to draw together a wide range of women's structures, including all the political parties. Despite internal tensions, the Coalition did provide a platform for women's organisations to come together, share information and discuss policy positions. These were also championed inside the political movements affiliated to the NWC and taken into the multi-party negotiations by civil society structures.

The Coalition was able to win broad support for a set of demands supported by women from a diverse range of organisations (see for example Albertyn 1994). The Coalition was available to provide legal formulations or policy options when required, and by lobbying at the multi-party talks, secured significant gains for women as well as deepening gender sensitivity among the future governing elite. Equally importantly, gender-focused civil society structures lobbied hard inside the ANC alliance and in the multi-party talks.

According to one study:

> The shift from resistance to negotiations politics saw the consolidation of women as a political constituency within political parties and in civil society as they joined forces across racial, class and political divides to fight for inclusion

within the new democracy. This movement was bolstered by a strong women's leadership that had been fostered by the struggles and debates of the 80s and which was to demonstrate its capacity to intervene strategically in the interests of women in the 1990s (Albertyn, Goldblatt, Hassim, Mbatha and Meintjies 1999, 11).

The strategy worked because of the growing international context of gender sensitivity, which had begun to impact on the ANC while still in exile; the ability of the Women's Coalition (despite internal problems) to present a sector-based voice; the history of organising around women's issues, including during the anti-apartheid struggle; the use of lobbying as a strategy; and the existence of senior women (and some men) within the ANC who would push a gender-sensitive agenda (Albertyn, Goldblatt, Hassim, Mbatha and Meintjies 1999, 11). One key result was that the RDP contained a fairly coherent set of recommendations for women in some sectors (but not all) as well as reflecting general gender sensitivity; sensitivity to gender in government's policy formulation has been marked since 1994.

The youth sector also thought it was well-positioned, with senior ANC leaders on its side, an agreed policy platform and set of recommendations. But the youth sector failed to mimic the women's movement. It lacked the contextual advantages that the growth of an international women's movement and gender consciousness gave the NWC, but enjoyed others. However, the NYDCC was racked by political squabbling, and failed to rise above party politics in support of a set of youth development demands other than on an *ad hoc* basis. Decisions were gradually and painfully achieved usually in the face of grand-stand politicking. The NYDF did not follow a supra-political strategy of taking a youth development platform into the multi-party talks. No lobby group existed to push for specific, sector-based demands or counter inappropriate proposals with alternatives. As a result, little of substance for youth emerged from the negotiating process.

The NYDF Collapse: The Final Nail in the Sector's Coffin

If there was a failure at the level of policy and a negotiating strategy, the National Youth Development Forum (NYDF) failed at the level of implementation. In part, this was because the NYDF suffered from the political tensions that bedevilled the sector. Furthermore, youth occupied virtually all the positions in the NYDF. While this lived out the development maxim that beneficiaries of development need to be at the centre of their own development, it also meant that experience in critical areas – notably finance and controlling (often older white male) consultants – was lacking. Although significant resources were made available to the NYDF, which employed a large number of staff, the institution collapsed after barely three years amidst allegations of corruption, mismanagement and political croneyism. The appropriateness of assuming only youth can staff institutions dealing with youth is discussed below. But it is evident that the NYDF sorely lacked experience in the delivery of development programmes, a fatal flaw in its make-up (see "Should youth manage youth development?", pp. 312-313).

The NYDF was founded by a wide range of organisations, many of them youth organisations. But the non-youth organisations in the NYDF, drawn from various key sectors, did not play an active role in the NYDF. They too must bear some responsibility for the collapse of the NYDF.

The broader context was also gloomy, as donors cut back their funds, re-directed money to Eastern Europe, and youth development slipped onto the back-burner. After corruption was exposed at the NYDF, the situation got worse for youth-focused NGOs, many of whom closed or slashed staff and programmes. Many others lost key staff to the newly formed government, a process which has continued unabated.

By the mid-1990s, the youth sector was in disarray. The gains of the early part of the decade had been lost. No significant policy commitments to youth were made. Although a Council was proposed to oversee youth affairs, youth development was not rooted in any government department. The collapse of the NYDF cost a great deal in terms of donor goodwill as well as reinforcing negative views of the ability of young people to manage their own affairs. When youth were addressed as a sector, it was generally in the context of the threat they were seen to represent, rather than the complexities and needs of the generation. The funeral of assassinated Communist Party leader Chris Hani saw street battles between police and youth (among others). Within weeks, more than fifteen proposals for organising youth had been produced by a wide range of organisations, ranging from community service corps (along American lines), to enforced physical exercise, to straightforward labour camps for black youth. Despite many newspaper column inches, however, nothing concrete was done. A few weeks later, as the national focus shifted back from "youth violence" to negotiations, the proposals disappeared, and South Africa's youth returned to the *status quo ante*, where they have remained ever since.

1997 Onwards: Institutionalisation, Policy Formulation and Drift

It was in this context that the National Youth Commission (NYC) was inaugurated on June 16th 1996,[6] the anniversary of the Soweto uprising and commemorated as Youth Day. The period from 1996 to the end of the decade was dominated by the creation of the NYC, and later the South African Youth Council (SAYC), and the existence for the first time of a formal mechanism for youth voices to reach the ears of those in power. The period was also marked by the failure of those institutions to translate this into programmes that benefit significant numbers of youth. The positive result, emerging more clearly as the decade closed, was that youth NGOs are once again (as in the early years of the 1990s) playing a central role in designing innovative programmes and piloting them via partnerships with government departments.

The Failure of Formal Youth Structures

The NYC became a target of media criticism almost from inception, initially because of the salary package of its chairperson, set considerably higher than those of the Human Rights Commission chairperson, for example. The notion that the sector was being bought off in return for quiescence was widespread.

It was telling that the media criticism focused not on the fact that the salary packages for all Commissions created by the Constitution were extravagantly high, but on the age of the NYC chairperson. The implication was apparent: she may have to do the same amount of work as the chair of any other Commission, but she should be paid less for doing so. Media representations of youth retained the prejudices of adults: youth should know and stick to their place.

More useful criticism of the NYC would have pointed to the National Youth Commission Act – hastily and badly drafted to meet the June 16th deadline, and poorly conceptualised. The Act defined youth as comprising everyone between the ages of 14 and 35,[7] a serious error. Youth in South Africa has always had a higher upper age limit than international definitions (16 to 24 is a more common age definition) because of the effects of the struggle on youth and students between 1976 and 1990. This group however cannot endlessly be recreated as youth or kept within age definitions.

By the same token, no explanation has been given for making 14 the age at which people turn from child to youth. Fourteen year-olds cannot vote, or legally have sex, or earn a living. An unfortunate parallel is that boys can be held responsible for rape at the age of 14 but not younger. Under ANC policies, a fourteen year-old should still be (compulsorily) at school. The life experiences, context and needs of a 14 year old are radically different from a 35 year old. When we add the complications of gender, race, class, urban/rural location and others that underpin South African society, the complexity becomes impossible to contain within an already blurry concept such as "youth". In practice, the definition is observed in the breach more often than not.[8]

Another weak point the NYC shares with other Commissions in South Africa is the political bartering that precedes the appointment of Commissioners. Political parties all insist on being represented, with the result that sectoral knowledge is a secondary concern to party affiliation. There has also been an on-going insistence that only youth can be Youth Commissioners and NYC staff, itself a questionable proposition. Over time, media criticism of the NYC moved from the salary issue to that of non-performance. The *Mail & Guardian,* which has consistently rated the NYC among the worst performing of governmental institutions, argued:

> Launched in 1996 with much fanfare – and criticism about the R30 000 per month salary and perks of chair Mahlengi Bhengu – the commission has faded from the public landscape as concerns about the future of the country's youthful generation have moved into the foreground.[9]

Should youth manage youth development?

Analysing the waxing and waning of the youth development movement since 1990 raises a difficult question: is it appropriate to assume youth have to staff and manage any institution dealing with youth development? The track record of such institutions to date is unimpressive.

The youth movement since 1990 has been based on the truism of good development, that project beneficiaries must be at the centre of their own development. This became a slogan: youth must drive youth development.

At the level of youth NGOs, this has worked well. But youth NGOs tend to be small, focused, and thrive on commitment, idealism and an on-going sense of struggle for their target group. Critically, most youth NGOs try to stay in touch with the rapidly changing youth culture(s), and their success in outreach is often dependent on this closeness. Burn-out and turn-over of staff (and of NGOs) is also very high.

312

At a national level, the notion of youth driving their own development has been taken literally, with young people staffing the NYDF, the National and Provincial Youth Commissions, the Youth Council and others. And without fail, each of those institutions has at the very least failed to live up to expectations; at worst, like the NYDF, they have collapsed.

Age alone is not a significant variable: there are highly skilled young and old people, as well as their opposites. But with age come experience, status and power in the political hierarchies where decisions are taken. As South Africa has developed a stable political system, this becomes increasingly important. Disregarding politics, experience is critical when national or provincial development programmes are being designed. Closeness to "the youth" by age or political affiliation is less and less a requirement: planning, costing, programme management and similar skills are most needed.

The situation is self-fulfilling: youth find less and less being designed for and made available to them by government. Like adults, however, they face five-yearly calls for loyalty and voting support. Penny Foley has described the situation where a local politician visited a JEP project, raised a fist and shouted "Roar, young lions, roar!" The youth on the project stopped for a moment, looked up, ignored and carried on with their work, explaining later that they are sick of politicians wanting their vote but giving them nothing in return (see Foley forthcoming).

It may be time to carefully examine the notion that only youth can understand and drive youth development at this level. Youth have to be part of the process at all levels, certainly. But the prosaic insistence that only people within certain age limits can manage national and provincial youth policy and programme design and implementation has thus far failed to deliver substantive improvements to youth.

The article quoted the director of the South African Graduates Development Association, Vukile Nkabinde:

The (Commissioners) are too far away from the youth. We are not sure if they are really working or just enjoying the tax money. They need to come nearer so they can see that the very same youths who participated in the struggle, throwing stones, are disenfranchised. They must stop the rhetoric – what we need is action.[10]

A year later, criticism remained constant. A young interviewee noted:

The Youth Commission are a serious bunch of people who aspire to be intellectuals or future politicians. They lack ideas to draw more young people to their side and try to help the socio-economic issues faced by us.[11]

The problem was not unique to the NYC, and faced political parties as well. The ANC Youth League (ANCYL) deputy president had earlier noted that his constituency:

> are impatient with the slow pace of change, and want militant action to speed it up. But we want them to become soldiers of democracy, to utilise their militancy to deepen democracy.[12]

NYC Commissioners repeatedly assert that they "lead" the youth sector,[13] and yet the Commission has signally failed to capture the imagination of youth. The NYC works closely with formal organisations but as we see below, the vast majority of youth do not belong to youth structures. Outreach and dialogue are largely limited to a closed circle of youth activists, many of whom have subsequently found their way onto national or provincial Commission structures, while others wait their turn.

NYC chairperson Mahlengi Bhengu has argued that "declining youth activism is part of a global trend. It shows that we are becoming a normal democracy."[14] She went on to note that "we have to engage them in their own language" – something all political institutions, including the NYC, have yet to achieve. Although the RDP proposed the idea of national youth service in 1994 – the only youth-specific programme the tripartite alliance explicitly endorsed – the process has moved slowly. A White Paper was submitted to Cabinet in late 1999, and the 2000 budget speech made no commitment to funding the initiative. The NYC undertook a large consultation exercise when developing the Youth Policy 2000 document (National Youth Commission 1997), which was important in taking the existing youth development platform and turning it into a government policy document. Nothing of substance has flowed from it, however, and Youth Policy 2000 has not been widely distributed or utilised in the youth sector.

Some criticism of the NYC is unfair, since the Commission is not an implementing body and should not be judged as one. The NYC Act gave the NYC the task of developing a policy platform (Youth 2000) and monitoring its implementation. It could be strongly argued that the NYC has fulfilled its mandate and should now be closed, or if it is to have a monitoring role regarding the progress of the youth sector, this could be done from within the Human Rights Commission.

The NYC Act also called for a South African Youth Council (SAYC) to be formed, as a broad-based oversight body for youth affairs (echoing the commitment to a Youth Council in the RDP mentioned earlier). In the case of both the NYC and SAYC, structures were put in place without any budget. Their formative phases tended to comprise much talk, grand plans, equipping offices, and negative publicity based on non-performance (which in turn partly flowed from the lack of money). Prejudices against the ability of youth to manage their own affairs have been repeatedly confirmed during the decade.

Despite having the NYC and SAYC to bolster its work, for example, the government and Independent Electoral Commission (IEC) failed to ignite interest among youth in the second democratic general election in 1999. After three attempts at registering South Africans on the voters' roll, the IEC registered almost 80 % of South Africans – but only 48 % of 18 to 20 year olds. Age was a critical variable: as Melissa Levin has shown, 97 % of those over 80 registered to vote (Levin forthcoming). Last-ditch efforts by the IEC, involving the NYC, managed to raise youth registration to 48 %: prior to that it had been even lower. A refrain heard throughout the youth sector was common at the time of registration: "politicians only show up before an election" (*Mail & Guardian* 16/4/1999; Foley forthcoming).

By the same token, few development-focused youth NGOs have benefited from the formation of the NYC or SAYC. These structures have not been able to forge new partnerships between government and the youth sector. In part, this reflects the lack of interest in the youth sector on the part of government.

Much of the criticism of the NYC and SAYC fails to trace the source of the problem – the failure of the RDP to understand the scale and need of youth, and to ensure that government as a whole put these at the centre of policy development. The result has been the NYC pressurising government departments to take youth seriously, design appropriate programmes and so on – but without any power to enforce decisions. Their location – adjacent to but not in government – has left the NYC in a difficult position. Their mandate is to formulate and monitor policy but not to implement, and their position symbolises that of youth development: much lip-service is paid to it, but not much more than that. Even in its mandated areas, the NYC lacks power: it can formulate policy, but is entirely reliant on Cabinet to endorse, and then fund and implement, that policy. This weak position can be traced back to the RDP. It failed to locate youth concerns at the heart of policy design – it merely exhorted government departments to "more forcefully represent youth interests" (African National Congress 1994, 74). They have failed to do so.

Story 3. Youth making it: "…it doesn't mean you can expect anything without working for it"

S. comes from the royal bloodline in KwaZulu-Natal. Still in his late twenties, he is the confidant of government Ministers across party lines, and is embraced by ANC and Inkatha Freedom party (IFP) leaders alike. When S. arrives for our interview, waiters immediately defer to him, despite his age, and remain attendant throughout the interview. He has a dignitas that belies his age, and reeks of class – in the best possible way.

Like the previous stories of young people making it, S. too should not be where he is, if research and media stereotypes are a guide. Many of his relatives live and operate in the labyrinthine world of court politics, where the favour of the King or Chief Buthelezi are key determinants of success, and where the IFP is the normal party of choice. Others have dropped into a regional and ethnic exclusivity. But S. has a history of involvement in United Democratic Front (UDF) politics, which he maintained by telling some people and not others. (The UDF was the leading internal resistance movement in the 1980s.) He maintains his royal position, but lets me know that being royal means everything and nothing – "It's who I am but it doesn't mean you can expect anything without working for it". He has multiple identities, and glides between them as he does between the worlds of business, politics, royalty and being a young man in the now not-so-new South Africa.

S. tells me he doesn't care if someone is black or white – echoing Mbeki, he stresses the need for delivery as the basis of judgement. And, he says, "I hate people – black or white – being presented as perfect, faultless". Uncaring of expectations, S. can frequently be found listening to his Walkman – playing classical music.

Youth are in limbo, S. believes. The struggle filled their (and his) lives with excitement and the chance to exert control over their circumstances. Crucially, according to S., the struggle had noble goals – but now there is nothing to rally around, nothing to focus on, except narrow, materialistic concerns. He believes that we need something on a grand scale, using American-style razzmatazz to "sell" its message. "We mustn't be ashamed of the big sell", he tells me.

S. is a new breed of young South African. In the late 1980s he was involved in UDF resistance politics, mainly via the civic movement. He has had his encounters with police, with poverty – despite his royal status – with racism and with violence. But he has also been highly successful, running his own large business while consulting to three or four national Ministries. He participates in royal affairs, and maintains homes in Durban and Johannesburg. He is not showy and doesn't flash money around. He is overseas every other month, setting up and signing deals throughout Europe and elsewhere. He is polished, presentable, and extremely good at what he does.

Why did he make it? S. tells me he spent a lot of time with older people,

316

while growing up, and they gave him something very important: a knowledge of right and wrong, and the perspective to see his own life unfolding as it happens rather than merely in retrospect. The common theme to the stories of youth making it is a strong moral identity – knowing what's right and wrong – and the drive (which may flow from knowing what's right and wrong) to achieve. This can overcome key obstacles in the lives of young people.

Perhaps what we missed, in our research and organising work in the early 1990s, was the fact that youth didn't have to be like us to make it – they were already gearing up to outstrip us.

A New Era?

The last years of the decade saw a new emphasis on youth programmes. The Presidential Jobs Summit saw government, labour and business commit themselves to youth brigades. The Department of Public Works began working on a youth Reconstruction Workforce (which subsequently stalled) aimed at creating a South African equivalent of Roosevelt's Civilian Conservation Corps. The NYC has pushed ahead with a proposed National Youth Service. A partnership between the NYC and the Department of Public Works should see R50m being spent on a pilot programme for youth service during 2000.

At a more modest level, the JEP and other youth NGOs are once again playing an important role in promoting integrated youth development programmes, this time in partnership with government departments. The Youth Development Initiative in Gauteng, for example, seeks to provide lifeskills and technical training while nurturing youth business ventures. The model is an innovative one, but still in its pilot phase (for more detail on JEP programmes, see Foley forthcoming). The School Leavers Opportunity Trust has had considerable success on a small scale in training and nurturing young business people but the challenge is replication at a scale large enough to make an impact on need, something the Department of Labour has been looking into.

However there is a danger that the current, low-level resurgence of interest in youth is again reflecting a short-term ad hoc commitment based on the potential threat youth pose, which in turn is a constant refrain in media coverage of both crime and HIV/AIDS. Moreover, as long as single-issue programmes are mounted from separate government departments, which fail to acknowledge the multiple needs of youth, so programmes will fail to meet their targets.

317

In the 1980s, youth felt themselves at the forefront of change. By the end of the decade, as Presidential spokesperson Parks Mankahlana observed:

> The leadership of the organisation (the ANC) shifted from the young lions to the old guard. The youth took a back seat. Today the national leadership of the ANC is characterised by old men whose traditions and conventions are deeply entrenched.[15]

These "old men" have to try and understand the youth sector. Here is the real problem, which informs the "what's wrong with the youth?" question: youth and youth culture have changed dramatically in the short space of a decade. The new youth were described by one journalist as follows:

> (Youth) feeds off a diet of MTV, Nikes, Aids consciousness, shopping malls, environmental awareness and a generous spirit of nihilism. It burps attitude without the idealism of its more politically earnest forebears. It is the generation of movies like Doom Generation and Kids.[16]

As young people create their own cultures and move further and further away from the anti-apartheid struggle, so political leaders and activists ask with increasing frequency: "what has happened to the youth?" In the final section, we try (partly) to answer the question.

Understanding South African Youth: 2000+

The main problem facing policy-makers is their ignorance of South African youth and the cultures they have created. "What has happened to the youth?" really means "why aren't they like I was?" – but in the democratic South Africa, struggle has been replaced by consumption. While government departments and political movements try to develop campaigns around HIV/AIDS, employment or crime, these tend to be somewhat stilted, well-meaning forays into alien territory. One unemployed teenager interviewed by a journalist complained that the NYC and others "lack ideas to draw more young people to their side.... Popular culture could be one way to lure young people", he added.[17]

At the core of youth culture lies a mix of music, fashion, risk-taking behaviour, social awareness, and – seemingly above all – consumption. But while many who spent years in the resistance movement tut tut about the drive for big brand labels among young people, they fail to acknowledge where it comes from – themselves.

The dramatic policy shifts navigated by the ANC, as it moved from the nationalisation and redistributive basis of the Freedom Charter to free market capitalism are well recorded (see Marais 1998; Saul 1999, 49-67). In the 1980s, Thabo Mbeki may have insisted that "the ANC is no socialist party. It has never pretended to be one, and it is not trying to be one. It will not become one by decree or for the purpose of pleasing its 'left' critics" (Saul 1999, 54), but many in the struggle either disbelieved him or were content with the leftwing social-democracy inherent in the Freedom Charter.[18] By the late 1990s, the ANC was implementing the Growth, Employment and Redistribution (GEAR) macro-economic strategy, emphasising foreign investment, deficit reduction and a flexible labour market.

Fetishising market forces is not simply a policy shift but a lifestyle choice. The new ruling elite adopted many of the unsavoury habits of their predecessors, most notably conspicuous consumption. Black empowerment deals have created a thin stratum of black multi-millionaires who live like their white counterparts. No "revolutionary discipline" was applied to ANC cadre as they took over government, and imported cars, houses in the wealthy suburbs, cigar-smoking, designer label clothing and complaints about MP's salary levels rapidly became the norm. The signals have not been lost on young people.

Eunice Komane, the MEC for Safety and Security and Public Works in the Northern Cape is a rarity. She lives in the "servant's quarters" of a house in a downmarket Kimberley suburb, and argues "Youth must understand the values that are really important in life, it is not money, fancy houses and fancy cars".[19] Her voice is drowned by the Ministerial injunction that blacks should get "filthy rich",[20] and the sound of people obeying.

Youth share the consumerism of South Africa's wealthy classes, but many lack the history of participation in the struggle or the ability to argue that current consumption is an extension of or reward for earlier political sacrifices. As one unemployed youngster put it:

> We are not revolutionary youth that threw petrol bombs at some informer's house in the 1960s. We are fun-loving people but that does not mean we have no ideas. We listen to kwaito, we are into the latest fashion, abuse of booze and drugs is also taking its toll.[21]

It has long been argued that youth are a lens that reflects society in sharper detail: the negative trends are amplified, as are the positive. The fascination with the trappings of wealth is by no means restricted to youth. It merely reflects – possibly in accentuated form – that of South African adults.

Profiling South Africa's Youth 2000+

Journalistic claims of the size of the youth population vary hugely, from one in three to seven in ten of all South Africans. In fact, youth between 14 and 35 years of age comprise four in ten (39.8 %) South Africans, numbering 16 million people.[22] Of these, 52 % are women. Youth are more likely than adults to be found in rural areas, where many in the younger cohorts are sent to be cared for by older relatives, and attend school. Youth are also more likely to be found in informal settlements, often because of the desire to set up their own household coupled with an acute shortage of housing stock.

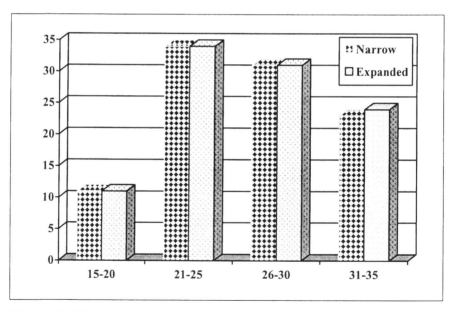

Figure 21.2 Unemployment among youth (narrow and expanded definitions)

The target group for most youth programmes are those who are neither in work nor school: they comprise 21 % of youth, totalling 3.5 million people (this should not be mistaken for the rate of unemployment which stands at just below 50 %). The scale of need is enormous. African youth dominate this group, comprising 3.1 million of the total. Women are more likely than men to be out of work and school: 60 % of the 3.5 million are women. In a recent national survey, only a quarter (27 %) of youth (18 to 35 year-olds in this instance) said they had gone as far in their education as they had wished: that leaves three-quarters of all young people aged between 18 and 35 feeling they have an incomplete education (data are taken from Strategy & Tactics 1999).

Two definitions of unemployment are used in South Africa (see p. 320, Figure 21.2). The narrower definition defines as unemployed those out of work but taking active steps to find work (in the 7 days preceding the survey). The expanded definition does not require the unemployed respondent to have sought work. Whichever definition is used, unemployment among youth is worryingly high, standing at 28 % (narrow) or 29 % (expanded). As we have already seen, this is skewed by race and sex. Young black women suffer disproportionately high levels of unemployment. In general, as youth age, levels of employment increase. Among women, the increase in employment is significantly slower than among men (data taken from Statistics South Africa 1997).

Urbanisation in South Africa was found by the 1996 census results to have increased considerably, so that 54 % of the population live in an urban area. This is slightly lower among youth – 51 % live in urban areas, 49 % in non-urban areas. The urban/rural axis is another cleavage within the somewhat amorphous "youth" group.

Among young women aged under 19, one in three (35 %) have been pregnant. While this places an enormous burden on women, far more worrying is the fact that 21 % of women under the age of 20 are HIV positive (Department of Health 1998a). This 1998 figure is almost double the number from the previous year (the 1997 figure was 12.7 %), showing that the HIV/AIDS epidemic has yet to reach its plateau. Condom use during the most recent sexual experience among youth stood at one in five (Department of Health 1998b).

The "lost generation" notion suggests that youth have disengaged from mainstream social processes, and are either anomic or involved only in their own sub-cultures. However, four in ten youth have seen a copy of the South African Constitution, higher than among any older age cohorts. Over half (57 %) have heard of the Bill of Rights, again the highest of all age cohorts.

Asked about organisational membership, youth emerged as concerned with spiritual, social and economic issues – but not with political ones. Less than one in ten young people belong to a political organisation, underscoring the dramatic shift in values and attitudes over a decade. The churches in particular retain a critical place – as they have throughout the decade – in the lives of young people. For programmes to achieve significant outreach among young people, the churches are critical partners (see Figure 21.3).

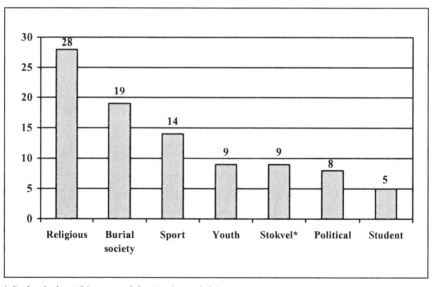

* Stokvel: the African word for 'savings club'.

Figure 21.3 Youth membership in South Africa (main mentions, 18-35 year olds)

Values and Optimism

Although young people may not be politically active to the extent their predecessors were, they remain politically aware and engaged. Asked a series of questions about the extent to which politics was seen as a waste of time or a civic duty, youth were least likely (at 10 %) to agree that politics is a waste of time. They were most likely (at 38 %) to agree that it is very important to keep in touch with politics, while the remaining 52 % felt that while politics was unpleasant it was important to stay in touch.

In answer to all of these questions, there was of course a group giving negative answers – but in most instances it was smaller than those aged 36 and above giving the same negative answers. For example, when asked which tier of government (national, provincial or local) was performing best, 15 % of youth replied "none of them" – lower than any other age cohort. The same number (15 %) of youth had "no confidence" in government's ability to solve problems – again the lowest of all age cohorts.

As we saw earlier, youth are not engaging with the political system to the same extent as adults. Many were children while the anti-apartheid struggle was being waged, did not participate in the constitution-making process, and may not have the same sense of ownership that adults have. On the other hand, however, the data suggest that youth treat politics very seriously: only 7 % of youth agreed that voting is a waste of time compared with twice that number of respondents aged above 60. The major failing may be the political parties that consistently fail to address youth concerns and fail to communicate with youth in appropriate ways. None followed the advice of the young respondent who suggested using popular culture – not deploying the odd pop star or soccer player, but penetrating youth culture in order to communicate with youth.

Social Attitudes

There is some cause for concern. A third (32 %) of 18 to 35 year old respondents agreed or strongly agreed with the notion that if a community supports a particular political party, no other parties should be allowed to campaign in the area. This was higher than among older age cohorts. But it should not be over-analysed: 75 % of youth – again the highest of all age cohorts – agreed or strongly agreed that a strong opposition is vital for good government. In short: searching for evidence of a "lost generation" (as opposed to some disaffected elements within a generation) by examining attitudes to politics seems to be fruitless.

Moving away from politics, we find that one in five (20 %) youth reject the death penalty – far higher than among older respondents. Youth were also least likely to offer an outright rejection of abortion, and most likely to agree that abortion is a woman's right and should be available on request. Despite "missing" the anti-apartheid struggle, many young people have notably more progressive social views than their elders.

The most striking fact about youth responses to survey questions about the future of South Africa is their enormous optimism. Asked about the quality of life, the economy, race relations, education, crime, and health care, in every instance respondents between 18 and 35 were significantly more positive than older respondents, and expect improvements in all these areas in the next half decade.

On the key issue of race relations and national unity, youth again showed more optimism than their elders. Two-thirds (67 %) of youth agreed that although it will take time, South Africa will become a united nation. Only a fifth (compared with a quarter to a third among older respondents) believed that we will always be divided. Asked a more pointed question – whether respondents would mind their children marrying someone from a different race group – one in two young respondents (48 %) said they would not mind. Less than a third (29 %) of those aged above 60 said the same.

This must not be taken to mean there are only minor problems facing young people in South Africa. However, it should be taken to mean that sloppy commentary allows for sloppy observations – such as the "lost generation" – to take root in the minds of both public and policy makers. Youth face real hurdles – they suffer high levels of unemployment, massive numbers believe their education was incomplete, HIV prevalence is very high and still growing, and they are hard hit by the housing shortage. The myriad youth cultures share one attribute: hostility to adults and their rules, or at best a disregard for the adult way of doing things. South African youth scarcely differ from their counterparts elsewhere in the world in this. But South African adults are unused to "teenagers" – they know about politically engaged "youth". A major problem lies in the way older people interpret the behaviour of youth.

Youth also cause many social problems. There are too many young men like Tefo, who tells girls "I'll buy you a big boat called the Titanic. And they believe me ... they're convinced 'this man really loves me'. But in actual fact I'm not even there. I just want to get some sex and move on."[23]

Youth also form a high (if disputed) proportion of the prison population (figures taken from National Youth Commission forthcoming). Juveniles aged 21 or younger are defined as offenders by the Department of Correctional Services. According to the 1997 Correctional Services Annual Report, juveniles constituted 15 % of the total prison population. Statistics South Africa reports that of the 218 394 convictions for serious offences in 1995/96, 8 % were juveniles between the ages of 7 and 17; 14 % or 30 565 were young adults between the ages of 18 and 20. Different age definitions make it difficult to gain an accurate picture. However, what the figures do show is that youth are disproportionately represented among the prison population – that is, they are disproportionately *under*-represented. They form 39 % of the total population but 22 % of those convicted for serious offences. Pick up any newspaper in South Africa, and the precisely opposite impression will be given.

Without the precise measures of marginalisation designed in 1992 it is impossible to directly compare youth at the entry and exit points of the decade. But it is clear that many of the youth problems of yesteryear are the adult problems of today. The problems deriving from repression and resistance are now unique to adults. A new generation of youth has come, created its own culture and style, and developed its own particular problems – but they relate to poverty, growing up in a transitional society, and living with the reality of HIV/AIDS. Some they share with adults. Some they do not.

Conclusion

The 1990s will go down in history as a lost decade for youth. Key moments in the shaping of South Africa came and went, and youth development – so carefully analysed and managed in the early 1990s – slipped further and further off the agenda. But is it really so terrible? Part of the problem lies in misplaced expectations of youth – that they will remain politically active, disciplined and a force for good. Their parents certainly were, largely, such a group. But youth of the past should not be idealised – they were also violent, and included criminals alongside ordinary, committed citizens. And the youth of 2000? The worst thing they have done is become teenagers, retreat into their own cultures whose codes are opaque to adults, and mimic the consumerism that marks South African society.

The need for youth development is clear – unemployment is high and growing, HIV infection is extremely high, educational opportunities have been missed by many, and rape and violence is widespread. But those programmes have to be based on a sound understanding of youth cultures as they are – not as we want them to be or as we think they ought to be.

NGOs and youth organisations have a critical role to play in helping society as a whole understand what is happening with and to youth, and in helping design programmes that attract and benefit young people. Government must learn that youth development is multifaceted and complex, and commit significant resources to the task.

The 1990s may not have created a lost generation but is certainly the decade of lost opportunities. We cannot afford a second decade in the same mould.

Notes

[1] Many thanks to Penny Foley and Cathi Albertyn for insightful and helpful comments.

[2] The tripartite alliance included the ANC, South African Community Party (SACP) and Congress of South African Trade Unions (COSATU). The South African National Civics Organisation was also part of the alliance.

[3] *Business Day*, 26 January, 2000.

[4] The age definition of youth was 16 to 30.

[5] *Ibid.*

[6] National Youth Commission Act (19 of 1996).

[7] National Youth Commission Act (19 of 1996).

[8] Statistics South Africa, for example, fails to report on youth as legally defined.

[9] *Mail & Guardian*, 12/6/1998.

[10] *Ibid.*

[11] *Mail & Guardian*, 18/6/1999.

[12] Bheki Nkosi quoted in *Mail & Guardian*, 1/3/1996.

[13] Participant observation.

[14] Quoted in *Mail & Guardian*, 18/6/1999.

[15] Quoted in *Mail & Guardian*, 1/3/1996.

[16] Quoted in *Mail & Guardian*, 1/10/1997.

[17] *Mail & Guardian*, 18/6/1999.

[18] Drawn up in 1955, the Freedom Charter was the Congress Alliance statement of principle.

[19] Quoted in *Mail & Guardian*, 26/3/1999.

[20] Then Deputy Minister Phumzile Mlambo-Nguka.

[21] Quoted in *Mail & Guardian*, 18/6/1999.

[22] Census '96 data.

[23] Quoted in *Mail & Guardian*, 11/6/1999.

References

African National Congress (1994), *The Reconstruction and Development Programme*, Ravan Press, Braamfontein.

Albertyn, C. (1994), 'Women and the Transition to Democracy in South Africa', in *Gender and the New South African Legal Order*, Juta & Co., Braamfontein.

Albertyn, C., Goldblatt, B., Hassim, S., Mbatha, L. and Meintjies, S. (1999), *Engendering the Political Agenda: A South African Case Study*, Centre for Applied Legal Studies, Johannesburg.

Department of Health (1998a), *9th National HIV Survey of Women Attending Antenatal Clinics of the Public Health Service* (unpublished).

Department of Health (1998b), *South African Demographic and Health Survey* (unpublished).

Everatt, D. (1993), *Putting Youth on the National Agenda*, CASE, Braamfontein.

Everatt, D. (1994), *Creating a Future: Youth Policy for South Africa*, Ravan Press, Braamfontein.

Everatt, D. and Orkin, M. (1993), *Growing up Tough: A National Survey of South African Youth*, CASE, Braamfontein.

Foley, P. (2000), '10 Years of the JEP', in *Development Update*, Interfund, Johannesburg (forthcoming).

Joint Enrichment Project (1993), *National Youth Development Conference*, JEP, Braamfontein.

Levin, M. (2000), 'Youth and the Elections', in *Development Update*, Interfund, Johannesburg (forthcoming).

Marais, H. (1998), *South Africa: Limits to Change*, University of Cape Town Press and Zed Books, Cape Town.

National Youth Commission (1997), *Youth Policy 2000: National Youth Policy*, National Youth Commission, Pretoria.

National Youth Commission (2000), *White Paper on National Youth Service* (forthcoming).

Saul, J. (1999), 'Magical Market Realism and the South African Transition', *Transformation, Vol. 38*, pp. 49-67.

Seekings, J. (1993), *"Heroes or Villains?" Youth Politics in the 1980s*, Ravan Press, Braamfontein.

Sitas, A. (1991), 'The Comrades', *Reality, May 1991.*

Statistics South Africa (1997), *1997 October Household Survey* (unpublished).

Straker, G. (1992), *Faces in the Revolution: The Psychological Effects of Violence on Township Youth in South Africa*, David Philip, Cape Town.

Strategy & Tactics (1999), *Reality Check*, Strategy & Tactics, Johannesburg (unpublished).

Truscott, K. and Milner, S. (1994), 'Youth, Education and the World of Work', in D. Everatt (ed.), *Creating a Future: Youth Policy for South Africa*, Ravan Press, Braamfontein, pp. 36-66.